Martin Guitars

To my parents, who have always supported my interests and passions, except for not letting me get Beatle boots when I was eight.
—Jim Washburn

To my parents, who always encouraged my curiosity and love of music, and to Jon Lundberg, who was one of the first to seriously study the history of the American guitar.
—Richard Johnston

ACKNOWLEDGMENTS

THE AUTHORS WISH TO THANK THE FOLLOWING PEOPLE FOR THEIR ASSISTANCE AND SUPPORT IN WRITING THIS BOOK:

To everyone at C. F. Martin & Company, particularly Chris Martin and Dick Boak; Joan Baez; Jim Bollman; Scott Chinery; Leonard Coulson; Susan E. Dreydoppel of the Moravian Historical Society in Nazareth; Fred Dusel; Frank Ford; James Forderer; Travis Harrelson; Steve Howe; Stan Jay; Roger Kasle; David La Plante; Norman Levine; David Lindley; Mike Longworth; Leslie Lueck; Kennard Machol; Greg and Margie Mirken; Bob Mytkowitz; Willie Nelson; David Ogden; Hank Risan; Eric Schoenberg; Marc Silber; Steve Soest; Dugald Stermer; Stephen Stills; Marty Stuart; Kim Upton; Jennifer Vineyard; Stan Werbin; Mac Yasuda; and the staffs of Gryphon Stringed Instruments and the *OC Weekly.*

SPECIAL THANKS: To Fred Oster and Michael Simmons for research assistance.

BIBLIOGRAPHY

Douglas Back, *American Pioneers of the Classic Guitar* (Mel Bay, 1994); Walter Carter, *The Martin Book* (Miller Freeman Books, 1995); Scott Chinery with Tony Bacon, *The Chinery Collection* (Balafon, 1996); Country Music Foundation Staff, *Country: The Music and the Musicians* (Abbeville Press, 1994); Tom and Mary Anne Evans, *Guitars: Music, History, Construction and Players from the Renaissance to Rock* (Paddington Press, 1977); Jim Ferguson, editor, *The Guitar Player Book* (Grove Press, 1979); George Gruhn and Walter Carter, *Acoustic Guitars and Other Fretted Instruments* (Miller Freeman, 1993); George Gruhn and Walter Carter, *Gruhn's Guide to Vintage Guitars* (Miller Freeman, 1991); Chet Hagan, *Grand Ole Opry* (Henry Holt & Co., 1989); Steve Howe with Tony Bacon, *The Steve Howe Guitar Collection* (Balafon, 1993); Ernie Jackson, *The Music of Justin Holland* (Cherry Lane Music, 1995); *La Guitarra Espanola* (Opera Tres, 1992); Mike Longworth, *Martin Guitars, a History* (Four Maples Press, 1988); Tony Palmer, *All You Need Is Love* (Penguin Books, 1977); Lorene Ruymar, *The Hawaiian Steel Guitar & Its Great Hawaiian Musicians* (Centerstream Publishing, 1996); Robert Shaw, *Great Guitars* (Hugh Lauter Levin Associates, 1997); John Teagle, *Washburn* (Music Sales Corp., 1996); Tom Wheeler, *American Guitars* (Harper & Row, 1982); *Mandolin Quarterly,* fall 1996 (Plucked String).

TUNER
HEADSTOCK/ PEGHEAD
FINGERBOARD BINDING
UPPER BOUT
SIDE
NECK BLOCK
WAIST
X-BRACE
FINGER BRACE
BRIDGEPLATE
CENTER STRIP
EDGE BINDING
PURFLING
LOWER BOUT
END BLOCK

CONTENTS

Nut
Neck
Frets
Fingerboard/Fretboard
Fretboard inlays
Top/Soundboard
Soundhole
Pick guard
Neck heel
Rosette
Saddle
Bridge pin
Bridge
Back brace
Kerfed lining
Tone bars/
Transverse
braces
End pin
End wedge

They say it's the wood.

They say it's the drying technique, that it's the glue, the resins, or the finish. They say it's the aging. They say it's the scalloped braces or the step of the neck (like a boat). They say it's the regularity of the grain in the fretboard. They say it's the cross-grain ripple to the spruce. They say it's the density of the rosewood. They say it's the precision of the joining braces. They say it's the binding. They say it's a hype, a tradition marketed.

They're all right, but they're all wrong...

They left out one major element.

It's the magic.

It's one guy thumping and caressing and sanding and picking out what fits together, and steaming and molding and drying and waiting and touching and knowing when to do what.

Everyone has tried to mass-produce it. They think machine-tooled, X-rayed, laser-calibrated, mathematically perfect impersonations of the old craft will fly, and they are always wrong.

What is it that none of them get?

It's the old craft.

Like the Stradivarius violins, violas, and celli produced by craftsmen 400 years ago, Martin guitars—particularly those created between 1900 and 1945—are masterpieces of carefully chosen woods and handcrafted elegance.

Light as a feather, so finely tuned as to demand the most of a player, they respond with an authority that leaves nothing unexposed.

They have a crystaline high end that resonates with the purity of a waterfall in a mountain stream.

The mid-range produces overtones that can fill a theater with no amplification.

The bass is so rich it can overwhelm any microphone and is best enjoyed live.

Press your ear against the side of one, right above the waist, so that your head is in direct contact with the wood, and you'll think you're in a cathedral.

I have had the distinct honor of becoming intimately acquainted with 15 of these exquisite instruments, and to my mind they are all among the finest examples of the luthier's art form in existence.

Each one has its own singular voice, as distinctive and individually unique as the features of a human face. Yet they were so delicately crafted that each could, as was intended, mold itself and adjust its response to the touch and expressiveness of the musician into whose hands it fell, becoming a true extension of the player's personality and the inspiring conduit of a creative artist's passion.

Having been on the receiving end of an entire career's worth of such inspiration, I shall remain forever indebted to C. F. Martin and all of his works and to all of the artisans that followed him at C. F. Martin & Company.

These people carefully and deliberately conspired to provide me and every other artist fortunate enough to have laid hands on one of their creations with the opportunity to give voice to our very souls.

Accompanied, as we have been, by the voice of God.

Stephen Stills
Singer, Songwriter, Guitarist

Each one has its own singular voice, as distinctive and individually unique as the features of a human face.

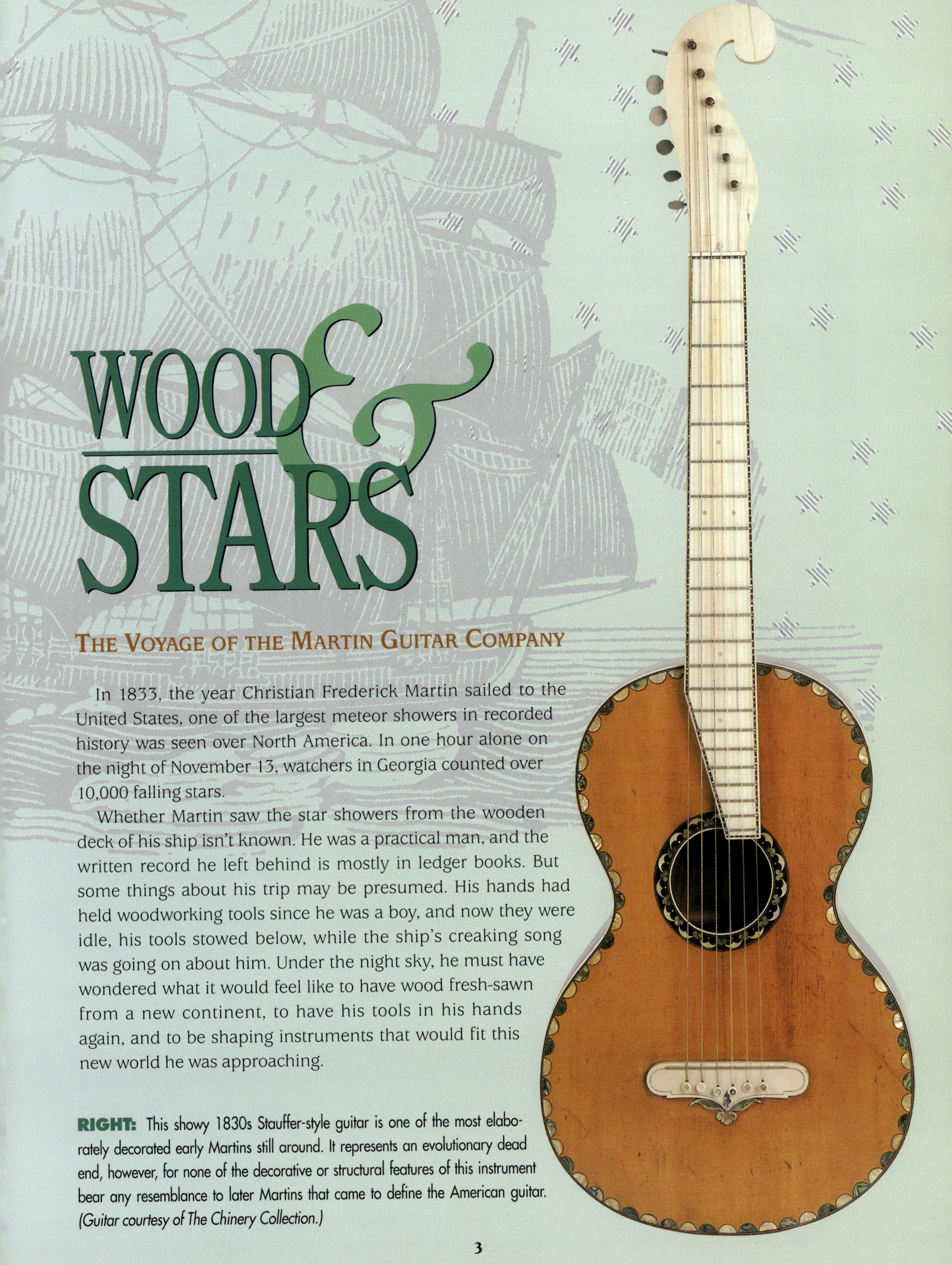

WOOD & STARS

The Voyage of the Martin Guitar Company

In 1833, the year Christian Frederick Martin sailed to the United States, one of the largest meteor showers in recorded history was seen over North America. In one hour alone on the night of November 13, watchers in Georgia counted over 10,000 falling stars.

Whether Martin saw the star showers from the wooden deck of his ship isn't known. He was a practical man, and the written record he left behind is mostly in ledger books. But some things about his trip may be presumed. His hands had held woodworking tools since he was a boy, and now they were idle, his tools stowed below, while the ship's creaking song was going on about him. Under the night sky, he must have wondered what it would feel like to have wood fresh-sawn from a new continent, to have his tools in his hands again, and to be shaping instruments that would fit this new world he was approaching.

RIGHT: This showy 1830s Stauffer-style guitar is one of the most elaborately decorated early Martins still around. It represents an evolutionary dead end, however, for none of the decorative or structural features of this instrument bear any resemblance to later Martins that came to define the American guitar. *(Guitar courtesy of The Chinery Collection.)*

An Instrument in Flux

By the time Martin was born in 1796, woodworking had reached such a level of refinement in Europe that many creations had already found their final, unimprovable form. The violin, for example, had reached a peak with the Stradivarius violin of 1700.

It was not so with the guitar, however. In the world Martin was leaving behind, both the instrument's design and its social acceptance were in flux.

Until nearly the 1800s most guitars had eight or ten strings, paired like a mandolin's in "courses." It was largely within Martin's youth that the now-accepted notion of the guitar emerged in Europe, moving to six courses, then six individual strings. Meanwhile, the guitar had passed in and out of fashion, gaining some small acceptance on the concert stage; but it was largely regarded as a parlor instrument, prized for gaudy ornamentation as much as for its musical viability.

There was no guaranteed place for the guitar in the new world, either, where the banjo was destined to be king through the 1800s. The guitar

ABOVE AND LEFT: This Stradivarius violin from the early 1700s looks, sounds, and plays very much like violins made today. Guitars made during the same period, including the one shown here, again by Stradivarius, would hardly suit any modern guitarist because of their inherent lack of volume. *(Photos from the Ashmolean Museum, Oxford, England.)*

LEFT: In the 1930s Martin cast its lot with the growing steel-string guitar market. The delicate pearl bordering and snowflake neck inlays of this 1933 OM-45 had just enough flash to attract singing cowboys like Roy Rogers and Tex Ritter. The decoration was subtle, but the tone was loud and robust, just what a cowboy needed to be heard over a stampede of banjos and fiddles. *(Guitar courtesy of C. F. Martin & Company.)*

BELOW: In the 1850s Martin began to give numeric designations to standard guitar shapes and decorative styles. This example from 1886 is a 2-40: a number 2–style body shape and Style 40 appointments, with ivory-bound body and neck and pearl-bordered top and soundhole. *(Guitar courtesy of C. F. Martin & Company.)*

wasn't to come into its own for nearly 100 years after Martin's arrival in America. Makers then started to fashion radical new instruments with metal resonators or electromagnetic pickups, in a rebellion against tradition. By then *tradition* largely meant the company bearing C. F. Martin's name, already the oldest musical instrument company in the United States. But those newer makers might not have had the luxury of traditions to rebel against if Martin had not boldly innovated them a century earlier.

In little more than a decade after setting up shop in a strange new land, Martin cast aside the filigree and conventions of the instrument he had learned to make in Europe, rethinking it from its internal braces to the austere beauty of its outward appointments, and so arriving at the American guitar.

He and his progeny were slow to improve upon his work in the following decades. There was little need. Martin had created an ideal instrument for a changing nation, with a design robust, responsive, and durable enough to hold firm while the country rode at breakneck speed into the future.

ancy mahogany, figured inlay
celluloid, figured inlay around fingerboard
ce, mahogany neck, rosewood fingerboard
, best American screw patent head.
No. 12R650 Our special price, standard size..........
No. 12R652 Same as No. 12R650, in concert size. Our special price..........

THE JULIEN.

Best quality rosewood back and sides, with top of resonant Eastern ruce; elaborate inlaying around sound hole and front edge and handsome inlaid strip in back; both edges bound in celluloid. Neck of solid mahogany; best quality ebony fingerboard, with beautiful pearl position marks. The head has rosewood veneer on front and back and best quality American made screw patent head. A wonderful instrument, highly finished and rich and powerful in tone.

No. 12R656 Our special price, standard size.......... $12.75
No. 12R658 Same as No. 12R656, concert size.......... 14.00
No. 12R660 Same as No. 12R656, grand concert size.......... 15.25

THE RICHARD.

Highly polished carefully selected rosewood back and sides, with fine quality Eastern spruce; elaborate ornamental inlay around sound hole and edges, and celluloid binding on both edges. Handsome inlaid strip in back, choice mahogany neck, head of which has rosewood veneer on front and back. Convex fingerboard of ebony, elaborately inlaid with pearl position marks. Bone nut and saddle and best quality American screw patent head. This guitar retails elsewhere at $30.00.

No. 12R664 Our special price, standard size...... $15.50
No. 12R666 Same as No. 12R664, concert size...... 16.75
No. 12R668 Same as No. 12R664, grand concert size 18.25

THE SEROCO.

Our Highest Grade Guitar—Nothing Better Made.

This guitar is made of the very finest quality of specially selected rosewood and only the most resonant extra seasoned choice Eastern spruce is used for the top, which is inlaid around sound hole and edges with colored wood and a broad strip of pearl, as shown in the illustration. Top and back edges are bound with white celluloid; handsome inlaid strip of variegated wood in back; convex ebony fingerboard, richly inlaid with pearl in fancy designs; edges of the fingerboard bound with white celluloid; the best grade of mahogany is used in the neck and the head is veneered on front and back with rosewood, finished to a point on the back ...ying the head of the instrument a handsome appearanc... the back as well as the front. The machine head is th... can be made, and the guitar is highly polished an... roughout as perfectly as the best mechanics ca... ing better in the market. This guitar is st... Acme professional strings and we inclu... so a first class perfect fitting canvas... valuable instruction book... regularly at $40.00 to... money refunded.

No. 12R672 Our s...
No. 12R674 Same...
No. 12R676 Same...
For Guitar Strings and...
For Folios and Instructi...

$18.75

Back

ABOVE: By 1902, when this Sears, Roebuck and Company catalog was printed, everyone accepted the fact that this was what the American guitar looked like. The long body with small upper bout, rectangular bridge with "pyramid" tips, square-shaped peghead, and multiring soundhole rosette seen on these guitars were all features that had been copied from C. F. Martin Sr.'s guitars.

RIGHT: The earliest Martin guitars were sent by stagecoach, then often by canal, to customers in the eastern United States. The young Martin company constructed not only the "coffin" cases for their instruments, but also the packing crates used in shipping. The cost of case, crate, and shipping was often over a third as much as the cost of the guitar itself. *(Guitar courtesy of The Chinery Collection.)*

Expanding with the Country

Initially, Martin guitars were delivered to their customers by stagecoach or canal in the young country's eastern states. The railroads were just starting, and most railroads in 1833 had horse-drawn wagons. By the end of the decade, steam locomotive rails outdistanced the nation's extensive canal system, and in 1869 the East and the country's new West Coast were joined by rail. As America expanded westward, the Martin company's greatest success was found in the boom towns of the West, such as Denver, Butte, Portland, and San Francisco.

ABOVE: In 1895 Martin began offering bowlback mandolins, described in its first catalog as made in "the finest Italian style." The mandolin replaced the banjo as America's most popular stringed instrument, with the guitar still in distant third place. *(Mandolins courtesy of C. F. Martin & Company.)*

Before the turn of the century, mass-producing competitors tied to huge mail-order houses were declaring Martin's obsolescence while freely appropriating the company's designs. Martin was a small, family-run firm in the out-of-the-way hamlet of Nazareth, Pennsylvania, whose advertisements were understated and few. Chicago-based Lyon & Healy, with its Washburn line of guitars, and newcomer Gibson were aggressively marketing their products. Washburn ad copy touted its more mechanized production methods as unapproachably superior to "others [Martin] depending to a large extent on their workmen, more or less at their mercy, never certain of the result, and often making dismal failures."

Somehow, Martin neglected to go out of business. Instead, the company was one of the first to recognize the musical potential of America's latest bit of expansion, the Hawaiian Islands, and

by the teens and '20s of this century, Martin's ukuleles and Hawaiian guitars were so popular that the factory had to be expanded to accommodate the surge in production.

But when the Depression hit in 1929, the company struggled to stay alive. At the same time, it entered what aficionados call its Golden Age. The method of internal bracing that C. F. Martin had developed for his guitars in the 1840s—the X-brace—turned out to be remarkably well suited for the steel strings that replaced gut strings by the 1920s. Coupled with a huge new body design named for British Dreadnought warships, Martin had an instrument that musicians embraced as a tool to stave off hard times. The Dreadnought has remained a staple in country, bluegrass, folk, and rock music and has become one of the most copied instruments on the globe.

The company today is still run by a man who shares its name, C. F. Martin IV, and it has now made well over half a million instruments. Along the way the still-small company in that still-small town has managed to make guitars played by many of the most influential musicians of their times, and it has seen its instruments become the first to reach the North Pole and the first carried to the top of Mount Everest. On March 4, 1994, a Martin Backpacker was the first American guitar to leave the Earth's atmosphere behind, orbiting the planet on the space shuttle *Columbia*, passing through the sky that had been filled with falling stars 160 years earlier, crossing in minutes the Atlantic that it had taken C. F. Martin and his family months to cross.

This is the story of the voyage of C. F. Martin & Company.

ABOVE: Adventurer Richard Konter shows his Martin ukulele to pilot Floyd Bennett. Konter, Bennett, and the Martin uke flew with Commander Richard Byrd on his first expedition over the North Pole in 1926. *(Photo courtesy of C. F. Martin & Company.)*

RIGHT: In 1990 Martin produced its 500,000th guitar—this HD-28P. To mark the occasion, all the employees signed the top. And if you look closely, you just might find the signature of C. F. Martin IV somewhere in the first column. *(Guitar courtesy of C. F. Martin & Company.)*

ABOVE: NASA astronaut Pierre Thuot finds time between his experiments in microgravity to strum his custom Martin Backpacker, made by Bob McNally, during a 13-day mission aboard the space shuttle *Columbia* in 1994. *(Photo courtesy of NASA Photo Archives.)*

RIGHT: *Dreadnought, Sir Knight!* Paul McCartney had to wait until 1997 to attain knighthood, but he and fellow Beatle John Lennon got their first Martin D-28s in 1967. He's shown here, several Martins later, on a 1990 *Rolling Stone* cover, with a model that accompanied him on his world tour of that year. Artists ranging from singing cowboys to screaming Seattleites have relied on Martins to facilitate their musical expressions. *(Timothy White/*Rolling Stone*, February 8, 1990, by Straight Arrow Publishers, Inc. All rights reserved. Reprinted by permission.)*

From SAXONY *to* AMERICA

1796 – 1838

Christian Fredrich Martin was born on January 31, 1796, in Mark Neukirchen, Saxony, son of Johann Georg Martin, a furniture maker who—in a town noted for instrument builders—also made guitars.

Saxony has a curious history. Once situated in northwestern Germany, it shifted boundaries as wars and political intrigues moved it to the country's far eastern borders. With wars, endless feudal and religious squabbling, and a succession of rulers with names like Albert the Bear, Henry the Lion, and Duke Maurice, the region could have qualified as a Wrestlemania event.

C.F.'s father was likely named for Elector Johann Georg I, who had ruled Saxony through the Thirty Years' War in the early 1600s, during which Saxony managed to change sides three times. It again changed allegiances in the middle of the War of the Austrian Succession and *again* in 1806 during the upheavals that followed the French Revolution. Since a few other wars—including the Seven Years' War—also spanned Johann Georg Martin's lifetime, one can see where there might have been a considerable need for new furniture.

There is no record of whether young C.F. became particularly adept at building credenzas, but his interest and skill in guitarmaking were sufficient to secure him an apprenticeship at age 15 with Johann Stauffer, 200 miles away in Vienna. Stauffer was recognized as one of the finest guitar

ABOVE: C. F. Martin Sr. was the founder of the Martin legacy. He was able to adapt the guitars of his Stauffer apprenticeship to the needs of a changing America. His wife, Ottilie, is shown here. *(Photos courtesy of C. F. Martin & Company.)*

RIGHT: Though Mark Neukirchen was oozing in Old World charm, beneath the surface were bitter disputes among competing guilds, who controlled what craftsmen could make. The Violin Makers Guild sought to extend its power by claiming the exclusive right to build any musical instruments made of wood. Their harassment of cabinetmakers who also wished to build guitars, including C. F. Martin, is the primary reason the Martin guitar is an American, rather than German, phenomenon.

RIGHT: Today the shape of this headstock reminds guitarists of the solid-body electrics of Leo Fender or the earlier custom necks made by Paul Bigsby; but the scroll-shaped peghead dates back to at least the early 1800s in Germany and Austria. Though commonly called a Stauffer headstock, other European makers also used the design. The "thumbprint" inlays bordering the top of this Martin (made before 1839) possibly came from pearl button blanks. *(Guitar courtesy of The Chinery Collection.)*

builders in the world, having made a guitar for Paganini, one of the few composers then writing for the instrument.

Johann Stauffer was one of the more original makers of his day. He expanded the guitar's upper range by extending the fingerboard over the body, up to the soundhole. Previous makers had stopped where the neck met the body, at most tapping a few frets into the guitar's top.

Stauffer's fingerboard was actually suspended slightly above the top because the neck was made to pivot where it joined the body. Adjusted by a clock key, the movable neck joint enabled guitarists to change the neck angle and string height to suit their playing. The most immediately recognizable feature of Stauffer's guitars was the peghead, where the scroll shape and six-on-a-side tuners prefigured Leo Fender's electric guitars of the 1950s. When C. F. Martin started making guitars in the United States, his early works were almost wholly derived from Stauffer's distinctive designs.

In his 14 years in Vienna, C.F. rose from apprentice to shop foreman before eventually leaving Stauffer to work for another Viennese, Karl Kühle, whose daughter, church harpist Ottilie Lucia Kühle, he married.

Shortly after Christian Fredrich Martin Jr. (both father and son later Americanized their middle names to Frederick) was born on October 2, 1825, C.F. moved his family back to Mark Neukirchen, just in time to become embroiled in a turf war between the cabinetmakers and the Violin Makers Guild.

ABOVE: The similarities between these two guitars are startling and clearly show the strong link between Johann Stauffer and his former employee, C. F. Martin Sr. Though the instrument directly above has no label and can only be attributed to Stauffer, the one at the top is clearly labeled with the Hudson Street address of Martin's new home in New York City. Note the almost identical bridge, soundhole rosette, and angled cut at the end of the fretboard, as well as the adjustable neck with fretboard floating above the soundboard. Both guitars also have maple backs and sides, though Martin would soon shift almost exclusively to rosewood. *(Martin guitar courtesy of C. F. Martin & Company; Stauffer guitar courtesy of The Chinery Collection.)*

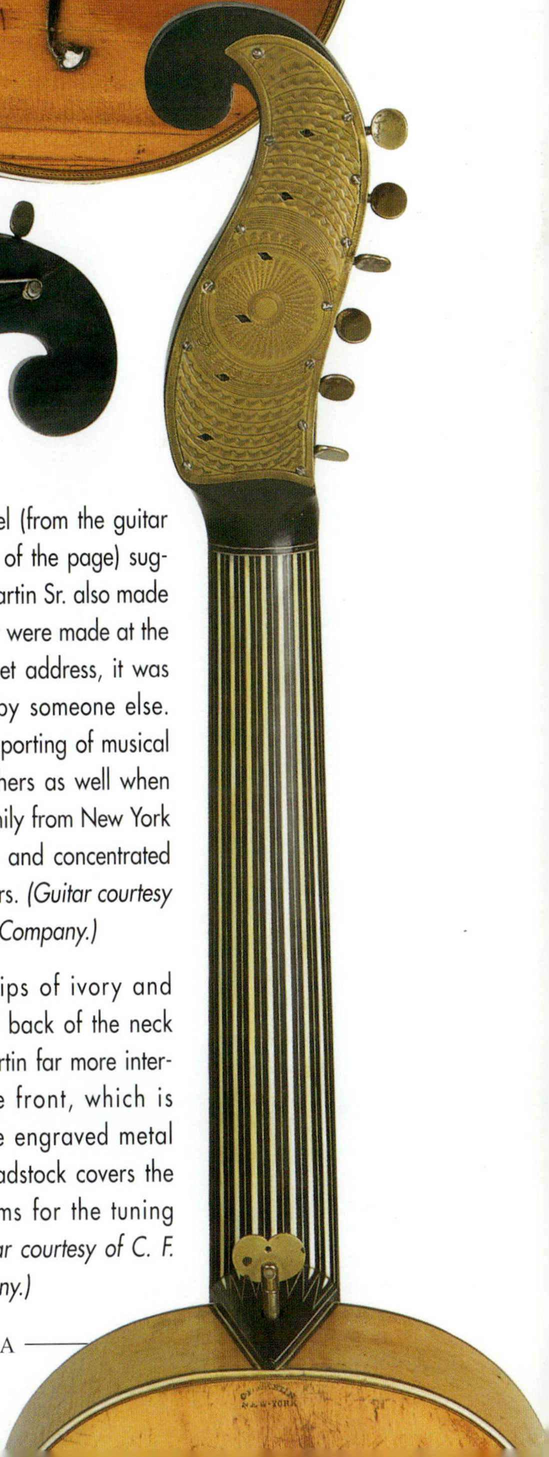

LEFT: This label (from the guitar shown at the top of the page) suggests that C. F. Martin Sr. also made violins; but if they were made at the 196 Hudson Street address, it was probably done by someone else. Martin left the importing of musical instruments to others as well when he moved his family from New York City to Nazareth and concentrated on building guitars. *(Guitar courtesy of C. F. Martin & Company.)*

RIGHT: Strips of ivory and ebony make the back of the neck on this early Martin far more interesting than the front, which is unadorned. The engraved metal plate on the headstock covers the gear mechanisms for the tuning machines. *(Guitar courtesy of C. F. Martin & Company.)*

THE CHANGING GUITAR

While not the illegitimate creation that some musicians claimed it was, the guitar is of uncertain parentage. Some trace it to the ancient Greek kithara, though there is little more than the similarity in names to suggest that. Others suggest a Mesopotamian, Egyptian, or Central Asian origin.

In Europe, references began springing up in the thirteenth century to instruments named the gitere, guiterre, quinterne, and gittern. In the 1400s the lutelike four-course guitar emerged, gaining a more guitarlike shape in the 1500s and finding favor in France. It and the five-course guitar that appeared in Spain by the mid-1500s had strings that were paired like a mandolin's.

The Spanish also led the way with the six-course guitar by the 1780s. Though it is disputed whether a French builder or one in Dresden was the first to develop it, the guitar as we know it, with six individual strings, arrived only a few years before C. F. Martin's birth. It wasn't universally acknowledged as the last word: Some went on to make seven-course guitars.

Through these changes, the guitar waxed and waned in popularity. The four-course guitar of the 1500s was widely used in the theater and by strolling musicians in Spain, while it was popular for dance music in France. There, King Henry II was reputed to have serenaded his mistress with a guitar, and it set off a brief fad. Others

LEFT: The five-course guitar enjoyed considerable popularity in the seventeenth century, and the Sellas family dynasty of Venice contributed many fine examples that have survived. This example, made by Domenico Sellas, circa 1670, displays unusually heavy pearl decorations, even for the period. Similar guitars were popular in Germany, France, and England. Most have long, narrow bodies with a gentle curve at the waist, a shape similar to what Martin would make for the Ditson company starting in 1916. *(Photo from S. R. H. Spicer, The Shrine to Music Museum, Vermillion, South Dakota.)*

ABOVE: Lyre guitars were quite popular in the early 1800s, especially in France, and were some of the first guitars to be made routinely for six single strings with the tuning we use today. Most had flat bases at the bottom for display purposes, though they probably weren't often played in the impossible position shown here. Though rather plain and quite functional lyre guitars do exist, most were intended to be primarily decorative displays of the owner's culture and refinement. *(Photo from Miki Slingsby—London.)*

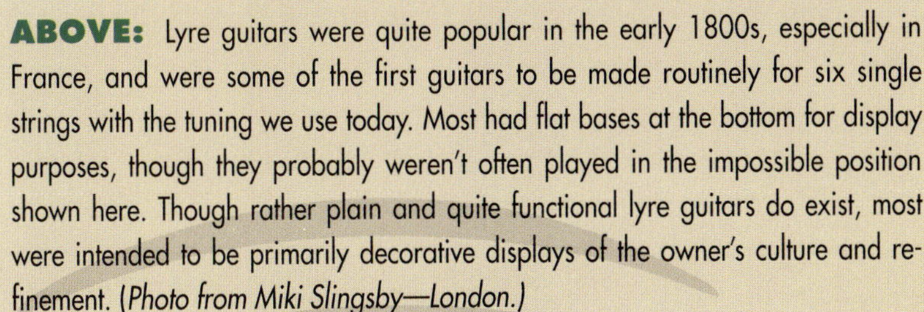

bemoaned the guitar's replacing the more courtly lute and vihuela. Spanish Inquisitor Don Sebastian de Covarrubias Orozco wrote in 1611, "The guitar is no more than a cowbell, so easy to play that...there is not a stable lad who is not a musician on the guitar."

It became popular in several royal courts but was just as quickly abandoned for the harpsichord or a newfound royal passion for opera. For many, by the 1700s the guitar had become a mere fashion statement, a "lady's trifle," heavily adorned for display in the parlor. Many of these instruments were so laden with gaudy ornamentation that they could scarcely be recognized as musical instruments. Evidently some of the fanciest

ABOVE: Hybrid guitars are nothing new, as evidenced by this version of a "harp guitar" made in 1827 by Josef Laurent Mast of Toulouse, France. Most later harp guitars had extra strings on a guitar-shaped body, but this French maker chose the opposite approach. *(Photo from Miki Slingsby—London.)*

guitars look too gaudy to be real, but some were actually played by royalty and were highly regarded as musical instruments at the time.

Much of the early music for guitar was written for a general, amateur audience, rendered in simple tablature form not unlike what one finds in modern rock music volumes. There were serious composers for the instrument, including Corbetta, Granata, and Sanz in the 1700s. At the end of the century, in C.F.'s time, guitarist/composer Fernando Sor did both of his jobs so well that the guitar was taken far more seriously in his wake. Another prime player, Italian Mauro Giuliani, resided in Vienna from 1809 to 1819, and it is hard to imagine that C.F. hadn't seen him perform during his time there with Johann Stauffer.

BELOW AND RIGHT: The maker of this three-necked "harpo-lyre," Jean-François Salomon, specified that the six-string neck in the center be tuned like an ordinary guitar, while the seven-string neck on the left was to be tuned in semitones from low A to high D-sharp. The eight-string neck on the right was tuned to a diatonic C-scale. Salomon also patented the "sound unit," an early "Marshall stack" that was connected to the harpo-lyre with special "bars"; the bars helped support the instrument for the player and transmitted vibrations to the box itself, "producing at least twice the sound of ordinary guitars." Mechanical methods of making a guitar louder kept recurring for the next hundred years or so, until the problem was finally solved with magnetic pickups and electric amplifiers. (*Photo from Miki Slingsby—London.*)

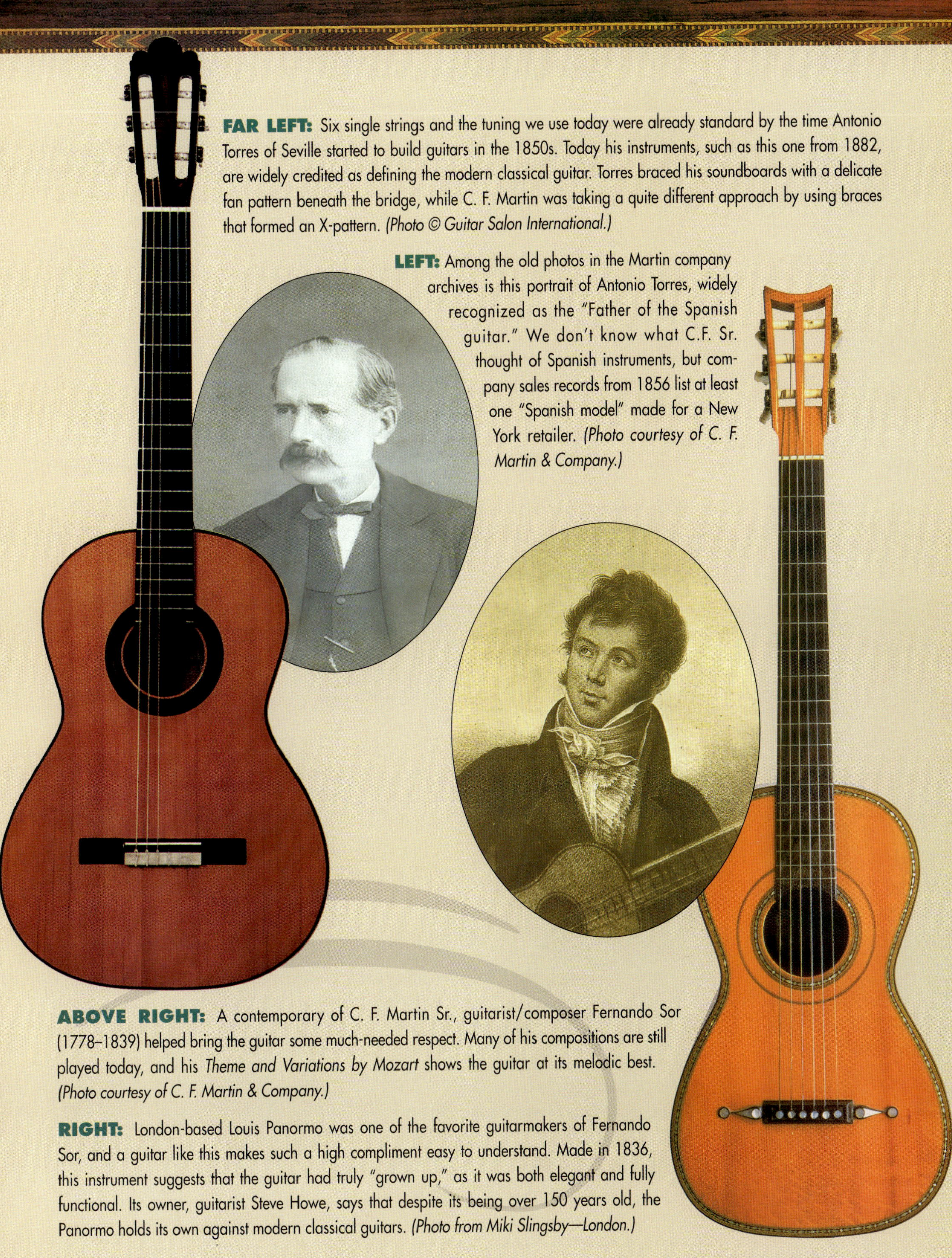

FAR LEFT: Six single strings and the tuning we use today were already standard by the time Antonio Torres of Seville started to build guitars in the 1850s. Today his instruments, such as this one from 1882, are widely credited as defining the modern classical guitar. Torres braced his soundboards with a delicate fan pattern beneath the bridge, while C. F. Martin was taking a quite different approach by using braces that formed an X-pattern. *(Photo © Guitar Salon International.)*

LEFT: Among the old photos in the Martin company archives is this portrait of Antonio Torres, widely recognized as the "Father of the Spanish guitar." We don't know what C.F. Sr. thought of Spanish instruments, but company sales records from 1856 list at least one "Spanish model" made for a New York retailer. *(Photo courtesy of C. F. Martin & Company.)*

ABOVE RIGHT: A contemporary of C. F. Martin Sr., guitarist/composer Fernando Sor (1778–1839) helped bring the guitar some much-needed respect. Many of his compositions are still played today, and his *Theme and Variations by Mozart* shows the guitar at its melodic best. *(Photo courtesy of C. F. Martin & Company.)*

RIGHT: London-based Louis Panormo was one of the favorite guitarmakers of Fernando Sor, and a guitar like this makes such a high compliment easy to understand. Made in 1836, this instrument suggests that the guitar had truly "grown up," as it was both elegant and fully functional. Its owner, guitarist Steve Howe, says that despite its being over 150 years old, the Panormo holds its own against modern classical guitars. *(Photo from Miki Slingsby—London.)*

"Nothing More Than Mechanics"

Guilds had emerged in medieval Europe as a means for merchants and craftsmen to bolster their economic and social clout by establishing quality standards and trade agreements and by fixing prices, limiting membership, and buying off bothersome nobles.

In Mark Neukirchen the 120-member Violin Maker's Guild had begun complaining about the "bungler" cabinetmaker's guitars in 1807, and in May 1826 it filed a petition seeking to forbid them from making guitars. The guild named Johann Georg and Christian Fredrich Martin, their friend Heinrich Schatz, and six others, maintaining that the guild alone belonged to the "class of musical instrument makers and therefore to the class of artists, whose work not only showed finish but gave evidence of a certain understanding, a cultured taste." The cabinetmakers were "nothing more than mechanics...their product consisted of all kinds of articles known as furniture.... Who is so stupid that he cannot see at a glance that a grandfather's armchair or a stool is no guitar, and such an article appearing among our instruments must look like Saul among the Prophets?" The guild also warned that the ungoverned cabinetmakers posed the danger of carrying the guitarmaking industry into foreign lands.

This petition was refused, but in 1831 the guild raised the matter again, claiming that the guild's 150-year history imbued it with "the exclusive right of making everything under the category of violins and related instruments, being all such as have a soundboard and strings in the manner of a violin and

LEFT: This European guitar from the early 1800s, attributed to Stauffer of Vienna, has a top border that should look familar to die-hard Martin fans—it is nearly identical to purfling used as the backstrip on some late-nineteenth-century Martins and on Style 42 and 45 models in the 1920s and 1930s. This pattern is still in use today on many contemporary Martin guitars. The conservative nature of Martin's stylistic evolution has left many continuous threads connecting Martin's features to Old World luthiers. *(Guitar courtesy of The Chinery Collection.)*

LEFT AND BELOW: The elaborate gear mechanism was relatively expensive for C. F. Martin to import, which may have prompted him to simplify the necks of his guitars to the style we see today. *(Tuning gears and guitar courtesy of C. F. Martin & Company.)*

LEFT: The label in this guitar reads "C. F. Martin & Schatz, Manufacturers of the celebrated Spanish and Vienna warranted Guitars, Violins, Violincellos, and Double Bass. Made in the best Italian style." Despite the confusing combination of countries mentioned on the label, Martin was already brewing his uniquely American guitars. This example has the bridge and neck of the Stauffer-style, but the body shape is slimmed down more like later Martins. Henry Schatz, who looms large in the Martin family's decisions, was already settled in Mill Grove, Pennsylvania. His influence brought Martin to nearby Cherry Hill. *(Guitar courtesy of The Chinery Collection.)*

by the combination of the two produce tone." One became a master in the guild by building—here's where the term originated—a *masterpiece* to prove his skill. The cabinetmakers had no such requirement, and the violin guild argued that their work would lower the reputation of local products.

The violin guild said it already furnished the cabinetmakers a good trade, making the cases for its instruments, and alleged that the cabinetmakers had stolen its guitar designs from patterns furnished by the guild for the purpose of making cases.

The cabinetmakers' response to this cranky lot included a testimonial from instrument wholesaler Christian Wilhelm Schuster that C. F. Martin "for a number of years had been foreman in the factory of the noted violin and guitar maker Johann Georg Stauffer of Vienna," and had made guitars "which in point of quality and appearance left nothing to be desired and which marked him as a distinguished craftsman."

On July 9, 1832, the authorities rendered in favor of the cabinetmakers, citing that guitars had not originally been part of the guild's articles of confederation. Had C. F. Martin stayed in Mark Neukirchen, he eventually would have seen the cabinetmakers permitted to form their own guild in 1853, for which a guitar was the required masterpiece. But by then he was half a world away, setting his own new standards for what constituted a masterpiece.

Starting Over in New York

Even though C.F. and his father had prevailed against the guild, it must have been a debilitating process fighting against narrow-mindedness and jealousy just to get their work done. Meanwhile Heinrich—now Henry—Schatz had immigrated to the United States and had written to his friends of the new country.

FAR RIGHT: Martin's first address—196 Hudson Street—is now the entrance to the Holland Tunnel. Though the guitar company started by one man in New York City in 1833 now makes over 125 instruments each working day, that's still small by the standards of international big business. It took the little Martin company 50 years to make its first 10,000 instruments—that would be a bit over one week's production for a large guitar manufacturer in Asia today. *(Photo from Library of Congress/Corbis.)*

RIGHT: Martin ledgers from the 1830s suggest that most of C.F. Sr.'s guitars were small and plain. The eye-catching inlays on this fancy model probably ensured its survival, while most of the simple guitars from this period were discarded long ago. *(Photo © J. Whipple photography/Lark Street Music.)*

BARNET
RUBIN
RUSSIAN
26
TRUSS MAKER.
בארנעט
רובין
רוסישער
26

BELOW: A page from C. F. Martin Sr.'s 1836 ledger shows that he kept incredibly detailed records in meticulous, flowing script. It was an obsession he would also pass on to his son. More than a century later, C.F. III remembered that his father, Frank Henry Martin (C.F. Sr.'s grandson), would be at his workbench during the day, then go home and do bookkeeping after dinner, and read before going to bed, a daily schedule that must have been a ritual for C.F. Jr. as well. Except for civic duties, there is little mention of any hobbies or other pastimes in the first four generations of Martins in America, probably because they didn't have the time.

Whether C.F. believed there was an American market for his guitar, as a late 1800s company history supports, or whether he was simply lured by the adventure and risk of a new land, he took his family, which now included an infant daughter, to the United States. They embarked on September 9, 1833; since steamships were not yet plying the Atlantic, such journeys by sail often took over 100 days on pitching seas.

Nor was solid footing guaranteed in the New World. The United States then was more a land of uncertainty than it was of opportunity. Just 18 years earlier, the nation had been isolated from Europe by a British blockade in the War of 1812, and several New England states had nearly seceded from the Union over their opposition to the war. In 1833 the nation was so young that there had yet to be a president who wasn't born under the British crown. The infamous former vice president and duelist Aaron Burr still practiced law in New York City and was scheming to enlist new German immigrants such as Martin to start a settlement in Texas.

When immigrants arrived in New York in 1833, there was no Statue of Liberty or skyscraper to greet them, nor would there be for more than 50 years. Instead newcomers like the Martins found a bustling and none-too-tidy city of about 100,000, distinguished by painted brick buildings and pigs still running wild in the streets.

ABOVE, LEFT, AND RIGHT: Not all early guitarmakers named Martin lived in Saxony, as indicated by this French guitar made by Charles Martin in 1829. The body shape, peghead style, bridge design, and fretted soundboard are all typical of early-nineteenth-century French guitars. The guitar shown here is a rather late example of a style that was already on the wane. *(Photo courtesy of Fred Dusel; guitar courtesy of James Forderer.)*

Steve Howe

Eclectic *Yes* Man

Just by coincidence, when Steve Howe answered the phone at his London studio, he was playing his venerable 00-18. Not that it's a huge coincidence; the British guitar wizard and mainstay member of Yes says he's had Martins in his bloodstream since before he even knew what one was.

As a lad he'd seen the first Elvis Presley album, with its cover photo of the King and his leather-enshrouded Dreadnought. "The impact on me was so subtle, because here's this guitar with a strange, anonymous-looking headstock. It's an instrument that didn't try to make an impression, but somehow it was so *right*," he recalls. Skiffle sensation Lonnie Donegan also played a Martin, and Howe soon noticed photos of other musicians playing them as well. The guitars themselves remained elusive, though.

"It was one thing to know *of* Martin guitars, but there were very few of them around. They just weren't spilling off the shelves of every shop, and by our standards they weren't cheap. American guitars were very sought after here in the early '60s; and although you *could* buy them, they were expensive, and only the really elite players had serious ones.

"But then in 1968 I saw Paul Simon playing a Martin at the Albert Hall, and that was the end of it. That made me say, 'All right, I'm going out and getting a Martin.' It was really a very powerful impression. And once I could afford a Martin, I went out the next

ABOVE: Though he's renowned for his electric guitar work with the supergroups Yes and Asia, Steve Howe also collects—and plays—rare acoustic guitars, some dating back three centuries. Shown here with his workhorse acoustic, a 1953 Martin 00-18, Howe owns a number of Martins including his early Stauffer-style. *(Photo from Miki Slingsby—London.)*

LEFT: Steve Howe's collection includes rare instruments such as this Martin 0-28 from around 1875, the Martin & Coupa guitar shown on page 35, the hybrid guitar shown on page 15, and the "harpo-lyre" shown on page 16. *(Photo from Miki Slingsby—London.)*

day and got one."

Since that day, Howe has owned all manner of Martins, from a recent MC-28 and electric model to one of the earliest Stauffer-style models. But it was the first guitar he played and bought—the 1953 tortoiseshell pick guard 00-18 used through his Yes and solo career—that told him all he needed to know about the guitars.

"Playing it was a shock. I realized that I'd run into an industrial standard, if you will, one which I didn't think that you could go above. It was an optimum kind of guitar, so simple and clear, with a certain kind of resonance that I felt, and was to discover in later years, you really couldn't get from other guitars. On it I could combine my folk playing with my rock playing; I could play blues and classical-style pieces. It's a very adaptable sort of guitar. What drove me to play it and what differentiates it from other guitars, is that basic inherent standard, a certain governing virtual perfection. I know it sounds like I'm overdoing it, but there was a kind of rightness about the Martin that I was lucky enough to get in touch with so early on," he says.

Howe has published his own book on guitars, called *The Steve Howe Guitar Collection,* and it is distinct from other guitar volumes in that its pictured instruments not only are rare but are also his musical working tools. Hence, you won't find such collectors' staples as a herringbone Brazilian rosewood D-28 in his collection.

ABOVE: Here Scott Chinery's 1936 00-40H gets a bit of exercise during the recording session for *The Chinery Collection: Masterpiece Guitars.* It may not be what C. F. Martin Sr. had in mind, but the 00-40 is a nineteenth-century style, beefed up for the steel strings and high action required by the Hawaiian playing style shown here. *(Photo courtesy of The Chinery Collection.)*

"I'm an '0' sort of guy—00 or 000. I never got on with the Dreadnoughts—I couldn't get my elbow in a comfortable position. And I prefer the tone of the mahogany Style 18," he said.

His Yes tour staples remain the 00-18 and a 1980s 12-string. Other Martins in his arsenal include backup 00-18s from various years, an SOM-45, sundry ukuleles, and a Style C mandolin, of which he says, "It's a fantastic mandolin. I use it whenever I want a warm sound."

Howe is one of the few contemporary guitarists to have played examples of C. F. Martin Sr.'s earliest American instruments. When he picks it up, his Stauffer-style Martin practically compels him to play in a restrained manner befitting its era. "There is a wonderful antiquity in it, and one has a tendency to not want to go too far on it," he says. "I don't work it very hard. It's delicate, and I've got it tuned quite low. I treat it more as a museum guitar."

But even museum guitars should have fun once in a while: Howe and jazz guitarist Martin Taylor collaborated on a project for collector and budding record-label owner Scott Chinery, recording an album—*The Chinery Collection: Masterpiece Guitars*—employing about 100 guitars from Chinery's collection. One of the pair's collaborations is "Smile," on which Taylor plays a Gibson built by Orville Gibson and Howe plays a C. F. Martin Sr.–era Stauffer-style Martin of Chinery's.

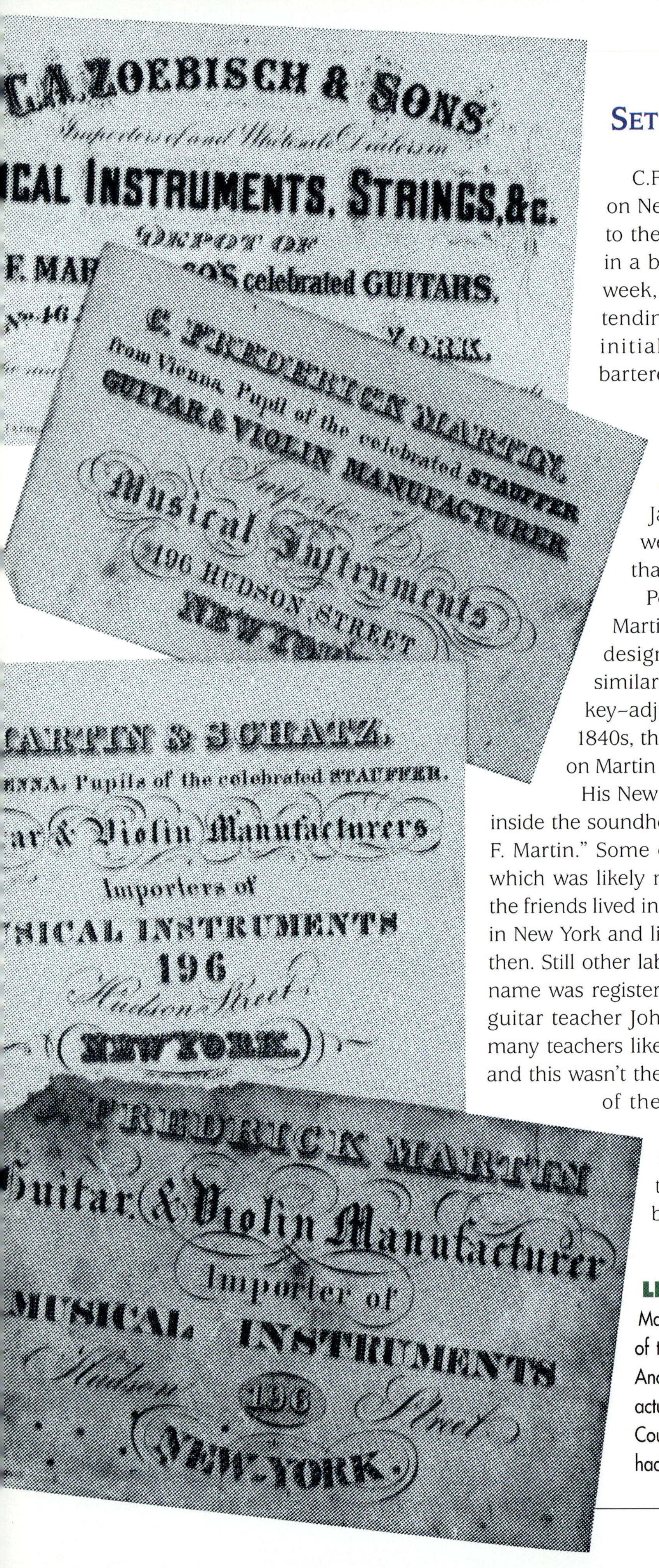

Setting Up Shop

C.F. opened a music store at 196 Hudson Street on New York's Lower East Side, where the entrance to the Holland Tunnel now stands. He built guitars in a back room there and sold an average of one a week, and he evidently spent much of his time attending to business in the front as well. Records—initially kept in German—show he sometimes bartered goods, obtaining items such as children's clothing and a case of wine by such trades.

The store sold all manner of musical instruments and supplies, from horns and harps to one-half of a violin string, as noted in a January 2, 1836, ledger entry. (Violin strings were made in triple length at the time; halving that length yielded a guitar string.)

Perhaps because his attention was also divided, Martin's guitars of that time differed little from the designs he had learned from Stauffer, featuring a similar paisley-shaped peghead as well as the clock key–adjusted neck joint. (He abandoned both by the 1840s, though the clock key feature remained an option on Martin instruments into the 1890s.)

His New York guitars often can be identified by a label inside the soundhole, reading "Christian Frederick Martin" or "C. F. Martin." Some of his guitars bear a "Martin & Schatz" label, which was likely merely a cooperative business relationship, as the friends lived in different states for most of the time Martin was in New York and likely didn't actually build instruments together then. Still other labels read "Martin & Coupa," and a firm of that name was registered at 385 Broadway, which was the studio of guitar teacher John Coupa. Coupa was not a guitarmaker; but many teachers liked to market guitars bearing their own names, and this wasn't the last time Martin would so oblige one. Neither of these labels was backed by a formal business agreement, though in 1838 Martin did enter into a brief seven-month partnership with distributor Charles Bruno, selling instruments bearing the "C. F. Martin & Bruno" label.

LEFT: Considering his short tenure in New York City, C. F. Martin went through a lot of changes in labels. Note that two of them state "from Vienna, pupil of the celebrated Stauffer." Another label lists an address of 212 Fulton Street, which was actually the business address of Charles Bruno. The Martin & Coupa label and the Zoebisch label were used after Martin had moved to Nazareth, Pennsylvania.

A Cold and Lonely Place

Business aside, the Martins were not happy in New York. An event that has reached near-mythic proportions in Martin family lore is the Miserable Christmas of 1833. The company's current head, C. F. Martin IV—known as Chris—heard the tale passed down from his grandfather, C. F. Martin III.

"I was told about how that first Christmas they were all in tears. They may not have been in a tenement, but they weren't living in the Upper East Side. They were scraping by. A little bit of money never went very far in New York City. And they felt really out of place, coming from a place with German traditions, where Christmas was one of those things where everybody participated."

Along with being a city not yet accustomed to the German tradition of Christmas trees, New York in the 1830s wasn't the smiling town of warm hospitality we all know it to be today. In 1834 mobs violently attacked anti-slavery meetings. There were murder attempts on abolitionist leaders Arthur and Lewis Tappan, and the Episcopal African Church was burned. Stonecutters rioted. The following year, half of the city's first ward—including Wall Street and the original Dutch part of town—burned to the ground. As this occurred during a chilly December, water froze in the firemen's sewn-leather hoses.

In Mark Neukirchen, Martin's livelihood may have been threatened, but not his family's entire sense of who they were. In correspondence from the time, C.F. even pondered moving back to Germany. Then he found he didn't have to go quite that far.

TOP RIGHT: The label inside this guitar (shown in its entirety on page 28) lists Martin's 196 Hudson Street address. *(Guitar courtesy of The Chinery Collection.)*

RIGHT: Dionisio Aguado y Garcia was one of Spain's most celebrated guitarists and teachers. He invented the "tripodium," which was designed to hold the guitar in the proper position for playing. It also served to keep the guitar away from the muting effect of the player's body to produce a louder tone.

THE TECHNICAL SIDE OF EARLY MARTIN GUITARS

There is so much variation among Martin's earliest guitars that it is difficult to describe them as a group. C. F. Martin Sr. apparently experimented with a variety of structural and stylistic details. And as his descendant and the current Martin head C. F. "Chris" Martin notes, "I have to believe that, selling direct in New York City, he certainly had contact with players, and they would specify to him what they wanted when they ordered a guitar." Some of

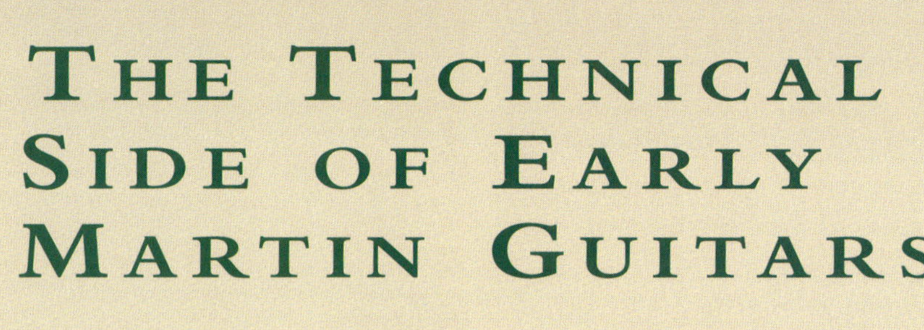

the wide variation is no doubt due to the fact that Martin had immigrant guitarists from different parts of the world arriving at his door requesting guitars; and there was very little agreement in the early nineteenth century as to what this young instrument, especially in an even younger nation, was supposed to look like. Martin also had short-lived partnerships—with John Coupa, Henry Schatz, and Charles Bruno—that may also have influenced the guitars he constructed before he settled upon what would become the Martin guitar.

ABOVE: Using a fret for a bridge saddle was common in this era. It was used as a shortcut on inexpensive guitars years later, but it appears only on the earliest Martins. *(Guitar courtesy of The Chinery Collection.)*

LEFT: Impressive as this 1830s Martin may be, virtually none of the stylistic features displayed on this model survived to the Civil War era. The angled cut at the end of the fretboard disappeared before Martin left New York, and the rounded bridge shape was apparently dropped in the 1850s. The Stauffer-style peghead lasted only slightly longer than the fancy "thumbprint" pearl bordering around the top and the elaborate soundhole rosette, both of which quickly gave way to simpler narrow bands of pearl. *(Guitar courtesy of The Chinery Collection.)*

RIGHT: The clock-key neck adjustment on many early Martins allowed the height of the strings above the frets to be easily adjusted. Called simply a "screw neck" in Martin price lists, it was offered as an option until the 1890s. The herringbone trim seen around the sides of this Martin & Schatz and other early Martins would later become the identifying top border on Style 28 models. *(Guitar courtesy of The Chinery Collection.)*

A few of the early guitars were made with maple backs and sides, and others had a thin veneer of spruce on the interior of the rosewood back. Some of Martin's showier pre-1850 custom-ordered models featured a strip of wood purfling inlaid as a center strip along the guitar's Brazilian rosewood sides. (One such custom model came with a case also made of the now fabulously rare wood; it, too, featured the purfling.) There are other anomalies, such as instruments made with aluminum nuts and one model with a fingerboard entirely covered with pearl. (At $17 a pound, aluminum was an exotic and expensive alloy then, not stuff used to keep your TV dinner from leaking onto the couch.) Common details did start appearing in the 1830s, however, such as the herringbone trim around the sides and back that later became the identifying top trim of Style 28 Martins.

Some of the differences between the earliest models and later Martins are apparent in any photograph: the older models' Stauffer-influenced long, paisley-shaped peghead with tuners all on one side, for instance, or the almost figure-eight shape of the body. Less noticeable is the fact that most of the early guitars had necks made of a close-grained, light-colored hardwood, such as birch or maple, stained black to look like ebony. Also, the neck heel was usually shaped like a half-cone, tapering to

LEFT: The cittern was another early lute-shaped relative of the guitar that had nearly vanished by the late 1600s. Similar instruments did survive in England for at least another century, and the Portuguese guitar still retains some of the cittern's features. The fact that C. F. Martin Sr. built a cittern-shaped six-string guitar, apparently in the 1830s, indicates the wide range of styles he was willing to accommodate. The neck inlays were added much later, and though the ebony bridge probably has the correct outline, it is not original. *(Guitar courtesy of Fred Oster.)*

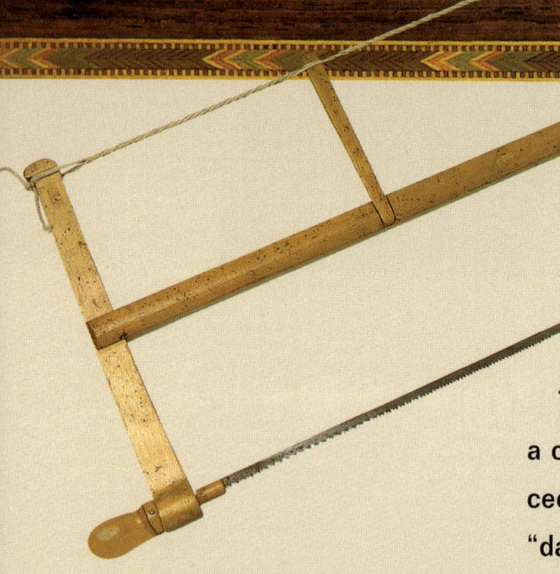

a small point near the back of the guitar. These were three-piece necks—both the peghead and heel being joined to the main portion of the neck with a joint so complex and beautifully fitted that it's a shame it's essentially invisible.

The stained neck with "ice-cream cone" heel would be replaced by a cedar neck, at least on most higher models, by the late 1840s. The cedar neck was two-piece, with the peghead grafted on with a long "dart" or "diamond" behind the nut to support the joint. However, the black neck with cone-shaped heel continued to appear on the smaller, very plain Style 17 Martins until the 1890s. Some of those smaller models also retained the fan-pattern top bracing that C.F. Sr. had used before he began to use X-bracing in the 1840s.

It was as if the rest of the Martin line continued to evolve toward the twentieth century, leaving the little Style 17s behind in the pre–Civil War era. This approach to change was typical of the Martin company during the nineteenth century, and to a certain extent even today. When changes occurred to one model or style, it is not safe to assume that similar changes were necessarily made to other models at the same time.

Other common internal features of nineteenth-century Martins, as compared to later models, are less dramatic in appearance and importance. Despite the smaller sizes and ultralight construction, most early Martins had five back braces instead of four. Since Martin was not yet using mahogany, the neck and tail blocks were also cedar. Whereas modern makers use a continuous kerfed wood lining strip to join a guitar's sides to the top and back, early Martins had either a

ABOVE AND BELOW: These tools almost undoubtably date from a time well after Martin's New York period, but they are similar to tools widely used in early–nineteenth-century instrument making. Today luthiers can count on the accuracy of power tools for many of the tasks that these simple implements performed, provided they have the knowledge and practice required to use them. This accounts for the large number of very young luthiers producing first-rate guitars today, even when they have recently come to the craft. However, 150 years ago the sheer manual skill and practiced eye needed to pilot hand tools like these took more years of experience. A slight misjudgment of the grain of the wood, especially if it happened in the final stages of a guitar's completion, could ruin several days' work.

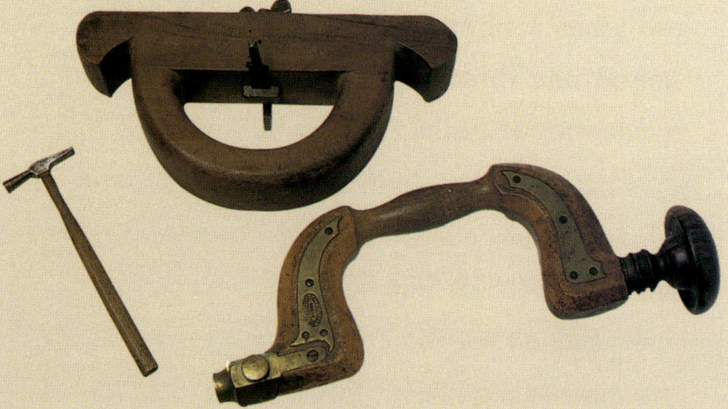

LEFT: These individual lining blocks are from a Style 40 guitar made in the 1880s, but they are identical to linings on Martins from much earlier and much later. It is actually the edge binding and lining blocks that hold the sides and soundboard together—you can even see a gleam of light coming through the ivory binding. *(Photo courtesy of Frank Ford.)*

BELOW AND INSET: One of the most curious Martins from the 1830s, this guitar has a number of innovative guitar-maker/inventor William Tilton's patented features from the 1850s, with his name all over them. The assumption is that someone couldn't resist the chance to try the latest "scientific" improvements on what was already an old standard. Countless Martins have been modified in numerous ways over the years, frequently with disastrous results. *(Photos from Jon Sievert © 1997.)*

solid, half-round lining or individual lining "blocks" that were glued in one at a time. That would be about 250 individual little pieces of wood for each size 2 guitar. The solid linings would have to be steamed and bent before being glued to the sides, and then shaped; so installing either of these linings was far more laborious than the current method. Typically slow to change, Martin continued to use individual lining blocks decades after other American makers were saving time with kerfed strips.

The cedar linings and blocks inside the early guitars may still smell faintly of the aromatic wood today. Combined with the slightly musty odor common to ancient, nearly closed wooden boxes, this accounts for the marvelous scent when you put your nose to the soundhole of many old Martins. Since the unfinished spruce and cedar inside the guitar are highly absorbent, old Martins often retain traces of perfume, cologne, or even incense from their previous owners, resulting in a "patina" for one's nose, just as signs on an old finish of previous owners' use can delight the eye. The Martin company continues to use cedar linings, and even the most recent models can still be identified by their scent as well as their sound.

THIS PAGE AND INSET: For C. F. Martin and his young family, life in Nazareth was far more comfortable than the melting pot hustle and bustle of New York City. But it kept Martin out of the mainstream of music and commerce. This would prove to be a disadvantage later. This late-nineteenth-century photo shows the view of the Cherry Hill Hotel from the Martin family home. Inset is the Martin House as it appears today. *(Photo courtesy of the Cherry Hill Hotel, Nazareth, PA; inset photo by Robert A. Yoder.)*

Finding a NEW HOME

1839–1873

February 21: Beautiful concert in church. A strange lady played on a harp, heard for the first time by many of the listeners.

From the diary of the Nazareth, Pennsylvania, Moravian congregation, 1839. Translated from German.

In 1836 C. F. Martin Sr.'s friend from Saxony, Henry Schatz, purchased 55 acres near Nazareth, Pennsylvania, a rural town north of Bethlehem. Ottilie Martin, C.F.'s wife, visited there and perhaps brought some pressure to bear on her husband, for in 1838 he sold his New York City store to the firm of Ludecus & Wolter. On December 21, 1839, he bought 8 acres on Cherry Hill—an area then known as Bushkill Township—situated above Nazareth on a road that was at that time the major route from Philadelphia to the north.

Nazareth had been settled by Moravians, one of the first Protestant sects, which in 1457 formed in what is now the Czech Republic after religious reformer Jan Hus was burned at the stake. Persecuted themselves, many Moravians found sanctuary in Saxony, not far from Mark Neukirchen.

Unlike other religious groups that settled in tolerant Pennsylvania, the Moravians weren't fleeing oppression. Rather they came to America as missionaries from their Saxony refuge. They initially settled in

RIGHT: C. F. Martin moved his family to rural Pennsylvania, but Martin guitars would continue to be sold primarily through New York for decades to come. This one has a Martin & Coupa label, and the loose partnership with New York City guitarist and instructor John Coupa lasted until at least 1850. *(Photo courtesy of Fred Oster.)*

Georgia in 1735, but the unworkable swampland and their pacifist beliefs (the British and Spanish were then battling in the region) led them to look elsewhere. They founded Nazareth in 1740.

From the diary account given on page 33, two things might be discerned about the Martins' new community: that Moravians quite liked music, and that they drew a definite line between themselves and others. On the first count, some of the first performances of Bach and Mozart pieces in America were by Moravians, and they possessed the first trombones heard in the New World. On the second count, what their diary entry meant by "a strange lady" was "she's not a Moravian." (It's even possible that the "strange lady" was Ottilie Martin, as she had been a church harpist in Vienna.)

Nazareth was a town—initially a commune—wholly owned by the church, and only church members could reside in it. That is why C. F. Martin Sr. bought a house on Cherry Hill overlooking Nazareth rather than one in town.

Cherry Hill was a far more agreeable setting than New York City had provided. Nazareth had only a couple of hundred residents—far fewer than the 500 persons today employed at the Martin factory—an inn, and a couple of stores and small industries, such as two carriage shops. The stores, operated by the church, carried many things imported from Germany. German and English were spoken in equal amounts in church and school.

LEFT: Though similar to the Martin & Coupa shown on page 33, this guitar represents the later stages of Martin's evolution of the American guitar. The three-ring soundhole rosette and straight-sided peghead go beyond Stauffer's influence. The top trim is an early use of herringbone on the face, though with extra lines of white and black purfling as is usually seen with Martin's pearl bordering. This body shape had been in use in Spain since the early 1800s, and a guitar built then by Augustin Caro of Granada had an identical peghead, complete with a carved "dart" behind the nut. C.F. Sr. may have arrived at these shapes independently, but details from his experimentation at Cherry Hill suggest that he was well aware of Spanish guitars. *(Photo © John Peden.)*

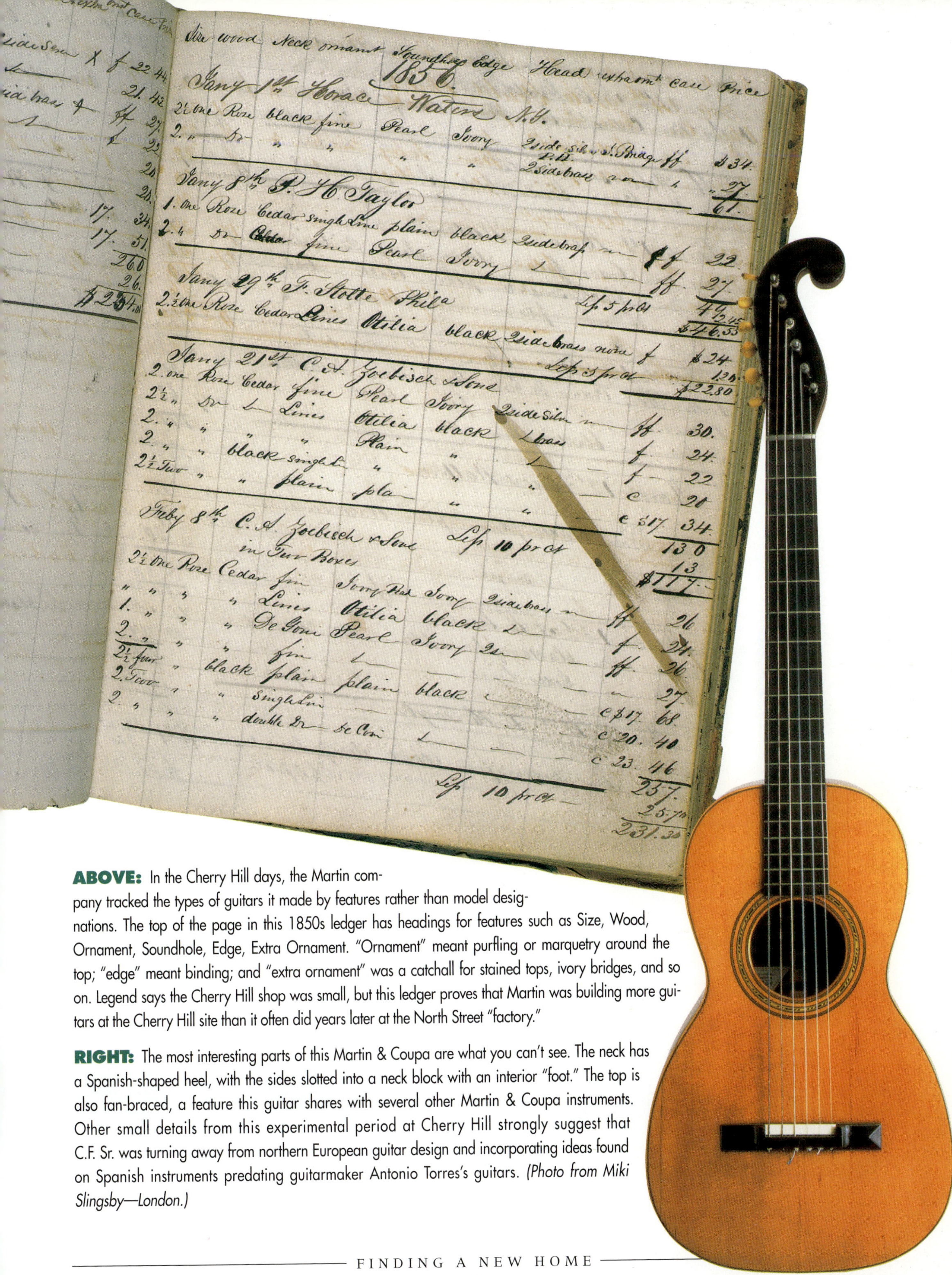

Size wood Neck ornament Soundhole Edge Head extra orn.t case Price

1850.

Jany 1st Horace Waters N.Y.

Jany 8th P. H. Taylor

Jany 29th F. Stotte Phila

Jany 21st C. A. Zoebisch & Sons

Feby 8th C. A. Zoebisch & Sons in Two Boxes

ABOVE: In the Cherry Hill days, the Martin company tracked the types of guitars it made by features rather than model designations. The top of the page in this 1850s ledger has headings for features such as Size, Wood, Ornament, Soundhole, Edge, Extra Ornament. "Ornament" meant purfling or marquetry around the top; "edge" meant binding; and "extra ornament" was a catchall for stained tops, ivory bridges, and so on. Legend says the Cherry Hill shop was small, but this ledger proves that Martin was building more guitars at the Cherry Hill site than it often did years later at the North Street "factory."

RIGHT: The most interesting parts of this Martin & Coupa are what you can't see. The neck has a Spanish-shaped heel, with the sides slotted into a neck block with an interior "foot." The top is also fan-braced, a feature this guitar shares with several other Martin & Coupa instruments. Other small details from this experimental period at Cherry Hill strongly suggest that C.F. Sr. was turning away from northern European guitar design and incorporating ideas found on Spanish instruments predating guitarmaker Antonio Torres's guitars. *(Photo from Miki Slingsby—London.)*

LEFT AND RIGHT: The mystery of which is the first X-braced guitar will probably never be solved, but these two early candidates were clearly made by builders who were aware of each other and may have even been acquaintances. The fact that two very similar guitars—both sold in New York in the latter 1840s and both made by German immigrants—have nearly identical X-patterns under the top suggests that there was a considerable pool of talent at work. Whether X-bracing was a concept shared among compatriots or pirated by competitors is the only question left unanswered. Schmidt & Maul were in New York from the late 1830s to about 1860, and the guitar on the right is dated 1848 on the underside of the top (the hole in the peghead is not original). The other guitar bears a Martin & Coupa label, and Martin historian Mike Longworth's research into insurance policies held by C. F. Martin Sr. on Coupa's 385 Broadway address suggests that Martin had guitars there as late as 1851 and certainly for several years before that. Regardless of which came first, Martin was the firm that went on to make X-bracing a standard feature of the American guitar. *(Guitar on left courtesy of The Chinery Collection; photo on right courtesy of Fred Dusel, guitar courtesy of Joseph Grubaugh.)*

The Moravian congregation diary depicts a placid, pastoral life: "January 1839: Weather very mild first part of month. January 7: Brother Christian Brunner elected head diener in place of Brother Jack Eckensburger, latter not very pleased thereby. April 8: Potato planting in gardens. April 11: Stone block laid across our street. April 15: Trees pruned..."

Current company chairman and CEO Chris Martin has traveled to Mark Neukirchen, and he found the area very similar to Nazareth. "You look at the lithograph of Mark Neukirchen in our museum and it looks a lot like Nazareth, but in person it's really stunning. You can see Neukirchen was a more prosperous town at one time—the buildings are more formal—but the countryside couldn't be more like this place," he says.

LEFT AND ABOVE: This Martin & Coupa size 3 guitar from the 1840s shows Martin's sense of refined elegance. Besides ivory binding, this guitar has an additional band of ivory bordering the top, much like the later Style 44 guitars made for performer Vahdah Olcott Bickford. The label lists the company's business address as 383 Broadway, New York—John Coupa's teaching studio and guitar showroom. Coupa claimed to offer "the largest assortment of guitars that can be found in the United States," but in the 1840s that could still have been only a few dozen guitars. *(Guitar courtesy of The Chinery Collection.)*

X-BRACING

Put a mirror in the soundhole of most steel-string guitars today, and you'll almost certainly see an X-brace. It's nothing to write home about, but you'd be looking at the thing that made the now-ubiquitous steel-string guitar viable.

European guitars of C. F. Martin Sr.'s day had an internal structural support known as ladder bracing—strips of wood glued to the underside of the top at right angles to the string length—or the more elaborate fan bracing developed earlier by builders in Cadiz and perfected by C.F.'s Spanish contemporary Antonio Torres. The fan brace would go on to define classical guitar design up to the present, becoming accepted in the United States only after Andrés Segovia popularized the Spanish-design guitars when he toured the United States in 1928.

In the 1800s, though, the Atlantic was a sufficient divide to separate the styles of construction, and the prevailing American bracing design was one that C.F. developed in Cherry Hill, Pennsylvania. It was called an X-brace because its spruce braces crossed in an X-pattern in the space between the soundhole and the bridge.

Though it's the least visible part of an acoustic guitar's construction, the bracing is of paramount importance. It functioned as a crucial balance between supporting the thin tonewood top—usually of spruce or cedar—and assisting the strings' vibration in radiating from the bridge over the entire top of the guitar. Err on the side of lightness, and the guitar's top caves in under the pressure of the strings; err on the side of stability, and you kill the tone of the instrument. With the X-brace, Martin hit a balance that is the standard to this day in nearly all but the Spanish-school guitars.

It is well established that C.F. developed his X-pattern top bracing by the 1850s, but there was no clear evolution in his earlier guitars leading to that specific bracing design. The earliest Martins were ladder-braced, with braces glued perpendicular to the strings. Some

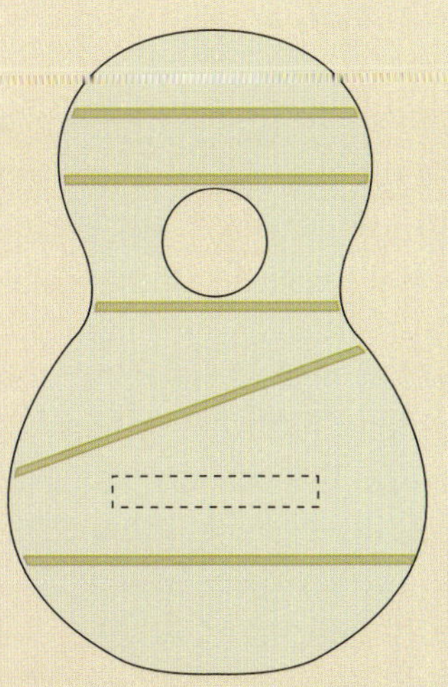

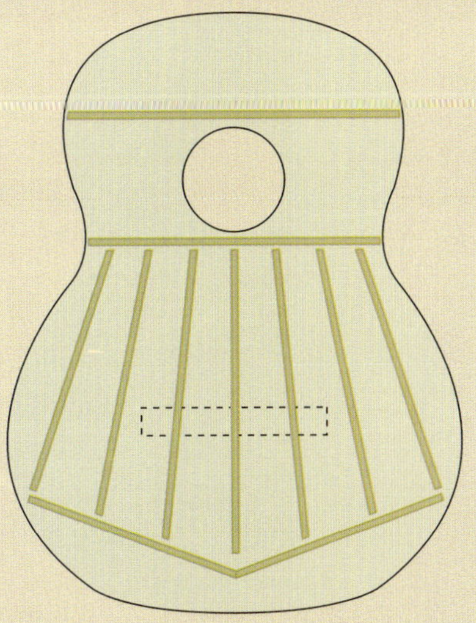

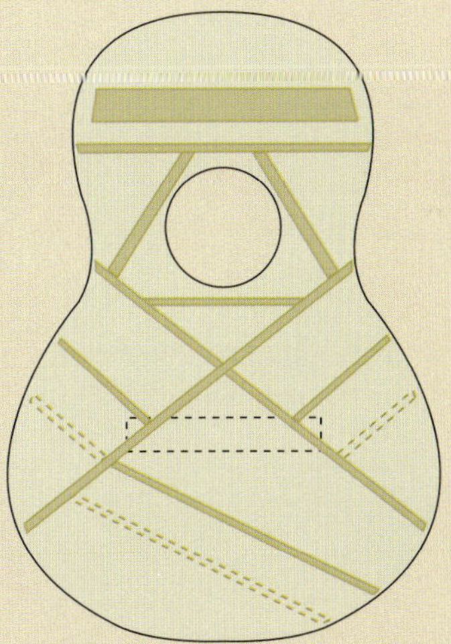

also had braces in a simple fan pattern, suggesting that C.F. was aware of the guitar's development in Spain. At least one guitar with a Martin & Coupa label has braces that cross. But the Martin company continued to use a simple fan-braced pattern for many of its smaller models into the 1890s.

There are some accounts claiming that other makers preceded Martin in using X-bracing, which is certainly possible, though hard to prove. Regardless of whether C.F. devised X-bracing on his own, devised it with compatriot guitar-maker Henry Schatz, or modified an X-pattern devised by others, it was C.F.'s work alone that went on to help forge the guitar's future.

ABOVE: The bracing pattern at left is a variant of "ladder bracing" as found on a French guitar by Rene Lacote made in 1852. Put the angled brace parallel with the others and you have a bracing style similar to that used in Stauffer-style Martins of the 1830s.

The fan bracing pattern in the middle was the contribution of Antonio Torres, also in the 1850s, and it is still widely used on classical guitars today. The X–bracing pattern at right appears in the early 1850s on Martin guitars. The dotted lines indicate braces added later for 00 and larger sizes. The strength and stability of the X-braces were just what was needed for the extra tension of steel strings.

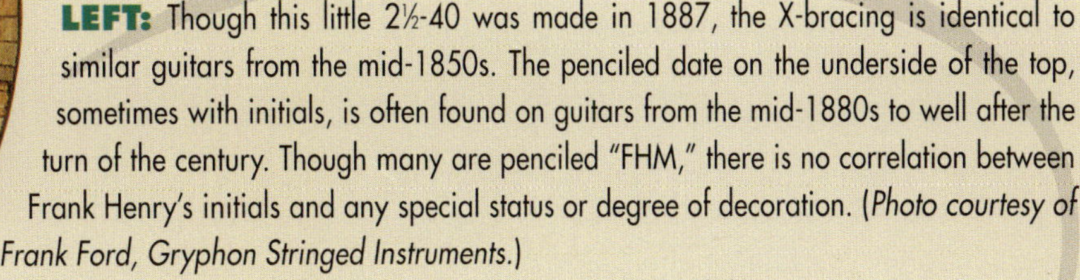

LEFT: Though this little 2½-40 was made in 1887, the X-bracing is identical to similar guitars from the mid-1850s. The penciled date on the underside of the top, sometimes with initials, is often found on guitars from the mid-1880s to well after the turn of the century. Though many are penciled "FHM," there is no correlation between Frank Henry's initials and any special status or degree of decoration. (*Photo courtesy of Frank Ford, Gryphon Stringed Instruments.*)

The X-Bracing Breakthrough

At some point through the years, a legend developed that Martin guitars were built in the kitchen at Cherry Hill. Chris Martin thinks it is more probable that they were built in a barn on the property. The labels and stamps on the guitars of this period identified them as being from New York City, an address that doubtless carried more cachet than "in a barn somewhere you've never heard of."

It was at Cherry Hill that C.F.'s genius for guitar design came into its own. The nearly equal-sized upper and lower bouts of his Stauffer-influenced New York models gave way to smaller upper bouts and narrow waists, while the fancy headstock and bridge were replaced with plain rectangular shapes. Instead of ornate inlay work, the soundhole was graced with concentric rings of light and dark purfling. His most significant change took place inside the instrument, with his X-shaped bracing of the top.

Within a few years at Cherry Hill, Martin had set the standard for American guitars for the next half-century.

ABOVE: By sometime in the late 1840s, the three-ring design became the standard rosette for Martin guitars. The string of pearl diamonds, as seen on this Martin & Coupa, disappeared in favor of a continuous band of pearl. Soon C.F. Sr. would reserve the pearl soundhole ring for higher models only, and most Martins were given ivory bands or delicate wood marquetry in the center soundhole ring. *(Guitar courtesy of C. F. Martin & Company.)*

RIGHT: The bridge ornaments and Stauffer-style head on this beautiful transitional Martin from the early 1850s suggest Martin's New York City days, but the narrow upper bout and sleek shape are of a standard size 2, Martin's best-selling size through the 1870s. More importantly, it has an X-braced top, though more plain size 2 Martins would still be made with fan bracing for decades to come. The lavish use of pearl bordering, shown here in detail, is already less common by this date, and the multiple rings of pearl in the rosette are rarely seen on later Martins, no matter how fancy. Pearl bordering on the face of the fretboard doesn't appear again until the "over Style 45" Limited Edition models of recent years. *(Guitar courtesy of The Chinery Collection.)*

OPPOSITE PAGE: The *Baltimore Olio and Musical Gazette* was a publication that catered specifically to women and their increasing influence in American music. C. F. Martin Sr. could and did specifically target a female guitar market by advertising his instruments in the *Olio*.

ADVERTISEMENTS.

NUNNS & CLARK,
NEW YORK,
Have opened an Agency for the sale of their PIANO FORTES at No. 352 *Baltimore street, Baltimore*, Where they constantly keep on hand a full assortment of 6, 6¼, 6½ and 7 octave instruments at New York prices. tf

A. H. GALE & CO.
NEW YORK,
Respectfully inform their friends and the public generally, that they have appointed W. C. PETERS their sole Agent for the sale of their PIANO FORTES in Baltimore. A full assortment at New York prices, can at all times be had at No. 352 *Baltimore street, Baltimore.* tf

LEE & WALKER,
Successors to G. Willig,
162 *Chesnut street, Swain's New Building,*
PHILADELPHIA,
Publishers and Importers of MUSIC, MUSICAL INSTRUMENTS and STRINGS of every description. Constantly on hand, a general assortment of PIANO FORTES at lowest prices. The Trade, Seminaries and Professors supplied on accommodating terms.

Franklin Institute.
The Judges, after a careful and laborious examination, recommend the following awards which...

P. FLAVIO,
MEMPHIS, TENNESSEE,
Dealer in
Piano Fortes, Music,
AND MUSICAL MERCHANDISE GENERALLY.
New Music received weekly.
Orders from Schools and Teachers filled on accommodating terms. tf

E. WEBER & CO.
LITHOGRAPHERS

Splendid Daguerreian Gallery.
Electro Daguerreotypes.
AN EXTRAORDINARY IMPROVEMENT!
The subscriber begs leave to inform the public that his new and extensive Gallery is now in operation at 207½ BALTIMORE STREET, two doors below the dry goods store of Hamilton Easter & Co. ...
J. H. WHITEHURST.

...l and Instrumental Tuition.
HEWITT & DAUGHTER,
...ors of Vocal and Instrumental Music,
...und at No. 143 N. HIGH STREET; or, ...tion to the stores of W. C. Peters or F. ... Terms reasonable. tf

Heads of Seminaries.

F. MARTIN,
Guitar Maker,

H. ANDREWS,
Copperplate Printer,

THE

BALTIMORE OLIO,

AND

AMERICAN MUSICAL GAZETTE.

A Monthly Parlor Companion for the Ladies,

DEVOTED CHIEFLY TO MUSIC, THE ARTS, AND MUSICAL INTELLIGENCE GENERALLY.

Each Number will contain at least Six Pages of closely printed Music, arranged for the Piano Forte, Guitar, Flute and Violin.

PUBLISHED BY
W. C. PETERS,
OFFICE—No. 352 BALTIMORE STREET,
BALTIMORE.

TERMS.
One Dollar and Fifty Cents per Annum,
SINGLE COPIES TWENTY-FIVE CENTS.
To be paid in Advance.

Vol. 1. Baltimore, January, 1850. No. 1.

Entered according to act of Congress, in the year 1850, by W. C. PETERS, in the Clerk's Office of the District Court of Maryland.

The BALTIMORE OLIO can be obtained by order at the office of publication, of the authorised Agents, or of any Music Seller or Periodical Dealer in the United States

BALTIMORE OLIO,
AND
AMERICAN MUSICAL GAZETTE,

Devoted chiefly to the cultivation of *Music, Musical Literature*, the Arts and Musical Intelligence generally.

Each number will contain, at least twelve pages of matter, (royal quarto,) six of which will be Letter-press, and six closely printed Music, divided thus:

Two pages Vocal Music, with Piano Accompaniment.
Two pages Instrumental Music, for the Piano Forte.
One page (Vocal or Instrumental Music) for the Guitar.
One page of Music arranged for Flute or Violin, with an occasional Duet for two voices, two performers on the Piano, or a Duet for Flute and Guitar.

The work will be printed on fine paper and new type. The price (the quality of the matter taken into consideration) will be put much lower than any similar publication.

The expenditures connected with this undertaking will be much greater than usual, as many of the Songs will be illustrated by the best American artists. A magnificent embossed Vignette or presentation plate will accompany the twelfth number, to those who subscribe for the year. The music will be stereotyped, and no pains or expense will be spared to make the "OLIO" a favorite Parlor Companion for the Ladies.

The Editorial Columns of the Olio will be divided, and the different departments confided to, and placed in separate hands.

The Musical Editor will be assisted by several distinguished American and European writers and composers.

The Literary Department will be confined to a gentleman of acknowledged ability.

The Business Department will be entrusted to a gentleman who will take charge of the Correspondence, and attend to the Financial arrangements.

TERMS:

The OLIO will be Mailed to Subscribers at the following rates:

Yearly Subscribers, each, payment in advance $1 50

The work will be sold to Music Dealers, Booksellers, Periodical Agents and Clubs, and forwarded to one address.

Four Copies, per annum, payment in advance,			$5 00
Nine do.	do.	do.	10 00
Fourteen	do.	do.	15 00
Twenty	do.	do.	20 00

ADVERTISEMENTS of a Musical or Literary nature will be inserted at the following rates:

One Insertion, six lines payment in advance,			$1 00
Three do.	do.	do.	2 50
Six Months,	do.	do.	5 00
One Year,	do.	do.	10 00

☞ Music Dealers, Musical Instrument Makers, Publishers, Professors of Music, and those in want of Teachers, will find the Olio a good advertising medium.

☞ All Letters, Orders and Communications should be *post-paid*, and addressed to "Baltimore Olio," care of W. C Peters, 352 Baltimore street.

W. C. PETERS, PUBLISHER AND PROPRIETOR.

PRINTED BY JOHN W. WOODS, 184 BALTIMORE STREET.

Contents.

Our Agents.

☞ Persons wishing to subscribe to ... directly to the subscriber, or to the follow... kindly consented to act as Agents.

New York, Firth, Pond & Co: Wm Hal... E. L. Walker, Philadelphia; Henry Kle... Pittsburg; C. F. Martin, Nazareth: *Mass...* & Co., Boston: *Delaware*, James L. Roche... *of Columbia*, Mrs. G. Anderson, Washi... Lanhert, Fredericksburg: *Ohio*, Peters & Fi... *tucky*, Peters, Webb & Co, Louisville: J. ... *Indiana*, J. R. Nunnemacker, New Albany: ... Weber, St. Louis: *Tennessee*, John B. West... *ana*, W. T. Mayo, New Orleans.

W. C. PETERS, 352 Baltimore...

To Correspondents.

"S. C. F." Cincinnati.—"Summer Longings," w... our second number.

"J. S." Pittsburg.—Thanks for your kind letter, we are ... clined to publish it.

"G." Cincinnati.—"A Duet for two Flutes," is declined, ... alterations will not do. We admit we promised to give a preference to *music* written by Americans, but we did not mean thereby, to publish *trash* because it was American.

"P. F." New York.—Every thing inserted in the Olio, whether Prose, Poetry or Music, will be paid for if desired—we prefer paying.

"O." Lexington, Ky.—As we intend publishing our very best copyright music in the Olio, we are compelled to take out a copyright for each number, as the different pieces will be issued in sheet form on the first Monday in each month. We shall insert such Songs only as may have been, or shortly will be, set to appropriate music. We...

...French language is also ... who has had much experience a... tress. The best of references can be ... tters (post-paid) directed to Wm. C. Pe... Music Publisher, Baltimore, will meet w... prompt attention. tf

C. F. MARTIN,

Guitar Maker,

Respectfully informs the Musical public generally, that the great favor bestowed on him has induced him to enlarge his Factory, in order to supply the increasing demand for his instruments.

A full supply of each pattern, always on hand, at the Music Stores of W. C. Peters, Baltimore; Peters & Field, Cincinnati; and Peters, Webb & Co., Louisville, Ky. tf

EDWIN H. ANDREWS,

...usic & Copperplate Print...

No. 7 *Liberty street, Baltimor...*

...left at the Music S...

* The above lines w... Smith, of Virginia, and were suggested by the departure of some friends (commonly called the Parkersburg Exiles) to the West. They will be fully understood by any of the CLAN McIVOR.

ABOVE, LEFT, AND BELOW: The fancy soundhole decoration, extra marquetry on the sides, and ivory-sided peghead make this an unusually fancy Martin for the 1850s. Existing sales ledgers for 1855 through 1858 indicate that Martin was selling mostly plain guitars with little ornamentation beyond a pearl soundhole and ivory bridge. The unique combination of details on a guitar like this was probably the result of a special order. *(Guitar courtesy of The Chinery Collection.)*

GROWING

In the America of C. F. Martin Sr.'s time, a great many guitarists, both professional and amateur, were women. This was a holdover from the European parlor music tradition and in keeping with the prevailing view that women were only suited for the gentler arts. Unlike in Europe, where women's fretboard skills remained confined to the parlor, American women may not have been allowed to vote, but they could earn a living by teaching music or performing publicly on the guitar. One publication devoted to female musicians carried the weighty moniker *The Baltimore Olio and Musical Gazette, a Monthly Parlor Companion for the Ladies, Devoted Chiefly to Music, the Arts, and Musical Intelligence Generally.*

Martin's sales to female customers were high enough that certain of the guitars C.F. made—the models 2 and 2½ initially—were specifically intended for women's typically smaller hands. In part due to the women's trade, he was successful enough that in 1850 he ran an ad in the *Olio* (shown on page 41) that announced his factory's expansion to meet demand.

By 1850 C.F. was able to say, in his *Olio* ad, "A full supply of each pattern [is] always on hand," having begun to standardize the line of guitars he offered. (See "Martin Models: Mid-Nineteenth Century" on page 52.) Prior to that time, he had exercised the craftsman's prerogative and rarely made two instruments precisely alike. But consistency in manufacturing—beginning in the 1830s with the mass production of Colt's revolvers—was coming to be

ABOVE: You don't often find Hawaiian koa on mid-nineteenth-century guitars; in fact, you don't find much koa on anything at that early date. Around 1915, when the Hawaiian music craze swept the nation, Martin began to make lots of instruments from this beautiful wood, but one can only speculate why C.F. Sr. chose to try it on this Martin & Coupa from the 1840s. *(Guitar courtesy of The Chinery Collection.)*

regarded as an American virtue, and buyers at distant stores wanted to know exactly what they'd be getting before they placed orders with Martin. As a result, Martin's sales were expanding to the point where C.F. needed set patterns for his models in order to produce them on any scale.

By 1850 a typical Martin guitar would have had its back and sides made of Brazilian rosewood, a three-piece neck of a light, close-grained wood (usually birch or maple) stained black, an ebony fingerboard, and a spruce top (from a variety of locales, but often from the Pocono Mountains north of Nazareth) with dark rosewood binding. This was standard throughout Martin's line, with the models set apart only in size and degree of ornamentation. Higher-priced models, for example, would have ivory trim and Spanish cedar necks. The bodies were still very small by modern standards; and with very rare exception, the decoration was restrained, typified by the elegant but reserved band of abalone inlay for which the company is still famous.

Some early Martin advertisements claim that the company also made violins and other stringed instruments, though there is no record of its doing so. But C.F.'s nephew, employee, and later partner, Christian Frederick Hartmann, did, and it's possible C.F. was just advertising his services. A viola and bass made by Hartmann reside today in the Moravian Historical Society Museum in Nazareth.

Charles A. Zoebisch Jr. was another Mark Neukirchen immigrant. He had been a brass instrument maker there before sailing to the United States in 1842 and settling at Cherry Hill, near the Martin home/workshop. Five years later, when his father, C.A. Sr., arrived from Europe,

(continued on page 48)

RIGHT: Even after leaving New York City, C.F. Sr. took more than a few sidetracks when it came to the shape of his guitars. Yet perhaps the most unusual feature of this 1840s Martin is its condition. It looks as if it had been made a decade or two ago and then stored without ever having been played. Classical style bridges (without pins) and ivory-sided pegheads were found on other 1840s Martins, including a few with Martin & Coupa labels. *(Photo © Kim Stephenson.)*

ABOVE: This elegant peghead has been seen on only a handful of early Martins, including another exotic one with an unusual shape and on a very early size 0. The ivory sides, as seen here, later evolved to a thin border on only the uppermost edge of the peghead. *(Photo © Kim Stephenson.)*

ABOVE: The compound curve of the guitar sides where they meet the neck is sure to inspire admiration from any serious woodworker. Although a common feature of later mandolins, no other Martin guitar has surfaced in which the sides form a continuous, smooth transition into the neck. The low-profile shoulders would make playing in upper positions on this guitar almost as easy as on a cutaway guitar. *(Photo © Kim Stephenson.)*

ABOVE: The bridge with Spanish-style tie block and fixed saddle appears on several early Martins, and it is the earliest version of the "pyramid" bridge that became the standard for many American guitars. The holes in the top of this ivory example are probably not original. *(Photo © Kim Stephenson.)*

ABOVE: This shield-shaped block, similar to the "foot" in a Spanish guitar, shows up on lots of early Martins. Like most of the features on this guitar, this block disappeared in the company's evolution. *(Photo © Kim Stephenson.)*

MARTIN COLLECTORS— ARE THESE GUYS NUTS?

ABOVE: Mac Yasuda: businessman, country singer, guitar collector, and owner of 14 prewar D-45s. *(Photo © Mac Yasuda Enterprises.)*

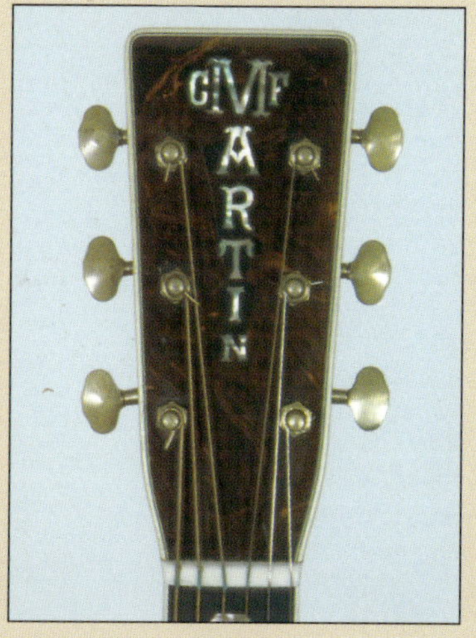

ABOVE: The tortoiseshell celluloid headstock veneer on Mac's 1940 D-45 makes it rare even for a D-45. *(Photo © Mac Yasuda Enterprises.)*

A Martin is not a purchase most guitarists take lightly. They save, ponder, and eventually buy one guitar in which they'll find a lifetime's worth of music.

Others, however, just keep going.

Consider Mac Yasuda. Growing up in Kobe, Japan, he glued a pick guard to his nylon-stringed guitar, hoping to make it sound like the guitar he saw pictured on albums by his hero Hank Snow. Mac was later befriended by Snow, who told the aspiring singer he needed a Martin guitar to go with that pick guard.

He saw plenty of Martins when he came to the United States in 1970. They were still beyond the reach of a poor college student, but he vowed that would change. As he became successful in business he started collecting rare Martins, and today he has 250, including 14 of the 75 or 80 prewar D-45s presumed to still exist.

One—formerly Eagle Bernie Leadon's—has a tortoiseshell celluloid peghead. Mac also owns a D-28 believed to have been Hank Williams's, Norman Blake's D-18H and 1934 D-28, and Webb Pierce's '46 D-28, with garish inlay that looks as if it was applied by a horse.

Mac uses several of the guitars—he's appeared on the Grand Ole Opry and recorded CDs with them. He restores and preserves the instruments, authors books on them, plans to share them in a museum, and supposes his wife is going to enjoy selling many of them off when he dies.

Scott Chinery's passion for guitars began when he first heard the Beatles. Like Yasuda, he worked his way into wealth and began amassing a collection, now about 1,000 guitars, some 10 percent of them Martins. While Yasuda focuses on "golden age" Martins, Chinery is documenting the entire history, from New York–made Stauffer styles to an X-braced 1852 model (with steel strings!) that he declares "the best sounding guitar I've ever heard" to the firm's current models. He's also helping to make some Martin history: He's ordered a custom 19-

RIGHT: Mega-collector Scott Chinery holds one of the finest examples of an 1830s Martin in his right hand, and his brand-new "Goliath" custom model in his left.

inch guitar—a company first—which Chinery hopes will be the prototype for a new model.

Chinery feels that, "Martin is making guitars as good or better than at any point in its history. Pick one up and you can't help but feel there's 150 years of family pride in it, that they take an exceptional pride in producing something extraordinary, not just something that can produce a dollar."

Chinery plays his guitars three to four hours a day, and has guests such as Steve Howe over to record with them. Several instruments have been loaned to the Smithsonian. Chinery says, "What I want is to tell the story of the American guitar, to share the instruments in public exhibitions, concerts, recordings, and publications."

Is he nuts, or compensating for some childhood lack?

"You know, I can't come up with a deep-rooted explanation to it all, other than that I love guitars," he says.

While it helps to be rich if you're collecting rare Martins, it's not crucial. California collector Travis Harrelson is retired and on a fixed income, but he has 60 Martins, mostly ukuleles. The attraction? "Martins are perfect, not like me, but pretty close," he laughs. He and his late ukulele partner, Don Wilson, took their ukes to convalescent homes, playing for free; to rock clubs; or sometimes they'd just hop a bus and play for the passengers. Even two weeks before Wilson passed away in a care facility, the duo entertained the other patients with their ukulele feats.

"I've had every model uke Martin has made," Harrelson says, "and it always amazes me how much joy you can get out of these tiny things."

ABOVE: Uke collector Travis Harrelson goes to bat with a Martin soprano uke while cutting up with his late bandmate Don Wilson. *(Photo courtesy of Jim Washburn.)*

New York, Aug 6th 1855

Mr. C. F. Martin

Bought of C. A. ZOEBISCH & SONS,

Manufacturers, Importers and Wholesale Dealers in

163 WILLIAM STREET, UP STAIRS.

MUSICAL INSTRUMENTS, STRINGS, &C.

No 1 — 1 Guitar pat. head . . . . 4 | 3.31
" 2 | 3.18
" 3
" 4
" 5
" 6
" 7
" 8
" 9
" add 3½% for Co

C. A. ZOEBISCH & SONS,

Importers of and Wholesale Dealers in

MUSICAL INSTRUMENTS, STRINGS, &c.

46 MAIDEN LANE, NEW YORK.

Depot of C. F. Martin & Co.'s

"CELEBRATED GUITARS"

ACKNOWLEDGED TO BE THE BEST IN THE WORLD.

C. F. MARTIN & Co. have received Testimonials from the following Professors of the Guitar:

MADAME DE GONI, MR. S. DE LA COVA,
MR. J. B. COUPA, MR. CHARLES DE JANON,
MR. WILLIAM SCHUBERT, MR. H. WORRELL.

WHO ARE CONSIDERED THE BEST SOLOISTS KNOWN.

All the Newest Styles of Brass & German Silver Instruments constantly on hand. or made to order.

ABOVE AND RIGHT: C. A. Zoebisch & Sons of New York City was Martin's exclusive distributor for nearly 40 years. The guitars were shipped from remote Nazareth to Zoebisch by stagecoach.

LEFT: Here is another, though somewhat less-refined, example of a "Renaissance-shaped" Martin guitar from around 1840. The shape of this and other similarly shaped guitars was probably derived from a French guitar of the Renaissance period. The odd metal bridge—screwed into the top—seems to be original. *(Guitar courtesy of C. F. Martin & Company.)*

both relocated to New York City, where as C. A. Zoebisch & Sons they established themselves as "Manufacturers, Importers, and Wholesale Dealers in Musical Instruments, Depot of C. F. Martin & Co.'s Celebrated Guitars." They remained Martin's exclusive distributors for nearly a half-century. Zoebisch and C.F. Sr. were also friends, with a long correspondence between the families that often strayed from business to such matters as the kidney trouble caused by New York beer.

Martin's guitars were shipped to New York by stagecoach via Somerville, New Jersey, then later through Easton, Pennsylvania. Packed in cases that looked like a variation on a child's coffin, they must have made an eerie image, those little black caskets with a faint musical humming emanating from them as the rough roads caused the strings to vibrate. Many also were delivered via canal barge or ship to stores in Richmond, New Orleans, Nashville, St. Louis, Boston, and other ports. No matter how well built or packed they were, some guitars arrived at their destinations cracked.

ABOVE AND LEFT: To protect his guitars for the rough travel to his distributor in New York City, C.F. packed them in cases that resembled little coffins. Bolts of "Canton flannel" and large amounts of "case trimmings" regularly appeared in Martin's expense records, so it is clear the company spent considerable effort building these cases. Martin used #2 grade poplar for the cases and "cull" grade for the packing crates.

The Move to Town

C. F. Martin Sr.'s Cherry Hill home was on the stagecoach route, so his business likely wasn't burdened by his out-of-town location. But for life's amenities or for socializing, it was far enough from town that the Martins needed to hitch up the wagon every time they needed butter or soap.

The family had joined the Moravian church around 1857, the same time the church had decided to open the town to outsiders. Martin bought a piece of property at the corner of North and Main streets in Nazareth and around 1859 built a home and then a small factory there. Within a decade his log books would show 11 men working there, each earning from $1 to $3 a day.

As Nazareth was going sleepily along, the rest of the nation was tumbling into violent discord. The slave forebears of future Martin players such as Lightnin' Hopkins, Skip James, and Brownie McGhee were still being sold and worked as livestock in southern states; and in 1861 the nation split in its most deadly war.

In many burgs, the Civil War decimated the male population. Though it raged to within 100 miles of Nazareth—including the decisive battle at Gettysburg—the war is barely mentioned in the Moravian records. The Moravians were pacifists and—as they had done in the Revolutionary War—were allowed to avoid conscription by paying a heavy fine, which was used to hire other men to go in their places.

Curiously, Martin's sales were strong throughout the war. In 1867, in recognition of his expanding company and advancing age, C.F. took on his son, C.F. Jr., and his nephew C. F. Hartmann as partners and renamed the business C. F. Martin & Company. Two years later they weathered an economic slump that gripped the nation.

ABOVE: Once the Martin family had joined the Moravian church, they quickly moved down from Cherry Hill into Nazareth proper. This is the restored family house in Nazareth as it appears today in its new role as home to the Nazareth Historical Society. *(Photo by Robert A. Yoder.)*

The End of a Generation

On February 16, 1873, after 77 years—some 62 of those years spent fashioning mute wood into singing guitars—C. F. Martin Sr. died.

A few months later, the company received a letter that, with hindsight, can be viewed as something of a skewed testimonial to C.F.'s guitars. It was from the Boston firm of White & Coullaud, music publishers, importers, and dealers in music and musical instruments. On the envelope, in place of an address, was the instruction: "Will the Post Master please hand this to the forman [sic] of the late Mr. C. F. Martin's Guitar Factory or any of his workman [sic] if the forman [sic] is not to be found."

The letter inside offered a paragraph of condolence on the death of Mr. Martin, and then it abruptly proceeded to attempt to induce the foreman to jump ship with Martin's designs:

"We write you hoping that some arrangement can be affected [sic] by which you and our selves can be benefited thereby.... What we want is to inquire of you if we can make any arrangement with you by which we can be supplied with guitars of Mr. Martin's pattern. Also if you would come to Boston and make them for us here.... We are greatly in need of a first-class instrument. An early answer stating your views of the case would greatly oblige us, as we mean business."

In the years to follow, C. F. Martin Sr.'s progeny were to find that several competitors meant business, as the guitar found a voice in the growing nation.

LEFT: This was the first section of the Martin Guitar factory to be built on North Street in Nazareth. Today it houses a parts shipping warehouse and the Guitarmaker's Connection, where aspiring luthiers can buy guitar parts and tools. *(Photo by Robert A. Yoder.)*

ABOVE: Shortly after C. F. Martin's death, White and Coullaud sent this letter to the foreman at the Martin factory, hoping to lure him to Boston with Martin's designs.

LEFT, MIDDLE AND RIGHT: This 2½-17 was purchased from the estate of Colonel John Hancock III, who both played and collected guitars. He reportedly bought this one from the family of Samuel Clemens, better known as Mark Twain (a name tag on the case has been authenticated as being in Clemens's handwriting). Clemens purchased the guitar used in 1861, and he took lessons from his older sister, who was a music teacher. He kept it until his death in 1910. The wear on the top and neck of the guitar shows that it received lots of use, and unpublished letters by the young Clemens suggest that he made considerable effort to become an accomplished guitarist. The young writer wrote that he found the instrument to be quite useful in meeting young women. Some things haven't changed. *(Guitar photos from Hank Risan; photo of Mark Twain from Corbis/Bettmann.)*

Martin Models

Mid-Nineteenth Century

For those not familiar with Martin guitar terminology, a conversation among acoustic guitarists may sound like a secret code. What does "triple oh twenty-eight" mean in plain English? With the addition of new models over the years, Martin's identification system gets confusing even to insiders, but the earliest nomenclature was quite logical—provided you knew the rules.

Martin model designations originally consisted of a number indicating the size, then a hyphen, followed by a two-digit number representing the style. With a few rare exceptions, from the 1850s until after

RIGHT: Model 2-27 shows up often in the 1850s sales ledgers, and it sold well until the style was discontinued in the late 1890s. The pearl soundhole ring and ivory-bound fretboard ($1 each) were sometimes added to the plainer Style 26 or 28. Though considered tiny today, this was a full-size guitar for women in the nineteenth century. *(Guitar courtesy of The Chinery Collection.)*

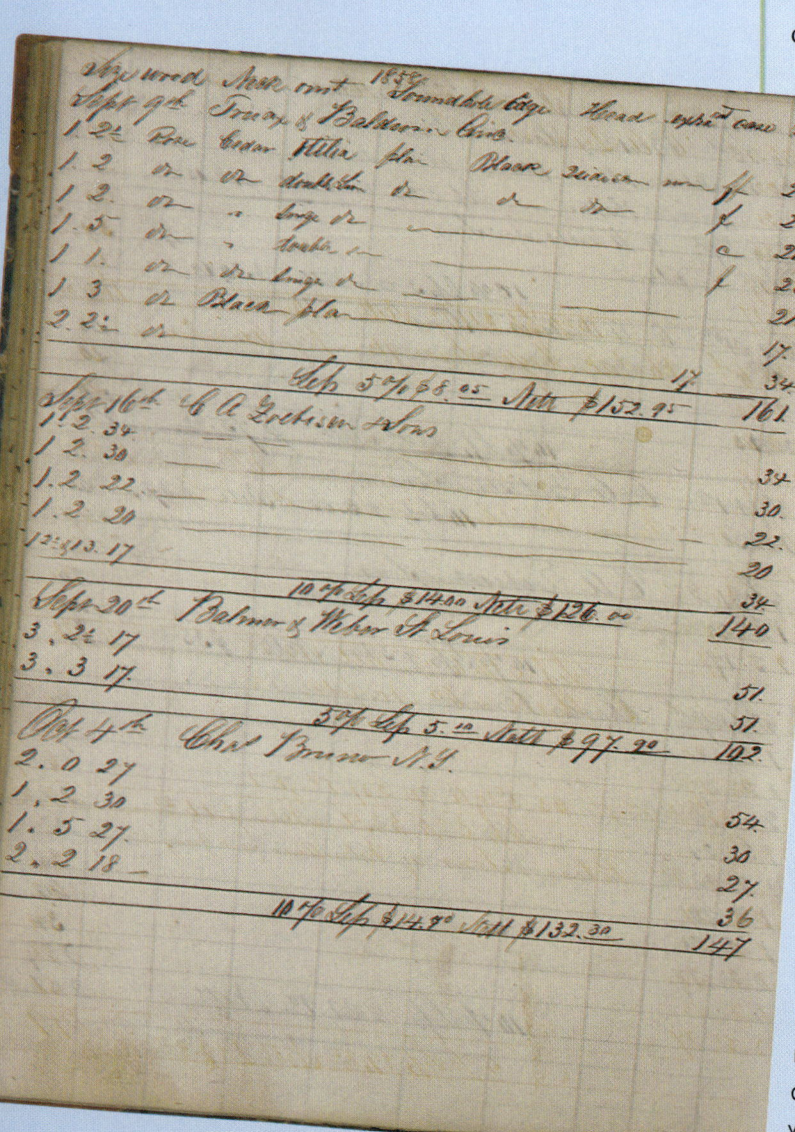

1858

Sept 16th C A Zoebisch & Sons
1.2 34 — 34
1.2 30 — 30
1.2 22 — 22
1.2 20 — 20
Sep 5% $8.05 Nett $152.95 — 161

Sept 20th Balmer & Weber St Louis
3.2½ 17
3.3 17
10% Sep $14.00 Nett $126.00 — 140

Oct 4th Chs Bruno N.Y.
2.0 27
1.2 30
1.5 27
2.2 18
5% Sep 5.10 Nett $97.90 — 102

2.0 27 — 54
1.2 30 — 30
1.5 27 — 27
2.2 18 — 36
10% Sep $14.70 Nett $132.30 — 147

LEFT: Martin used the style/price shorthand more and more through 1857 and early 1858; and by the dates shown here the written descriptions for each guitar were clearly dying out. Styles 18, 21, and 42 were already in use, and the number of models offered was soon simplified. Earlier entries for the 0-27 describe an ivory soundhole decoration, so the larger Style 27 was more plain than the 2-27. A price increase later made Martin's largest "concert model" the only guitar with a $28 wholesale price, and Style 28 has been with us ever since.

1900, all standard guitar models had rosewood sides and back and a spruce top; so the style number—such as 17 or 28—would indicate only the level of decoration. That generally boiled down to differences in the guitars' body decoration.

MARTIN SIZES

The largest guitar that C. F. Martin Sr. offered initially was called size 1, and the higher numbers—2, 2½, and 3—indicated progressively smaller sizes. The bigger the number, the smaller the guitar. Makes sense, doesn't it? To C.F. it probably made perfect sense, since in a machinist's world, wire gauges, among other things, get smaller as the number gets larger. At least by the early 1850s, the Martin company had added a larger "Concert Model," called size 0. These five sizes—0, 1, 2, 2½, and 3—were Martin's line of standard guitars for over three decades. Also listed were the tiny size 4 and size 5; but these were considered "terz" [third] guitars, tuned a musical third higher (G-C-F-Bb-D-G) than a standard guitar. The 00, "Extra Large Concert," first built in the early 1870s, wasn't added to the Martin price lists until the 1890s.

RIGHT: Size 0 was Martin's concert guitar, added to the smaller sizes by the early 1850s. Considered a serious performer's instrument, it wasn't offered with the pearl bordering or colored purfling of "parlor guitars" such as the 2-27 or 2-42. Though larger sizes were added as demand grew for more volume and bass, Martin still recommended size 0 for solo playing as late as 1930, when steel strings and 14-fret necks made all the old designs obsolete. *(Photo courtesy of Fred Dusel; guitar courtesy of James Forderer.)*

FAR RIGHT (TOP): The case label was the only place the model designation would appear on early Martins. Not until 1930 did the company finally stamp the model code inside the instrument. *(Photo courtesy of Fred Dusel; guitar courtesy of James Forderer.)*

FAR RIGHT (BOTTOM): The silver name plate suggests that this 0-28 was made in the 1870s, as similar plaques are dated from that period. It is literally "tacked on." Martin was at least half a century away from personalizing guitars with the owner's name inlaid in the fretboard. *(Photo courtesy of Fred Dusel; guitar courtesy of James Forderer.)*

Even the 00, described as being "rather loud for a small room," wasn't a large guitar at all by today's standards. At just over 14 inches wide and 4 inches deep, the 00 was still smaller than a typical Spanish classical guitar. The most popular sizes during the late 1800s were sizes 2, 1, and 0, with size 2 a mere 12 inches wide at the lower bout.

ABOVE: Before Martin used style numbers, the word "fine" described any top purfling with a pattern, while "lines" referred to the alternating black and white lines as seen on Style 18. But the pattern used on the $24 model (usually size 2 or 2½) was often called Otilia, listed as a decoration for the top edge, the soundhole, or both. The guitar above is a 2½-24 from the 1880s, but it may not be the pattern called Otilia in 1850s records. Mrs. Martin's first name was Ottilie, but we'll probably never know whether the model was named after her. *(Guitar courtesy of C. F. Martin & Company.)*

MARTIN STYLES

Martin's style numbers are so readily associated now with the guitars' features that few people ever wonder how the firm first came to affix a particular number to a particular style. But the sales ledger of late 1856 suggests that the origin of the style numbers was each instrument's wholesale price: C. A. Zoebisch & Sons was billed $20 for a size 2/20 and $17 for a 3/17. Note that the descriptions were written as fractions, and included on the same bill to Zoebisch was a pair of 2½/17 guitars for $34. This simple style-to-price correlation worked because certain styles were then specific to only one size of guitar.

This designation by style/wholesale price appears to be a shorthand used only in Martin's dealings with Zoebisch, though it would later become a common language among Martin fans around the world. Sales to other accounts on the same ledger page do not use this system. Rather, they are identified by the size number, followed by a brief description, such as a size 1 "rosewood (with) ivory edges, 2 side screw & case," billed at $26. This was apparently a 1-26 model, which for years would be the least expensive Martin with ivory binding. Other entries have identical descriptions and prices, suggesting that some Martin models were already standardized. The unusual "2 side screw" phrase appears often, referring to the geared tuners on a slotted headstock as opposed to the Stauffer-style tuners, or the solid "peg head" with friction pegs. By late 1858 descriptions are no longer found in the sales ledger, and the size/style code is used throughout. Each style number corresponds exactly to the wholesale price, though this convenience wouldn't last very long.

RIGHT: The gospel has always been that Martin did not build mahogany guitars until after 1900, but there were some early exceptions. In 1855 and 1856, size 2½ and size 3 guitars were sometimes listed in Martin sales ledgers as "mahog" and in one entry "mahogany." When rosewood size 2½ and size 3 Martins had a wholesale price of $17, the mahogany versions like the one shown here cost dealers $16. *(Guitar courtesy of Fred Oster.)*

Soon C. A. Zoebisch & Sons became Martin's sole distributor and printed the earliest price lists found to date. In the price list from the early 1870s, each style is specific to one body size only (except for Style 17, the only style offered for the two smallest Martins). Price was determined by both size and decoration. Hence, the Style 28 is plainer than Style 27—Style 28 was offered only on the largest size and so was more expensive than the much smaller 2-27. "All the above numbers...and any size desired made to order" suggests that Martin encouraged requests for other combinations of styles and sizes, but those listed were the stock models representing most of Martin's production until the 1890s.

Price increases had scrambled the handy style-equals-wholesale-cost equation; but because the distributor was given a hefty discount and prices were stable, the style numbers still represented figures close to Zoebisch's cost. Zoebisch paid $30.00 for an 0-28 and $22.50 for a 1-21. Today, relating Martin style numbers to dollars seems unimaginable.

PRICE LIST

OF

C. F. MARTIN & CO.'S GUITARS.

No. 3 – 17	Rosewood, plain,	$36 00
" 2½–17	" "	36 00
" 2 – 18	" double bound,	37 50
" 2 – 20	" Cedar neck,	42 00
" 1 – 21	" "	45 00
" 2 – 24	" " fancy inlaying,	50 00
" 1 – 26	" " Ivory bound,	54 00
" 2 – 27	" inlaid with Pearl, Ivory bound,	58 50
" 0 – 28	" " " "	60 00
" 2 – 30	" " " "	63 00
" 2 – 34	" " " " Ivory bridge,	72 00
" 2 – 40	" richly " " " "	84 00
" 2 – 42	" " " " " Screw Neck,	90 00

No. 3.—Small Size. No. 2½ and No. 2.—Ladies' Sizes. No. 1.—Large Size. No. 0.—Largest Concert Size.

Terz Guitars made the same Style and Price

All the above numbers, with Patent Head or Peg Head, and any size desired made to order.

If not specially ordered with Peg Head, Guitars with Patent Heads will be sent.

The prices above include wood case.

No extra charges for packing.

ABOVE: This 1870s price list lasted for over two decades due to stable prices and C. A. Zoebisch's reluctance to change. No words are wasted, as Martin described guitars more fully in its ledgers than Zoebisch did in selling them. The dittos suggest that an 0-28 has a pearl soundhole, but it does not. The 2-40 has pearl bordering around the face as well as the soundhole, quite a difference to be covered by "richly." Evidently pearl bordering was intended for ladies, as sizes 1 and 0 were not offered in the 40 series. Martin records show many orders for larger guitars with fancy pearl, suggesting that men chose to ignore the hint.

LEFT: Conventional wisdom says the herringbone on this pre-1867 size 1 makes it a 1-28 with pearl rosette, but is it? There are many entries in the mid-1850s sales ledgers for $26 (wholesale) size 1 guitars with pearl soundhole, so perhaps this is an early 1-26. Though sizes were already standardized, decorative details were not yet fixed, and Martin probably saw no reason to use the same top purfling or backstrip on guitars of the same size and price. The top purfling for the 1-26 was often listed as "De Goni" in the 1850s. But 150 years later we can't be sure what that meant, although a Madame de Goni was a prominent guitarist who endorsed Martin guitars before 1870. *(Guitar courtesy of C. F. Martin & Company.)*

A SECOND GENERATION Takes Hold

1874 – 1898

Not long after C. F. Martin Sr.'s death, some unscrupulous competitors spread the rumor that since its founder had passed on, "the Martin guitar isn't made anymore, only an imitation."

Nothing could have been further from the truth. Judging from the guitars each made, the only difference between father and son was the *Junior* at the end of the latter's name.

Born in Vienna on October 2, 1825, Christian Frederick Martin Jr. had his eighth birthday on the mid-Atlantic, as his family crossed to America. When his father died 40 years later, he was more than primed to run the family business, having worked alongside C. F. Martin Sr. since he was old enough to hold tools.

He sat still for a basic education in New York

INSET: C. F. Martin Jr. ran the guitar business started by his father for only 15 years; but during that time, he kept the company on solid financial footing, even through the panic of 1873. During his tenure, he brought the company into the industrial age with new, steam-driven machinery. *(Photo courtesy of C. F. Martin & Company.)*

RIGHT: C. F. Martin Jr. and C. F. Hartmann were not only cousins and business partners but also next-door neighbors, as shown in the upper right block of this drawing. Though there were some bruised feelings when Hartmann left the Martin company after C.F. Jr.'s death, the Hartmann and Martin families remained close. *(Courtesy of Moravian Historical Society.)*

NAZARETH HOTEL Wm H. WHITESELL, PROPR.

S REESE'S STABLE. S.REESE'S STORE. S.REESE'S RES.

GUITAR MANUFACTORY. C.F. MARTIN'S RESIDENCE. C.F. HARTMANN, RES. R. SCHUSTER'S RES.
C. F. MARTIN & CO. GUITAR MANUFACTURERS.

H.F. KINGINER, WHOLESALE & RETAIL CONFECTIONER & BAKER

R. F. BAGS. BRICK BLOCK.

NAZARETH HALL. NORTHAMPTON COUNTY PENN.

NAZARETH.

PENNSYLVANIA.

O.H. BAILEY & CO. LITH. & PUB. BOSTON.

1885.

NAZARETH HALL.
WHITEFIELD HOUSE, COMMENCED IN 1740.
FIRST HOUSE BUILT IN NAZARETH IN 1740.
PUBLIC SCHOOL.
FAIR GROUNDS NORTHAMPTON COUNTY.
CEMETERY.
NAZARETH HOTEL, Wm H. WHITESELL PROPR.
FRANKLIN HOUSE, Wm R. KIEFER. "
AMERICAN HOUSE, DAVID WAGNER "
NAZARETH AGRICULTURAL WORKS, R.I. SCHLABAC.
A. WUNDERLY & BRO. PLANING MILL.

12 J.H. KRIEBLER & CO. CARRIAGE MANUFACTURERS.
13 T.D. ROTH & CO. " "
14 REUBEN HAHN, WAGON & BLACKSMITH SHOP.
15 C.F. MARTIN & CO. GUITAR MANUFACTURERS.
16 ROBERT HAAS. MARBLE WORKS.
17 CHAS. E. MIKSCH. COAL YARD.
18 J.W. TRUMBOWER. " "
19 MORAVIAN. CHURCH.
20 LUTHERAN. "
21 METHODIST. "
22 BANGOR & PORTLAND, R.R. STATION.

J. J. UNANGST & SON. MERCHANTS.

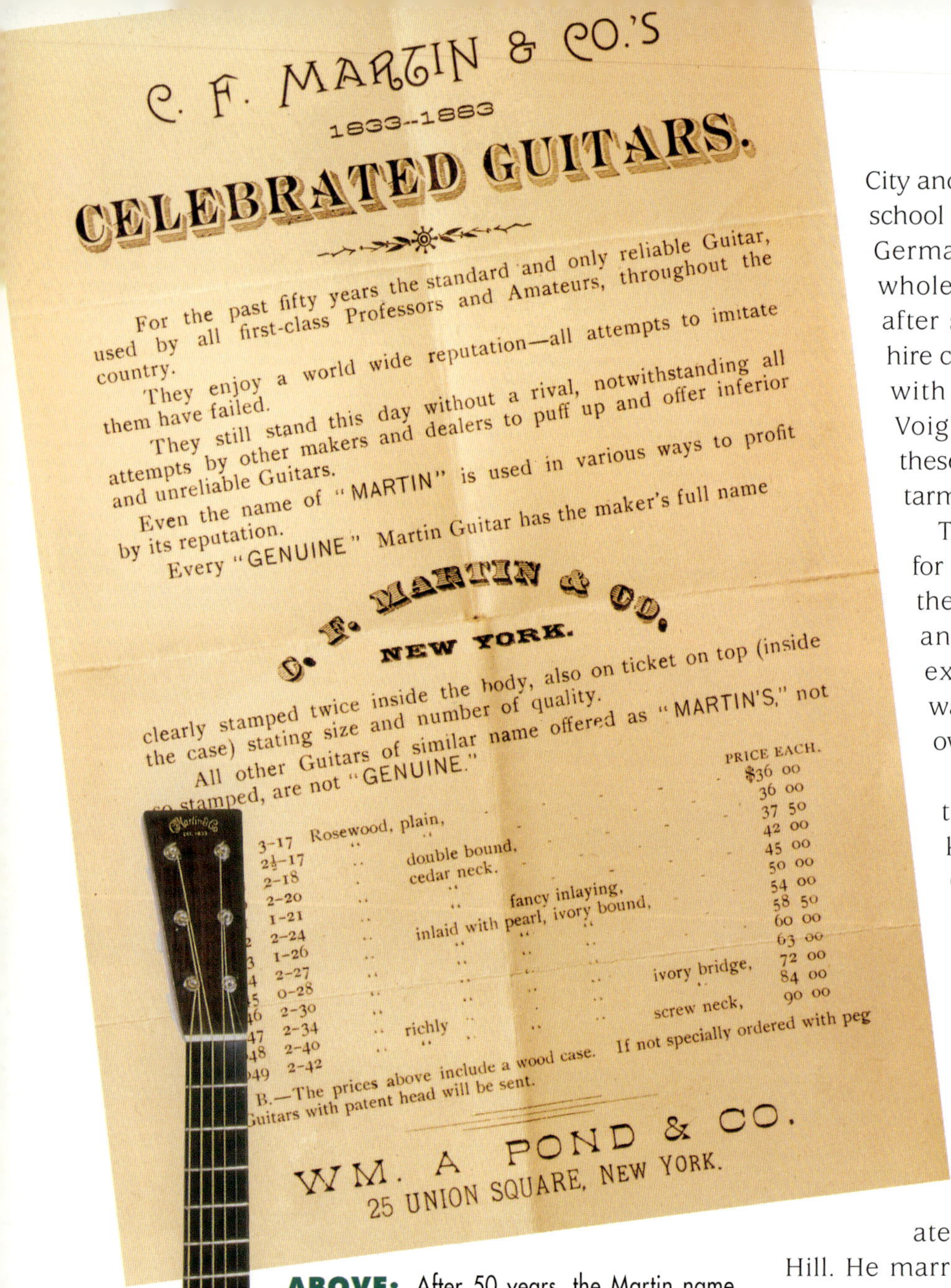

C. F. MARTIN & CO.'S

1833–1883

CELEBRATED GUITARS.

For the past fifty years the standard and only reliable Guitar, used by all first-class Professors and Amateurs, throughout the country.

They enjoy a world wide reputation—all attempts to imitate them have failed.

They still stand this day without a rival, notwithstanding all attempts by other makers and dealers to puff up and offer inferior and unreliable Guitars.

Even the name of "MARTIN" is used in various ways to profit by its reputation.

Every "GENUINE" Martin Guitar has the maker's full name

C. F. MARTIN & CO.
NEW YORK.

clearly stamped twice inside the body, also on ticket on top (inside the case) stating size and number of quality.

All other Guitars of similar name offered as "MARTIN'S," not so stamped, are not "GENUINE."

3-17 Rosewood, plain,
2½-17 " "
2-18 " double bound,
2-20 " cedar neck.
1-21 " " fancy inlaying,
2-24 " inlaid with pearl, ivory bound,
1-26 " " " "
2-27 " " " "
0-28 " " " " ivory bridge,
2-30 " " " " "
2-34 " richly " " screw neck,
2-40 " " "
2-42

PRICE EACH.
$36 00
36 00
37 50
42 00
45 00
50 00
54 00
58 50
60 00
63 00
72 00
84 00
90 00

B.—The prices above include a wood case. If not specially ordered with peg Guitars with patent head will be sent.

WM. A POND & CO.
25 UNION SQUARE, NEW YORK.

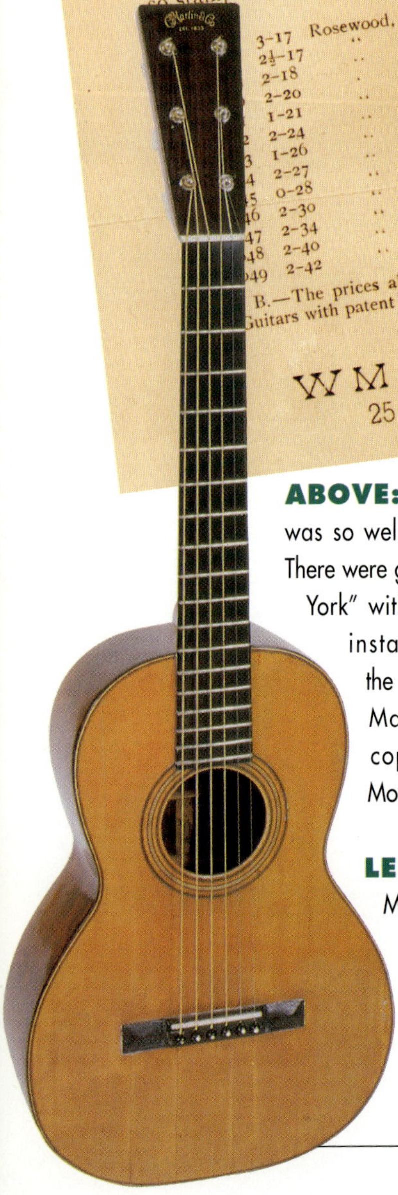

ABOVE: After 50 years, the Martin name was so well established it was being pirated. There were guitars marked "George Martin, New York" with the same semicircular stamp, for instance, which probably prompted the warning shown here. A century later, Martin also saw its peghead decal copied, with brands like "C. F. Mountain" being common.

LEFT: Size 5 was the smallest-size Martin offered in the nineteenth century. It wasn't a travel guitar but a "terz" model, tuned a third higher than a standard guitar. The decal is not original. *(Guitar courtesy of Roger Kasle.)*

City and in Nazareth, where at the Moravian school they spoke English half the time and German the other half. He also heard a whole lot of umlauts on the shop floor after school, as the company tended to hire craftsmen from the old country, men with names like Beitel, Schuster, and Voight. From his father and men like these, C.F. Jr. learned every aspect of guitarmaking.

This knowledge had been enough for his father. C. F. Martin Sr. had been the complete luthier, building guitars and managing his small factory so exactingly that every instrument was shaped by his will if not by his own hands.

Martin's control ended at the factory door, however, because marketing and distribution were left to C. A. Zoebisch & Sons in New York. Ultimately that arrangement was to become a millstone to Martin's success, but it did leave father and son free to do what they did best.

So they made guitars, and when C.F. Sr. died in 1873, C.F. Jr. went on making guitars.

Back when C.F. Jr. was 24, he had bought the house immediately north of his parents in Cherry Hill. He married Ann Marie Alleman of Cherry Hill, and they had a daughter, Emma Natalie Martin, in 1854. Ann died in 1861, and C.F. Jr. wasted little time in remarrying, to Lucinda Leibfried in 1862. Frank Henry Martin was born October 14, 1866.

When C.F. Jr. inherited the company, he also inherited a partner, his cousin C. F. Hartmann. In 1867 C. F. Martin Sr. had turned 71 and taken on C.F. Jr. and Hartmann as partners in the newly formed C. F. Martin & Company. (C.F. Jr. had a brother and two sisters, who took no place in the business.) Hartmann, another Mark Neukirchen native, had come to the United States in 1839 and had worked in Martin's shop for several years. The partnership lasted into the mid-1880s, when C.F. Jr. became sole owner, though Hartmann stayed with the company into the early 1890s.

PROPORTION RULES

The timeless beauty of Martin's early guitars is the result of careful attention paid to the details of proportion—resulting in a vast sea of measurements that would drive any modern manufacturer crazy. Today guitarmakers producing a range of instruments use the same soundhole diameter, rosette spacing, and bridge size, regardless of the body size.

Not so with Martin. In its size 2 through 000 guitars, each successively larger size has a soundhole 1⁄16 inch larger in diameter, with the rosette similarly scaled. Smaller models have scaled-down bridges and other altered details to maintain proportion. Rather than standardize the parts for all its guitars, Martin instead chose to standardize their aesthetic harmony.

Considering the small production runs, Martin workers must have spent as much time measuring and changing tool settings as they did cutting and gluing. Minor changes in side depth and internal bracing for the different sizes were also noted as being required for proper tone. Why else would Martin have made the lower bout 4 3⁄16 inches deep for size 1 and 0 guitars but only 4 1⁄16 inches deep for sizes 00 and 000?

This attention to things rarely noticed cut into the company's profit and added countless hours to the workload, time that could have been spent adding more inlays, or simply building cheaper guitars. Yet there is no indication Martin ever considered such alternatives. Their painstaking approach was simply the only way they could be satisfied building guitars.

GUITAR SOUNDHOLE MEASUREMENTS 2/16/
SINGLE RING STYLE

SIZE	HOLE	RING
TIPLE	2-5/8	2-7/8
5	3-1/4	3-1/2
3	3-11/32	3-19/32
2½--2	3-1/2	3-3/4
1	3-9/16	3-13/16
0	3-5/8	3-7/8
00	3-3/4	4
000	3-7/8	4-1/8

INSET: This index card of soundhole measurements shows the detailed adjustments made between different guitar models. If the size of the guitar body changed, so did the size of the soundhole and the inlay spacing. This extreme attention to details would be a modern manufacturer's nightmare.

RIGHT: These wooden forms show the outline of the old 12-fret models (a more modern shape is at the back). Today for special orders of the smaller sizes, the sides are still bent over a heated pipe—using these forms as a guide.

Moving Slowly but Surely

To the outside world during C.F. Jr.'s tenure, the guitar company must have seemed like a stone set amid a racing stream. In 1876 Bell made the first telephone call, and Heinz first bottled ketchup; in 1877 Edison patented the phonograph, a device that would play a pivotal part in Martin's twentieth-century success; in 1879 Edison followed that with the electric light. And what did the Martin company do during that time of bold innovation? It introduced the 00 model, a guitar only incrementally larger (⅝ inch at the lower bout) than the 0 size it had been making since the mid-1850s. Talk about taking a walk on the wild side.

However plodding the little firm may have seemed, the surety of its footing is inarguable: Not only is the company still viable over a century later but more of its 1800s guitars still exist, in playable condition, than remain of all its high-output contemporaries combined.

Martin's production in 1873 totaled 245 guitars, with all but 29 of those sold through C. A. Zoebisch & Sons of New York. (Though Zoebisch was the "sole agent," Martin had a small number of direct accounts, selling to teachers, professional musicians, and a couple of dealers.) Of the 216 that went through Zoebisch, there were very few of the higher models (one 0-34, three 2-34s, and fourteen 2-27s). Most were smaller, plainer models, with the 2½-17s being the best-selling with 64 sold. In the price lists, this model was sold as a

ABOVE: C.F. Jr. made a few zithers in the late 1870s or early 1880s for Professor Louis Brachet of Philadelphia. This one, from the Martin museum, is nearly identical in shape, construction, and trim to European zithers. The five strings over a short fretboard distinguish this as a "concert zither," whereas the common zither has just the harplike strings. *(Zither courtesy of C. F. Martin & Company.)*

LEFT: Early Martins had more colorful wood marquetry than twentieth-century models, a feature that gradually disappeared as style choices were simplified. Green and white herringbone was not unusual on small models, like this 2-20 from before 1867, and the top edge of Styles 27 through 34 might have had three or more colors. When the neck and fretboard are removed, the colors of this wood purfling are much more vivid where it has been protected from the light, suggesting that some "parlor" models were quite colorful when new. *(Photo from Hank Risan.)*

ABOVE: Over a century ago, Martin was already making reissues! This guitar is dated 1892 on the underside of the top, but the soundhole inlay and Spanish-style "foot" on the neck block are features dating back to the 1850s. Even before the use of serial numbers Martin often reproduced its earlier styles, which can result in errors in dating. The purfling around the top is the same pattern later used as the backstrip on post-World War II Style 28 models. *(Guitar courtesy of Fred Oster.)*

RIGHT AND INSET: The elegance of Martin's Style 42 may have been confined to the ladies' size 2 on the price list, but that didn't keep people from ordering them in larger sizes. Though this example is from the 1890s, similar special orders of 1-42 and 0-42 models show up in Martin sales records in the early 1880s. With gleaming ivory bridge and ivory friction pegs but a blank fretboard, these abalone-bordered guitars make quite a fashion statement. *(Guitar courtesy of The Chinery Collection.)*

ABOVE: This elaborate joint connecting the headstock to the neck shows the original purpose of the carved "dart" and displays Martin woodworking at its finest. The joint was completed and glued before the rosewood veneer was added to the face. Visual appeal was secondary to function and the result, despite the soft cedar, is far stronger than any one-piece neck. *(Photo courtesy of Frank Ford.)*

"lady's guitar," so Martin's success was relying in large part on female guitarists, or on cross-picking men.

While C.F. Jr. was content to go on building his father's guitars, he did radically change the manner in which they were built.

There's a tendency among Martin collectors today to picture the old North Street factory as some kind of Keebler Elves enclave of hand craftsmanship. While the human hand still plays a large part in shaping Martins today, that wasn't a characteristic that was revered as much in the 1800s, when they had to build things that way. Instead, America was optimistic about progress, and progress meant mechanization. Machines would free us from drudgery, it was believed. Mass production would mean consistency and economy. And so Martin mechanized, too, when it was to their instruments' advantage.

Initially Martin's single-story brick workshop on North Street was half the size of the adjacent family house. But in 1887 C.F. Jr. built an addition to the factory and invested in band saws and all manner of steam-driven tools, having ordered a boiler engine from the Pennsylvania Iron Works in Reading, Pennsylvania. The machines were driven by belts and pulleys installed under the floorboards. Quaint though all this may seem today, it was risky business at the time, as evidenced by an insurance company's tersely worded rejection note: "We cannot insure the contents of Martin's Guitar Factory as our company takes no risks on wood-working with steam power."

C.F. Jr. himself unfortunately ran out of steam shortly after his 63rd birthday, on November 15, 1888, dying after running C. F. Martin & Company for only 15 years. Hartmann had ceased to be a business partner a few years earlier—though he remained a top-paid employee there—so Frank Henry Martin and his mother became the owners.

LEFT: This peculiar guitar was made by a Martin employee sometime in the 1890s, but it never became part of Martin's guitar line. The exaggerated waist and fingerboard raised above the soundboard harken back to Martins made some 50 years earlier. The strangest feature of this guitar is its forward-pitched neck. A guitar's neck usually angles about 2 degrees back from the soundboard, but the neck on this guitar angles forward the same amount. This forward pitch puts some unusual, harplike stresses on the soundboard. *(Guitar courtesy of The Chinery Collection.)*

FRANK HENRY MARTIN

Frank Henry Martin was only 22 when the responsibility of supporting his family and helming Martin landed on him. Though young, he proved strong willed, and he actually steered the company rather than letting it drift along in the backwaters of commerce. He brought C. F. Martin & Company into the twentieth century, nearly on time.

Frank Henry's son, C. F. Martin III, would later recall of him: "He was a classic student. He never went to college. He didn't have that opportunity, but he studied Latin, Greek, and history. When I was growing up, he would work all day in the shop making guitars, do the bookkeeping in the evening, and read a book before he went to bed. He read Gibbon's *Decline and Fall of the Roman Empire* all the way through, and that's a big book."

The position he inherited at 22 was a mixed blessing. On the one hand, he had the nation's oldest guitar firm, with a newly improved factory, as well as a respected name and the endorsements of top players.

On the other hand, his business was reliant upon the moribund C. A. Zoebisch & Sons; new competitors were leaping ahead of his company in the marketplace; and America was heading toward the worst financial crisis of the century.

A pay ledger from 1890 shows ten employees

ABOVE: Frank Henry Martin—pictured with his wife, Jenny Keller Martin—was only 22 when his father died, and he found himself in charge of the family business. He proved up to the challenge, bringing the traditional German company into the twentieth century with some bold business decisions. *(Photo courtesy of C. F. Martin & Company.)*

RIGHT: C. F. Martin Jr.'s contribution to the styling or structure of Martin guitars is unknown, since he lived for only 15 years after C.F. Sr.'s death. But he did bring the Martin company into the machine age by enlarging the factory and installing a powerful steam engine. This allowed the use of modern woodworking machinery, such as is shown on these envelopes.

working under Frank Henry, paid between 50 cents a day and $3 a day. Though Martin was doubtless friends with some of his employees, and probably regarded others from his father's generation as uncles, he worked them hard, as he did himself. They worked a six-day week. During Christmastime of 1890, they had Thursday the 25th and Friday the 26th off, but it was back to work on Saturday. In 1893 Charles A. Zoebisch Jr. (then nearly 70 years old) wrote to Frank Henry, urging him not to let his men take holidays or picnic too much at noonday, to get the most work out of them before hard weather set in.

Zoebisch's frequent correspondences with Martin often assumed an avuncular tone. The Martins had been dealing with Zoebisch so long that they were practically family. It was a curious relationship, too, with a fair percentage of their trade being bartered. In payment for guitars, Zoebisch would supply them with everything from French shellac and tuning machines to imported wine. Along with tissue paper for Martin to wrap its guitars in, he also sent Martin an inexplicable number of instrument parts, such as six dozen violin tailpieces and dozens of French horn mouthpieces in the span of a year. Martin did do violin repairs, and Hartmann built a number of violin-family instruments, but not in quantities like that. And you can only give away so many French horn mouthpieces as gifts.

Martin actually gave very little

ABOVE: No, the photo isn't reversed. Dugald Stermer is playing an original lefty 000-45 from 1931, one of his newest Martins. Stermer is an illustrator—flowers are his favorite subject—and the refined elegance of old Martins isn't lost on someone who makes his living by careful observation. Since he's left-handed, another bonus is the nonangled saddle and lack of pick guard on the numerous nineteenth- and early-twentieth-century Martins pictured here. By simply changing the nut and reversing the strings, he can play them as well. *(Photo © Kevin Bond; on loan from Dugald Stermer.)*

LEFT: Though pearl-bordered models get the press coverage today among guitar collectors, little 2½-17 models like this one paid the bills from the mid-1850s to well into the 1880s. Style 17 guitars lacked binding on the back and had a black-stained neck and a simple fan-braced top, but their spartan features didn't prevent them from often outselling all of Martin's ivory-bound models combined. *(Photo courtesy of Fred Dusel.)*

away. People wonder today why the company doesn't give guitars to prominent musicians the way most other manufacturers commonly do. The reason may be that, unlike the other manufacturers, Martin has endured over a century and a half of musicians trying to hit them up for free instruments. Had they honored many of those requests, the company—which in some years in the 1880s was making only a couple of dozen instruments a month—would have gone out of business.

ABOVE: With the introduction of guitar-type finger picking in the 1860s, the banjo began to shed its minstrel roots and moved uptown. Though the other two guitars in this photo of the M.I.T. banjo club are hard to identify, the one in the center is clearly a Martin, probably a size 2. Even though the banjos were probably also strung with gut, the little Martin would have been hard to hear in any combination of these instruments. Notice the short-necked banjeaurines, popular variants of the five-string banjo at this time. *(Photo from The MIT Museum.)*

The Brown University Glee, Banjo, and Mandolin Club wrote the company in 1892 asking for two free 00 guitars in exchange for an ad in their program and the group's endorsement. "We are continually asked about the excellence of various guitars, and would take pleasure in booming 'the Martin,'" wrote director G. N. Norton.

Green Bay, Wisconsin, performer and teacher Emma Miller Harger got her father to write Martin for her, asserting that if Martin would send two guitars at cost, "she will exert her utmost influence to introduce your instruments here, and this is in her power to do, as she has already a great number of pupils who are ready to order a Martin guitar as soon as they can see, and also hear the good tone of, one of these instruments."

Martin Models

Martin's First Mandolins

Although the guitar was steadily gaining in popularity in the late 1800s, the mandolin, already a favorite in Europe, was the instrument that was taking America by storm.

The musical fashion for mandolins was initially fueled by instruments imported from Italy, and the most highly regarded were made by long-established family companies such as Vinaccia and Calace. But the growing number of mandolin ensembles prompted a rapid change in America's fretted-instrument manufacturing as well, and factories in New York and Chicago rushed to meet demand. Despite the head start Italian luthiers in America had and the vast production potential of Martin's more industrial competitors in this country, young Frank Henry Martin led his small company into the fray.

Mandolins occupy a unique position in the history of the Martin company. Other than a few special-order instruments and a limited number

Martin

STYLE G 5. Rosewood, with ivory strips at joints, 37 fluted ribs with continuous binder, mahogany neck and head, white face inlaid at sound hole, border, nd fingerboard with pearl, butterfly guard solid pearl fingerboard, ivory bridge, extra fine machine tail piece. Every available part being bound with makes a magnificent showing.

Price . . . $80.00

TOP LEFT: Martin's first catalog was published in 1896, introducing its new line of bowlback mandolins and only briefly mentioning guitars. Style G mandolins came in five grades, 1 through 5, and the G 5 shown here was quite unlike later high-grade Martin bowlbacks. The butterfly pick guard and mother-of-pearl fretboard with abalone inlays were stock items from pearl cutters who supplied the industry, and identical examples of such fancy work are found on other mandolin brands from around the turn of the century. These early bowlbacks were the first stock Martins to get pearl inlays on the fingerboard and peghead.

LEFT: The Italian-style mandolin (more precisely the Neapolitan style) is much older than the guitar, but the bowlback type of body, similar to that of the lute, was relatively new to most North American instrument makers. It brought the challenge of a new type of body construction to the Martin company and a level of decoration far more demanding than what the company had presented on its guitars. *(Mandolins courtesy of C. F. Martin & Company.)*

of zithers, it was the first time it had tried producing something other than the flat-top guitar. Mandolins were also the first Martin instruments to get serial numbers, and the expensive Style 5, 6, and 7 models were the most elaborately decorated production Martins ever made, predating Style 45 guitars by several years.

It has been suggested that mandolins caused the split between the Martin company and its sole distributor, C. A. Zoebisch & Sons of New York. After reviewing what has survived of the distributor's correspondence, however, the cause of the separation appears to have been more complex. Building mandolins was an indication of not only young Frank Henry Martin's ambition but also his impatience during the long recovery from the economic panic of 1893. With a mother and unmarried sisters to support, along with a wife and very young family, Frank Henry couldn't ignore the chance to make money with the most popular instrument of the time.

The company had been repairing other makes of mandolins since the late 1880s, and Frank Henry doubtless was aware of the success that other makers were having with them. Washburn catalogs were awash with bowlback mandolins, touted with characteristic hyperbole by their manufacturer, Lyon & Healy of Chicago.

After the split with Zoebisch, Martin produced the company's first-ever catalog, in 1896. It didn't picture its guitars, only the new line of mandolins. Mandolins were given a

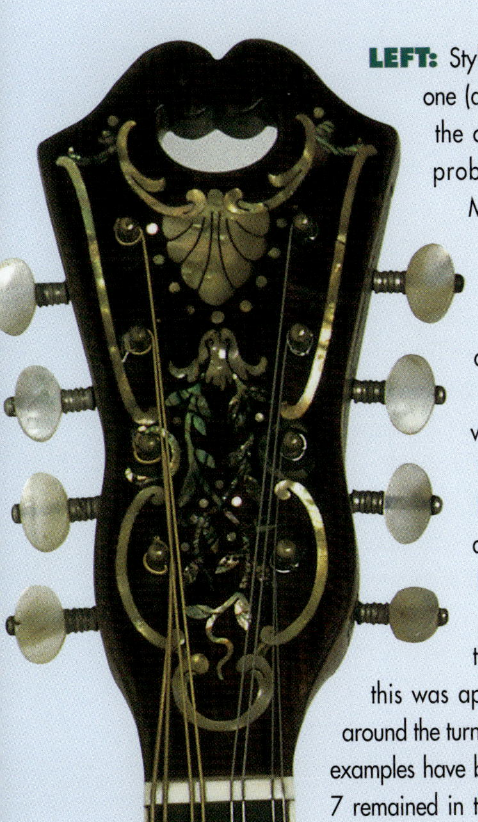

LEFT: Style 7 mandolins like this one (also shown at bottom on the opposite page) are still probably the most ornate Martin instruments of all time. That's a mother-of-pearl vine inlaid into a ½-inch-wide abalone border around the face! This example was made in 1902 for Douglas Little, of Easton, Pennsylvania, a town just a few miles from Nazareth. Though this Style 7 has an over-the-top, custom-order look, this was apparently a stock model around the turn of the century, and other examples have been found. Though Style 7 remained in the catalog until 1917, it had long since ceased to be as elaborate as earlier versions. *(Mandolin courtesy of C. F. Martin & Company.)*

ABOVE: Style 6 and 7 Martin mandolins had 42 ribs of Brazilian rosewood, each separated by a thin strip of ivory. After the bowl was completed, each rib was scalloped, or fluted, with a gouge (curved chisel) and a curved scraper. The separate apron of rosewood, bordered in abalone only on the Style 7, is called the "cap." The detailed workmanship shown here indicates why current Martin company head Chris Martin estimates that mandolins like these would be the most difficult and expensive Martin instruments to duplicate today. *(Mandolin courtesy of C. F. Martin & Company.)*

RIGHT: This Style 5 from the Martin museum is nearly identical to the mandolin pictured with John Santschi on page 78. Style 5 was the most popular of Martin's ornate bowlback styles, and despite the lavish inlay, it was less expensive than the somewhat plainer Style 6 models because it didn't have the labor-intensive scalloped ribbing on the back. *(Mandolin courtesy of C. F. Martin & Company.)*

separate serial number sequence from guitars, which gives us the opportunity a century later to track the success of Frank Henry's new venture.

Judging by the number of styles made and the production totals, Martin mandolins were an almost immediate success. Over 150 were sold each year in 1898 and 1899, while the sales of the long-established Martin guitars were only a little over twice those numbers. Mandolin sales more than doubled in 1900, bringing the company's total production out of the rut it had been in for almost 50 years; and in 1906 to 1909, sales of mandolins would surpass sales of guitars. After over 60 years of building the same thing, the Martin company had followed a new fad and, at least by its modest standards, hit the jackpot.

Mandolins also represented Martin's first tentative step toward higher production: In 1906 the company produced 144 of its lowest-priced Style 0 mandolin. This was almost three times the yearly production of any single guitar model. This new emphasis on higher production would come in handy when Martin tackled the ukulele fad a decade later, though the company's building methods were still slow and old-fashioned compared to those of the manufacturing giants of the era like Lyon & Healy.

The Martin company's early catalogs suggest that the rapid development of its bowlback mandolins was achieved by a time-tested method—copying other instruments that were already popular. The 1898 catalog states, "The model is a well-tested

LEFT: Martin's greatest sales in mandolins came from the very plain models, and this 1909 catalog illustration of the Style 000 was a sign of things to come. It was simple, it was mahogany, and it was cheap—this mandolin sold for only $12 when the least expensive Martin guitar (the 1-17, also mahogany) cost $20.

INSET: Judging by Master Kenneth Robbins's small size in relation to his mandolin, not to mention the chair, he was something of a child prodigy. He's holding a Style 5, which had alternating blocks of tortoiseshell and pearl around the top edge, called "corded binding in the Italian style" in Martin's catalog. Robbins was a pupil of C. D. Schettler, a noted guitarist, instructor, and Martin endorser from Salt Lake City, one of many music teachers who purchased strings and instruments from Martin direct. *(Photo courtesy of C. F. Martin & Company.)*

RIGHT AND ABOVE: In the introduction of the mandolin section in the 1904 catalog, Frank Henry stated, "The Martin mandolin takes its ideal from the best known Italian makes and from the Martin guitar..." and uses "the standard Italian system of bracing...." Yet Martin's version of the Italian original is uniquely its own. The elaborate fingerboard inlay as shown on this 1899 Style 6 (*above*) was soon changed to "snowflake" inlays like those found on Martin guitars. The plainer mandolin is a higher model, a Style 7, but from 1908. The pearl decorations on all of Martin's bowlback models became less ornate after about 1904. *(Photo of Style 6 mandolin © Alicia Stratton, from the collection of David Ogden, Keene CA; Style 7 mandolin courtesy of C. F. Martin & Company.)*

ABOVE: This Style C bandurria, now in the Martin museum, was shipped to the Clark Music Company of San Francisco in 1904. There are notations of only three being made, all for the same retailer in the same year, and this was the most ornate. With 12 steel strings, and only friction pegs, tuning must have been a nightmare; it is no wonder this bandurria saw so little use. It was found in a San Francisco antique shop 90 years later. *(Bandurria courtesy of C. F. Martin & Company.)*

one. No novelty is claimed for it, as we believe that by adding to the good qualities of standard Italian makes the finish for which our work is known, and the safety from warping which this climate affords, we gain a degree of perfection unknown before."

Despite the structural inspiration from Italian models, the Martin bowlback mandolins were definitely American in their appearance, and later versions were distinctly Martin in their ornamentation. With the success of its venture into mandolin production, the C. F. Martin company gained new confidence to follow popular music trends, using its long-established reputation as guitarmaker to help market the new types of instruments with slogans such as "Martin quality prevails." This new flexibility and wider reputation allowed the company to better survive changes in America's economy and the rise and fall in popularity of the guitar. During the far more dramatic economic panic beginning in 1929, the Martin company would again spur sales with new models and innovations, coupled with large numbers of less-expensive instruments.

RIGHT: Early Martin instruments with the company name on the headstock are highly unusual; stock instruments with Martin decals or the name in pearl letters didn't appear until steel-string guitar models of the early 1930s. This 1907 Style 4 mandolin is an early exception, though Martin records list two guitars with "Martin" inlaid into the peghead a few years earlier. At least one had the period after the name, as shown here. *(Photo © Alicia Stratton, from the collection of David Ogden, Keene CA.)*

RIGHT AND ABOVE: Most American mandolin manufacturers filled out their catalogs with mandolas and mando-cellos, the deeper-voiced companions to the mandolin, hoping to appeal to those who wanted to duplicate the instrument voices of the classical string quartet. Martin made little effort to appeal to the string ensemble market during the first wave of the mandolin's popularity—only 16 mandolas and 4 mando-cellos were made in the bowlback style, according to factory records. *(Mandolins courtesy of C. F. Martin & Company.)*

Martin's Loyal Fans

Along with the musicians and teachers in search of a soft touch, the company heard from Martin partisans, many of whom maintained that it was the only guitar worth playing. Endorsers included Justin Holland, William Schubert, early Martin partner J. B. Coupa, a Madame de Goni, and others.

Perhaps the first old-Martin collector was Leadville, Colorado, newspaperman Stanley G. Fowler, who in 1880 wrote to Martin of finding a "50-year-old Martin, in great shape" in a barbershop.

In the same letter he ordered "one of your best" 1-26 guitars. Fowler also taught guitar and occasionally ordered an instrument for a student. In August 1881 he wrote about one such guitar: "It is an elegant, magnificent instrument. I played it for a full two hours and was so charmed with its brilliant resonance and singing quality of tone that I could hardly leave it there."

The next year Fowler became managing editor of the Leadville *Democrat;* on May 5 he wrote: "I am pestered quite frequently by applicants to teach, but I tell one and all that the first requisite is a fine instrument and unless they have a Martin or will buy one, I will give no instruction whatever."

In 1884 distraught guitar owner C. G. Wright of Bay Head, New Jersey, sent a damaged guitar for repair, and she felt the need to let Martin know that the fault wasn't hers. "Mr. Martin, I bought one of your invaluable guitars from your factory in '81 and I have taken such care of it. But this morning a stupid servant knocked it off the table onto the floor and cracked the top.... I am so devoted to the guitar that you can imagine my distress at such an accident."

In 1889 Detroit attorney and land speculator Robert N. Bell, pleased with a Martin that his uncle

ABOVE AND RIGHT: The 00 size first appears in Martin's sales records on August 1, 1873, just a few months after C.F. Sr.'s death. Inasmuch as a "00-28" is matter-of-factly listed alongside standard models, they may have been making the 00 even earlier, with its origin lost in the spotty records that remain from 1858 to 1873. Demand for the larger Martin was steadily increasing by the 1890s, thanks to groups like the one above, where guitars were expected to keep up with the greater volume of mandolins and banjos. Always concerned with tonal balance, Martin believed that its 00 was "rather loud for a small room" but advertised it as "excellent for club use." Shown here is a 00-34 from just before the new century, when Martin finally began to put position markers on the fingerboard. Style 34 was like Style 30, but with an ivory bridge. *(Photo © 1997 Centerbrook Archives; guitar photo courtesy of Roger Kasle.)*

— THE —

YODLERS

— AND —

Instrumental Artists.

PROGRAMME.

PART I.

1. Philippovic March — by M. Hruby
2. Gasparoni Selections — by Milloeker
3. Tyrolese Song with jodel
4. Stradella, Bandonion Solo — by Flotow
5. T. K. Emmett's Song

PART II.

6. Poldi, Polka Mazurka
7. Tyrolese Song, with jodel
8. Mandolina, Duett on two Yankee Zithers

[Never before Played in the City.]

6. Tyrolese Song with jodel
10. Potpourri
11. Alpine Rover

PART III.

12. Levy's Cornet Solo, Hyppodromme Polka

Immitation on the Bandonion.

13. Tryolese Song
14. Dreams on the Ocean, Waltz — by Gungl
15. The Lazy fellow
16. My Austria, March. — by Schmidt

CARL. DURSTMUELLER,
Leader and Manager.

The Banjolin (Yankee Zither) used by this Company in their Concerts, is invented and manufactured by Mr. John Farris of Hartford, Conn.—The Guitar manufactured by Mr. C. F. Martin of Nazareth, Pa., the best for Concert purposes and the best in the market. The Bandonion, an instrument with 264 different notes comes from Germany, and as fine effect may be produced as on the Largest Church Organ. This Company claims to have the only one Gentleman who performs on this difficult instrument here in America.

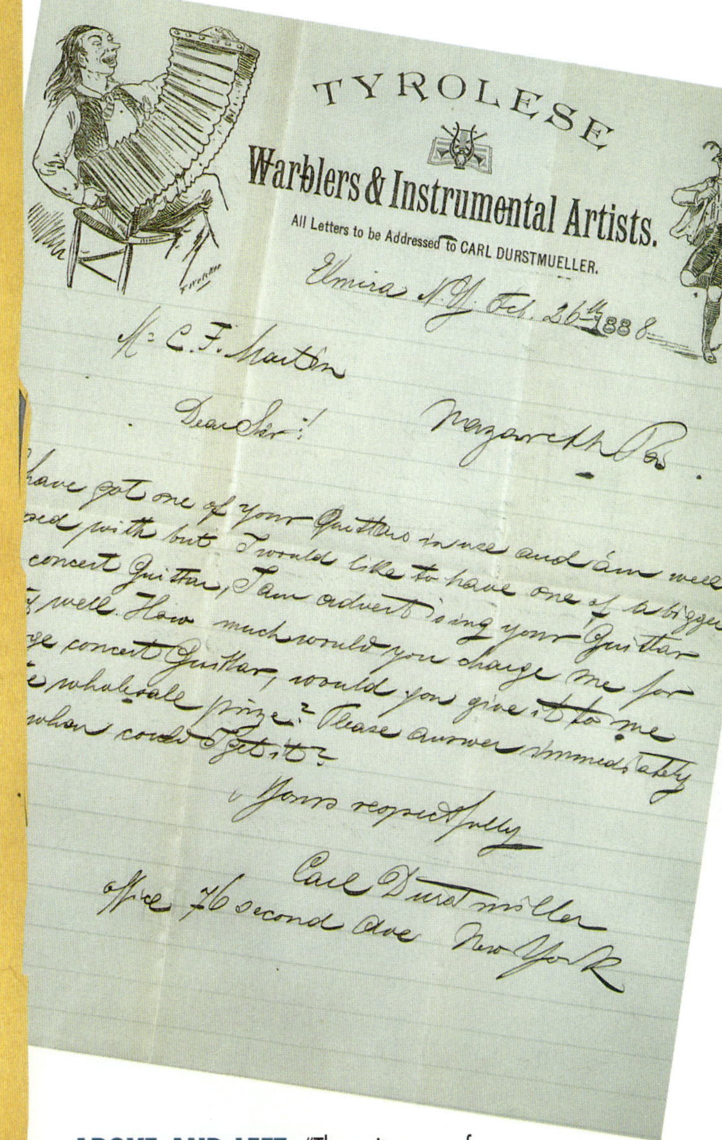

TYROLESE
Warblers & Instrumental Artists.
All Letters to be Addressed to CARL DURSTMUELLER.

Elmira N.Y. Oct. 26th 1888

Mr C. F. Martin

Dear Sir! Nazareth Pa.

have got one of your Guitars in use and am well
sed with but I would like to have one of a bigger
concert Guitar, I am advertising your Guitar
y well. How much would you charge me for
ge concert Guitar, would you give it to me
e wholesale prize? Please answer immediately
when could I get it?

Yours respectfully

Carl Durstmüller
No 76 second ave New York

ABOVE AND LEFT: "The guitar manufactured by Mr. C. F. Martin of Nazareth, Pa., the best for concert purposes and the best in the market," reads this 1888 program of the Tyrolese Warblers & Instrumental Artists. Their director, Carl Durstmueller, wrote Martin to ask for a larger guitar, a frequent and largely unheeded request from musicians in this period. He was one of many performers who promoted Martin in hopes of getting a better deal on a new guitar. The banjolin or "Yankee Zither" mentioned at the bottom of the program is probably an early version of the mandolin-banjo, a hybrid that remained popular through the 1920s.

had, wrote to order a custom model. The company's most expensive production model at the time was $90. Bell was quoted $275 for a size 1 with "fingerboard of genuine white ivory to be from 3/16 to ¼ of an inch in thickness. Frets to be made of 14-karat gold, bridge and tuning pegs of ivory. Outside edge of guitar, all the way around, ½ to ¾ of an inch in width, to be as richly inlaid with pearl as possible. Rosette also very richly inlaid with pearl...." Bell said that he was "willing to pay up to $50 extra for the best tone. If it is impossible to have gold frets, you can make your price covering sterling silver ones, but I would greatly prefer gold."

Like Leadville's Mr. Fowler, many of Martin's new customers were in the expanding western half of the nation. In the early 1880s Billy the Kid and Jesse James had been shot dead, Sitting Bull had surrendered, and additional rail lines linked the West Coast to the East. By 1883, the Old West was effectively dead, and it was first mythologized that year in Buffalo Bill's Wild West Show, which in New York alone was soon to be performed for over two million patrons one season.

ABOVE: As these wood purfling samples suggest, the reserved decorations on Martin instruments were not due to a lack of fancier options. Most of the more colorful patterns of purfling used on nineteenth-century Martins are in the two far-right columns, while several versions of herringbone and other styles still used today are on the ledger's left page.

LEFT: These samples of pearl inlay were first sent to Martin as part of a sales pitch in 1890, and many of the designs were already being used by Martin's competitors. As with wood purfling, Martin chose the most conservative styles. Despite the profusion of animals and foliage, sharp-eyed readers will be able to find the "snowflake" and "cat's-eye" motifs that first appeared on Martin's bowlback mandolins and Style 42 guitars in the late 1890s.

The Martin Files

C. F. Martin and his nineteenth-century associates and descendants left little record of what they were thinking or feeling. But while not much for diaries, they were ferociously good record keepers. In safes and cabinets in the company's present factory and in the attic of its old Nazareth factory are at least a ton of old documents.

They didn't just keep their mail from the 1850s, but the envelopes, too, as well as an 1855 shopping bill for butter and woolen yarn, an 1869 IRS receipt for a $10 "special manufacturers tax," an 1891 bill for lightning rods, 1920s Easter Seal form letters, handwritten notes from a not-yet-famous Gene Autry, and an 1892 letter from a Pennsylvania Railroad executive asking Frank Henry Martin to send him some local pretzels.

There are glowing testimonials from long-dead musicians, written in flowing script with quill pens or their steel replacements, stored in envelopes still bearing 2-cent stamps. A 1901 ledger reveals an accounting process that factored in every little expenditure, from $156.75 for a 57-pound Zanzibar ivory tusk to 25 cents for six pieces of Lava brand soap. In a 1926 inventory, Martin employees counted 14 pieces of partially used soap, valuing the lot at 70 cents.

Even Martin's trash is fascinating: Letters in old German were found wrapped in crumpled newspapers relating Civil War battles—"Attack on United States Steamer Ceres!" shouts one headline—while elsewhere an 1850s classified section touts sexual potency tonics.

Firms like Coca Cola or Campbell's Soup may come to mind when one thinks of the elder icons of American business, but C. F. Martin & Company predates them by more than a half-century, and Martin's files could provide the raw material for a uniquely rich history of American business conducted in two centuries. And unlike those of most other firms, many of Martin's old records wear a fine patina of rosewood dust.

BELOW: One could spend months in the Martin company ledgers. They cover not only six generations of the family's business but bits of America's musical history as well—from dealings with Madame de Goni and Vahdah Olcott Bickford to Jimmie Rodgers and Gene Autry. Financial panics and musical fads are all reflected in the barometer of Martin's production.

The Guitar's Competitors

When they're scoring documentaries and films of the Old West, composers today often rely on the sound of the steel-string guitar, ignoring both the gut strings of the day and the fact that the guitar was still a second-class instrument while the banjo ruled.

The banjo, African in origin, had been popularized by minstrel shows, in which whites would grotesquely parody black language and culture. The banjo was an instrument in flux. Most banjos made before the 1870s were fretless. Even in that harder-to-play form, the banjo had a huge advantage over the guitar. It was louder, and in a time before microphones, that was the whole ball game.

In the 1880s the banjo's half-century fad was still in full swing. A nation can only stand so much banjo, however, and America was opening up to other sounds. It might have been a splendid time for the guitar to pick up the slack. Instead the country became infatuated with a musical group of Spanish students, ingeniously named the Spanish Students, who played the mandolin-like bandurria. Their arrival in the United States in 1880 did for the mandolin what Fess Parker later did for coonskin caps.

By 1888 a great many communities had mandolin orchestras, and magazines such as *Cadenza* were devoted to the instrument. There are accounts of several groups of Italian-American musicians masquerading as Spaniards to get gigs, peeved that others were cashing in on an instrument the Italians had been playing in America for decades. Longtime Martin correspondent Justin Minor Holland (son of the notable guitar composer Justin Holland, profiled on the opposite page) wrote the company in 1889 suggesting that Martin and other firms fabricate a group along the lines of the Spanish Students, but with guitars, to help promote the instrument.

ABOVE: Martin competitor Washburn introduced Model 308, shown at right, in its 1889 catalog; it was the largest version of Washburn's fanciest style. Though it was far more elaborate than a Martin Style 42, Washburn added an even fancier guitar to its line by 1892, featuring a continuous "vase & vine" pearl inlay covering the length of the fretboard. By the mid-1890s, the top Washburn had a solid pearl fretboard, like the model on the left. Most of these elaborate features were borrowed from bowlback mandolins, which had a long tradition of lavish decoration. Martin's response? It added three small "snowflake" inlays on the fretboard of Style 42 guitars, beginning in the late 1890s. *(Photo from Hank Risan.)*

Justin Holland

One of Martin's First Stars

Guitarists had a limited audience through the 1800s, playing second fiddle, at best, to the banjo featured in the wildly popular traveling minstrel shows. But while painted whites strummed banjos in a crude mockery of black culture, an African-American was using a Martin to compose the most rigorously American guitar music of that century.

Justin Holland was born on July 29, 1819, to freed former slaves in Norfolk County, Virginia. Though solidly a slave state, that part of Virginia had many free blacks, and Holland received an education at church. In 1831 Nat Turner, who also had a religious education, led a slave revolt in that state. As a backlash, Virginia outlawed the teaching of blacks. So two years later, at age 14, Holland moved to Boston to continue his education while supporting himself doing manual labor.

After hearing Mariano Perez perform, Holland began taking guitar lessons from early American guitar arrangers Simon Knaebel and William Schubert. At age 22 Holland moved to Ohio to attend Oberlin College, one of the few colleges in America to admit black students then. But in 1844, his devotion to the guitar led him to Mexico, where he learned Spanish to study guitar method books by Fernando Sor and others.

Holland settled in Cleveland, started a family, and supported himself by teaching guitar. The compositions and arrangements he wrote for his students were in such demand that he published over 300 pieces. Though he rarely performed and never toured, Holland's compositions and two widely respected method books made him the most influential American guitarist of his time. His pieces reveal a distinctly American character when compared to his European counterparts. There is an arid humor, playfulness, and vitality to his clean lines that at times reminds one of present-day guitarist Leo Kottke.

Along with being the most prolific guitar arranger of his time, Holland was politically active for most of his life. In the 1850s he worked with Frederick Douglass in the abolition movement, and he was active in the Underground Railroad and a plan to purchase land in Central America for a black colony. Later, he was a leader in the black Freemasons in Cleveland.

Holland's long correspondence—from 1868 to 1884—with the Martin company, however, is pure guitar chat. He certainly wasn't shy. In the flowing script of an 1869 letter, Holland chastised Martin for allowing an unhelpful, overpriced store to have a monopoly on Martins in Cleveland (the fault was certainly Martin's distributor, Zoebisch). Less than a week later Martin offered to sell direct to him. Later that year C. F. Martin Jr. wrote to him requesting a few pieces of music for his teenage daughter Emma, which Holland gladly provided.

Over the years he ordered several guitars, for himself or for students, including a 1-21 with ivory friction pegs and a 5-20 terz guitar. Martin apparently didn't keep much stock on hand, as Holland noted of some purchases, "sometimes the guitars had to be made after being sent for." In 1884 he organized a guitar club in Cleveland and reported, "They all have Martin guitars and are getting along very well."

In 1887 he died of "brain fever" (encephalitis), leaving a grand legacy of music and a guitarist son, Justin Minor Holland, who also had a long relationship with Martin.

(Photo courtesy of International Guitar Research Archives.)

No Support in New York

Rather than creating an artificial Spanish guitar band and counting on them to spur guitar sales, the more obvious thing would have been for Martin to start making mandolins. They certainly knew how to, since the only benefit Martin had thus far derived from the craze was from music stores sending them other makers' mandolins to repair.

But in 1892 Frank Henry Martin saw the company he'd inherited still standing on the sidelines. The reason was C. A. Zoebisch & Sons, the company's sole distributor, whose head, Charles A. Zoebisch Jr., was opposed to the Martin company's entering the mandolin market. This may have been due in part to Zoebisch's being old and set in his ways, but it probably had more to do with his already being supplied with imported mandolins. Though Zoebisch ran ads proclaiming his firm to be the "Depot of C. F. Martin & Cos. Celebrated Guitars," that was just one small part of his business.

The Martin company at this point was also doing a goodly amount of special-order work, for people wanting custom appointments on larger-model guitars. Frank Henry likely suspected that Martin would be getting far more of this lucrative work if Zoebisch weren't still making people order from the same limited choices on a decade-old price list.

Customers needed bigger Martins to not be entirely drowned out by steel-stringed mandolins, but that wasn't the company's biggest challenge. There was a growing market for the guitar, but that market was being both created and filled in large part by the aggressive marketing of Chicago's Lyon & Healy Company. As Sears, Roebuck was to general merchandise, so Lyon & Healy was to music. It recognized that in the expanding nation, many Americans were living beyond the reach of stores, and it serviced them with a mail-order catalog, selling everything from Steinway pianos to nose flutes.

Once a customer of Martin's, the huge mail-order music house was now a competitor, making instruments similar to Martin's in construction but with flashier appointments, which is a nice way of

~~The Old Standard—The Old~~ Reliable

MARTIN GUITARS.

1833. Manufactured by C. F. Martin & Co. 1895.

NO CONNECTION WITH ANY OTHER HOUSE OF THE SAME NAME.

For over sixty years the **MARTIN GUITARS** were and are still the only reliable instruments used by all first-class Professors and Amateurs throughout the country. They enjoy a world-wide reputation, and testimonials could be added from the best Solo Players ever known, such as

Madame De Goni, Mr. J. P. Coupa, Mr. Wm. Schubert, Mr. Ferrer, Mr. S. De La Cova, Mr. Chas. De Janon, Mr. H. Worrell, Mr. N. W. Gould, Mr. N. J. Lepkowski, Mr. Luis T. Romero,

and many others, but we deem it unnecessary to do so, as the public is well aware of the superior merits of the **MARTIN GUITARS**. Parties have in vain tried to imitate them, not only here in the United States, but also in Europe. They still stand this day without a rival, notwithstanding all attempts to puff up inferior and unreliable guitars.

Depot at C. A. ZOEBISCH & SONS, 19 Murray St., near Broadway, NEW YORK.

Importers of all kinds of Musical Instruments, Strings, Etc.

ABOVE: Regardless of whose guitars sounded best or lasted longer, competitor Washburn was certainly winning far more attention with its up-to-date ads. The Washburn catalog was much more direct: By the mid-1890s, each page had two picture-endorsements of teachers or performers from around the country praising the superiority of Washburn guitars and mandolins. *(Advertisements courtesy of John Teagle.)*

saying you could blind a crow with them. Martin guitars had been imitated since the 1860s, when distributor C. Bruno was importing Martin knock-offs from, of all places, Mark Neukirchen. But Lyon & Healy was another animal entirely. The firm started off big, organized in 1864 by music publisher Oliver Ditson to be his Chicago distributor. It began manufacturing Washburn guitars (named for co-owner George Washburn Lyon) in 1883, and by 1899 it claimed to have sold 20,000 guitars. The previous year Martin had begun stamping serial numbers on its guitars, starting with the number 8,000 because that was its best estimate of how many instruments it had made since 1833.

Along with mail-order, Washburns were sold direct to dealers, pushed with flashy rhetorical advertising, and their business practices were not altogether decorous.

"I wish to tell all about the Washburn guitar.... They proposed to give me a guitar under the condition that I denounce your guitar and that I use their name for our program and advertise their instrument. Their guitar is a model like yours and it is a fine instrument. It is a dangerous opponent," wrote touring guitarist Otto Schwemberger to Martin in 1888. He, naturally, then proceeded to hit Martin up for a guitar.

ABOVE: No matter how you feel about a vast flock of mandolins tremoloing their way through light classics, groups like this one helped bring fretted instruments up to the level of popularity that brass bands and string orchestras enjoyed. Mr. and Mrs. late–nineteenth-century-America wouldn't take grandma and the kids to hear a guitarist on Saturday evening, but they would take them to hear a mandolin club perform. Seventy years later, C.F. III remembered this photo from Martin's archives as being of the Jersey City Mandolin Club. *(Photo courtesy of C. F. Martin & Company.)*

Meanwhile, one can only presume that the previously mentioned Emma Miller Harger wasn't sent the two Martins she asked for, since Frank Henry was informed on August 24, 1892, by Cleveland Guitar Club president L. H. Prescott that Mrs. Harger "has gone to work for Lyon & Healy to teach and promote their guitar."

ABOVE: John Santschi, from Goshen, Indiana, was one of many performer/instructors who purchased instruments and strings direct from Martin. Though teachers didn't receive the full discount that music stores did, they could still profit from selling Martin's goods to their students. (Gibson sold through instructors exclusively until the 1920s.) Here Santschi is holding an 0-30 guitar, and the Martin mandolin beside him is probably the Style 5 sent to him in November of 1898 "on trial," according to Martin's sales ledger. The music tucked behind the mandolin is *Tyroler Alpenlieder. (Photo courtesy of C. F. Martin & Company.)*

With Zoebisch doing the marketing, Frank Henry could do little to counter the competition.

Cutting the Strings

In 1893 the nation entered a depression in which the stock market crashed and 15,000 businesses failed. That November, Frank Henry considered laying off workers and closing his shop until the following April. Zoebisch reported that accounts weren't paying and that he had 80 unsold Martins lingering in his warehouse.

Finally, after consulting with his mother (who was still co-owner), Frank Henry terminated the exclusive distribution deal with C. A. Zoebisch & Sons and took on additional dealers.

Frank Henry's take-charge manner had evidently already rubbed one-time Martin partner C. F. Hartmann the wrong way. Hartmann left Martin to open a shop in New York in 1892, and letters reported a "strained relationship."

It is unclear exactly when Martin ended the exclusive relationship with Zoebisch, but by 1895 Martin was making and selling mandolins, doing very well with them.

Even in New York, where Zoebisch was based, Frank Henry discovered a greater demand for his guitars than Zoebisch had been supplying. But eastern dealers coming out of the Depression were ordering only small guitars and parts. Frank Henry put more effort into servicing the burgeoning West Coast and was soon receiving orders for his larger and fancier models from Denver, Spokane, Butte, Portland, San Francisco, and elsewhere.

For a company used to selling only 260 instruments a year, these western accounts were a marvel to Martin. In 1898 the Wiley B. Allen store in Portland alone placed an initial order of 3 mandolins and 7 guitars and months later followed with orders for another 24 guitars and more mandolins.

And for the first time, in 1898, these guitars were being shipped not with a stamp bearing the New York location of his old distributor, but with one proclaiming "C. F. Martin & Co., Nazareth, Pa.," as Martin guitars do to this day.

Martin Models

Late Nineteenth Century

The first Martin style designations, as found on the C. A. Zoebisch & Sons price list of the 1870s, were based on the wholesale price. There were lots of style numbers, often with very minor differences between them, because each style represented only one model. But as demand for larger guitars grew in the 1880s, new Martin models overran the simple system. Rather than continue to add new style numbers just to account for the larger-size instruments the company began offering, Frank Henry Martin made each style represent a specific set of decorative features that remained constant regardless of size. For example, a standard model from Civil War days such as the 1-21 would have big brothers, the 0-21 and 00-21, that had identical trim.

The 1897 price list was organized by size, not by price. It showed four styles for both the 0 and 00

ABOVE: Though usually seen as the backstrip on the Style 28, this zigzag pattern was used around the face of some early Martins. *(Photo courtesy of Gryphon Stringed Instruments.)*

BELOW: The "5-9-5" pattern of soundhole rings used on the Style 28 became the standard rosette for all Martins except those with a pearl ring. The wider rings in the center were ivory until 1917. Thanks to Martin, the herringbone top border seen here is now found on more guitar brands than any other wood purfling. *(Photo courtesy of Gryphon Stringed Instruments.)*

ABOVE: Elegant multicolor purfling was common for the backstrip on the more expensive nineteenth-century Martins, but unlike later in the 1900s, one particular pattern was not necessarily associated with just one or two styles. The pattern above is from an 1890s Style 27 but is also often found on Styles 30 through 42. *(Guitar courtesy of Fred Oster.)*

ABOVE: Although early Style 18 guitars had a narrow rope-pattern rosette, shortly after 1900 the pattern was simplified to a combination of black and white strips of wood similar to those around the top. The binding on the outer edge is rosewood. *(Guitar courtesy of Fred Oster.)*

guitar sizes, and five styles for sizes 1 and 2. Styles 24 and 40 had disappeared; and Styles 17, 20, and 26 were gone before the 1898 catalog appeared, though Style 17 would return in later years. (See “Pre-1898 Martin Styles” on page 251 to see what these numbers all mean.) Other styles were deleted by 1901, and of those that remained—18, 21, 28, 30, and 42—all but Style 30 would continue for decades. Flat-back mandolins, ukuleles, and other later additions to the family of Martin instruments might not have the same style numbers, but the progression from plain to fancy would display the same combination of decorative elements as the guitar models.

Paring down the number of designs was probably necessary if the Martin company was to compete with the new industrial giants in Chicago, for it made both production and promotion more economical. A craftsman could put the same purfling on the edges of different-sized guitars, while the catalog could show one guitar of that style and then simply list the other sizes available.

Style 18 was quite plain, with rosewood binding and simple black and white lines for the soundhole rosette. Style 21 was also bound in rosewood, with herringbone around the soundhole and up the center seam of the back. Style 28 was bound in ivory with herringbone around the top edge and a fancier backstrip, while Style 42 had a thin line of abalone bordering the top and soundhole and was the first to get delicate "snowflake" inlays on the ivory-bound fretboard. Style 45, added in 1904, had more of everything, including an elaborate headstock inlay and all body edges bordered in pearl and ivory.

Though the Martin guitar would go through a dramatic transformation in the next few decades, the styles remained remarkably constant. Despite changes in woods, strings, body shape, and neck length, these five styles—18, 21, 28, 42, and 45—would continue to define Martin aesthetics until World War II. Renewed interest in the classic designs would bring them back 30 years later, and today they again define the subtle beauty of the original Martins.

LEFT INSET: The famous "pyramid" bridge used by the Martin company from the 1840s to the early 1930s is unique to the company, though other brands have tried variations on that theme. The name comes from the peaks at each bridge tip; but a close examination reveals that they aren't quite pyramids after all—only three sides are a flat plane, while the fourth is rounded. *(Guitar courtesy of C. F. Martin & Company.)*

LEFT: By late in 1898, the Martin company had settled on the inlay pattern shown here for Style 42, and this pattern would last almost half a century. On early examples such as this 0-42 guitar from 1902, the neck inlays were of white mother-of-pearl; but later versions were cut from sea snail pearl, and later, abalone. *(Guitar courtesy of C. F. Martin & Company.)*

RIGHT: The Martin company's response to the lavish neck inlays on Washburns and other brands was even more modest and understated than the rest of their decorations. This 0-42 from mid-1898 shows Martin's tentative step toward putting pearl inlays on the guitar fretboard. The darkened top, appropriately called "orange" in the 1897 price list, is not typical of Style 42, though it is commonly seen on less ornate Martin styles like the 0-28. The abalone top border is also wider than usual, indicating that this was not a typical 0-42. Considering the serial number (8165), the orange face, and the ivory pegs, it is probably the guitar Martin shipped on August 10, 1898, to C. D. Schettler of Salt Lake City, a Martin endorser in later catalogs who sent the company a photo of one of his prize students (see page 68). *(Photo from Hank Risan.)*

Slow GROWTH *and* EXPERIMENTATION

1899–1929

"I like to think of the wood in a guitar as the voice of the tree. At our home on North Street when I was a small boy, we had a spruce pine tree on the south side of the house. It stood there alone. It did very well. It grew much taller than the house, and at one point my father said, 'We'll take that tree down. It's mature now, and it'll make good guitar braces.'

"So we took it down, and when we opened it, we found it wasn't suitable at all because the grain was too wide. And the reason for that, as I see it and as Father saw it, was that the tree grew alone under ideal conditions and it grew too fast. Good, close-grain spruce grows on the north side of the mountain in a forest, not by itself. Maybe there's a moral there. I won't try to preach a sermon on it, but that's what I mean about wood. It does have personality. I love wood. My father loved wood, and I think all my ancestors did."—C. F. Martin III in 1985.

Like the best trees, the Martin company grew slowly and under adverse conditions. But the moral might have ended there, for if money were sunlight, the other growths in Martin's forest—including Gibson, Lyon & Healy, and its fellow Chicago firms Harmony and Groehsl (which later became Kay)—were

LEFT: Though Martin may have preferred that its guitars be associated with the refined elegance shown by Vahdah Olcott-Bickford *(right)* and her friends in the La Banduria Trio, the phonograph and radio instead opened a vast market for more popular and less polished types of guitar music. *(Photo courtesy of International Guitar Research Archives.)*

RIGHT: C.F. III's 1911 000-45 is clearly a custom model, and the blank fretboard and peghead may be the result of Vahdah Olcott-Bickford's influence. Though the back and sides are inlaid like a Style 45, the top bordering doesn't extend around the end of the fretboard. *(Guitar courtesy of C. F. Martin & Company.)*

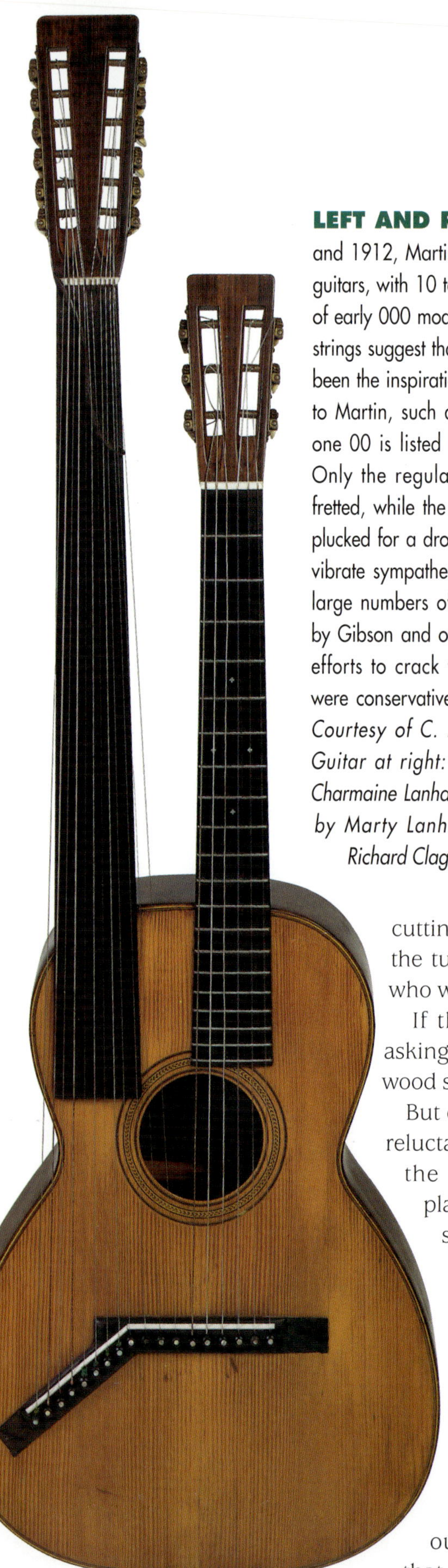

LEFT AND RIGHT: Between 1902 and 1912, Martin made at least 10 harp guitars, with 10 to 18 strings. The number of early 000 models made with additional strings suggest that harp guitars may have been the inspiration for what was, at least to Martin, such an oversized body (only one 00 is listed with additional strings). Only the regular 6 strings were to be fretted, while the bass strings were either plucked for a droning effect or allowed to vibrate sympathetically. Compared to the large numbers of harp guitars marketed by Gibson and other companies, Martin's efforts to crack the harp guitar market were conservative at best. *(Guitar at left: Courtesy of C. F. Martin & Company. Guitar at right: Photo by Dan Loftin/ Charmaine Lanham, Nashville; restoration by Marty Lanham; guitar owned by Richard Claggett.)*

cutting out Martin's light. The company was scarcely growing at the turn of the century, and it was dwarfed by its competition who were adept at flashy advertising and aggressive marketing.

If things hadn't changed, people might soon have been asking, "Say, whatever happened to those fellows who admired wood so much?"

But change did come in the new century, in the form of some reluctant inspiration on Martin's part and in the championing of the company's instruments by unexpected new types of players. Martin had been making guitars of exacting precision and detail: Each of its successive sizes, for example, had soundholes exactly 1/16 inch larger than the preceding size did. The company was accustomed to seeing its instruments played with equal precision by instrumentalists applying themselves to music that at least aspired to classical standards. In the twentieth century, Martin's success would instead be tied to its instruments' finding favor in the less-exacting hands of Hawaiians, hillbillies, and eventually hippies.

The first two members of this 3H club reached previously impossible levels of exposure via the phonograph that Thomas Edison had invented in 1877. As if to make up

for the ages of human history when sound recording was impossible, Edison and his competitors started recording everything: opera, animal sounds, and humor sketches, as well as ethnic and regionally peculiar music. By the early 1920s, commercial radio stations expanded audiences again by broadcasting an endless fountain of free entertainment into homes.

Recording and radio would ultimately have a homogenizing effect on the nation, but initially the opposite was true. Previously, most people came to know songs via sheet music, and those little black dots never imparted an artist's accent. The new media for the first time brought regional voices to a mass audience. And for the first time, listeners heard real folk music—country music, "race" music, Hawaiian music—simple, direct stuff often sung by voices not unlike the listeners'. And when those hayseed voices were making it onto the hit parade, it was a huge inducement for listeners to try making music themselves.

For Martin, there was a new market for instruments waiting to be filled, if the company could find a way out of its own backwoods.

ABOVE: Early record companies were often a part of a parent company that manufactured, or at least marketed, phonographs. The goal was not so much to sell millions of records, but to sell phonographs, as that was where the real profit lay. Local phonograph shops would broadcast records of Greek, Italian, Polish, or other ethnic music into the street in immigrant neighborhoods, and those longing for the sounds of their homeland would scrape together hard-earned cash to be able to hear familiar music once again.

The Flat Line

Looking back from the turn of the century, Frank Henry Martin could trace his firm's long and respectable history. He also was looking at a flat line. In 1864 the Martin company had sold just over 300 guitars, reaping an average wholesale price of $20. Forty years later, in 1904, the company sold a total of 349 guitars and mandolins for $8,717 wholesale, averaging $25 an instrument. In 1907 production was up to 621 instruments, but many—including 144 of the Style 0 mandolins—were inexpensive models, bringing the average price to only $16.28. (Martin also lowered its prices: An 0-28 listed for $60 in the 1870s but dropped to $45 from 1898 until World War I.) In 1911 the company barely sold 200 guitars, and only 150 were sold the year following.

Had Frank Henry not split with C. A. Zoebisch & Sons, Martin's sole distributor, things would have been truly grim; but mandolin sales and the new accounts in the prosperous West kept C. F. Martin & Company at a sustenance level. But even that wasn't enough when competitors were trying to eat Frank Henry's lunch.

Frank Henry tried a number of things to increase the revenue trickling into Nazareth. He debuted the size 000 guitar in 1902, the biggest Martin yet. Its 15-inch width at the lower bout made it ⅞ inch wider than the next-biggest 00 model, though it was still dwarfed by other makers' guitars. The 000 has since become the

favorite Martin size of many players, but in 1902 the guitar—still strung with gut—still couldn't cut the competition from the louder mandolin and banjo.

Around the same time, Martin had an unsuccessful go at making strings, not the top three gut ones, but the silk-cored, copper-wound bottom three. When not busy cleaning up the shop, Frank Henry's son, young Christian Frederick Martin III, worked at the winding machine, and the string envelopes were made at home by the Martin family. They got out of the string business by 1918 because they couldn't compete with other makers who had made large investments in winding machinery.

Ahead of the Curve

In late 1907, perhaps buoyed by Martin's relative success with the mandolin, Frank Henry decided to try building ukuleles. The ukes were simple compared to the company's bowlbacked mandolins. The bowlbacks were so labor-intensive that current company CEO Chris Martin estimates the more elaborate models would cost upward of $30,000 if marketed today. But Frank Henry built the early ukes like guitars, with spruce tops and lots of internal bracing, which made them too heavy to respond to the light tension of typical ukulele tuning. There also was the little problem that nobody especially wanted ukuleles in 1907, and the Martin company quickly gave up making them.

The look of several Martin guitar models had evolved by that time. The post-1898 instruments, of course, all were stamped C. F. Martin & Co., Nazareth, PA, and were given serial numbers, beginning the most accurate and continuous record-keeping of any American instrument manufacturer. But Frank Henry also began cutting loose on the aesthetics, letting at least a bit of the pearl lavished on his mandolins spill over into the guitar line. In 1898 the Style 42 gained snowflake-shaped pearl fret markers at three frets, while Styles 34 and 30 also received distinctive patterns.

The twentieth century dawned with most models gaining position marker inlays on the fingerboard. The special-order Style 42 of 1902 reached the limit of Frank Henry's catalog dictum, "ornate but never ostentatious." The pearl border on the face of the guitar was joined by pearl borders on the side and back. Two more fret markings adorned the neck, and the slotted peghead acquired a scroll inlay. If this sounds like

(continued on page 90)

ABOVE: The Martin company was often requested to build special-order instruments with more ornamentation than Style 42. This 00-42, made in 1902, features mandolin-style pearl work and extra pearl bordering. About a half-dozen Style 42s with extra helpings of pearl were made before such models were designated Style 45 in 1904. The vine-pattern fretboard inlay and fancy pick guard were rarely used again, probably because such inlays are in a thin veneer, making future fretwork nearly impossible without damaging the design. Except for the pearl bordering on the body, all the inlay was done by the George H. Jones Company of New York, which supplied Martin with the inlaid veneers. *(Photo from Hank Risan.)*

MARTIN'S FLAT-BACK MANDOLINS

Thanks to changes in the mandolin market, the Martin company's success with the bowlback mandolin didn't last very long. In the years following 1910, American mandolinists began to abandon the bowlback style in favor of flat-back models. The aggressive marketing of the Gibson company to promote its carved-top mandolins probably also contributed to the growing sentiment that the Neapolitan mandolin was simply old-fashioned, and the fact that it was harder to hold couldn't have helped. Martin did not follow Gibson into production of carved mandolins but instead began producing the flat-back style in 1914. The binding and inlay on Martin's flat models, unlike the bowlbacks, was roughly equivalent to its guitar line. Though far simpler to make, the flat-back mandolins sold for only slightly less than the bowlback models, as Martin realized that making lots of mandolins was of little use if it wasn't making a decent profit on them. Martin mandolin production peaked in 1920, with over

ABOVE: The Martin "flat-model" mandolins, introduced in this special 1915 catalog, soon replaced the Italian bowlback style that the company had first produced 20 years earlier. The Style A shown here was by far the most popular of all Martin's mandolins, and it was the only model to have a peghead shaped like that of a guitar. Style A was switched from rosewood to mahogany by 1917, and the body was later made wider. The pick guard shape of this Style A mandolin disappeared almost immediately, replaced by one much like what would appear on Martin guitars of the 1930s.

LEFT: Martin's flat-model mandolins were given letter designations A through E with the plain Style A being roughly equivalent to a Style 18 guitar. This 1931 Style B is a rosewood model with the same trim as a Style 21 guitar, including dark binding and herringbone purfling for the rosette and backstrip. The shaded top was an option beginning in the late 1920s. Ironically, Martin never made a flat mandolin equivalent to the ever-popular Style 28. *(Photo courtesy of Fred Oster.)*

RIGHT: Except for the bend in the top, a feature shared by the Neopolitan mandolin, the flat-back mandolin is constructed much like a small guitar. This may be one of the reasons Martin was keen to switch from the bowlback style, which was waning in popularity by 1910. The Style E, shown here, was the only flat-back style to approach the ornate decorations commonly found on the bowlback styles, but it was really just a mandolin version of a Style 45 guitar. *(Mandolin courtesy of The Chinery Collection.)*

LEFT: Martin made more mandolas in the flat style than it had in the bowlback mandolin style. The mahogany version was called AA, while the rosewood model (shown at left) was given the BB code. Later versions were just listed as A or B mandolas. When guitars with an all-koa body were popular, Martin offered all-koa mandolins as well. About 1,000 of the simplest style, like the AK shown on the right, were sold in the 1920s. A higher model with herringbone soundhole and backstrip, the BK, did not fare nearly as well. *(Photo courtesy of Steve Szilagyi/Elderly Instruments.)*

RIGHT: The 2-30 was the highest-priced of three f-hole mandolins Martin introduced in 1936 (the 2-20 was the same shape with less binding). But the addition of more modern soundholes and a beautiful shaded finish were not enough to make up for the fact that the mandolin craze was well past its expiration date. Note the tortoiseshell celluloid peghead overlay of this 1940 example, a common feature on Martin's carved mandolins in the last years before production was halted by World War II. *(Mandolin courtesy of C. F. Martin & Company.)*

BELOW LEFT: Introduced in 1929, Styles 15 and 20 were the Martin company's first carved-top instruments, and mandolins would be the only Martin arch-top instruments to receive a fully carved back. (Style 15 didn't have the points on the body.) These arch-top mandolins would have been worthy contenders around 1917, when Lyon & Healy had introduced similar models, but by 1929 they were already old-fashioned in the rapidly fading mandolin market. *(Photo courtesy of C. F. Martin & Company.)*

1,500 sold that year alone. This included nine bowlback styles and five flat-back models, with a few mandolas made as well. Mandolin sales began to fall in the mid-1920s as the tenor banjo and the ukulele became America's new favorites. Martin responded by dropping production of all bowlback models by 1925, when it was busy making thousands of ukuleles. When uke sales plummeted in 1929, Martin tried to revive enthusiasm in the mandolin ranks by adding two models with carved tops, oval soundholes, and maple backs and sides. Designated Styles 15 and 20, they were closer in appearance to the Lyon & Healy (Washburn) Style C and B mandolins than they were to Gibson's, for America's leading mandolin maker had already progressed to f-shaped soundholes for most of its mandolin line. Gibson wasn't paying much attention to mandolins then anyway, having realized that the instruments' popularity was fading fast.

In 1936 Martin added more modern models with f-shaped soundholes and shaded finishes on the top. These belated attempts to follow Gibson's success with carved mandolins were doomed to failure as more exciting musical styles like jazz and swing captured the nation's attention. When it came to arch-top mandolins, Martin had been so busy building ukuleles that the company missed the bus. By looking back at a 1929 letter to O. F. Bitting, for whom Martin had made a special line of flat-back mandolins a decade earlier, we can see what F. H. Martin was thinking. Frank Henry explained his company's late arrival on the carved-top mandolin scene by stating, "We are counting on a return of mandolin playing to a considerable extent." Evidently F.H. was better at noticing the birth of new musical trends than he was at recognizing their demise.

All but the simplest carved model, the 2-15, were discontinued in 1942 when mandolin production was suspended for three years because of the war. The 2-15 and the mahogany Style A flat-back were the only Martin mandolins produced in the postwar era, except for three dozen Style B flat models in 1946 and some special-order Style 20 models around 1950. The Style 15 lasted until 1964. The flat-back Style A, though not highly regarded today, was by far the most popular Martin mandolin of all and sold well throughout the 1950s and 1960s. Even in the mid-1970s, Martin was able to sell 200 Style A mandolins per year, and a total of almost 14,000 were made in the 60-plus years it was made. Production dropped off after 1976, bringing to a slow close almost a century of Martin mandolin production.

ABOVE: Bill and Earl Bolick performed as the Blue Sky Boys, singing old-fashioned songs in a relaxed style that might best be described as pre-bluegrass. Though Earl later moved up to a D-28, Bill used his Martin Style 20 mandolin on through the 1950s, and its smooth tone is distinctly different from the more commonly heard Gibson mandolins. Earl is shown here with one of the transitional late 1920s 00-28 Martins built for steel strings—it has a pick guard (possibly added later) but the old-style pyramid bridge. *(Photo from the Frank Driggs Collection.)*

LEFT: Ironically, the unassuming 2-15, like this one from 1947, sold in greater numbers in the decade following the war than the previous combined sales of all Martin's carved models. This is perhaps because Gibson mandolins suffered a decline in quality compared to 20 years earlier, whereas the Martin Style 15 was consistent to the end. *(Photo courtesy of Intermountain Guitar and Banjo.)*

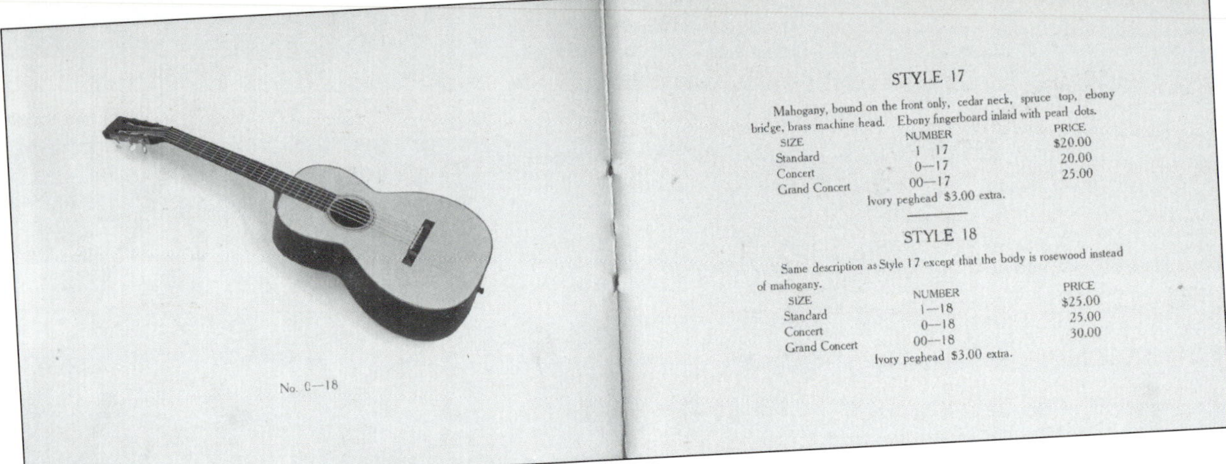

No. 0—18

STYLE 17

Mahogany, bound on the front only, cedar neck, spruce top, ebony bridge, brass machine head. Ebony fingerboard inlaid with pearl dots.

SIZE	NUMBER	PRICE
Standard	1 17	$20.00
Concert	0—17	20.00
Grand Concert	00—17	25.00

Ivory peghead $3.00 extra.

STYLE 18

Same description as Style 17 except that the body is rosewood instead of mahogany.

SIZE	NUMBER	PRICE
Standard	1—18	$25.00
Concert	0—18	25.00
Grand Concert	00—18	30.00

Ivory peghead $3.00 extra.

ABOVE: After a few years' holiday, Style 17 returned to the Martin line in 1906, this time as a mahogany version of Style 18. In 1917, when the Style 18 was switched from rosewood to mahogany, the 17 would disappear again, only to reappear in 1922 as an even plainer steel-string guitar with a mahogany top.

LEFT: C. F. Martin III (1894–1986), shown here steering the tricycle, would eventually end up steering the company bearing his name into the space age. To this day he is still remembered fondly as "Mr. Martin" by Martin employees. He truly loved playing the guitar and the craft of guitarmaking, traits that were shared by his tricycle-hitching brother, Herbert Keller Martin (1895–1927). *(Photo courtesy of C. F. Martin & Company.)*

Martin's famed Style 45, that's because the special-order Style 42 was renamed that in 1904. For all that it sold at the time, though, the company might as well have gone back to making zithers.

In 1906 Frank Henry tried another idea that wasn't an immediate success, this time at the low end of his price scale. He reintroduced the Style 17 guitars with a mahogany back and sides instead of the more expensive rosewood the company had always used. Mahogany is now one of the most commonly used woods in guitarmaking, but it was generally found only on budget makes then. Only 15 of the $25-list Style 17s were sold in the first three years of production, but they opened the door to Martin's later success with the mahogany Style 18 series, still popular today.

QUALITY *AND* QUANTITY

Christian Frederick Martin III—born on September 9, 1894, and known as Frederick, or Fred if you really knew him—had a large maple plaque that his father had hung in his bedroom when he was a child. It had inlaid rosewood letters reading "Non Multa Sed Multum," or "not many but much." "In plain English," Frederick later interpreted, "quality rather than quantity."

ABOVE: It could have been a big slab of beautiful rosewood or fancy maple with the same message, but Frank Henry instead gave his son an intricately worked background for the words "not many but much" (quality not quantity). *(Courtesy of C. F. Martin & Company.)*

In 1985 Frederick recalled, "That was his philosophy.... He did want to make as many guitars for as many people as possible. [But] it wasn't so much the quantity as it was the fact that he could put a good guitar in the hands of many people. So in our early catalogs we emphasized and put up front the cheaper guitars, which was contrary to the rules of advertising and marketing. You should put your high-priced stuff up front and your lower-priced stuff in the back, right? Well, he didn't do that. He wanted to make as many plain guitars as possible so that more people could use them, because they were lower in price."

Frederick was inducted into the family business at an early age. "One of my first journeys away from Nazareth was a trip with my father to New York City. It must have been about 1903 or 1904, and we visited the lumberyards between 6th and 10th Streets, where East River Drive is now," he said.

There, his father would choose logs. Martin believed in using quartersawn

ABOVE: In C.F. III and Herbert Keller, the Martin family had the makings of a typical guitar-and-mandolin duet. Besides playing in college, they both performed in the Aetna mandolin club in Nazareth and in similar clubs in the neighboring towns of Allentown and Bethlehem. There is no mention of the previous three generations of Martins having been musicians. *(Photo courtesy of C. F. Martin & Company.)*

LEFT: Ivory friction pegs in a solid headstock were available at no additional charge on all models until 1900, when Martin began charging an extra $2.50 for the "peghead" option on Styles 21 and 28. Certain retailers, such as Clark Music of San Francisco, ordered all their better Martin models with these friction pegs. The option was still free on Style 42 guitars, such as this 1903 1-42; and the strap button, made of horn, was also standard. *(Photo from Hank Risan.)*

ABOVE: Here is the evolution of the Style 45 headstock inlay. With very few exceptions, inlaid headstocks on Martins began with the fancy pattern at left, which appeared on special Style 42 models and on the first guitars designated Style 45, as seen in the 1904 catalog. Sometimes called the "fern" inlay, it also appeared in the 1909 catalog, but only because Martin used the same photo-engraving for several years. The design in the middle, now commonly called a "torch," appears at least as early as 1905 and was in use until about 1927. Martin paid 75 cents for this pattern at the time, inlaid into a rosewood veneer. The variant on the right, with simplified upper portion, was used on both slotted and solid headstocks from 1927 until late 1933, when it was replaced by letters spelling "C. F. MARTIN" on the 14-fret model 45s. The old "torch" inlay was still used on slotted Style 45 headstocks and a very few special order models, until the late 1930s. Martin's typically vague catalog descriptions referred to this design as a "pearl scroll." *(Photo from Hank Risan.)*

wood; and to get a guitar back half 8 inches wide required a Brazilian rosewood log 20 inches in diameter. Years later, when Frederick took a position with the company, he would follow the same route his father had taken, from lumberyard to sawmill:

"I would have the logs I selected, usually only one or two, delivered to the sawmill, then I'd go there and talk to the sawyer. I'd make sure he understood how we wanted that log cut, and the exact thickness, and we got a good close relationship with our wood sawyers."

Frederick had a brother one year younger, Herbert Keller Martin, who also grew up in the business. Making up for the previous generations of Martins, who had no more than a high school education, both brothers went to Princeton. They were in the glee club together there, where Frederick played a 000-45 guitar that his father had given him.

Though Frederick was also the first generation of Martin to play a guitar as well as to make them, when he graduated from Princeton in 1916, "I had ambitions at the time of getting away from the family business," he told *Music Trades* magazine in 1983, considering instead a graduate degree in business administration from Harvard. "But my brother was still in college, and my father needed help managing things, so I came home and went to work making guitars, on what I thought would be a part-time basis."

When Herbert graduated the following year, he, too, entered the business. They weren't long at it before both rallied around the flag in World War I, along with plant foreman John Deichman and two other Martin employees. Neither brother came close to action: Herbert was stationed in Kentucky, while Frederick's poor eyesight kept him out of the service altogether. Instead he served as secretary of the YMCA at

RIGHT: This leather case with Princeton decal housed C. F. Martin III's 000-45 (shown on page 83) while he was at college. Martin had begun phasing out its black wooden "coffin" cases around the turn of the century in favor of leather cases like this one. Though handsome and lightweight, the opening at the bottom can send a guitar to the ground if the leather strap holding the lid breaks or comes unfastened. Less expensive canvas-covered cardboard cases were also available, with a similar opening at the bottom. These styles are sometimes called "bottom dumpers" today. *(Photo courtesy of C. F. Martin & Company.)*

BELOW: In this view of the inside of the factory around 1912, note the stacks of wood screw-type guitar frames under the workbench and the line of glued guitar sides above. *(Photo courtesy of C. F. Martin & Company.)*

ABOVE AND INSET: The photo at the top was probably taken about 1906, as C.F. III, wearing knickers, appears to be in his early-teens. His father, the clearly all-business Frank Henry, stands in the doorway. The inset photo, probably taken around 1910, shows the now-promoted-to-trousers C.F. III at the far right with his knickered brother Herbert Keller at the far left. Both photos are taken at the main entrance of the Martin factory with the sign stating "C. F. Martin & Co. Guitars and Mandolins." These photos show the imposing figure of Frank Henry Martin in his prime. Most of the older men shown were born in Germany, as it wasn't until after the turn of the century that Martin hired its first native-born craftsman. Considering the company's low production at the time, these groups may well have represented most of Martin's workforce. (*Top photo courtesy of Old Salem; bottom photo courtesy of C. F. Martin & Company.)*

ABOVE: In 1928 performer/instructor Vahdah Olcott-Bickford conducted the American Guitar Society Orchestra. She is shown at the far right holding the batton. Not all, but most of the guitarists in this group played Martins, probably under Vahdah's influence. *(Photo courtesy of International Guitar Research Archives.)*

Camp Hancock in Augusta, Georgia. He transferred to North Carolina to work in a program teaching illiterate soldiers to read, and there he met Daisy Allen, whom he would later marry.

After the war, Frederick oversaw production. He rarely completed a guitar himself, but he worked at many stations of the factory. His more outgoing brother was soon on the road handling sales.

The thing necessitating Frederick and Herbert's help at the company was the "bouncing flea," the translation of the Hawaiian name—*ukulele*—given to a sprightly, toylike little instrument from the islands.

Hawaii Triple-0

In the 1910s the news arriving from across the Atlantic Ocean was unremittingly grim. Europe was gripped by a plummeting economy, petty political squabbles, and then a horrific war for which no one could fathom the reason. No wonder, then, that the United States chose to become fascinated with what was going on off its other shore.

In 1912 the first Hawaiian Broadway show, "Bird of Paradise," had taken New York by tsunami, with exotic scenery, dazzling costumes, and the authentic music of five Hawaiian musicians. After a successful run at Daly's Theater, the show went on the road throughout the United States and Canada, playing to packed houses everywhere. An even bigger boost for the captivating new sound came from California, where the Hawaiian Pavilion at the 1915 Pan-Pacific Exposition in San Francisco staged Hawaiian music shows several times a day, drawing the highest attendance of the exposition. Soon Hawaiian bands were criss-crossing the continent, putting mandolin-laden Spanish Student groups out of work.

While the Martin company usually had a knack for catching trends as they were dying, for once it had been too early with its 1907 ukes. But when its new, more Hawaiian-styled ukuleles went on the market in January 1916, the company was right on the money. The instruments were an immediate success and continued to grow in popularity far beyond the company's most hula-intoxicated expectations.

Martin was pushed to the limit keeping up with the demand for the leisure-time instruments. In the company's second year of ukedom, one disgruntled employee with a sharp sense of humor posted the following notice: "The Martin Guitar factory will work on Friday, April 6th, 1917. Good Friday. Evidently."

The tiny instruments outgrew the factory, necessitating its expansion that year, and again in 1924, and yet again in 1925. The company, which had been selling barely a couple of hundred instruments a decade before, now turned out 14,000 ukes in 1926.

Up to this point, Martin had been aiming its guitars at the admirers and students of classically bent performers such as William Foden, Vahdah Olcott-Bickford, and Sophacles Papas. But with guitar production stuck at around 200 instruments a year, it was the Hawaiians who came to the rescue.

Islanders had an utterly distinctive method of playing the guitar, sliding a metal bar over raised steel strings tuned to an open chord. When the Hawaiian guitar fad struck around 1915, Gibson and other companies had long since embraced steel strings. With Martin's guitar sales going nowhere despite the company's widespread recognition, it was clear that Martin had done far more for the gut-string guitar than players of that instrument had done for Martin.

Frank Henry must have realized this, and in

LEFT AND ABOVE: Lots of love-struck guys gave ukuleles to their sweethearts or wives, but not many were able to assist in building the highest-grade uke from the country's top-rated ukulele factory. The Style 5 shown above was a gift from C.F. III to his wife, Daisy. Style 5 ukes were usually made of figured koa, but the curly mahogany seen here is considered its equal. Stock Style 5 ukes were offered in mahogany only in 1941 to 1942, just before the model was dropped due to the war. *(Photo courtesy of Jim Bollman; ukulele courtesy of C. F. Martin & Company.)*

RIGHT: Sometimes playing Hawaiian music just isn't enough, so Lois Phillips deepened the mood with a penknife on her Style 1 mahogany taropatch. Tuned like a uke but double-strung, the taropatch wasn't easy to tune with friction pegs, as seen on this example. *(Ukulele courtesy of C. F. Martin & Company.)*

William Foden

A "Special" Customer

Born in 1860, this well-known concert guitarist and instructor had a long career with the guitar, and his instruction book, titled "The Grand Method," was widely used for decades. Martin's close relationship with Foden dates back to around 1900, when sales records list many guitars sold directly to him. He frequently ordered 0-42 models with an ebony bridge instead of the ivory bridge that came standard. Beginning around 1912, Martin made at least four guitar models, "Foden Specials," which had a number of unique features.

The Foden A was equivalent to Martin's Style 18; and Foden B, C, and D corresponded to Styles 21, 28, and 30, though with minor differences in the purfling and rosette. Foden Style E had features placing it somewhere between Martin Styles 40 and 45. Production records are not complete; so although fewer than 30 Foden Specials have been found in the sales books from 1912 to 1917, more may have been produced.

William Foden was the first to suggest that Martin guitars should have 20 frets instead of 19, and 20-fret fingerboards later became a standard feature on most Martins. This required moving the soundhole closer to the center of the guitar and resulted in one of the most visible differences between most twentieth-century Martins and those guitars made to the original patterns from over a half-century earlier. William Foden died in 1947.

RIGHT: William Foden appeared in the 1897 Washburn catalog, endorsing Washburns as "none finer," but later he must have had a change of heart. By 1900 he was ordering Martins for himself and his students, and he eventually was given a line of "Foden Specials" with unique features. *(Photo courtesy of International Guitar Research Archives.)*

BELOW: The Style D Foden Special shown here was equivalent to a Martin Style 30, but with different marquetry and fretboard inlays and a single ring rosette. The inlays were later revived for use on the Martin koa guitars, D-37K and D-37K2, introduced in 1980. *(Photo © J. Whipple Photography/Lark Street Music.)*

Vahdah Olcott-Bickford

Elegant Classicist

Of all the performing artist/instructors who championed Martin guitars, none had as long a relationship with the company as Vahdah (born Ethel) Olcott-Bickford. A child prodigy, when she was only 20 she became the first American guitarist to perform *Giuliani's 3rd Concerto with string quartet*. Vahdah and her husband, mandolinist/conductor Zahr Bickford, were founding members of the American Guitar Society, and struggled to gain fretted instruments recognition as serious vehicles for classical music.

Vahdah preferred the highest grade Martins but disliked pearl bordering, so in 1913 Martin offered special order Style 44 Olcott-Bickford Artist Models. Made in size 2 through 000, these guitars had an ivory-bound body, fretboard, and peghead, but had the soundboard edged in black and white lines rather than the elaborate patterned wood purfling usually found on high-quality American guitars of the day. The top border was later used on Martin's arch-top guitars, and also replaced the herringbone trim on Style 28. Unlike other lines made for instructors, Style 44 was sold in retail stores, especially Ditson's New York branch.

Style 44 was plain but expensive, and existing records suggest that fewer than 35 examples of her special models were made. Letters between Vahdah and the Martins went beyond business; she once sent hollyhock seeds from her garden, and C.F. later reported on the plants' height and color.

The last Style 44s were made in 1938. In later photos, Vahdah is shown holding a Spanish guitar, as by then classical guitarists and American guitar manufacturers had gone their separate ways. She died in 1980 and so lived to see her beloved guitar accepted at last as a true classical instrument (thanks largely to Andrés Segovia). Though Martin returned to building guitars for nylon strings the company Vahdah had so championed in her youth was no longer favored by classical guitarists.

RIGHT: On this sheet music, "In Happy Days" refers to when "the guitar and lute reigned supreme in the Courts of Europe", while the "Lament" was since "fretted instruments were cast aside because of the...piano." "Song of Triumph" celebrates "the victory of fretted instruments over ignorance and prejudice." No wonder folks abandoned such stuffiness for Nick Lucas playing "Teasin' the Frets." *(Photo courtesy of International Guitar Research Archives.)*

LEFT: Though few style 44 Martins were made, they cover a wide range of sizes. This is a 1930 size 2, but others were made in sizes up to 000. The solid headstock with banjo tuners is a adaptation of the ivory friction pegs Vahdah Olcott-Bickford had preferred in years past, though usually associated with Martin's earliest OM models today. *(Courtesy of The Chinery Collection.)*

(Photo courtesy of International Guitar Research Archives.)

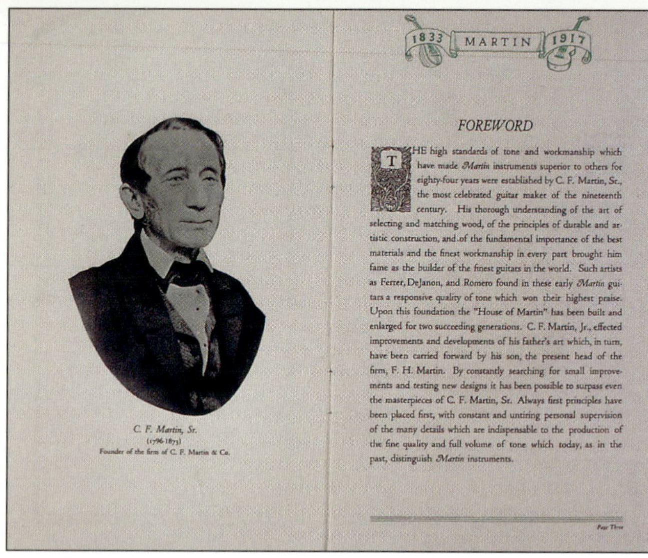

C. F. Martin, Sr.
(1796-1873)
Founder of the firm of C. F. Martin & Co.

1833 MARTIN 1917

FOREWORD

THE high standards of tone and workmanship which have made *Martin* instruments superior to others for eighty-four years were established by C. F. Martin, Sr., the most celebrated guitar maker of the nineteenth century. His thorough understanding of the art of selecting and matching wood, of the principles of durable and artistic construction, and of the fundamental importance of the best materials and the finest workmanship in every part brought him fame as the builder of the finest guitars in the world. Such artists as Ferrer, DeJanon, and Romero found in these early *Martin* guitars a responsive quality of tone which won their highest praise. Upon this foundation the "House of Martin" has been built and enlarged for two succeeding generations. C. F. Martin, Jr., effected improvements and developments of his father's art which, in turn, have been carried forward by his son, the present head of the firm, F. H. Martin. By constantly searching for small improvements and testing new designs it has been possible to surpass even the masterpieces of C. F. Martin, Sr. Always first principles have been placed first, with constant and untiring personal supervision of the many details which are indispensable to the production of the fine quality and full volume of tone which today, as in the past, distinguish *Martin* instruments.

Page Three

ABOVE: In 1917 C. F. Martin Sr.'s image appeared for the first time in a catalog, along with some tasteful artwork reminding potential customers how long Martin had been in business. Ukes and Hawaiian guitars weren't even mentioned yet, but brisk sales of these newcomers were already changing the old Martin company.

BELOW: Earle Hartzel sands ukulele bodies in the "new building" in 1925. By that time the old drive belts and gasoline engine were gone as the countryside was equipped with veins of cheap electricity. Apparently ukulele production was in full swing, as evidenced by the pile of uke bodies stacked on the table. Earle's granddaughter works in the even newer Martin factory today, where she scallops braces for new Martin guitars. *(Photo courtesy of C. F. Martin & Company.)*

1917 the company started manufacturing steel-string guitars capable of Hawaiian-style playing. (They weren't entirely his first; in 1914 he had built a single 00-21 Hawaiian guitar.) These guitars had heavier tops and bracing and came with a "nut adjuster" that would raise the strings high above the frets to facilitate playing them with a steel bar. Without the adjuster these guitars could be played normally, though it wasn't until 1922 that Martin would advertise one of its steel-string guitars as suited for normal play. At about the same time, Martin's Hawaiian guitars became specifically Hawaiian, with permanently raised nut and bridge. By the late 1920s the company was even filing these instruments' frets flush with the fingerboard to facilitate the Hawaiian slide style of playing.

Exotic Koa

Along with the boost in sales brought by the newly mahoganized, low-priced Style 18 guitars, the Hawaiian guitar craze proved to be just what Martin needed. Prodded by a request for a custom line from the Southern California Music Company of Los Angeles, Martin began making guitars of Hawaiian koa wood, including a koa top. The mahogany-like koa had an appealing reddish brown tint, was often highly figured, and was a commonly used wood in Hawaii until the cattle industry decimated the groves later in the twentieth century.

Sales of over 250 koa guitars to this one retailer in less than a year was a clear message, and by late 1918 Martin added an 0-18K to its own line. In 1920 Martin sold 270 0-18K models, its highest annual production of one guitar model up to that date, and it wasn't even in the catalog. This was greater than their entire yearly guitar output just four years earlier.

The new guitars proved so popular that when longtime Martin supporter Vahdah Olcott-Bickford moved to Los Angeles in 1923 she was appalled to report, "I found the real guitar very, very dead out here and the Hawaiian or steel guitar very much of a fad." She blamed California's "close proximity" to the islands and the "propaganda" of a local steel guitar manufacturer.

Her style of playing the *real* guitar wasn't threatened only by island music. In 1922 Nick Lucas recorded the instrumentals "Pickin' the Guitar" and "Teasin' the Frets," featuring hot guitar solos played using a flat pick on steel strings. Lucas's radio appearances soon made him America's first guitar hero, and imitators found that their guitar picks shredded gut strings in no time—and the strings weren't cheap.

Though typically referred to as "cat gut," guitar strings were actually made from sheep intestines. In either case, you probably wouldn't want the factory tour. It was a messy process and hence expensive, as was winding wire around the silken core of the three lower strings. Steel strings cost only a fraction of what the oft-breaking gut strings did, which may also have hastened the demand for steel-strung guitars.

Martin finally began making a standard guitar for steel strings in 1922, more than two decades after Gibson did. "We were late to give up gut strings," Frederick Martin later admitted. The company started cautiously, with only a small, inexpensive 2-17 being offered initially. The $25 guitar sold 344 in its first year, rising each year after that until it peaked at 1,300 in 1926.

ABOVE: By 1924 C. F. Martin Sr. would barely have recognized what had become of the one-story brick guitar workshop he had built in 1859. First, his shop was expanded and had a second story and attic added (*far right*); then around 1880 a two-story frame building was tacked on the west side (*center*). The crawlspace below the frame addition housed a gasoline engine that drove pulleys to power the shop's machinery. By 1925 the Martin factory expanded once again by adding a large one-story brick building to accommodate the ukulele craze (*far left*). Within two years Martin needed to add a second story to the addition to meet the demand for new instruments. *(Photo courtesy of C. F. Martin & Company.)*

LEFT: Koa guitars were the first Martins with hardwood tops, and the dense koa wood gives these instruments a distinct tone quite unlike similar Martins with spruce soundboards. The success of these models led to the use of mahogany tops on the 17 series steel-strings in 1922. This example is a 00-28K. *(Photo © Mac Yasuda Enterprises.)*

RIGHT: Low cost and durability, not to mention the flat pick, were major factors in the triumph of steel strings over gut. $2.25 was a lot for a set of strings—think of being able to buy a new Martin guitar for the price of a dozen sets of strings! (A Style 17 Martin was available for $25.) Many pickers, unable to pay the high price, tied broken strings together or found ingenious alternatives. Chet Atkins recalls using wire from window screens.

The HOUSE *of* MARTIN

STRINGS

The strings used on Martin instruments are made by string specialists according to Martin specifications. They are right in gauge, true in tone, and as durable as the best materials can make them.

SPANISH GUITAR STRINGS

	EACH	DOZEN
No. 101-E, 1st, Silvered Steel	$0.10	$0.70
No. 102-B, 2nd, Wound Steel	.15	1.50
No. 103-G, 3rd, Wound Steel	.15	1.50
No. 104-D, 4th, Wound Steel	.15	1.50
No. 105-A, 5th, Wound Steel	.20	2.00
No. 106-E, 6th, Wound Steel	.25	2.50
No. 107 Set of Six	.90	9.00
No. 121-E, 1st, Gut	.40	4.50
No. 122-B, 2nd, Gut	.45	5.00
No. 123-G, 3rd, Gut	.50	5.50
No. 124-D, 4th, Wound on Silk	.30	3.50
No. 125-A, 5th, Wound on Silk	.35	4.00
No. 126-E, 6th, Wound on Silk	.40	4.50
No. 127 Set of Six	2.25	25.00

HAWAIIAN GUITAR STRINGS

	EACH	DOZEN
No. 201-E, 1st, Silvered Steel	$0.10	$0.70
No. 202-C#, 2nd, Silvered Steel	.10	.80
No. 203-A, 3rd, Silvered Steel	.10	.90
No. 204-E, 4th, Polished Copper Wnd	.20	2.30
No. 205-A, 5th, Polished Copper Wnd	.25	2.80
No. 206-E, 6th, Polished Copper Wnd	.30	3.50
No. 207 Set of Six	1.00	10.00

ABOVE: The Martin company announced that it would discontinue the use of ivory in early 1918, "in favor of celluloid." Since the celluloid used for rosettes and binding had a distinct ivorylike grain—it was often called "ivoroid"—few customers noticed the difference. This marked the end of the gleaming ivory bridges that had been a distinctive feature of Styles 34 and higher. Pratt, Read, and Company, which had been in business even longer than Martin, probably didn't suffer as a result—the biggest demand in ivory was for billiard balls. *(Courtesy of C. F. Martin & Company.)*

ABOVE: Guitarists could earn big money playing Hawaiian guitar, as long as they didn't have hay fever.

ABOVE: Frank Ferera (Ferreira) was a contemporary of Joseph Kekuku, born in Honolulu of Portuguese parents. He recorded and toured extensively in the early days of the Hawaiian "steel" guitar's popularity and always favored Martin guitars. Of the hundreds of Hawaiian recordings made before 1930, Ferera is estimated to have been included on about a quarter of them, often using the name "The Hilo Hawaiian Orchestra." (*Photo © 1997 Centerbrook archives.*)

That was enough to convince Frank Henry, and Style 18 was made with steel strings in 1924. By 1928 the entire line had the heavier tops and bracing necessary to perform with steel strings.

1928 was also the year the C. F. Martin company made what would become one of the most famous guitars of all time—the "Blue Yodel" 000-45 for "The Singing Brakeman," Jimmie Rodgers, America's favorite musical entertainer of the day.

A number of potentially interesting Martins wound up *not* being made, such as the special-order request of Jack Pennewell, who performed as "Jack Pennewell and His Talking Guitar!" He requested a double-necked guitar for two different steel guitar tunings. The company wrote back to him, "Our factory is so crowded with work and we are so far behind orders in our regular stock styles that we are not in a position to handle special work of this kind."

Along with offering a wide range of ukes, guitars, mandolins, and the ill-fated tenor banjos, Martin was making tiples (a ten-string mini-guitar from Argentina) and taropatches (an eight-string ukulele; in 1924 Martin custom-made one for silent-screen comedian Buster Keaton, with his name inlaid on the headstock).

LEFT: Richard Wesley Konter took his ukulele on a ride over the top of the world along with Admiral Byrd's arctic expedition. Along the way he picked up a few autographs, and on the uke's top you should be able to find the scratchings of Calvin Coolidge, Charles Lindburg, and "Commander & Navigator R. E. Byrd. *(Guitar courtesy of C. F. Martin & Company.)*

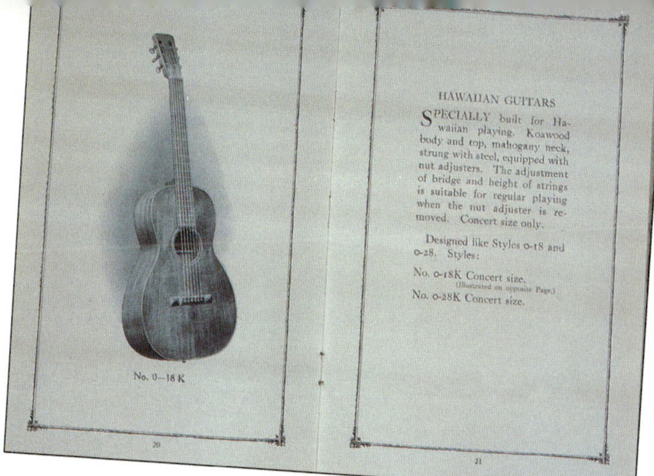

No. 0—18 K

20

HAWAIIAN GUITARS

SPECIALLY built for Hawaiian playing. Koawood body and top, mahogany neck, strung with steel, equipped with nut adjusters. The adjustment of bridge and height of strings is suitable for regular playing when the nut adjuster is removed. Concert size only.

Designed like Styles 0-18 and 0-28. Styles:

No. 0-18K Concert size.
(Illustrated on opposite Page.)
No. 0-28K Concert size.

21

ABOVE: 1923 was the last year Martin used a removable nut adjuster on its Hawaiian guitars. Later Hawaiian models had a permanent high nut and bridge saddle, making it far more difficult to switch to regular playing. Martin had been building these "convertible" koa guitars since 1918, making them the first production Martins built for steel strings.

ABOVE: Martin's first steel-string guitars were called "Hawaiian Steel Guitars" because they were played by sliding a steel bar across the strings with the left hand. By coincidence, you need to use steel strings as well. Flat steels like the ones at left came first, the round "bullet" shape didn't become popular until most Hawaiian players were using resonator guitars, which often had steel (or alloy) bodies as well. A nut extender, which made it possible to play any guitar with steel strings in the Hawaiian style, is pictured at right. *(Photo courtesy of Gryphon Stringed Instruments.)*

RIGHT: Gibson wasn't the only competition Martin had to face as the steel-string guitar rapidly gained in popularity. The Larson Brothers of Chicago, Karl and August, were perhaps the first to build a wide range of 12-fret old-fashioned guitars fully reinforced for use with steel strings. Here is one of their top-of-the-line models, built under the Maurer brand. *(Photo from Hank Risan.)*

In 1920 Martin made 1,336 guitars with serial numbers (not counting the guitars made for the Ditson company, which had a separate serial sequence until mid-1921) and an uncounted number of others made under other labels. The company made 430 mandolins that year and 3,000 ukes. Though the 14,000 ukes sold in 1926 was a definite spike, the other years certainly weren't bad: 3,500 sold in 1919, 10,000 in 1925, and 5,860 in 1927, slowly tapering off to under 1,000 per year from 1932 on.

Shipping records showed hundreds of pounds of Martins being shipped to Hawaii each month through the Panama Canal, as well as shipments to Australia, though most of the company's success with the Hawaiian music craze was in the United States.

There was at least one ukulele destination that no one had anticipated. On May 9, 1926, Arctic aviator Richard Byrd's three-engine Fokker airplane flew over the North Pole, with expedition volunteer Richard Wesley Konter's Martin uke along for the ride, making it the first musical instrument ever to fly over the North Pole. These men were the first humans to do so as well, but let them get their own book. The famed koa ukulele was signed by the expedition members as well as by Charles Lindbergh and various White House swells, and it now resides in the Martin Museum.

Big Sales from the Small Fry—The Martin Ukulele

ABOVE: Rock stars and blues artists didn't start the trend of stashing a cigarette on the peghead after all! Cliff Edwards, better known as "Ukulele Ike," was a vaudeville hotshot whose high tenor, scat singing, and jazzy uke licks made him an early recording star as well. Unlike many vaudeville stars, Edwards found a second career much later in Hollywood; he was the voice of Jiminy Cricket in *Pinnochio,* and his soaring vocals on "When You Wish upon a Star" opened the Disney TV show every week for years. *(Photo from the Frank Driggs Collection.)*

Martin had first tried building ukuleles in 1907, but with little success. For the second attempt, the company tried using thinner woods, an all-mahogany body (including top), and a minimum of bracing, resulting in a good-sounding uke. By 1916 Martin was selling hundreds and then thousands of highly affordable instruments small enough to take anywhere.

Unlike the guitar or mandolin, the uke wasn't difficult to play—basic chords could be mastered in a few hours even by those with no musical experience. Magazine covers led Americans to believe that a front porch or lawn swing was uncivilized without a uke handy, while on back pages ads offered a "5 Minute Ukulele Course" for only a nickel. Though vaudeville hotshots like Cliff Edwards (Ukulele Ike) and Roy Smeck performed amazing musical gymnastics on the instrument, for most players it was easy fun on four strings.

The first Martin ukuleles, all of mahogany, were offered in Styles 1, 2, and 3, with Hawaiian koa models added in 1920. The fancy pearl-bordered 5-K (a whopping $50), was added in 1922, but the majority of sales were of plainer models such as Style 1. An even simpler mahogany model without any binding, Style 0, was offered in the early 1920s for only $10, allowing Martin to

RIGHT: Though plain mahogany ukes were far more popular, Martin's koa models, like the 3K and 5K shown here, established the company's reputation as America's premier ukulele manufacturer. *(Ukuleles courtesy of The Chinery Collection.)*

compete with cheaper mail-order ukes from Sears, Roebuck and Montgomery Ward. The public's acceptance of the couldn't-be-plainer Style 0 showed approval of no-frills value with the Martin name, and the same formula was used on Style 17 guitars during the Great Depression.

A tremendous number of ukuleles were sold during the initial fad, allowing Martin to enlarge the North Street factory in 1925 and again in 1927. Uke sales tapered off in 1928, before slowing dramatically as the Depression deepened in the 1930s. Though the improved Martin factory could be called "the house that ukes built," the downside was that Martin had little time to modernize their ancient guitar and mandolin designs until uke sales began to falter.

Ukuleles were given another boost when Hawaiian music became prominent again after World War II. This was partly due to Arthur Godfrey's celebrity, but more to the renewed popularity of Hawaiian music spurred by servicemen returning from the Pacific.

Martin rarely builds ukuleles today, primarily because the vast numbers made earlier are sufficient to supply the current demand at lower prices than the cost of a new one. When sales slowed to a trickle in the 1960s, C. F. Martin III was asked why he didn't drop ukuleles from the catalog. His reply was that the little uke had supported the Martin company more than once and so deserved to stay. Such loyalty meant that Martin continued to offer high-quality ukuleles long after every other American manufacturer had abandoned them altogether.

ABOVE: Whoever ordered this custom tenor ukulele was clearly not interested in the Hawaiian ukulele tradition. With a deep Brazilian rosewood body, sunburst face, pin bridge, and pearl bordering, this dramatic-looking uke is a show-stopper wherever Martin fans gather, even if they don't normally care about ukuleles. *(Photo courtesy of Steve Szilagy/Elderly Instruments.)*

[MARTIN]

CONCERT UKULELE

Style 1-C

MAHOGANY body, neck and bridge. Rosewood fingerboard with white position dots. Ebony nut and bridge saddle. Body bound with rosewood, bordered and inlaid with black and white wood. Lacquer finish, dark mahogany color. Nickel-plated patent pegs. The body is larger than a regular ukulele and the strings are longer, increasing the volume of tone.

Price

No. 1-C.......................... $18.00

TARO-PATCHES

Body same as concert ukulele, but with four pairs of strings. Style descriptions same as ukuleles (see pages following).

Prices

No. 1 Mahogany	$18.00
No. 1K Koa	22.00
No. 2 Mahogany	24.00
No. 2K Koa	28.00
No. 3 Mahogany	35.00
No. 3K Koa	40.00

Thirty-three

ABOVE: In 1925, just as ukulele sales were peaking, Martin introduced the concert uke, with the larger body and longer string scale of the taropatch, but with only four strings. Tuned the same as a soprano uke, the extra volume of the larger body and the greater string tension made the concert model the powerhouse of ukes.

TOP: Judging by the cover of this 1927 catalog, Martin was no longer just a guitar company.

Jimmie Rodgers

THE SINGING BRAKEMAN

Though the Martin company had seen many famous guitarists choose its guitars, and pay for them, the first major recording star to give Martin lots of free publicity was one of the most influential recording artists of all time, Jimmie Rodgers. Many of his songs are standard fare for any bluegrass band or retro country act today, but Rodgers actually preceded the time when popular music in America was pigeonholed into strict categories. He recorded sentimental songs about Mother, plaintive love songs, comedy numbers, and bawdy blues, borrowing elements from sources as diverse as minstrelsy and light opera. Now credited as "the Father of Country Music," his recordings rarely bear any relation to the current style of music marketed under that name, and his wide range of material was often recorded in sessions with Hawaiian bands and even early jazz bands (a few included Louis Armstrong). But many of his biggest hits, and the songs most often heard today, had simple guitar accompaniment.

Jimmie Rodgers was not a great guitarist, even by the standards of his day, but he played guitar with an unabashed enthusiasm that inspired thousands to take up the instrument. The dropped beats, overlong measures, and muffed notes of his where-is-this-going solos are almost a necessary part of his relaxed, accessible style, often punctuated by his signature "blue yodel."

Photos of Rodgers as a young man show him holding an all-mahogany Martin, probably one of the early Style 17 models built for steel strings. Photos taken soon after his first recording sessions in 1927 show him with a 00-18. Not long after he began to make serious money, he ordered a custom 000-45, with his name in the fretboard and "Blue Yodel" inlaid in the peghead.

Rodgers died from tuberculosis at age 35 in 1933, the day after his final recording session. Exhaustion had forced him to record while seated earlier in the session, with others playing backup, but he performed the final song just as he had begun his career—on his feet, playing his Martin alone. His widow later loaned the guitar to Ernest Tubb, who appeared with it at every possible photo opportunity and played it on tours that crisscrossed the country. (It was once even stolen briefly.)

ABOVE: Jimmie Rodgers, known as "The Singing Brakeman," first recorded in 1927 at the same Bristol, Tennessee, sessions where the Carter Family was discovered. Though credited as "the Father of Country Music," some of his biggest hits, such as "Frankie and Johnnie," went on to become staples of the folk revival. Other Rodgers songs, such as "In the Jailhouse Now," "Mississippi River Blues," and his first "Blue Yodel," (T For Texas) have become standard fare for country artists from Hank Snow to Merle Haggard. *(Photos courtesy of the Jimmie Rodgers Museum.)*

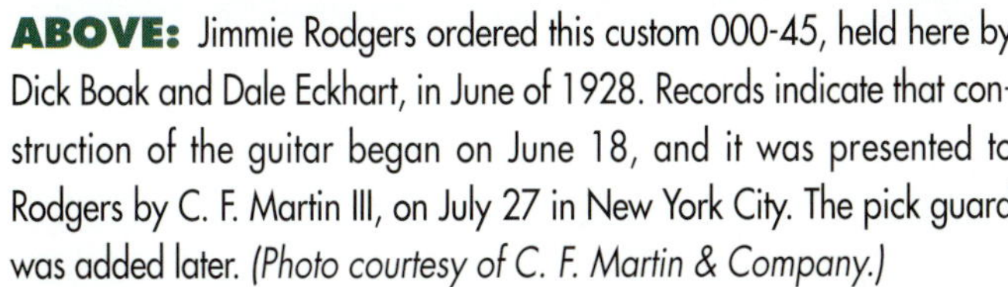

ABOVE: Jimmie Rodgers ordered this custom 000-45, held here by Dick Boak and Dale Eckhart, in June of 1928. Records indicate that construction of the guitar began on June 18, and it was presented to Rodgers by C. F. Martin III, on July 27 in New York City. The pick guard was added later. *(Photo courtesy of C. F. Martin & Company.)*

RIGHT AND ABOVE RIGHT: What better way for Jimmy Rodgers to thank an audience for their applause than to flip over the guitar and flash this message, along with that famous "shucks, it was nothin'" grin. Martin produced a limited edition of 100 reissues of the Jimmie Rodgers model, the 000-45 JR in 1997, complete with Brazilian rosewood back and sides and "Blue Yodel" inlaid peghead. *(Photo courtesy of C. F. Martin & Company.)*

Though Jimmie's career lasted less than five years after he acquired his "Blue Yodel" Martin, the guitar went on for another four decades before being retired to a glass showcase in the Jimmie Rodgers Museum after Ernest Tubb's death.

Gene Autry idolized Jimmie Rodgers and was covering his songs as early as 1929. After sending his 0-42 back to Martin to have "Gene Autry" inlaid in the fretboard, Autry ordered a custom Dreadnought with a similar neck inlay. Within a few years, every singing cowboy had his name on the fretboard of his guitar, turning the instrument into a tireless promoter at every appearance. The Blue Yodel 000-45 may not have been the first guitar with such an inlay, but it was undoubtedly the one that started a long tradition that continues to this day.

Martin Models

Early Twentieth Century

In the first years of the new century, Martin guitar styles were more simple and easy to understand than they had been in the past. The Martin catalogs offered Styles 21, 28, 30, and 42, in only three sizes—"standard" (size 1), "concert" (size 0), and "grand concert" (size 00). Style 45 was added in 1904.

Styles 17 and 18 (Remember them? The homely models had dropped from sight by 1901) reappeared in 1906, and by 1909 Style 17 was listed with mahogany back and sides (it may have been mahogany as early as 1906). In 1917 Style 17 disappeared again, having been made redundant by Martin's switching the Style 18 to mahogany back and sides. Mahogany would soon rule the lower end of Martin's guitar line, and the most significant increases in the company's production would be in mahogany, not rosewood, instruments.

Around 1917 Martin nomenclature was still easy to fathom—after the plain

ABOVE: Martin's Style 42 and 45 have the abalone pearl bordering extending around the end of the fingerboard, a bit of elegance left over from the days when the fingerboards on "screw neck" models were suspended above the face of the guitar. *(Guitar courtesy of C. F. Martin & Company.)*

LEFT: Martin's classic Style 28 soundhole rosette and herringbone trim got a dramatic new setting in the koa tops of Style 28K models first ordered in 1917. *(Photo from Hank Risan.)*

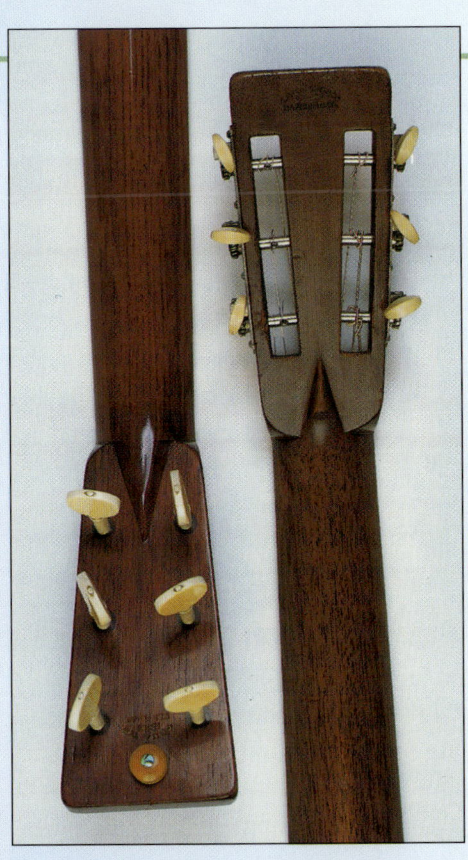

RIGHT: Once the Style 18's rosewood back and sides were changed to mahogany, Style 21 guitars like this one were the least expensive rosewood Martins. This is still the position of Style 21 today. The herringbone around the soundhole shown here lasted until after World War II, while the rosewood binding was changed to celluloid in the mid-1930s. *(Guitar courtesy of Fred Oster.)*

LEFT: Around the same time that Style 18 became a mahogany guitar, Martin phased out its cedar guitar necks when the company began buying mahogany lumber of greater thickness. This allowed one-piece mahogany necks, ending the need for the complex peghead joint. The hand-carved "dart," or "diamond," as shown here, was no longer necessary and was deleted from the one-piece mahogany necks on Style 18, disappearing on Style 21 shortly thereafter. True to Martin conservatism, however, it remained as a stylistic touch of elegance on the higher rosewood models, even though the one-piece mahogany necks made it unnecessary. The classic Martin neck dart has remained on Styles 28, 42, and 45 to this day. *(Photo from Hank Risan.)*

LEFT: Tuning machines on Martin guitars became less elaborate as the new century wore on, and beautiful gear plates like these disappeared during World War I. Martin could not import from its favorite German sources during the war, and the company continued to use American tuning machines with stamped plates in the 1920s. The inlaid celluloid buttons as seen on this 000-45 from 1906 were used only for a few years. The metal seen here was called German silver (nickel silver) regardless of its country of origin. *(Photo from Hank Risan.)*

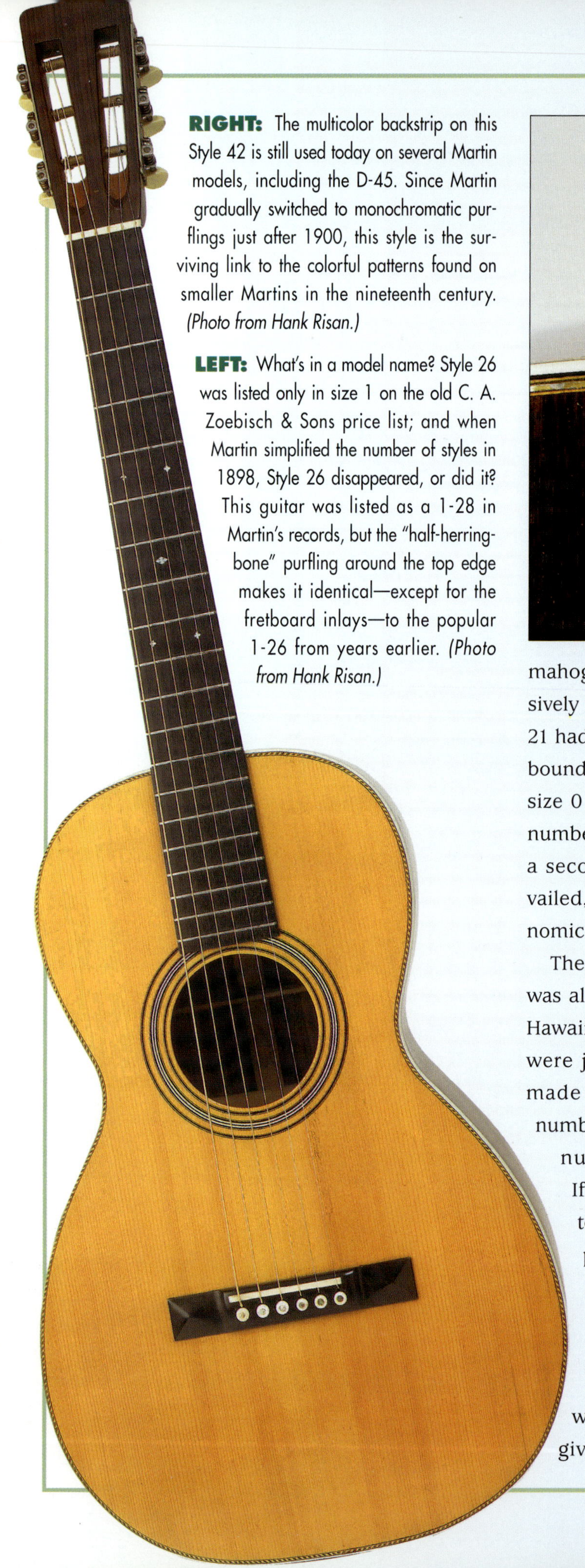

RIGHT: The multicolor backstrip on this Style 42 is still used today on several Martin models, including the D-45. Since Martin gradually switched to monochromatic purflings just after 1900, this style is the surviving link to the colorful patterns found on smaller Martins in the nineteenth century. *(Photo from Hank Risan.)*

LEFT: What's in a model name? Style 26 was listed only in size 1 on the old C. A. Zoebisch & Sons price list; and when Martin simplified the number of styles in 1898, Style 26 disappeared, or did it? This guitar was listed as a 1-28 in Martin's records, but the "half-herringbone" purfling around the top edge makes it identical—except for the fretboard inlays—to the popular 1-26 from years earlier. *(Photo from Hank Risan.)*

mahogany Style 18, the rosewood guitars got progressively fancier from Styles 21 through 45. Styles 18 and 21 had dark binding, while Styles 28 and higher were bound in ivory. Guitars got progressively larger from size 0 to 000. Each Martin could be described by a number indicating the size, followed by a hyphen and a second number indicating the grade. Logic prevailed, but it did little good for the company's economic health.

The system was simple and too good to last. Martin was already brewing new models in response to the Hawaiian music craze, and stock steel-string models were just around the corner. (Some were already made on a special-order basis.) Resultingly, the number of Martin models exploded, with letters and numbers flying on both sides of the hyphen. If the nomenclature gibberish that follows gets too confusing, we strongly recommend that you put down this book and go back to playing guitar.

About the same time that Style 18 became mahogany, Martin began to build guitars out of Hawaiian koa, including the top, for use with steel strings. Plainer grades of koa were given binding and other details like a Style 18,

RIGHT: Martin listed Style 18 models as steel-string guitars in the 1924 catalog; and until 1928, 000-18 models like this one (from 1927) were the biggest, loudest Martins available for use with steel, unless you placed a special order (which many people did). The pyramid-shaped bridge tips are flat by this date, but the delicate wood purfling and rosewood edge binding would remain on Style 18 for another few years before being replaced with celluloid. This guitar, though in excellent condition, shows why Martin began adding pick guards in the late 1920s. *(Guitar courtesy of Fred Oster.)*

BOTTOM RIGHT: In 1929 Martin began making models with 14 frets clear of the body, like this 1931 OM-28. This would begin the most confusing decade of Martin nomenclature, as the company made a rapid transition to the new longer necked style of steel-string guitar, while still building many of the old models. The shaded top, an option first offered a few years earlier, became more popular in the 1930s. *(Photo from Hank Risan.)*

TOP RIGHT: Stamping the model designations inside the guitar took much of the guesswork out of identifying Martin's instruments. The practice was begun in late 1930, and just in time, for the next few years saw an explosion of new models that transformed the entire Martin line. *(Guitar courtesy of C. F. Martin & Company.)*

while curly koa was considered more on a par with rosewood and got the ivory-color celluloid binding and diamond and square fretboard inlays of the Style 28. For the first time, Martin used a letter to indicate the wood used, so 0-18K meant the guitar had a koa body instead of mahogany.

In 1929 Martin confused matters further by introducing guitars that were the same size as a 000 but a different shape with a longer neck. These were called OM-18 and OM-28, and the OM stood for "Orchestra Model." The old nomenclature system was still being used, but now Martin began using letters on the left side of the hyphen to indicate new types of guitars. Starting in late 1930, Martin began stamping model designations just above the serial number on the neck block, inside the guitar. This was a big help but only if you knew what the increasingly complex code of letters and numbers meant.

CABLE ADDRESS:
DITSON BOSTON

FOUNDED 1835
INCORPORATED FEBRUARY 1889

Oliver Ditson Company
Music Publishers

DEALERS AND IMPORTERS OF
Music, Music Books and Musical Instruments.

178-179 TREMONT STREET

DEPARTMENTS:
A-SHEET MUSIC & BOOKS
B-MUSICAL INSTRUMENTS
C-PRINTING
D-EDITORIAL
E-BOOKKEEPING
F-THE MUSICIAN
G-ADVERTISING
H-VICTOR-VICTROLA
K-BAND AND ORCHESTRA MUSIC

AGENCIES:
CHAS. H. DITSON & CO. NEW YORK.
LYON & HEALY, CHICAGO.

Boston, July 17, 192

JUL 20 19

ABOVE: In 1916 the giant Oliver Ditson Company began a joint venture with tiny C. F. Martin & Company. Today the Ditson name is all but forgotten, except as the company responsible for the birth of the oversized guitar called the Dreadnought.

The Custom-Brand Business

We may never know exactly how the trend started, but around 1915 Frank Henry probably made his long-standing accounts aware that Martin was willing to build special instruments that could be sold under their own brand names. The wholesale accounts who took advantage of this new flexibility had been selling Martin guitars and mandolins for many years, making it hard to believe that around 1915 a half-dozen guys all spontaneously said "Hey, let's have Frank build special stuff nobody else can get."

It is difficult to determine how many "custom brand" instruments were made, but we do know that in the decade following 1915, a lot of Martin's production left the North Street factory headed for other retailers under assumed names. The complete list of companies who had contracts for special Martins made with other names is in "Instruments Made by Martin for Other Firms" on page 254, but the most important ones are Ditson, Southern California Music Company, and Wurlitzer.

OLIVER
DITSON
CO.
BOSTON
NEW YORK

Ditson

Of all the companies that Martin built instruments for, none offered as wide and unusual a range as the Oliver Ditson Company of Boston. Ditson was one of the oldest names in American music publishing and one of Martin's oldest and

RIGHT: Dreadnoughts are usually thought of as massive, imposing, and masculine; but this small Style 45 with the Ditson shape is just downright cute. Though only four like this were made, plainer versions of this size sold far better than the big Dreadnought back in the late teens. Known today as a "baby D-45," its designation when made was 1-45, the smallest of the standard Ditsons. *(Guitar courtesy of The Chinery Collection.)*

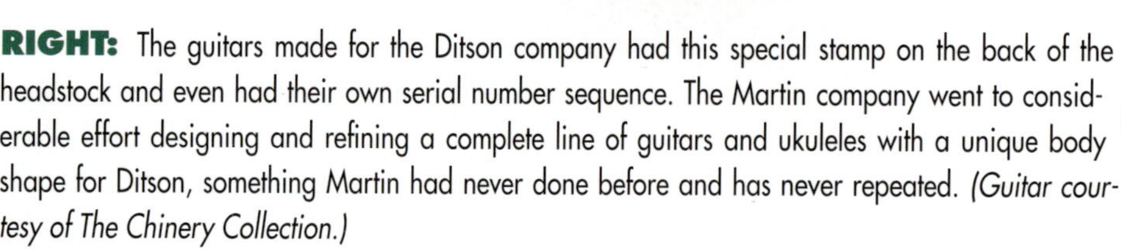

RIGHT: The guitars made for the Ditson company had this special stamp on the back of the headstock and even had their own serial number sequence. The Martin company went to considerable effort designing and refining a complete line of guitars and ukuleles with a unique body shape for Ditson, something Martin had never done before and has never repeated. *(Guitar courtesy of The Chinery Collection.)*

ABOVE: Even soprano ukes were made with the unique Ditson shape, making this 5K the littlest "baby D-45" of all. *(Photo © J. Whipple Photography/Lark Street Music.)*

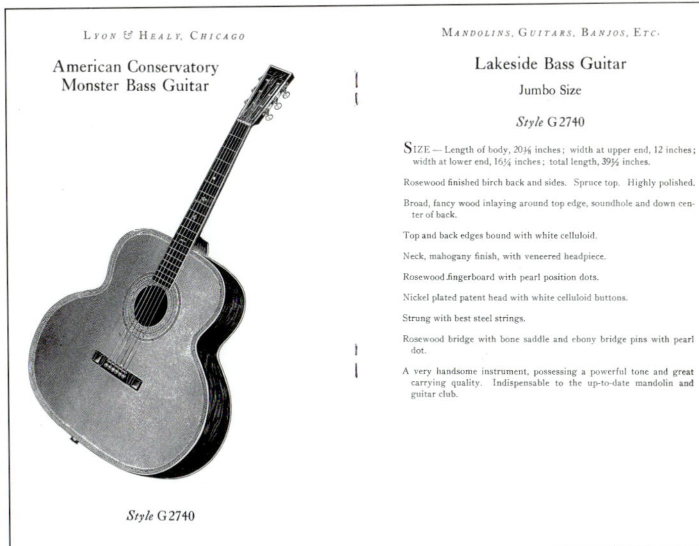

Lyon & Healy, Chicago

American Conservatory Monster Bass Guitar

Style G2740

Mandolins, Guitars, Banjos, Etc.

Lakeside Bass Guitar

Jumbo Size

Style G2740

Size — Length of body, 20⅛ inches; width at upper end, 12 inches; width at lower end, 16¼ inches; total length, 39½ inches.

Rosewood finished birch back and sides. Spruce top. Highly polished.

Broad, fancy wood inlaying around top edge, soundhole and down center of back.

Top and back edges bound with white celluloid.

Neck, mahogany finish, with veneered headpiece.

Rosewood fingerboard with pearl position dots.

Nickel plated patent head with white celluloid buttons.

Strung with best steel strings.

Rosewood bridge with bone saddle and ebony bridge pins with pearl dot.

A very handsome instrument, possessing a powerful tone and great carrying quality. Indispensable to the up-to-date mandolin and guitar club.

ABOVE: "Indispensable to the up-to-date mandolin and guitar club" was Lyon & Healy's sales pitch for this Monster Bass Guitar, as shown in its 1917 catalog. Martin's equally monstrous Chicago competitor had been marketing similar oversized guitars for several years. In comparison to this behemouth, the Ditson Dreadnought isn't so big after all.

largest accounts. (The New York branch was called Chas. H. Ditson & Company.) Starting in 1916, Ditson and Martin embarked on an ambitious venture to market guitars and ukuleles under the Ditson brand. (Martin was already making bowlback mandolins with Ditson's label.) These would carry the stamp "Oliver Ditson Co. Boston, New York." Most of the correspondence about these instruments was with Harry L. Hunt, manager of the New York store, who seemed to be the man with the ideas.

Hunt's plan for the Martin-made Ditson line of instruments was ambitious; besides numerous uke models, it included six different guitar shapes made in various styles. Frank Henry Martin must have shared his enthusaism, for the Martin company's spec sheets from 1917 list "Martin models" and "Ditson models" side by side. Three were very small guitars: a child's model, a slightly larger version called ¾ size, and a terz model (so designated because these small guitars were tuned a minor third, known as *terz* in German, above the standard). The larger guitars, called "standard," "concert," and "extra large," were first listed on Martin's spec sheets as "Ditson Hawaiian Guitars," though these may not have been shipped with the high nut and saddle that would later

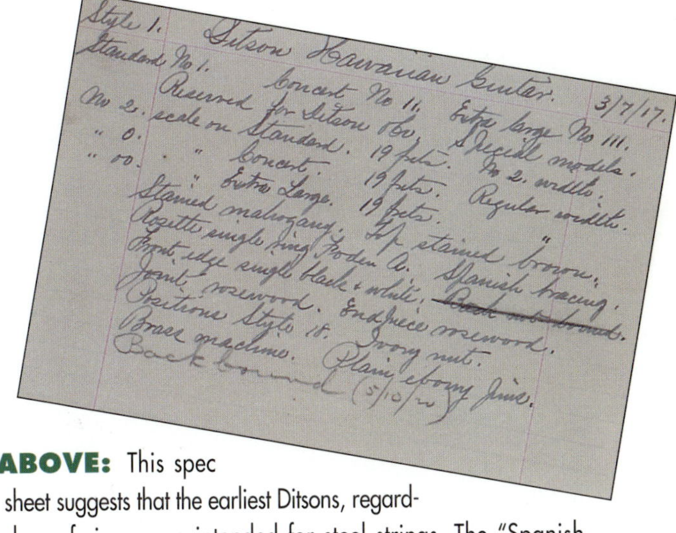

Style 1. Ditson Hawaiian Guitar. 3/7/17.
Standard No 1. Concert No 11. Extra Large No 111.
Reserved for Ditson Co, Special models.
No 2. scale on Standard. 19 frets. No 2. width.
" 0. " Concert. 19 frets. Regular width.
" 00. " Extra Large. 19 frets.
Stained mahogany; top stained brown.
Rosette single ring Roden Co. Spanish bracing.
Front edge single black & white;
Joint rosewood. End piece rosewood.
Positions Style 18. Ivory nut.
Brass machines. Plain ebony pins.
Back bound (5/10/20)

ABOVE: This spec sheet suggests that the earliest Ditsons, regardless of size, were intended for steel strings. The "Spanish bracing" referred to here was much heavier than the fan bracing used on small, gut-strung Style 17 Martins just a few years earlier. In fact, Ditson fan bracing is identical to that used on the koa-wood guitars made for the Southern California Music Company during the same time, and those were clearly sold with steel strings.

LEFT: Though the Ditson name is now almost synonymous with Dreadnoughts, most of what that company marketed were regular Martin models with the Ditson stamp, such as this Style A flat-back mandolin. *(Mandolin courtesy of Fred Oster.)*

characterize Martin's Hawaiian models.

The Ditsons were offered in three styles: Styles 1 and 2 were quite plain, while Style 3 was more like Martin's Style 28, though without the herringbone around the top edge. Ditson ukes and guitars featured a wide-waisted shape with gentle curves for the sides, rather than the narrow, "pinched" waist of most nineteenth- and early-twentieth-century guitars. The "standard" Ditson was quite small, about the same as a Martin size 3, while the "concert" was about the size of a Martin 0.

Called "Dreadnought," after the heaviest class of battleship at the time, the largest Ditson was huge by Martin's standards—both wider and much deeper than the 000. Today the smaller guitars and ukuleles with the unique Ditson shape are

ABOVE: Not bad inspiration for a guitar name: H.M.S. Dreadnought. *(Photo courtesy of National Maritime Museum, London.)*

RIGHT: We still don't know exactly how the earliest Dreadnoughts, like this Style 111 Ditson, were marketed. Were they sold as six-string "bass guitars" for use in mandolin and banjo clubs? For Hawaiian playing? The fan bracing on the top is identical to that used on the koa wood guitars made for Southern California Music Company during the same time. However they were intended, the fan bracing on the top wasn't as resilient under the tension of steel strings as the X-pattern, and most Ditson Dreadnoughts have needed extensive top restoration. *(Guitar courtesy of Fred Oster.)*

referred to as "baby Dreadnoughts," but at the time the extra-large model must have appeared like an overfed cousin who could barely fit through Martin's door.

The Ditson company had little luck selling the new extra-large model. Records at Martin indicate that over 500 Ditson guitars were sold by 1921, but only 14 were Dreadnoughts.

As with most of Martin's other "contract instruments," the Ditson guitar line didn't last long. After less than five years of production, Ditson went back to selling regular Martins. Though few were sold, the Dreadnought must have stirred some interest in New York, however, for in June of 1923, Harry Hunt asked Martin to build more of the plainest model, Ditson's Style 111. The first batch included one for Roy Smeck, the "Wizard of the Strings," and 18 more Dreadnoughts were built by 1930.

ABOVE, LEFT, AND BELOW: Manuel Nunes was a big name in Hawaiian instruments, so the Southern California Music Company must have thought this label and decal would have more appeal than any mention of C. F. Martin. It must have worked, for starting in late 1916, when this guitar was built, Martin shipped over 250 similar koa-wood guitars to Los Angeles in just over 18 months. This is Style 1400, similar to a Martin Style 21, and it has fan-pattern top bracing like the Ditson models. Guitars like this one were the first all-koa Martins and were the first regular-production Martins for steel strings. Their success prompted the introduction of the 0-18K in 1918. The bridge shown is not original. *(Photo courtesy of Intermountain Guitar and Banjo.)*

Southern California Music Company

One of Martin's largest retailers, the Southern California Music Company ordered three styles of guitars, all made with Hawaiian koa, including the top. These predated Martin's own koa guitars, and their popularity probably inspired Martin to add its all-koa line. At least a few of the earliest examples were sold with labels identifying them as made by Hawaiian instrument maker M. Nunes. Though listed as Hawaiian models, they had raised frets, and it is likely that many were sold set up for regular playing.

Style 1350 was roughly the same as the later 0-18K, while Style 1400 was similar to an 0-21K. Style 1500 was slightly fancier than the 0-28K Martin that followed it. Styles 1350 and 1400 had fan-braced tops until 1919. The series had its own serial numbers until mid-1918, but these were later mixed in with Martin's regular production and were given Martin serial numbers.

Wurlitzer

The Rudolph Wurlitzer Company had a chain of music stores and was another of Martin's large accounts. Between 1922 and 1924, Martin made a series of instruments with the Wurlitzer name stamped on the back of the peghead. Except for a single-ring rosette and a slightly different pattern of fretboard inlays on the higher models, these were identical to Martins of the time. Twelve styles were made in all, from Wurlitzer Style 2075 (2-17) to Style 2092, which was equivalent to an 0-42. These had no serial numbers for the first year or so but then had regular Martin numbers for the last year of production. By mid-1924 Wurlitzer had gone back to selling regular Martin models.

LEFT: This guitar from the Martin Museum is probably unique—at least Martin's records list only one. Wurlitzer Style 2092 was an 0 size with similar trim, but this is a 00. Except for minor differences in the fingerboard inlays, and the single-ring rosette, it is identical to a Martin 00-42. Most Wurlitzer models were plain mahogany styles, though rosewood models and even some all-koa guitars were included in the line. *(Guitar courtesy of C. F. Martin & Company.)*

LEFT AND BELOW: William L. Lange, owner and founder of the Paramount Banjo Company, was no stranger to marketing rather bizarre instruments. His company made tenor banjos with a spruce top, called "tenor harps" (not a joke), and double-decker banjos that looked like wedding cakes. As the public's tolerance for the banjo tone was waning, he enlisted Martin's help in the late 1920s to produce an instrument with the tone of a guitar and the volume closer to that of a banjo. Martin produced about 36 of these Paramount Style L guitars in all. Some had four-string necks and some had six, some had soundholes and some did not, but they all followed the dinosaurs into oblivion. *(Guitar on opposite page courtesy of C. F. Martin & Company; guitar below courtesy of The Chinery Collection.)*

Though some of these custom brand schemes were short-lived, they still had an impact on later Martin guitars. The Ditson Dreadnought, of course, would change Martin history. The Martin company was often lacking in imagination when it came to meeting new musical trends, but by building what retailers wanted and seeing the resulting sales, the company was led to build models under the Martin name that it probably would not have dreamed up on its own.

Building from the Top Down

As mentioned, the uke sales compelled Martin to enlarge its factory several times. According to current company head Chris Martin, the capital to do so came from the family's selling off orchard land adjacent to the Martin home and factory. In the final enlargement to the building in 1925, the factory gained a second story and attic, beginning the Martin's era of what some have called "the gravity system of manufacturing." Different processes would take place on different floors, with racks in

ABOVE: Herbert Keller Martin's years working out his great-grandfather's dream were cut short when he died suddenly of peritonitis in 1927. *(Photo courtesy of C. F. Martin & Company.)*

ABOVE: The tenor guitar found a welcome home as the accompaniment for a number of harmony groups in the 1930s, including the Mills Brothers, Ink Spots, and Three Cats and a Fiddle (*shown here*). The four strings and short, narrow neck made it easy to play fast, closed chords (no open strings) to drive the rhythm on up-tempo swing tunes, yet the tenor could still deliver smooth guitar tone for slower numbers.

Martin may have watched from the sidelines as companies like Paramount cashed in on the tenor banjo craze, but the conservative guitar company instead enjoyed a long success with the tenor guitar. Martin sold over 1,100 tenors in 1930 alone, and the 0-18T and all-mahogany 0-17T were often some of the company's best-selling guitar models. Such popularity was probably because many people who had learned to play the tenor banjo weren't about to let all their practice go to waste just because the banjo was rapidly fading in popularity. *(Photo from the Frank Driggs Collection.)*

the attic used to dry the wood. The same heat used to warm the workmen on the shop floor was used to dry the roughed-out guitar top, back, and side pieces in the attic.

"In the old factory, these drying racks were at the ceiling," Frederick Martin recalled in 1985. "There was no air conditioning; but the heat rose from the radiators to the ceiling, and there were openings in the attic floor above to vent the heat, and we got vertical circulation. It was very effective and very inexpensive."

By that time the machinery, once powered by steam and then gasoline engines, was powered by electricity. With all the heavy machinery on the ground floor, gravity wasn't exactly a help in the manufacturing process. Most of the instruments took several trips up and down the wooden stairs before they were completed.

On the first day of 1921, amid all this ukulele-spawned activity, Frank Henry sold his sole ownership of C. F. Martin & Company, making him, his wife, Frederick, and Herbert the sole shareholders.

HILLBILLIES ON THE AIRWAVES

On January 3, 1927, Herbert Keller Martin died of peritonitis in Nazareth, Pennsylvania. Within a month Frederick (C.F. III) had replaced him on the road. On February 3 Frederick telegraphed his father from Cleveland: "Detroit complains of unemployment but does not look it. All dealers ordered total about $1,500 net. Warm welcome awaits tenor guitar. Push samples. Tiple not strong in West. Regular guitar active. Ukulele not dead."

The tenor guitar mentioned was an offshoot from the tenor banjo, which had been just one more instrument that had threatened the guitar's ascension in the nineteen-teens and '20s. Martin had even made a brief foray into banjo making, offering the Style 1 tenor banjo from 1923 to 1926.

Martin made it easy for banjo players to switch to guitar with the similarly strung and tuned tenor guitar. Distributor Chicago Musical Instrument Company telegraphed an urgent request in January 1927 asking that Martin begin manufacturing two models immediately—suggesting one of mahogany to retail at $30 and one of rosewood at $50—and promising an initial order of 100.

On March 2 Frederick began a more extensive road trip, writing his father that night, "I made two calls, and sold two instruments!... So ends the first day. There is plenty of calamity howling in the coal regions, with the mines working less than half-time, so I'll be glad to get on to New York.... Love to Mother, Frederick."

The coal regions weren't the only ones experiencing hard times. Though the Depression didn't officially start until two years later with the stock

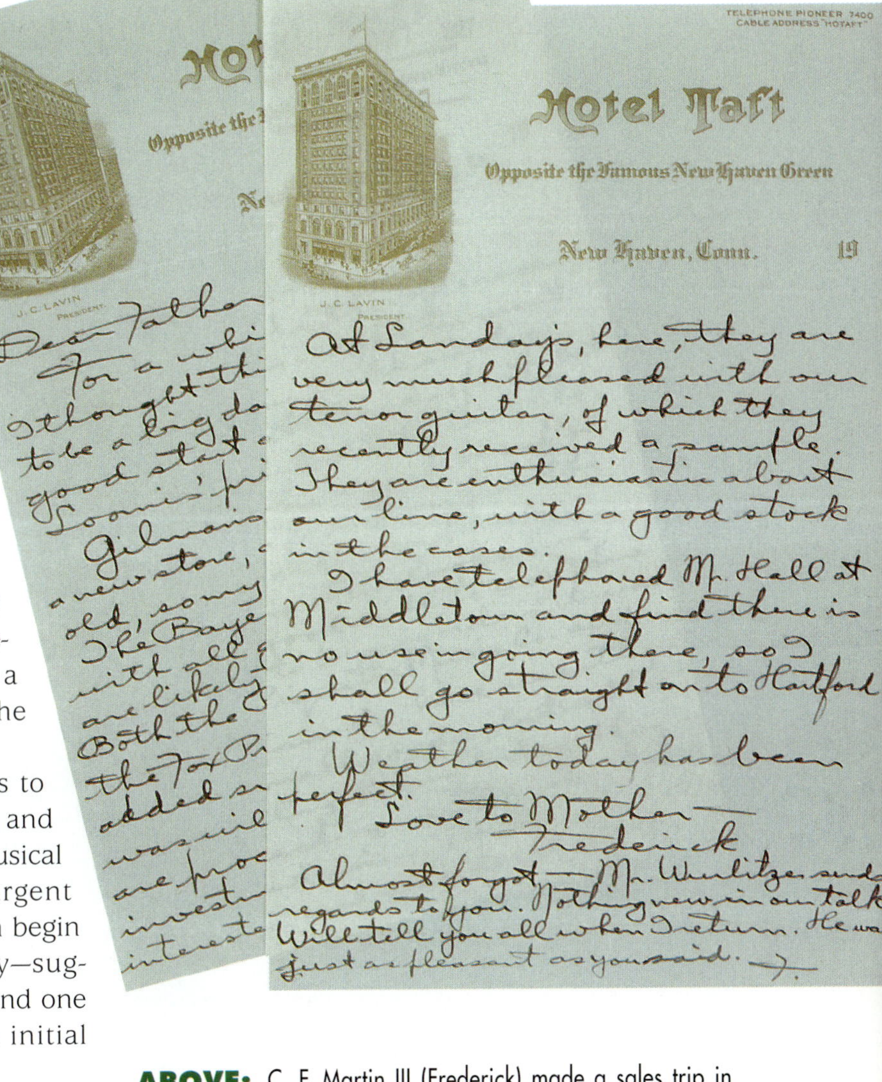

TELEPHONE PIONEER 7400
CABLE ADDRESS "HOTAFT"

Hotel Taft

Opposite the Famous New Haven Green

New Haven, Conn. 19

J. C. LAVIN
PRESIDENT

At Landay's, here, they are very much pleased with our tenor guitar, of which they recently received a sample. They are enthusiastic about our line, with a good stock in the cases.

I have telephoned Mr. Hall at Middletown and find there is no use in going there, so I shall go straight on to Hartford in the morning.

Weather today has been perfect.

Love to Mother—
Frederick

Almost forgot—Mr. Wurlitzer sends regards to you. Nothing new in our talk. Will tell you all when I return. He was just as pleasant as you said. —F.

ABOVE: C. F. Martin III (Frederick) made a sales trip in 1927 and found that the economy was starting to sag a bit. He wrote this report of his trip to his father, Frank Henry, from New Haven.

LEFT: The radio changed the way America perceived its music. With its advent, the music of the people came directly to the people, in their living-rooms and kitchens. It made stars of unlikely musicians, such as a singing cowboy from Oklahoma named Gene Autry.

market crash, it was already old news to a great many farmers and laborers in the United States, who had never shared in the raccoon-coated high life of the Roaring '20s.

But entertainment has always fared well in hard times, when moments of joy and release from one's troubles might seem as necessary as flour. That may be why—even as America's cities continued to prosper—there was a boom in entertainment aimed specifically at the rural poor. There are accounts from the time of families spending their limited income on milk, eggs, and the latest Jimmie Rodgers 78.

Record players had been commonplace in homes since before the war, and by 1916 industry had jumped on radio as well. Firms manufactured home radio sets, and by 1924 there were some 1,400 radio stations broadcasting to them. (Just as movie studios later feared the advent of television, record companies at first regarded radio as a deadly competitor and were able to block the playing of

BELOW: Besides this 1929 1-18, Martin made at least one other guitar with a five-string banjo neck. Their rarity is not too surprising since even banjo companies were making very few five-string models at this time. *(Guitar courtesy of The Chinery Collection.)*

FAR RIGHT: Style 45 Deluxe wasn't exclusively reserved for the six-string OM, and here it is seen on a 1930 tenor model. To a tenor banjo player, this isn't very fancy. The first Style 45 Deluxe was a 12-fret 000 (six-string) made earlier the same year. *(Photo © Mac Yasuda Enterprises.)*

records on the radio until the mid-1920s, when they caught on that airplay was essentially free advertising.)

Many stations were started by businesses, which saw them as a new marketing tool. Sears, Roebuck, which owed a great deal of its sales to rural customers, owned 50,000-watt clear-channel station WLS in Chicago (the call letters stood for World's Largest Store). Its *WLS Barn Dance* could be picked up in many states. It soon became a flagship program of the new National Broadcasting Company (NBC), and it was the far-reaching *Barn Dance* that made a young Gene Autry a star in the early '30s.

When WLS's program director moved to station WSM in Nashville, Tennessee, he brought the country music idea with him, debuting the *WSM Barn Dance* in the fall of 1925. It soon was given the name it has retained to this day, the Grand Ole Opry. Martin's guitars, particularly once the company switched to steel strings, became one of the prominent sounds heard on these broadcasts. By 1926 sales of the size 000 had picked up. Now equipped with steel strings, it was just what guitarists needed to vie for attention from the single microphones then used to capture radio broadcasts and recordings.

By 1929 Martin was sponsoring its own series of solo guitar programs on station WHAS out of Louisville, Kentucky. One of the numbers performed over the air was "The C. F. Martin March" by Kentucky guitarist J. Henry Brady.

The little guitar company from Nazareth was finally marching in step with the musical trends of the nation, and Frank Henry Martin had lifted production far above the company's 70-year flat line. But with the Hawaiian music craze fading like a South Pacific sunset, there was little knowing what lay ahead.

ABOVE: Another 1920s addition to Martin's stable of little instruments was the tiple, an American variant of a folk instrument from Argentina. With geared tuners and ten steel strings in four courses, it was both louder and easier to tune than the taropatch. Tuned like a uke, the first and fourth strings are doubled (like a mandolin), while the second and third are triples, with the center string tuned an octave below the outer strings in each course. *(Photo © Mac Yasuda Enterprises.)*

RIGHT: Martin made 96 of these tenor banjos between 1923 and 1926. The company apparently didn't know what to do with them—they never appeared in a catalog and showed up only on the 1924 price list. Even with full promotional fanfare they would have been doomed to failure, as the austere Martin style was not what banjo players were looking for. *(Banjo courtesy of C. F. Martin & Company.)*

Martin's Orchestra Model, the First Modern Martin

Martin had put its first steel-string guitar for regular playing in the 1922 catalog, and its immediate success was even greater than what the company was enjoying with the Hawaiian models introduced a few years earlier. Style 18 was given steel strings in 1924, and by 1928 all models were listed as steel-string guitars, with gut-string versions available on special order. Except for using slightly thicker woods and heavier braces, however, Martin's new steel-string guitars still looked just like the gut-string models. Until the late 1920s, Martin was too busy building ukuleles to worry about changing its guitars; and since the new steel-string versions of old Martin models were selling so well, why bother?

With uke sales continuing to plummet in 1929, however, Martin

FAR LEFT: Martin chose to modify this model in answer to Perry Bechtel's request for a longer-necked guitar. Possibly because of the company's aversion to larger guitars, Martin had apparently never thought much of its original 000 anyway. Introduced shortly after 1900, the 12-fret 000 appeared only rarely in a price list until after 1920 and didn't begin to sell very well until it was offered with steel strings. *(Photo courtesy of Fred Dusel; guitar courtesy of Tom Culbertson.)*

LEFT: The first version of the OM-28, as shown here, began to evolve immediately (the pick guard was added after the first batch of four prototypes). First to go was the narrow bridge, replaced by the "belly" bridge, which had a wider footing to better withstand the tension of steel strings. Pick wear around the edge of the soundhole prompted Martin to extend the small pick guard, creating the teardrop shape still used today. The solid peghead with straight-through banjo tuners was possibly an attempt to appeal to banjo players, as right-angle guitar gears for solid pegheads had been widely available for decades. The banjo-style gears didn't hold up well under guitar-string tension, and they were replaced by more ordinary guitar tuners by late 1931. *(Photo from Hank Risan.)*

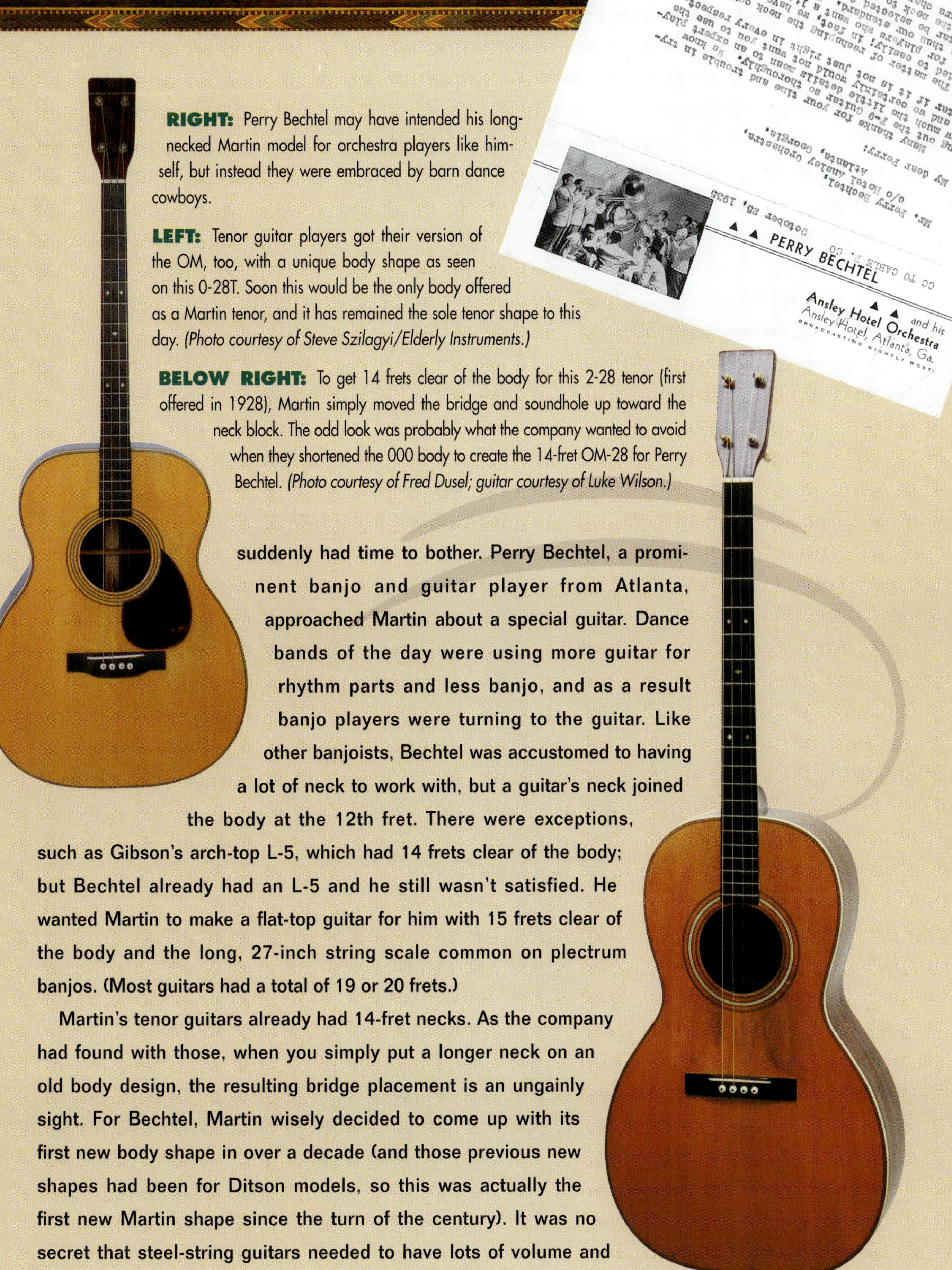

RIGHT: Perry Bechtel may have intended his long-necked Martin model for orchestra players like himself, but instead they were embraced by barn dance cowboys.

LEFT: Tenor guitar players got their version of the OM, too, with a unique body shape as seen on this 0-28T. Soon this would be the only body offered as a Martin tenor, and it has remained the sole tenor shape to this day. *(Photo courtesy of Steve Szilagyi/Elderly Instruments.)*

BELOW RIGHT: To get 14 frets clear of the body for this 2-28 tenor (first offered in 1928), Martin simply moved the bridge and soundhole up toward the neck block. The odd look was probably what the company wanted to avoid when they shortened the 000 body to create the 14-fret OM-28 for Perry Bechtel. *(Photo courtesy of Fred Dusel; guitar courtesy of Luke Wilson.)*

suddenly had time to bother. Perry Bechtel, a prominent banjo and guitar player from Atlanta, approached Martin about a special guitar. Dance bands of the day were using more guitar for rhythm parts and less banjo, and as a result banjo players were turning to the guitar. Like other banjoists, Bechtel was accustomed to having a lot of neck to work with, but a guitar's neck joined the body at the 12th fret. There were exceptions, such as Gibson's arch-top L-5, which had 14 frets clear of the body; but Bechtel already had an L-5 and he still wasn't satisfied. He wanted Martin to make a flat-top guitar for him with 15 frets clear of the body and the long, 27-inch string scale common on plectrum banjos. (Most guitars had a total of 19 or 20 frets.)

Martin's tenor guitars already had 14-fret necks. As the company had found with those, when you simply put a longer neck on an old body design, the resulting bridge placement is an ungainly sight. For Bechtel, Martin wisely decided to come up with its first new body shape in over a decade (and those previous new shapes had been for Ditson models, so this was actually the first new Martin shape since the turn of the century). It was no secret that steel-string guitars needed to have lots of volume and

BELOW: From Jimmie Rodgers to Roy Rogers, or "How to take an old fancy guitar and make it modern!" On the left is the "standard" Martin 000-45, first produced around 1906 (this one is from 1926), while on the right is the "orchestra model" Style 45, which first appeared in 1930. *(Photo from Hank Risan.)*

bass, so Martin and Bechtel chose the 000, or auditorium size, as the starting point.

Though Martin rejected the 27-inch scale and 15-fret neck as too extreme, Frank Henry, his son C.F. III, and factory foreman John Deichman did come up with a good compromise. Shortening the 000 body, especially the upper bout, and moving the X-braces and bridge up closer to the soundhole allowed a neck with 14 frets clear. The neck was made more narrow and with greater radius to the fretboard, resulting in a shape much like Bechtel's L-5. It was the first time Martin had modified one of its original designs, and the transformation of the 000 was only the first of many changes that would completely alter the look of the Martin guitar in the next decade.

The result was the 000-28 Perry Bechtel model, completed in early October 1929. With its new shape and long neck, it may have looked a bit odd to the old hands at Martin; but today it looks like a rather plain, modern guitar. It was in fact the first modern Martin, designed specifically for steel strings rather than simply beefed up to withstand them. Today this model is second in popularity only to the Martin Dreadnought and is also widely copied by other manufacturers.

Perry Bechtel must have voiced his approval, for ten more were completed that year. Since they were to be pitched to orchestra players like Bechtel, by 1930 the new model was designated OM, for orchestra model. Perry clearly wasn't the only one giving the new OM-28 a thumbs up, as Martin made 235 more in 1930, despite the frightening Depression. A mahogany version, the OM-18, was also added in 1930, and from 1931 onward it easily

RIGHT: The transition from 000 to OM resulted in more than a few guitars with a somewhat confused identity, at least by today's standards. This 000-45 has the old-style body and 12-fret neck, but the solid peghead with banjo tuners and small pick guard are features associated with the OM. *(Photo © Mac Yasuda Enterprises.)*

BELOW: Here's the 1930 000-45 (shown at right) in its original setting with "Two Texans," who must have provided some interesting duets with a Martin guitar and bass drum. Most cowboys, Texans or otherwise, quickly switched to the new long-necked OM models. *(Photo courtesy of Jim Bollman.)*

RIGHT: A pearl-bordered model, the OM-45, was added in 1930 to Martin's new line of "orchestra models," along with an even richer version, the OM-45 Deluxe. Many of these were sold through Sherman Clay Music in San Francisco and Southern California Music in Los Angeles. Leonard Slye, who wisely renamed himself Roy Rogers, was the most prominent cowboy star to play a Deluxe. The inlaid pick guard is unique to this model, of which only 14 were made, all in 1930. At $225, the Deluxe was the most expensive flat-top Martin ever offered in the 1930s; and today it is the only other Style 45 in the same price bracket as the D-45—meaning the sky's the limit. *(Photo from Hank Risan.)*

outsold the more expensive original. Once again Martin had been leading a trend in the rapidly changing American guitar market.

Yet Martin OM models don't appear in old photos of dance bands like Perry Bechtel's Ansley Hotel Orchestra. Those players continued to flock to the new arch-top guitars by Gibson or Epiphone. Once again, Martin aimed high on the cultural ladder and missed but struck paydirt in the radio station corrals far west of their original target. Rather than being dubbed OM for Orchestra Model, the new Martins should have been designated CG, for Cowboy Guitar. Especially on the West Coast, Martin OM models swept through the new Western Swing bands like prairie fire, where buyers were far more likely to wear ten gallon hats and pressed chaps rather than tuxedos. An OM-18 was quickly adopted by guitarist Karl Farr, who, with his brother Hugh on fiddle, provided the hot, swing-style accompaniment for the Sons of the Pioneers. In San Francisco, Haywire Mac McClintock's "Haywire Orchestry" used two of the new OM Martins.

Guitar players embraced the new Martin models so quickly that Martin was left holding the bag with some 12-fret guitars it had made in the early 1930s. Fifteen 0-45 models completed in 1931 were still in inventory in 1936, when they were offered at Style 28 prices and listed in Martin's inventory as "obsolete models." The last one wasn't sold until 1945. San Francisco retailer Sherman Clay Music wrote to Martin in 1932, hoping to return 12-fret models like the 00-28 for credit on purchases of the new models that its customers demanded. Martin's reply was polite but firm: "No, as we have too many of the older models in inventory as it is."

With the new models added to Martin's already considerable line, dealers and customers—and probably even many Martin workers—were increasingly confused. With over a half-dozen body sizes, an equal number of styles, and two different neck lengths, how was anyone supposed to know what model they were looking at? A request from a promi-

RIGHT AND BELOW: The less expensive OM-18 quickly surpassed the OM-28 in sales, and many were shipped with the new shaded finish shown here. The widespread acceptance of the new steel-string OM also prompted Martin to abandon another bit of classical stuffiness by adding its name to the front of the headstock. OM-18 and 28 models were the first to get the gold "C. F. Martin & Co." decal in 1932. The decal quickly spread throughout the whole line, prompting Martin to discontinue stamping the back of the peghead in 1935. Though nearly identical in style to the Martin decal used from the 1930s through the mid-1990s, the earliest version had no black border around the gold lettering. *(Guitar courtesy of Fred Oster; detail photo from Hank Risan.)*

nent California dealer for model designations inside the guitar prompted Martin to stamp the model code on the neck block, just above the serial number, starting in October 1930.

Realizing that most steel-string players wanted the longer, more narrow neck, in 1932 Martin offered dealers 14-fret "0-18 Specials," which had a solid peghead, shaded top, pick guard, and long-string scale. By 1934 most of the old 12-fret models in all sizes were redesigned and offered as new, 14-fret versions, including the recently adopted Dreadnought. Since the solid peghead of the OM models was easier to manufacture than the old slotted headstock, Martin took the opportunity to make the solid head a standard feature of all the new models.

Despite the many differences, the model stamps on the neck block remained the same as before, creating exactly the kind of confusion that model stamps were supposed to eliminate. Since the old 12-fret designs were rapidly fading in popularity, the original OM models were simply renamed 000 in 1934; and to Martin, anything with a 14-fret neck was an orchestra model. In factory records for 1934, for instance, the new 14-fret versions were often listed with the old model code followed by the initials "OM," so "D-28 OM" meant a 14-fret D-28.

A few months after renaming the original OM as a 000, Martin changed the string length to the 24.9 scale then in use on the 0 and 00. This left the Dreadnoughts as the only flat-top Martins with the long scale that is an industry standard today for guitars of all sizes. Even as late as World War II, Martin's catalogs were divided into "Orchestra Models" (14-fret) and "Standard Models" (12-fret), with the number of standard models offered decreasing with each year. Thanks to all the reissues and copies of the original OM models, however, today's guitarist associates the term "OM" with a 14-fret, long scale 000 size guitar.

LEFT: One of the first of the old standard models to get "modernized" as a result of the OM's success was the little 0-18. In early 1932 Martin offered dealers the "0-18 Special," with 14-fret neck, pick guard, and dark top. The first few were long-scale (25.4 inches), but these new, low-cost orchestra models soon went back to the shorter 0 scale of 24.9 inches. The modern 0-18 (dark-top versions are rare after the mid-1930s) went on to a long career as one of Martin's best-selling guitars. This one is from early 1933. *(Guitar courtesy of Fred Oster.)*

BELOW: Roy Bookbinder, who used to lead Reverend Gary Davis to gigs, has never strayed far from his country blues roots. Though he has used a wide range of guitars, for years he often relied on an early OM-28. *(Photo courtesy of John Sterling Ruth/C. F. Martin & Company.)*

The GOLDEN ERA
1930 – 1945

ABOVE: Frank Henry Martin (1866–1948) was the most innovative member of the Martin dynasty, bringing both the Dreadnought and the 14-fret neck to the market. *(Photo courtesy of C. F. Martin & Company.)*

Occasionally in history things come together in such a serendipitous manner that one can view the result and well imagine that there is a plan to the universe after all.

Such can be said of the serendipity raining on Martin as it neared its centennial. The company's traditional market bolted, the entire country was careening toward disaster, and Martin took to putting its name on products it previously disdained. Yet in years to come this time would be called C. F. Martin & Company's golden era.

Andrés Segovia's stunning U.S. tour in 1928 pretty well nailed the coffin case shut on the Martin school of gut-string guitarmaking. Segovia's virtuoso playing left little doubt that, for gut strings, the Spanish models he favored with fan-braced tops were superior to the X-brace design C. F. Martin Sr. had perfected in the 1850s.

But by the whim of fortune, 1928 was also the year that Martin's conversion of its line to steel strings was completed, a change the company had initiated to satisfy the demands of a musical style developed half a world away in Hawaii.

The confluence of Martin's venerable X-brace and steel strings made Martins sing with the fullest, loudest, growlingest voice imaginable. That was perfect for the new generation of American entertainers in the 1930s who owed their popularity to radio and records—two media that required a guitar loud enough for a microphone to pick out amid the clang of a band.

By this time Martin guitars were rarely heard in rarefied circles. The highbrow players who had previously favored them followed Segovia's lead, and by 1934 gut-strung Martins could be purchased only on special order. And the players of the new sound of the city—jazz—embraced the arch-tops made by Gibson and Epiphone.

The company that had once supplied the likes of Justin Holland and Vahdah Olcott-Bickford was now seeing its guitars instead in the hands of guys with names like Arkie, the Arkansas

ABOVE: C. F. Martin III (1894–1986) helped his father pilot the Martin company through the difficult years of the Depression. *(Photo courtesy of C. F. Martin & Company.)*

ABOVE: Zing went the strings: Martin packaged steel strings made by the Mapes Piano String Company of New York to accompany their newly steel-strung guitars.

RIGHT: Rabon and Alton Delmore were among the most popular early brother duets in country music, and they both played Martins. Rabon's hot leads on tenor guitar, here an 0-17T, inspired the flat-picking of Doc Watson, who also adapted their *Big River Blues* as his fingerstyle classic, *Deep River Blues*. Despite the straw hats and overalls, the Delmores were polished musicians; Alton wrote over 1,000 songs and helped Merle Travis learn to read music. *(Photo from the Frank Driggs Collection.)*

LEFT: Roy Rogers was still known as Leonard Slye when he bought this OM-45 Deluxe in 1930 and was still a member of the Sons of the Pioneers. Rogers went on to become the biggest cowboy star of all time. The inlay on the pick guard of Roy's Deluxe is the same as is pictured in the 1930 Martin catalog, while other OM-45 Deluxes that have surfaced have the pick guard design shown on page 123. *(Photo courtesy of Jim Bollman.)*

Woodchopper, and cowboy singers who sought Martin's exemplary pearl-inlaid models because they matched their pearl-handled revolvers.

Instead of for stately marches, Martins were now used to compose songs like "Hallelujah, I'm a Bum," a "Haywire Mac" McClintock song that became the hobo anthem for a dispossessed generation of American men who took to riding the rails.

Martin's guitars may have moved down the social ladder, but they couldn't have found a more noble purpose. In the thick of the Depression, Franklin Roosevelt said, "The only thing we have to fear is fear itself." Martin introduced its most daring guitar: the big, oddly shaped Dreadnought. Though the name came from a British battleship, "dread not" could have been the booming guitar's motto, echoing Roosevelt, when placed in players' hands. It facilitated the music of a host of country players—and some blues ones—who helped spread the word to people in the Depression that they weren't alone in their woes nor ever very far from the simple joys in life.

Dreadnoughts and Whatnot

In the 1930s, one would have had a hard time telling anyone at the Martin company that it was in its golden era. At that time Martin was just trying to survive. In fact, it had to lay off many of its workers. As the company had in other hard times, it dealt with a downturn in business by offering new products.

To create work, Martin made violin parts—tailpieces, mutes, and fingerboards. C. F. Martin III, known as Frederick, was dispatched to New York City to see if he could find a market for bracelets made with scrap wood. Some previously imported purfling and binding material was now made in-house.

Although the instruments the Martin company introduced at this time were prompted by desperation, some also had a simple perfection that would ring out for decades. The OM model built in 1929 was the first flat-top guitar where the neck had 14 frets clear of the body. It wasn't one of the great engineering feats of the century. Gibson already had a 14-fret neck on its L-5 arch-top. Martin merely shortened the 000 body a bit and moved the bridge and bracing. Guitarists embraced the resulting OM model for its balanced, responsive tone and more playable neck. By 1934 Martin had made the 14-fret neck standard across its line.

The new design was so popular that it took the company years to sell its leftover 12-fret models. (Players have since come to prize the 12-fret models, and Martin has been reissuing them since the 1960s. It is another irony that the OM, Martin's attempt at an ideal plectrum guitar, is now prized by many as the finest fingerstyle guitar ever.)

(continued on page 134)

LEFT: Some 1930s Martins were more colorful than ever before, or since. This 1936 000-28 looks quite different than the shaded-top OM-28 of five years earlier (page 109), and Martin was no longer staining the herringbone border. Martin continued to offer the shaded top, but after the early 1940s it was rarely requested. *(Photo from Hank Risan.)*

ABOVE: Lonnie Johnson was one of the most accomplished guitarists of his day, as indicated by the recordings he made in the early 1930s with jazz guitar pioneer Eddie Lang playing backup. Since Johnson was on a "Race" record label, Lang used the name Blind Willie Dunn on their duet recordings. Though Lonnie Johnson often recorded on a 12-string guitar, here he's playing a 00-21. *(Photo from the Frank Driggs Collection.)*

LEFT: Many of the steel-string guitarists of early radio were closer to proto-folk than early country. Bradley Kincaid was a star on the *WLS Barn Dance* in Chicago in the late 1920s, and his smooth tenor singing on old-time ballads soon brought him thousands of letters from fans. His version of the Childe ballad "Barbara Allen" was so popular that he sang it on the air every Saturday night for almost three years. Though he was billed as "The Kentucky Mountain Boy with His Hound Dog Guitar," it's doubtful many mountain boys from any state could have afforded $170 for the 000-45 Kincaid is playing here. *(Photo courtesy of Jim Bollman.)*

ARCH-TOPS

Gibson's Lloyd Loar–designed L-5, introduced in 1922, defined the modern arch-top guitar and set a standard other manufacturers were hard-pressed to match. Many certainly tried, however. By the time the Martin company had entered the arch-top market a decade later, it was a growing and refined field, with everyone from discount-king Harmony to banjomaker Epiphone to master builder John D'Angelico producing them.

The L-5 and its progeny borrowed even more from the violin-building principles that Orville Gibson had used with his turn-of-the-century oval-soundhole arch-tops. Like the violin, whose f-holes it now appropriated, the L-5 had a spruce top carved so that the bridge rested on an arch that curved down to the instrument's sides. The back was similarly carved, and the back and sides were typically maple. And, as on both the violin and Martin's earliest Stauffer-inspired guitars, the fingerboard extended over the body rather than joining it. The guitars tended toward the huge—in 1934 Gibson introduced the 18-inch-wide Super 400—so guitarists had at least a fighting chance of being heard amid the horns of a jazz orchestra.

ABOVE AND LEFT: Introduced in 1931, the C-series Martins marked the first time the company featured the Martin name on the peghead of a stock guitar. (The letters C and F appeared on either side of the M about a year later.) Today the C-series models are not considered worthy jazz guitars like Gibson's L-5, yet these round-soundhole arch-tops are excellent all-purpose guitars for all-purpose guys like actor James Cagney, who played this 1931 C-2 for many years. (*Photos from Hank Risan.*)

Martin's arch-tops give every indication that the company entered the market grudgingly. For its initial C-1, C-2, and C-3 models in 1931, the company essentially took a 000 and put an arched top on it, with the round soundhole that competitors were abandoning in favor of f-holes. (Martin followed suit with an f-hole version by 1934.) The back was nearly flat—only slightly more curved than on Martin's flat-tops—and was Brazilian rosewood (or mahogany on the C-1), as were the sides. Unlike most other arch-top makers, Martin glued the fingerboard to the top instead of suspending it. Because of the body's curious mix of flat-top and arch-top characteristics, the necks had to be set at an awkward angle that did no favors to either tone or playability. And, unlike guitars from other makers, Martin's arch-tops were a mere 15 inches wide until the modestly

ABOVE: Martin never grasped the central principle to arch-top guitar construction—that of suspending the fretboard out over the guitar's top, allowing a much larger and effective soundboard. Instead, Martin carved a large platform into the spruce top so the fretboard could be glued directly to it. *(Photo from Hank Risan.)*

RIGHT: Martin's arch-tops are considered failures by today's standards; but in the early 1930s, sales of plain models like the R-18 shown here helped keep the company afloat in the worst years of the Depression. Just under 500 of this model were sold per year in 1933 and 1934, at a retail of $55, the same price as a 000-18. *(Guitar courtesy of C. F. Martin & Company.)*

RIGHT: Martin's F-series arch-tops were shaped like 000 flat-tops, but an inch wider. Considering their low value at the time, inventive guitar repairmen in the 1960s, like Jon Lundberg in Berkeley, couldn't resist the temptation to replace the carved top on this F-9 and convert it to a Brazilian rosewood 0000 flat-top guitar. Martin issued its own version, the M-38, in 1977. *(Photo © Mac Yasuda Enterprises.)*

BELOW: According to Martin company records, only two maple F-series guitars like the F-5 at left were made, both in 1940. The F-7 at right was a less expensive version of the F-9; and with total production of 187 between 1935 and 1942, it was by far the best-selling F model. Both of these guitars have celluloid hexagons on the fretboard. Many C and F arch-tops of the period have celluloid imitation pearl (sometimes called "mother-of-toiletseat") for both hexagons and peghead letters. This plastic was considered high-tech at the time, and some expensive four-string banjos were covered with it. *(Photo from Hank Risan.)*

larger 16-inch F-size was introduced in 1935.

While moderate for an arch-top, the 16-inch width was bigger than even Martin's new Dreadnoughts and was differently contoured. Decades later, this inspired some guitarists to have their F-series Martins converted into flat-tops (which, in turn, inspired Martin to issue its similar M-series guitars in 1977).

At the time, though, arch-tops didn't do too badly for the company, accounting for 1,046 of the 3,595 guitars Martin sold in 1935. And the company gave some models features that were new to Martin and would later adorn Martin's standard models. The celluloid black and white lines bordering the tops of higher-model arch-tops would replace the herringbone trim on flat-top Style 28s a decade later. Both the hexagonal pearl position markers and the pearl "C. F. Martin" headstock logo made famous on the late 1930s D-45s got their start on the F-series arch-tops in 1935.

That year Perry Bechtel, the bandleader for whom Martin had devised the 14-fret OM model in 1929, tried out Martin's top-of-the-line F-9. He sent it back. Bechtel had been playing a Gibson L-5, and Martin's guitar gave him no reason to change. He complained, "Frankly, the neck will never have the 'feel' for me as it stands," and he said that the tone was wanting in "velvet." He also wanted a guitar with more ornamentation, writing, "Don't think I'm a baby, but I'm used to all that, you know."

Other professional players must have agreed, for Martin arch-tops showed up on few bandstands. By 1938 sales of the lower-priced arch-tops were only a third of what they'd been three years earlier, while the fancy F-series was dead in the water. Gibson had issued a

BELOW: Martin tried their arch-top designs on other guitar types, and the most successful, in terms of sales, were the arch-top tenors like this C-1T. About 300 C- and R-series tenor guitars were made in the 1930s. The version made as a mando-cello didn't fare nearly as well—only 7 were made in all. *(Guitar courtesy of C. F. Martin & Company.)*

ABOVE: This 000-28 from 1936 was ordered by someone who liked Martin's arch-top styling, even if they still preferred the sound of the standard flat-top guitar. The coloring and binding are like an F-7, as are the celluloid hexagons on the fretboard and Martin letters on the peghead. *(Photo © Mac Yasuda Enterprises.)*

RIGHT: Maybe Martin arch-tops didn't have the sound needed for big swing bands, but the maple F-5 shown here and on the opposite page did the job for country music group Benny and Vallie Cain. (*Photo from Hank Risan.*)

new, larger version of its L-5 and L-7 in 1936, and this "advanced" 17-inch-wide body, with similar Epiphones in hot pursuit, probably sounded the death knell for Martin's arch-top, flat-back hybrids. Though the restrictions of the Second World War were an incredible nuisance on most fronts, it did give Martin a good excuse to get out of the arch-top business.

In 1931, the Martin company responded to Gibson's encroachment on the flat-top market by issuing its first arch-top guitars. By Martin's standards, the guitars sold well at the time, though history has not been overly kind to them.

That same year, though, Martin's place in guitar history was assured by the introduction of its Dreadnought. Martin had not been in any hurry to meet that destiny. The company first made a small number of the distinctively wide-waisted guitars under the Ditson name in 1916 (in three styles and three sizes, with the largest, the 111s, 222s, and 333s, being the behemoth we know and love today). Martin showed no inclination to add the size to its own line, though.

Indeed, as late as mid-1929, the company responded to a dealer's request for a larger guitar with a firm assertion that Martin had taken size as far as it should go. To go any larger than the Auditorium size, or 000, the company said, would make the guitar too bassy, upsetting the tonal balance that had been a Martin byword for generations.

It would be interesting to have a time machine to go back and capture the exact moment Frank Henry Martin decided to give the playing public what it had been asking for. We do know the moment came sometime in the spring of 1931, when Martin introduced its D-1 and D-2 Dreadnoughts, which by year's end had been renamed the D-18 and D-28.

Though he turned 65 that year, Frank Henry Martin was still very much in charge of the company. In fact, in the 1980s his son Frederick told a symposium of luthiers that his father "does not get the credit he should for building up the business. It was his open mind that accepted the idea for the Dreadnought guitar. It was his open mind that accepted the idea for the longer neck. I was involved in that, but he was the main one responsible."

Martin's Dreadnought wasn't the immediate success that the OM was, perhaps because the company didn't include the new guitar model in its catalog, or perhaps because by 1931, people were getting the idea that the Depression was going to linger a while. A total of 8 Dreadnoughts were sold that first year, 9 the following year, and 22 in 1933. In 1935, though, production topped 200 and it climbed from there, reaching a high of 782 in 1941, before the war limited production.

100 Years

On April 20, 1933, the *Nazareth Item* newspaper devoted nearly its entire front page to Martin's centennial. Next to it was a story headlined "Family of Eight Found without Food or Bedding." That year the company received congratulatory letters from fellow instrument manufacturers, including this one from Gibson's general manager, Guy Hart: "You produce instruments of the very highest quality and workmanship, your dealings are fair and square.... I am certain that with the spirit and ideals behind the Martin product, the name will live on and on, and as each member of the family passes to the great beyond, they can feel proud of the monument left behind." Frederick, who handled most of the company correspondence, responded with thanks,

ABOVE: Martin survived the Depression in better shape than most of its competitors, but the hardships C.F. III had witnessed during that period made a lasting impression. Though his conservative fiscal management in later years limited his company's growth, it was prompted by his desire to protect Martin workers from ever having to endure the poverty and breadlines shown here. *(Photo from Library of Congress/Corbis.)*

RIGHT: Though not generally known for shaded finishes, Martin gave this 1933 C-3 the subtle coloring of a fine violin. Introduced in 1931, it was Martin's finest arch-top at the time, although they switched to more modern f-shaped soundholes shortly after this example was made. Today most players agree that the round soundhole versions are better guitars. If you stop expecting it to be like a Gibson L-5, this C-3 is a beautiful guitar with nice tone and lots of volume. *(Photo from Hank Risan.)*

NAZARETH ITEM

NAZARETH, PA., THURSDAY MORNING, APRIL 20, 1933

AN INDEPENDENT FAMILY NEWSPAPER DEVOTED TO LITERATURE, LOCAL AND GENERAL INTELLIGENCE

No. 21

zareth Service Clubs Fete C. F. Martin & Co., Inc. Officials Commemorating the 100th Anniversary of Successful Business

n The Manufacture of Mandolins and Guitars Are Honored For areer; Frank H. Martin, Senior Member of Firm, Relates History of Company; Handsome Engraved Loving Cup, Baskets of t Flowers Presented; Artists Render Musical Selections

S FOR MANUFACTURE OBTAINED FROM MANY COUNTRIES

Churchmen Meet In St. John's Reformed

CHAMBER OF COMMERCE DIRECTORS HOLD MEETING

LEGIONNAIRES TO ORGANIZE "SONS OF THE AMERICAN LEGION"

NAZARETH SCHOOL BOARD HOLDS REGULAR MEETING

continuing, "The consciousness of being a constructive factor in the music world is one of the greatest rewards any of us can hope for."

Fine sentiments, but Martin had laid off all but 30 of its employees. One of Martin's biggest West Coast accounts, the Southern California Music Company, wrote to apologize for the light orders, going on to explain that other stores in Los Angeles were going out of business and selling their instruments "at ruinous prices."

In 1933 Frederick also exchanged a series of letters with one Homer H. Simpson—no kidding—a Georgia woodworker who had traveled all the way to Nazareth in hopes of landing a job with Martin. Told that there was already a long list of laid-off employees to be hired back, Simpson returned home but kept pleading to be given a chance.

Simpson sent a sample of his work, a miniature guitar made with only a pocketknife, and then a more elaborate one made with a knife, file, and sandpaper. He asked to be hired on an unpaid trial basis, writing: "I am 24 years old with a father and mother past 60 years of age who depend on me for a living...I am in Gainesville, Georgia, now on the road not knowing where to go, but before starting thought I would make a final plea with you...I must prove myself to you before I can get a job in this Depression."

Someone at Martin—almost certainly Frederick—took the time to respond compassionately to Simpson's letters. While reiterating the company's first loyalty to its own employees, he seemed to realize that, like so many men without a livelihood, Simpson was hungry for someone to at least recognize that he had worth. Martin's letters praised Simpson's workmanship and sent him scrap pieces of ebony, rosewood, and mahogany for his carving. When Simpson seemed determined to build a

LEFT: In 1933, as Martin celebrated its 100th anniversary, the *Nazareth Item* devoted nearly an entire front page to a history of the company. *(© Nazareth Item.)*

RIGHT: Southern California Music was one of Martin's most aggressive retailers. Along with free lessons and a radio show featuring Martin instruments, the company was not averse to spreading a bit of folklore as part of the sales pitch. C. F. Martin Sr. did not build his first guitar in a cabin in the Adirondack Mountains as this 1933 ad suggests, but what do you expect from a store so close to Hollywood?

FAR RIGHT AND BELOW: Henry Hunt of the Ditson company had first requested eight-string bridges from Martin in 1925, "for a new style guitar that has been invented, called the Octa-Chorda," a variant of the Hawaiian steel guitar. Hunt included a drawing of the bridge, shown below, with the suggested tuning. He asked if Martin would use such a bridge on its guitars, but evidently the crush of ukulele orders ended the discussion. By the time Martin got around to making this Octa-Chorda in 1930, the Ditson company was about to be liquidated. Martin apparently didn't make other Octa-Chorda models like this one, but it did make other eight-string guitars, including a Ditson Dreadnought with a similar bridge. *(Guitar courtesy of C. F. Martin & Company.)*

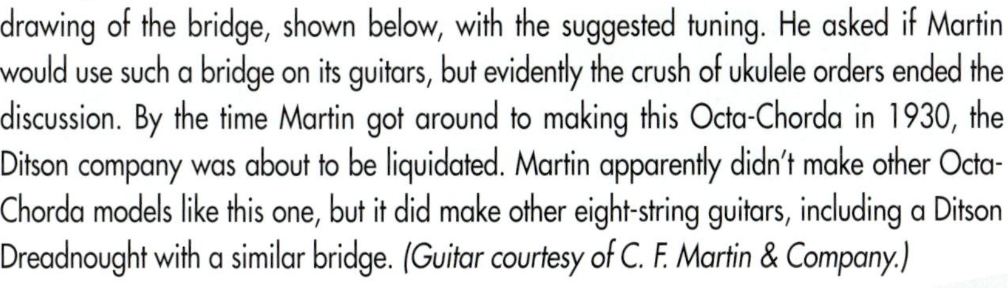

Gayble Theatre

North Judson, Indiana

Sunday, Jan. 31st One Day Only

ON THE STAGE

IN PERSON

Gene Autry

Oklahoma's Yodeling Cow Boy

Famous Radio Recording Artist From W-L-S Chicago

YOU HEAR HIM EVERY M
AT 9:20 A. M. ON THE
NOW FOR A REAL TREAT
HEAR HIM ON THE STAG
ING AND SINGING YOUR
ITE SONGS.

— On the Screen —

"Strictly Dishonorabl

LATEST NEWS and CARTOON Also COMEDY RIOT

BELOW: Nothing sells during depressed times like fantasy, and no image could be further from the realities of the mid-1930s than that of a handsome cowboy in hundreds of dollars' worth of clean clothes, playing an expensive pearl-encrusted guitar while riding a horse. During the grim news of World War I, Americans had turned their thoughts to grass-skirted hula dancers and coconut-strewn beaches. During the Great Depression, Americans flocked to movie theaters to see cowboys like Gene Autry tame the Wild West with six-guns and a song—all in 15 minutes—over and over again. The fact that such cowboys accompanied their sagebrush serenades with the guitar was better advertising than guitar manufacturers could have imagined. *(Photo courtesy of Jim Bollman.)*

ABOVE: Orven Autry bought his first pearl-bordered Martin, an 0-42, in 1927 when he was barely out of high school. About a year later he bought a 00-42. In 1929, with his singing career gathering steam (and fully under the influence of Jimmie Rodgers), Autry sent the 00 back to Martin for extra pearl befitting his new status. Martin seemed reluctant to add a new fretboard with his name (now Gene) in block letters ($20), gold-plated gears with pearl buttons ($10), and pearl bordering to the peghead (another $10). C.F. III wrote: "The expense of special pearl work is considerable and we do not advise it unless there is...a return to the player in increased publicity in his professional work. You understand...this would be purely ornament and would not improve the tone of your guitar at all." Despite the fatherly rhetoric Autry promptly sent the 00-42 back for as much pearl as Martin would load on. In 1931 his 0-42 was given the same treatment, but with his name in pearl script.

ABOVE: Nashville native Muriel Ellen Deason began performing in 1937, at the age of 18, when she married fellow Martin player Johnny Wright. Here as Kitty Wells she looks at home behind her big, booming D-28. After singing harmony with her husband's duo, Johnny and Jack, she became the "Queen of Country Music" in 1952 with the number-one hit "It Wasn't God Who Made Honky Tonk Angels." *(Photo © Robert Menasco, Shreveport, Louisiana.)*

full-size guitar at home, Martin broke its policy of supplying parts only for the repair of its own guitars and sent Simpson a prime-quality spruce top for $1.

Martin was doing all it could to keep its own workers employed. Oddball custom orders that the company had previously been too busy to undertake were now welcomed, such as the Octa-Chorda, shown on page 13. The company even considered producing a true bass guitar for another dealer.

Martin made its most famous custom-order instrument in 1933. Gene Autry had already been a good Martin customer, playing both an 0-42 and a 00-42 with his name in the fretboard, like his idol, Jimmie Rodgers. By 1933 Autry was a star on NBC's *National Barn Dance* (formerly the *WLS Barn Dance*) out of Chicago. He asked the Martin company to make him the biggest, fanciest guitar it could, with his name again inlaid on the fingerboard. The result was the world's first D-45, elevating the previously utilitarian Dreadnoughts (formerly available in only the plain D-18 and D-28 models) to Martin's pinnacle of style. In what might be called "lavish understatement," Martin craftsmen inlaid pearl on every edge of the instrument—the top, back, sides, and headstock—but in a thin, exquisitely precise band barely visible beyond the bandstand.

The D-45 was clearly a work of pride for the company, and though it didn't sell many at first, it kept it in its line. Until production was halted by World War II, only 91 D-45s—including Autry's—were made. That limited production later caused the prewar D-45s to become perhaps the world's rarest model of guitars. By the late 1990s they were selling for about $125,000 each. It is almost impossible to speculate how much more Autry's guitar might be worth, since it was both the first of its kind and a celebrity instrument. It presently resides in Autry's Western Heritage Museum in Southern California, hopefully under 24-hour armed guard.

COWBOY 45s

What did Gene Autry, Roy Rogers, and Tex Ritter all have in common besides cowboy hats and white teeth? The answer is that they all played Style 45 Martins. These top cowboy stars, and many others, paid for fancy Martins when other companies would gladly have given them guitars. Was it something about the number 45? Did Martin name its top model after a Colt revolver, or was it the other way around? Either way, it is no coincidence that the bang-bang strum-strum movies these soundstage cowboys were making often had titles like *Six Gun Rhythm*.

The most famous Martin of all is probably the D-45 belonging to Gene Autry. Built on special order in 1933, it was the first D-45 but the third pearl-bordered Martin with Autry's name on the fretboard. The next D-45 was made in 1934 for another cowboy star, Jackie "Kid" Moore, who was barely in his teens at the time.

That same year, the only D-42 ever made was built on special order for Tex Fletcher, the singing foreman on the *Bobby Benson*

ABOVE: The new Martin Dreadnoughts didn't escape the eye of Gene Autry, who ordered a fancy rosewood version that became the first D-45. Along with typical Style 45 appointments, Autry requested his name inlaid in the fretboard. Martin offered a limited edition of 66 Gene Autry D-45s in 1994. It is no small irony that the Holy Grail to Martin guitar collectors is still in the hands of its first owner. (*Photo courtesy of C. F. Martin & Company.*)

LEFT: Jackie "Kid" Moore was quite a celebrity in Milwaukee in the early 1930s, playing a custom Gibson arch-top with his name on the fingerboard. Martin's local retailer was able to interest him in a Martin Dreadnought, but surviving correspondence depicts an uphill battle getting Martin to make the guitar fancy enough to entice a young star looking for "a lot of flash." C.F. III wrote: "We have consistently stood out against the use of...(flashy ornament) because it has a tendency to interfere with the tone of the instruments and to detract from the fine dignity that is characteristic of Martin designs." Moore, quite wise in his youth, knew that dignified designs meant little to customers in the cheap seats. He was familiar with Gene Autry's D-45 and wanted a similar guitar, but with an OM-width fretboard and a solid peghead with the C. F. Martin letters in pearl. Martin was clearly less than swamped with work—in 1934 it promised "delivery in about three weeks after receipt of the order." *(Photos from Hank Risan.)*

B Bar B Riders radio show. A later D-45 was heard by thousands of radio fans of Nolan "Cowboy Slim" Rinehart. Martin's loudest, fanciest flat-tops were favorites with singing stars who chose guitars that matched their personalities—they liked to be heard and seen.

Other cowboys opted for their abalone bordering on a more compact package. Roy Rogers had been one of the first cowboys to succumb to 45 fever, purchasing an OM-45 Deluxe in 1930; and "Haywire Mac" McClintock, who really had been a cowboy, bought an OM-42 model the same year. Tex Ritter, one of the few movie cowboys with that name who was actually from Texas, chose a later 000-45 to serenade his leading lady in the movie *King of Dodge City*.

Gibson, realizing the high visibility of these cowboy stars, quickly went on the offensive. Gibson designed a large flat-top guitar with a cowboy's taste in mind, quickly placing its new Super Jumbo 200 in the hands of cowboy stars like Ray Whitley and Crash Corrigan. By 1938 both Gene Autry and Tex Ritter were pictured in the Gibson catalog with custom SJ-200 models. Unlike the conservative taste that prevailed at Martin, Gibson had no aversion to flash, and these early SJ-200s often had large horseshoes inlaid on the fretboard.

With the D-45, Martin had a potential flagship in its line but didn't seem to recognize the marketing bonanza that had landed in its lap. Even in 1937 there was no mention of the D-45 in the Martin catalog, and predictably Martin sold only

ABOVE: OK, so it's not a D-45, but what this D-42 lacks in pearl is more than compensated for by its rarity. Made for radio cowboy Tex Fletcher in 1934, it's the only prewar D-42 ever made. Tex held his guitar like most lefties, but learned to play on a right-handed instrument. So his D-42 has the pick guard and fretboard letters for a lefty but is strung like a typical right-hander's guitar. (*Guitar courtesy of C. F. Martin & Company; Tex Fletcher photo courtesy of Jim Bollman.*)

LEFT: Maybe Toby Stroud is a very small guy, or maybe his D-45 is one of the two wide-body versions made in 1936. Fewer than a dozen D-45s were made with the old snowflake inlays on the neck. Instead, in 1938 Martin began using the hexagon pattern introduced on its arch-tops in 1935. (*Photo courtesy of Jim Bollman.*)

RIGHT: The next two D-45 models after those for Autry and Moore didn't come until 1936, and they were no less unusual. Ordered by Wurlitzer in St. Louis, the guitars, including this one, have the typical, updated 14-fret design, but the bodies are just over a half inch wider than normal. Whatever the intent, Martin's records make no mention of ever repeating the effort on D-45 models or any other Dreadnoughts. (*Photo © Mac Yasuda Enterprises.*)

two. The D-45 got a one-line listing at the bottom of page 10 in the 1938 catalog, with the hard-sell description as "A very handsome guitar." Sales went up to nine for that year.

Over five years after Martin made the first D-45, the model was finally pictured in the August 1939 catalog. This was the first catalog appearance of the hexagon fretboard inlays on a flat-top Martin.

Once pictured in the catalog, sales improved significantly; 19 of the D-45 models were sold in 1940, and two dozen in 1941, with the Dreadnought version of Style 45 finally outselling the smaller 000-45. Despite a severe case of the war jitters, another 19 of the fancy Dreadnoughts were sold in 1942, but production began on the last batch of 6 in October of that year. Only 91 Style D-45s were made in all, making them the first Martins to gain widespread recognition as a rare and valuable vintage guitar. Barely 20 years after the last ones were made, the hunt would begin for any and all prewar D-45 Martins. The stakes have gotten higher every year.

Why Martin never bothered to revive its pearl-bordered models after the war was over is anybody's guess, but C. F. III's aversion to anything flashy may have had at least something to do with it. The fact that the D-45 never returned to the stage made Gibson's fancy J-200 the postwar cowboys' guitar of choice, though many of them con-

LEFT: Despite the motif on his sleeves, Ken MacKenzie was probably more familiar with cranberries than cacti. Based in Maine, Ken and his New Radio Revue represented Western music as the ultimate American melting pot—with accordions and yodeling from Europe mixed up with rhythms and song styles from south of the border. Some cowboy groups even added Hawaiian guitars and ukuleles to the mix as well. (*Photo courtesy of Jim Bollman.*)

ABOVE: No, that's not a rare 14-fret 00-45 Tex Ritter is holding in this comedy skit, it's a 000-45 in the hands of a big guy. Though Ritter was later wooed by Gibson with an SJ-200 that better suited his size, he made many appearances with this 000 in his early days as a singing cowboy. It was probably made between 1934 and 1937. *(Photo courtesy of Jim Bollman.)*

ABOVE: Proudly pictured in Martin's catalogs, the 000-45 was popular in the mid-1930s, and four dozen were sold each year in 1935 and 1936. Unlike the D-45, the 000-45 received the C. F. Martin letters in pearl on the peghead but retained the old-style snowflake pattern on the fretboard. *(Photo from Hank Risan.)*

tinued to record and perform with D-28s despite the contrast between their colorful outfits and the utilitarian look of all postwar Martins. In 1968 the D-45 was revived, and it has since proven to be a favorite of cowboys and city slickers alike.

Martin usually sells more D-45 guitars each year than were sold in the original nine years of production, with sales in the hundreds being the norm. Beyond stock models, it is the starting point for many lavishly inlaid Dreadnoughts from Martin's Custom Shop that would make Jackie "Kid" Moore green with envy. The D-45's appeal now stretches beyond cowboys and bluegrass singers, and its deep voice is heard in every kind of music that welcomes the acoustic guitar.

LEFT: Canadian singer and first-rate yodeler Wilf Carter, known in the United States as "Montana Slim," played a 000-45 to accompany his many songs about the West. A prolific songwriter, Carter was still performing in his 80s and got decades of service from his 1935 Martin. *(Photo courtesy of Jim Bollman.)*

NO DEALS

While Martin sales benefited from performers such as Autry being photographed with its guitars in films and on song folios, the company refused to take greater advantage by forming endorsement deals with artists.

In 1935 a large British account that was considering doing more business with the company asked Martin for a list of prominent players. Martin's response: "We are unable to furnish a list of players who are using the Martin guitars because we do not keep any records of that kind. Our sales to the players are made entirely through the dealers, and it is our policy not to use player's testimonials in our advertising."

While Martin had addressed the need for greater volume with a bigger guitar, other manufacturers were taking more drastic measures. In 1927 in Los Angeles, the Dopyera Brothers at National had introduced their metal resonator guitars, while Rickenbacker had topped that, volume-wise, with its electric guitars in 1931. By the time Gibson chimed in with its ES-150 electric arch-top in 1936, it was clear that the electric guitar wasn't just another fad. (There were plenty of fads at the time—one inventor even tried to

RIGHT: Martin wasn't pushing guitars to performers, but the company was willing to put forth considerable effort for this window display in the summer of 1934. Lyon & Healy of Chicago had once been a competitor, but by this time the retailing giant was a major Martin account after shedding all connections with guitar manufacturing. Its offer of a window display was well timed, since it was during the annual music trade show, and Martin's sales were still slow as a result of the Depression. The center pedestal was given to the new C-3 arch-top, Martin's most expensive guitar at the time. Flanking it are the C-1 and C-2. High on the left side is a D-18, with an 0-18K and 00-17 below, while a 000-45 is on the right-hand pedestal, with a 000-28 and sunburst D-28 underneath. On the left are various ukuleles and a Style 20 mandolin, while three old Martins from the previous century are on the right, including what appears to be a Martin & Coupa with Stauffer-style headstock. Also included is an Anniversary Cup from Martin's centennial the previous year. *(Photo courtesy of C. F. Martin & Company.)*

C.F. MARTIN & CO.
ESTABLISHED 1833
GUITARS
Mandolins Ukuleles
HAWAIIAN GUITAR
MARTIN
makers of fine
STRINGED
INSTRUMENTS
Since 1833
Visit the large
Exhibit of
Martin Instruments
Fourth Floor
A Martin Guitar
in the making
GREETINGS
to members of
MUSIC DEALERS
CONVENTION
LYON & HEALY
Martin Guitar
made in 1845
Martin Guitar
made in 1836
Martin Guitar
made in 1860

LEFT AND BELOW: The cover of Martin's 1936 catalog had a modern look uncharacteristic of the company, and the wide selection within gave no hint of hard times. The 32 pages listed arch-top models, both modern and old-fashioned flat-top guitars, and Hawaiian and tenor guitars. The flat-model mandolins had faded. But Martin was gamely hanging in there with new carved models, and ukes and tiples (a ten-string miniguitar from Argentina) were still well represented. This plush offering would continue, and even grow, in the next few years. However, the war already brewing in Europe, combined with changing tastes in music, would cut this selection to less than half by ten years later. Arch-tops, Hawaiian models, mandolins, tiples, koa-wood instruments, and anything with pearl bordering would disappear in 1942. Except for a couple of mandolins and tiples, those deleted instruments did not return after the war was over.

18 MARTIN

Tenor Guitar

ARCHED MODEL

These tenor guitars are the same in body size and construction as the six string styles C-1 and R-18 shown on pages six and seven. The string length is twenty-three inches, with adjustable bridge, internal gear pegs, pearl position dots and elevated pick-guard. Polished lacquer finish, dark color.

In style R-18T the spruce top is arched but not carved; in style C-1T it is carved and graduated in thickness like a violin.

PRICES

No. C-1T Auditorium.................... $80.00

No. R-18T Grand Concert................ $55.00

GUITARS 19

Tenor Guitar

FLAT MODEL

Mahogany body and neck, rosewood fingerboard and bridge, white position marks and side dots. Nickel-plated tuning machines. Polished lacquer finish, dark mahogany color.

This style is made in two sizes: Junior (No. 5) size is $11^1/_4$ inches wide, Concert (No. 0) size is $13^1/_2$ inches wide at the bridge; both have a string length of 23 inches.

PRICES

No. 5-17T Junior........................ $25.00

No. 0-17T Concert....................... $30.00

.... $40.00

12 MARTIN

Orchestra Model

STYLE D

This is the famous "Dreadnaught" bass guitar, originated by Martin in 1917 and now modernized for the plectrum style of playing. The extra wide and very deep body produces a tone of great power and smoothness, especially fine for broadcasting or recording.

Rosewood body, spruce top, ivoroid edges, re-enforced mahogany neck, ebony fingerboard and bridge, wide frets, polished lacquer finish. *Dark top on request at no extra charge.*

PRICES

No. D-28 Dreadnaught.................. $100.00

The same model with mahogany body, spruce top, dark edges, and less inlay:

No. D-18 Dreadnaught.................. $65.00

GUITARS

Hawaiian Guitar

STYLE 40H

Rosewood body with selected spruce top, bound with ivoroid and bordered with pearl. Mahogany neck, ebony fingerboard and bridge, fine pearl position marks. Genuine ivory nut and saddle. Nickel-plated single unit tuning machines; polished lacquer finish.

For Hawaiian playing only, with high nut, high and level bridge, frets flush with the finger-board. A fine guitar for professional use.

PRICE

No. 00-40H Grand Concert.............. $100.00

~~No. 0-18K~~ Concert size, Hawaiian koawood body, dark binding $40.00

No. 0-17H Concert size, mahogany body. $30.00

2 MARTIN

FOREWORD

More than a hundred years ago C. F. Martin, Sr., established the principles of construction and the ideals of workmanship that govern the manufacture of Martin guitars and kindred instruments today. His descendants of the third and fourth generations, mindful of changing times and new conditions, have added tested improvements in design and construction to meet the needs of modern players; but the old standards of excellent materials and careful workmanship are still the basis of Martin quality.

WARRANTY

All Martin instruments are warranted, without time limit, against defective material or imperfect workmanship.

C. F. Martin & Co., Inc.

ESTABLISHED 1833

GUITARS 3

Arched Model

STYLE F-9

This is the Guitar De Luxe. To brilliance in tone is added the beauty of rich pearl and ivoroid inlay, engraved gold plated trimmings, lustrous lacquer finish—a masterpiece of design and workmanship.

Grand Auditorium size, rosewood back and sides, carved spruce top, mahogany neck, re-enforced with steel bar, ebony fingerboard inlaid with pearl marks. All edges bound with ivoroid and bordered with fine black and white lines. Authentic 'cello F-scrolls, adjustable ebony bridge, ivory nut. Top shaded golden brown color to match the body and neck, all hand polished.

PRICE

No. F-9 Grand Auditorium.............. $250.00

interest Martin in his "Airelecroharp, which makes the piano as easy to play as a harmonica.")

Though Martin made no attempt to plug in, it evidently wasn't mortified by the thought of its guitars being amplified. In 1935 Bob Dunn, of Milton Brown and His Musical Brownies, had put a Los Angeles–made Volu-Tone pickup unit on his Martin. When Martin received inquiries about amplifying its guitars, the company recommended the Volu-Tone unit: "We have tested this unit and know that it can be used on our instruments."

As with most American manufacturers, the Second World War closed a chapter in Martin's history. On September 10, 1942, Martin informed its dealers that, due to government wartime restrictions, "priority in production goes to the instruments with the fewest metal parts, especially ukuleles and flat-top guitars. We are making relatively few carved-top guitars [which had metal trapeze bridges], and we shall discontinue temporarily all mandolins and tiples when the present stock is sold out.... A rigid ebony bar now gives guitar necks the same guaranteed strength as the steel bar it replaces."

Through the war Martin limited its dealers' orders to their 1941 totals and was often unable to fill those. Along with the mandolins, tiples, and arch-tops—whose discontinuation proved more than temporary—the war also killed off all the pearl-bordered models, including the D-45s.

The world would be a different place when it emerged from the war. Martin, however, would stake its reputation on remaining much the same.

ABOVE: One of country music's most endearing stars, Red Foley enjoyed a career that lasted over 30 years. The high point was hosting the *Ozark Jubilee*, one of the few country radio shows that successfully switched to TV. Foley recorded with Ernest Tubb, Kitty Wells, and even the Andrews Sisters, but his biggest draw was his sense of humor. *(Photo from the Frank Driggs Collection.)*

LEFT: No one knows how much of World War II this guitar actually witnessed, but the Army Air Corps insignia suggests that "Smoky," presumably named for the guitar's owner, was proud of his branch of the service. To its right is Smoky's brother, one serial number younger. These guitars were numbers 9 and 10 of a batch of 12 D-28s begun in late November of 1939. *(Photo courtesy of Steve Szilagyi/Elderly Instruments.)*

DREADNOUGHTS: BASS NOTES AND THE BOTTOM LINE

Martin guitars had never been faulted for their tone; but the company was so insistent on exalting tonal balance that it long ignored the poor guitarist whose gold-toned instrument was drowned out by banjos, mandolins, and nearly every other musical instrument.

Well before the twentieth century, guitarists were asking Martin for more volume. An 1889 letter from professional touring guitarist Otto Schwemberger said, "I must have strong, well-seasoned, deep-toned bass, as our orchestra consists of three pieces, a violin, flute, and guitar. We have to work under tent canvas this summer." You didn't have to be outdoors to need more volume than a gut-strung Martin could deliver.

Even after casting its high-toned principles aside and finally offering a steel-string guitar in the 1922 catalog, the Martin company offered only its smallest, cheapest model, the little 2-17. And while the 2-17 was selling like hotcakes (nearly 800 in 1923), Martin made musicians wait another year or two for bigger guitars like the 00-21 and 000-18 to be built to handle steel strings.

But in 1931 Martin's ukulele sales were dropping almost as fast as the stock market; and all those pleas for a bass guitar, from years past and present, were ringing in their ears. The OM, Martin's first model designed to be a steel-string guitar from the ground up, had been an immediate success just the year before. If the public wanted an even larger steel-string guitar, Martin was in a mood to give it to them.

LEFT: The most famous flat-top of all is the prewar D-45, like this one from 1940. Like most of Martin's successes, it was a blend of several styles, rather than the unique concept of a genius. The delicate pearl bordering came direct from Martins of a century earlier, while the neck inlays were borrowed from its arch-tops of the mid-1930s. The shape was originally made for Ditson, then adopted by Martin and redrawn to accommodate a slim, 14-fret neck. *(Photo from Hank Risan.)*

ABOVE: This guitarist for Shelly Lee Alley and his Alley Cats had his work cut out for him, trying to avoid being drowned out by the piano, violin, banjo, and amplified Hawaiian steel guitar, not to mention the saxophone. His choice? The Martin D-18. Though this was perhaps dictated by the price, the bright "cutting power" of the mahogany Dreadnought might actually have come through with this group more clearly than a D-28 would have. *(Photo from the Frank Driggs Collection.)*

ABOVE: The petite Vonny had her hands full with this big D-18, but at least the sound of her guitar could be heard through the microphone. The smooth bass and extra volume made Martin's Dreadnoughts instant favorites with vocalists of all kinds. *(Photo courtesy of Fred Oster.)*

Martin previously had made Dreadnoughts for the Oliver Ditson Company of Boston. Then when Ditson was sold in 1931, Martin wasted little time in adopting the Ditson Dreadnought as its own. Only a few months after the last extra-large Ditsons left Nazareth, Martin began building four more Dreadnoughts, in two styles, this time to be sold under the company's own name.

These were clearly going to be steel-string guitars, so the new "belly" bridge and long teardrop-shaped pick guard, features developed for the OM, were standard equipment, as was a heavier version of Martin's X-pattern top bracing. Otherwise, however, the slotted pegheads and wide 12-fret necks made the new Dreadnoughts look just like the old standard Martins—on steroids. Production started with a trial batch of four in 1931—the two mahogany examples were labeled D-1, while the rosewood models were called D-2. It's no coincidence that at least two of these first Martin Dreadnoughts were shipped to Chicago, home of the

RIGHT: Shaded finishes were quite popular in the 1930s, as on this D-28, probably because of all the sunburst Gibsons (and arch-tops in general) newly on the market. Though Martin's shaded finishes in the early 1930s were rather subtle, in a few years they became quite dramatic, as shown here. *(Photo © Mac Yasuda Enterprises.)*

WLS *National Barn Dance* radio program.

In March of 1932, one the biggest WLS stars, "Arkie the Arkansas Woodchopper," ordered a D-2 with his name (just the "Arkie" part) in mother-of-pearl script on the fretboard. Harty Taylor, guitarist for the Cumberland Ridge Runners and another WLS star, was soon keeping the beat with a rosewood Martin Dreadnought.

The D-1 and D-2 soon were renamed D-18 and D-28, respectively, and these two models would carry Martin to even greater glory in the years to come.

Barely a year after Arkie ordered his Dreadnought, Gene Autry ordered what has become the most famous Dreadnought of them all. His pearl-bordered Dreadnought would be not only the first D-45 but also one of the fanciest Dreadnoughts made before all the pearl-bordered Martin models were discontinued in 1942.

Despite the prominent performers who used them, Martin Dreadnoughts did not catch on as quickly as the smaller OM models had done a few years earlier. Part of the problem was the Depression, for the $100 it cost to buy a D-28 would feed a family for months. But the biggest problem was that Martin seemed reluctant to put Dreadnoughts in the catalog, and only 21 of the D-18 and D-28s combined were sold in 1933, the year Autry received his flashy masterpiece. By 1934, however, the popularity of the new 14-fret OM guitars prompted Martin to redesign all of the old models, including the Dreadnought.

The result was the instrument that came to define the steel-string

ABOVE: Though D-45 and D-28 models got all of the publicity, the hardy D-18 was by far Martin's best-selling version of the new Dreadnought. In the years before World War II, the D-18 outsold the D-28 by about 3 to 1. In the late 1930s, this D-18 sold for $65 when the D-28 was $100. *(Photo from Hank Risan.)*

RIGHT: Young Tony Rice rewrote the rules about flatpicking in the 1970s, and his blazing solos inspired bluegrass guitarists to demand their time at the mike for solos as well as rhythm chops. Tony's 1935 D-28 had received very unMartinlike modifications at the soundhole while owned by flatpicking pioneer Clarence White, and the look prompted the "beyond Martin" herringbone D-28 sold by smaller companies. *(Album cover from Tony Rice/Rounder Records 0085.)*

12 MARTIN

Orchestra Model

STYLE D

This is the famous "Dreadnaught" bass guitar, originated by Martin in 1917 and now modernized for the plectrum style of playing. The extra wide and very deep body produces a tone of great power and smoothness, especially fine for broadcasting or recording.

Rosewood body, spruce top, ivoroid edges, reenforced mahogany neck, ebony fingerboard and bridge, wide frets, polished lacquer finish. Dark top on special order at no extra charge.

PRICES

No. D-28 Dreadnaught..................$100.00

The same model with mahogany body, spruce top, dark edges, and less inlay:

No. D-18 Dreadnaught..................$65.00

LEFT: Despite the less-than-exciting language, this inclusion in the July 1935 catalog was just what the Dreadnoughts needed. Sales of the D-18 in particular jumped dramatically between 1934 and 1936. Frederick (C.F. III) must have been reluctant to tinker with the ad copy: Except for an added reference to "television work," this same description was used in catalogs for almost 30 years.

BELOW AND INSET: Somebody must have wanted a loud Hawaiian guitar with lots of bass, and that somebody got his or her wish with this 1936 special-order D-28. Hawaiian D-28s are certainly rare, and the shaded top and Style 42 neck inlays makes this a one-of-a-kind. The flat fingerboard with frets ground flush is typical of Martins set up at the factory as Hawaiian models in the 1930s. *(Photo from Hank Risan.)*

flat-top guitar. By squaring off the upper and lower bouts and shortening the body, Martin came up with a more boxy shape that allowed a neck with 14 frets clear of the guitar body.

As with the earlier OM models, the neck was made narrower, with a solid peghead. At this point, all of the elements of the modern Dreadnought were in place. Perhaps assured that it was on to something, Martin gave the Dreadnought a prominent spot in its 1935 catalog, and sales began to climb. In 1937 Martin sold over 400 D-18s, outperformed only by its budget 0-17 model. After years of preaching about tonal balance, Martin had finally learned to give guitar players what they wanted and let the bass notes roll.

Martin Models

Mid-Twentieth Century

Starting in 1931, Martin began making its big Dreadnought guitars under its own name, adding the letter D to the company's increasingly complex model code. Only the D-18 and D-28 were offered at first, with the D-45 chiming in shortly after. Beginning in 1932 Martin added arch-top guitars to its roster, beginning with the 000-size C-1 and C-2. The C-1 had a mahogany back and sides with Style 18 appointments, while the C-2 was a rosewood model with Style 28 details.

In 1933 a smaller, less expensive arch-top was added in the 00 size, called the R-18. This was later followed by an even plainer version with mahogany top, the R-17. Why these models were given the same style designations as comparable flat-top Martins is a mystery. An R-18 was very much like a 00-size version of the C-1, but the difference in the model code defies logic. Why not an R-18 and a C-18? Or a

LEFT: The 00-21 was the sole surviving 12-fret model after Martin's big switch to 14-fret designs in the 1930s. The 00-21 on the right is from 1898, with the high soundhole, 19-fret fingerboard, and long scale (25.4 inches) typical of the early 00 models (these are more commonly seen with a slotted peghead). The guitar on the left is a steel-string 00-21 from 1942, with shorter scale (24.9 inches) and 20 frets total. Soon the 00-21 would lose its ebony fingerboard and bridge and dots would replace the inlays shown here; but aside from these concessions to modern times, it would remain the same until the late 1960s. Though other 12-fret models came and went, the 00-21 is Martin's continuous link to the nineteenth century. *(Photo from Hank Risan.)*

C-1 and an R-1? Martin nomenclature often makes little sense around this time, and understanding the company's model designations becomes less an act of mastering the odd logic and more an exercise in blind faith and memorization.

The F series arch-tops were added in 1935. These were an enlarged version of the 000 shape, a body outline that would later be used for the M series flat-tops in 1977 (getting the new 0000 designation beginning in 1997). The appointments for the F-7 and F-9 did not correspond to the style of any contemporary Martin flat-tops, and the F models disappeared along with the rest of Martin's ill-fated arch-tops by 1942. (The letter C has reappeared in modern times, combined with a regular body designation, to indicate a cutaway, such as 000C-16 or DC-28. The F reappeared 20 years later as a series of shallow-bodied electric guitars, with the same body outline and f-scroll soundholes as the earlier acoustic arch-tops.)

In 1934 most of Martin's old "standard" models were redesigned in the new "orchestra model" style, with shortened bodies and narrow, 14-fret necks. At the same time, the OM models were renamed 000, and from then on "orchestra model" was only a general term used in the catalog and factory records to indicate any model with a 14-fret neck. But Martin continued to make the old 12-fret "standard" models as well, and as a result there was lots of model code confusion in the mid-1930s.

THE HOUSE OF MARTIN 7

Orchestra Model

STYLE 18

MAHOGANY body, finished dark, with natural color spruce top. Edges bound with black fiberloid; soundhole and top border inlaid with black and white lines. Mahogany neck, ebony fingerboard and bridge. Pearl position dots and white side dots. Nickel plated tuning machines, new single unit all-metal type. Hand rubbed, lacquer finish.

This style will be furnished with dark color top instead of natural finish on special order at no extra charge.

PRICES

No. 0-18 Concert........................$40.00

No. 000-18 Auditorium....................$55.00

(Formerly listed as No. OM-18)

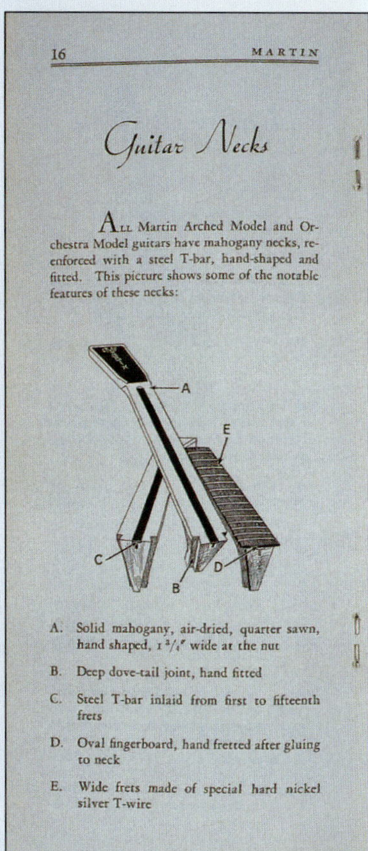
16 MARTIN

Guitar Necks

ALL Martin Arched Model and Orchestra Model guitars have mahogany necks, reenforced with a steel T-bar, hand-shaped and fitted. This picture shows some of the notable features of these necks:

A. Solid mahogany, air-dried, quarter sawn, hand shaped, 1 3/4" wide at the nut

B. Deep dove-tail joint, hand fitted

C. Steel T-bar inlaid from first to fifteenth frets

D. Oval fingerboard, hand fretted after gluing to neck

E. Wide frets made of special hard nickel silver T-wire

ABOVE LEFT AND ABOVE: Martin showed a 12-fret standard model on the cover of its 1934 catalog; but inside, the old style only got one page. Martin at least tried to reduce confusion by mentioning the earlier "OM" designation for the new 14-fret "orchestra model," as shown above left on the bottom of page 7 of the catalog. The number of standard models, such as the 0-28, steadily decreased in the next few years until only the 00-21 was left.

LEFT: Not all of the changes at Martin were as easy to notice as longer necks and shorter bodies. This 1935 catalog illustration shows the neck reinforcement first used in August 1934. Martin added the T-bar when it switched to modern T-shaped frets, partly because it could no longer rely on the wedging action of the solid "bar stock" frets to keep necks straight under tension. Most guitar manufacturers had been using T-frets since before 1900. Martin necks were made slightly narrower in 1939, resulting in the 1 11/16-inch width at the nut that we're used to today.

Eventually the letter S came to be consistently used to indicate the old 12-fret-style guitar, and if S had been used only to designate "standard," the code would have been fairly easy to understand. Unfortunately, what S really meant at this time was "Special," a catchall term that could mean almost anything. So a "D-28S" might mean a 12-fret model, but it could also indicate a regular 14-fret D-28 with a special wide fretboard, or that the owner's initials were inlaid at the 12th fret.

This period, 1930 to 1945, is known as Martin's Golden Age, when the most highly valued—and

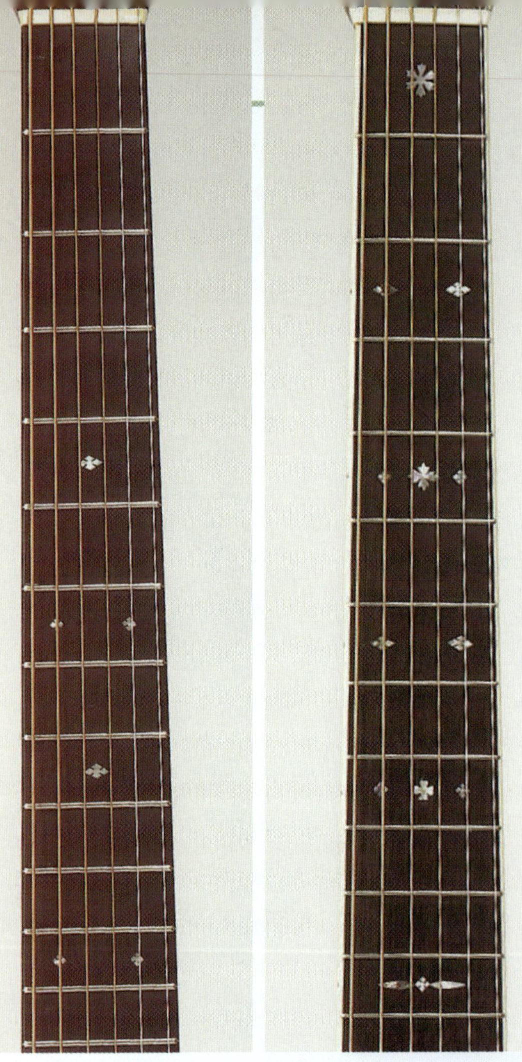

ABOVE: Martin changed the necks and bodies of old standards to create its new flat-top models but left the binding and neck inlays the same. Style 28 *(left)* got more of the delicate "diamonds and squares" fretboard inlays that had first appeared around 1900, while OM and later 000 Style 45 models *(right)* also displayed the snowflake inlay pattern of the past. Only the D-45 got inlays in the modern style. *(Photo of Style 28 © Mac Yasuda Enterprises; photo of Style 45 from Hank Risan.)*

RIGHT: Beginning in late 1933 Martin borrowed the peghead lettering of its arch-tops to modernize the style 45s. A few years later they borrowed the arch-tops' hexagon fretboard inlays as well for the D-45 only, perhaps starting with this one from 1938. The sunburst top and celluloid fretboard stripes of the F-9 are fitting additions to the D-45 on the left, and together with the 1937 F-9 these two represent the top-of-the-line for both Martin's arch-top and flat-top models in the late 1930s and early 1940s. The hexagon inlays have become one of the most recognizable features of the modern Martin flat-top, but the celluloid neck stripes disappeared with the arch-tops in 1942. *(Photo from Hank Risan.)*

some say the best-sounding—guitars were made. It could also be called the Decade of Chaos at Martin, as the company was making both long-neck and short-neck guitars, with either wide fretboards or narrow, with or without pick guards, for either gut or steel strings, often all with the same model designation. Martin also offered three sizes of arch-top models with either f-holes (FH in the factory ledger) or round soundholes, and four-string guitars of two neck lengths in both flat-top and arch-top versions. Throw in two types of mandolins in a dozen different styles, plus an amazing array of ukuleles, tiples, and taropatches; it's a wonder the shop foremen didn't go mad keeping production running smoothly.

By the early 1940s, however, the model code confusion resulting from the transition from gut strings to steel, and the evolution from 12-fret to 14-fret styles, was for the most part resolved. The 00-21 would soon be the sole surviving stock model in the old style, with everything else getting the new body shape and a 14-fret neck. As the arch-top Martins and pearl-bordered models disappeared, so did many of the special orders. The only addition during this period was the 0-15, which appeared in 1940. This all-mahogany model was an even plainer version of Style 17.

Models made for gut strings, given the G suffix, were an odd case of mistaken identity. Beginning in the late 1930s, the 00-18G and 00-28G were given wide, 12-fret necks on the shortened body designed a few years earlier to accommodate the long, 14-fret neck. Fan bracing and a Spanish bridge did little to make these hybrids acceptable to classical guitarists.

Why Martin continued to make the 00-21 as a 12-fret model for steel strings, but combined the new body with the old neck length in producing a model for gut strings, is anybody's guess. It was as if the company had forgotten, in less than a decade, how to make the very guitars that the founder had invented a century earlier. Martin's ungainly combination wasn't corrected until 1962, when the company's classic guitars were given the more elegant rounded shape of the old standard models.

D-45

DREADNAUGHT ORCHESTRA MODEL

THE selected rosewood and spruce used in this guitar, beautifully inlaid on all borders with mother-of-pearl and bound with ivoroid, give it the handsome appearance and the superior tone that professional players need. Easy fingering is assured by the thin hand-shaped neck and the oval ebony fingerboard. Gold-plated tuning machines, enclosed style.

PRICE
No. D-45 Dreadnaught $200.00

The fine spruce top, with its unique graduated bracing, gives Martin Tone the purity and power that players admire.

[8]

00-18G

CLASSIC MODEL

GUT and silk strings, classical style, very thin wood and light bracing, wide neck, flat fingerboard and loop bridge give this new model definite Spanish character in tone and in appearance. *Made for gut and silk strings only; not suitable for steel strings.*

STYLE 18G. Mahogany body and neck, spruce top, ebony fingerboard with white side-dots, wide frets, hand-polished lacquer finish.

PRICE
No. 00-18G Grand Concert $50.00

STYLE 28G. The same model in rosewood, with ivoroid bindings and more inlay; finer tone for solo playing.

PRICE
No. 00-28G Grand Concert $85.00

[9]

ABOVE: Ah, the cheap high of 20/20 hindsight! If Grandpa had purchased the D-45 at left in 1939, and kept it for you, you'd be rolling in six-figure clover today. Unless, of course, you decided to keep the booming guitar, in which case you'd be investing in a climate-controlled safe to keep it in. But if Gramps was the more cultured sort who went for gut strings and austere trim, you would barely be able to trade his $85 1939 00-28G for a new D-28 today. It takes more than a 1930s serial number and Brazilian rosewood to make a Martin guitar valuable.

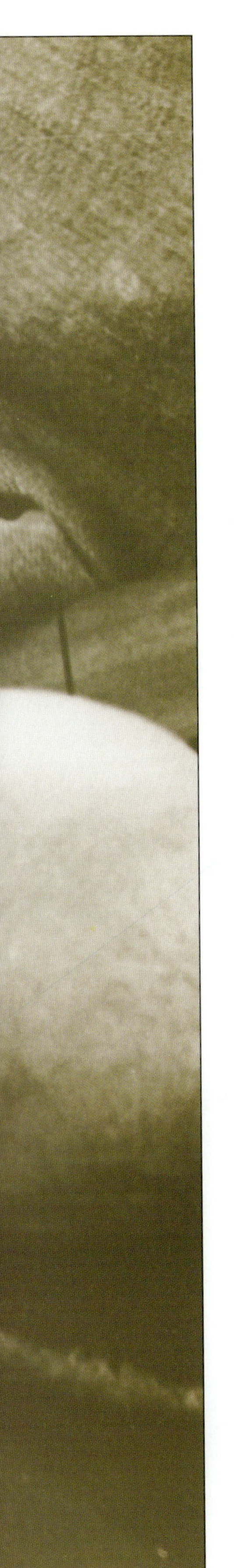

A Bold CONSERVATISM

1946–1969

During World War II and the years immediately following, Martin condensed its line, offering fewer instruments than at any time since 1915. In fact, the company introduced virtually no new instruments for two decades.

C. F. Martin & Company was essentially echoing what it had done nearly a century before. By the late 1840s, C. F. Martin Sr. had transformed the European guitar into a distinctly American guitar, with his X-brace and plainer, sturdier designs. Then he let his creative urges rest and left it to America to figure out what to do with its new guitar.

In the late 1940s, C. F. Martin III, often called Frederick, followed suit. His father, Frank Henry Martin, had introduced the Dreadnought models, the 14-fret neck, the tenor guitar, and other innovations during his long years helming the company. In 1945 Frank Henry turned the presidency over to Frederick, who was then 50 years old, and Frederick looked to trimming rather than new growth. Frederick didn't have to reinvigorate the catalog, since musicians were finding a sufficient number of new things to do with the guitars the

LEFT: The decorative details changed in the years following World War II, but the way Martin guitars were made remained much the same. *(Photo courtesy of John Rowe Photography, Fort Lauderdale, Florida.)*

RIGHT: Frank Henry Martin, shown with his wife, Jennie, successfully led his company through the Great Depression and into Martin's Golden Era. He retired in 1947 and died a year later. *(Photo courtesy of C. F. Martin & Company.)*

ORCHESTRA MODEL

Mahogany body, finished dark, with natural color spruce top. Edges bound with dark plastic; sound hole and top border inlaid with black and white lines. Mahogany neck with steel T-bar, rosewood fingerboard and bridge. Pearl position dots and white side dots. Nickel-plated tuning machines, single unit all-metal type, polished lacquer finish.

0-18—Concert $105
00-18—Grand Concert $115
000-18—Auditorium $135

D-28

DREADNAUGHT MODEL

This is the famous "Dreadnaught" guitar originated by Martin. The extra wide and deep body produces a tone of great power and smoothness, especially fine for radio or television work.

D-28—Rosewood body, spruce top, ivoroid edges, mahogany neck with steel T-bar, ebony fingerboard and bridge, wide frets, ivory nut and saddle, highly polished.

D-28 Dreadnaught $250

D-21—The same model with dark bindings, plainer inlays, rosewood fingerboard and bridge, black pins.

D-21 Dreadnaught $200

D-18—Same size, mahogany body, spruce top, mahogany neck with steel T-bar, rosewood fingerboard and bridge.

D-18 Dreadnaught $155

TENOR MODEL

These four-string tenor guitars have the regular 23-inch scale for A-D-G-C tuning; otherwise they are like the corresponding six-string models. All have the full-size guitar bodies except the 5-15T which is 11¼ inches wide.

5-15T—¾ Size .... $ 65
0-17T—Concert .... $ 80
0-18T—Concert $100

THREE-QUARTER MODEL

Three-quarter size dark-finished mahogany body with natural-finish spruce top. Mahogany neck, rosewood fingerboard, black and white inlays on the front edge and soundhole. Pearl position dots, nickel-plated machine heads, polished lacquer finish.

5-18—¾ Size $90

5-18

0-18

Martin

00-18G

CLASSIC MODEL

Nylon strings, very thin wood and light bracing, wide neck, flat fingerboard and loop bridge give this model definite Spanish character in tone and in appearance. Made for gut or nylon strings only.

00-18G—Mahogany body and neck, spruce top, rosewood fingerboard with white side-dots, wide frets, polished lacquer finish.

00-18G Grand Concert $130

00-28G—The same model in rosewood with ebony fingerboard and bridge and more inlay; finer tone for solo playing.

00-28G Grand Concert $215

000-28

ORCHESTRA MODEL

Rosewood body bound with ivoroid, bordered and inlaid with black and white marqueterie. Fine vertical grain spruce top, finished natural color. Ebony fingerboard, well rounded, with hard nickel-silver frets wide and low, mahogany neck with steel T-bar. Tortoise-shell plastic pick-guard, polished lacquer finish.

000-28—Auditorium $220

The same model with dark bindings, plainer inlay, rosewood fingerboard and bridge, and black pins.

000-21—Auditorium $180

ORCHESTRA MODEL SIZES

Size No.	0	00	000	D
Total Length	38⅜	38⅝	39⅜	40¼
Body Length	18[illegible]	18⅞	19⅜	20
Body Width	13½	14[illegible]	15	15⅝
Body Depth	4¼	4⅛	4⅛	4⅞

All Martin Guitars have solid mahogany necks hand-shaped and fitted to the body in a deep dove-tail joint. Dreadnaught and Orchestra Models have a steel T-bar reinforcement in the neck under the fingerboard. All necks are guaranteed not to warp.

ORCHESTRA MODEL

Dark mahogany body and top, black and white lines inlaid around sound hole. Mahogany neck re-inforced with steel T-bar. Rosewood fingerboard, well rounded for easy fingering, wide nickel-silver frets, white position dots. Polished lacquer finish, dark mahogany color. Nickel-plated tuning machines, single-unit style.

00-17—Grand Concert $95

The same model but with clear semi-gloss lacquer finish. Light natural color.

0-15—Concert $80

00-17

ABOVE: There were lots of mahogany instruments in Martin's late 1940s and 1950s catalogs, but not much else. Except for a rosewood classical guitar and a tiple, the 000-21, 000-28, D-28, and D-21 (added in 1955) were all that remained of the company's majestic lineup of rosewood guitars, which had enticed musicians in the 1930s. The 00-21, also rosewood and the only 12-fret model for steel strings, wasn't even shown in the late-1950s catalogs, but a few were still made each year.

company was already making. Along with country musicians, bluegrass, folk, and rock and roll musicians all took to Martins just the way they were.

Frederick's pruning of the company line and reluctance to create new products could have been seen as conservatism, but in so doing he gambled all of the company's chips on one thing: tone. Martin's biggest competitor, Gibson, was nothing if not diverse. Along with making very good-sounding flat-tops, their designers knew how to appeal to a player's eye, with instruments like the curvaceous J-200. But the company also made arch-tops, electric guitars, steel guitars, amplifiers, banjos, and sundry instruments, including marketing a primeval tube-powered synthesizer called the Clavioline. Meanwhile, on the West Coast, Leo Fender had launched his own little revolution in amplified sound that would soon yield jet age–shaped, metal flake–painted electric guitars that roared like hot rods.

And while all of this innovation was bubbling around, Martin made these plain wooden boxes, from which a tone emerged that was like no other.

The Ships of the Line

Because of cutbacks during World War II, Martin's arch-tops were gone, and soon forgotten. But the company's elegant flagship, the D-45, was also missing in action. The pearl inlay of Martin's upper-line models, once understated, was now nonexistent. Much of the skilled workforce had been drawn off by the war, and afterward the company simply didn't bother resuming its inlays, so it was good-bye to the Style 45, as well as to the less-laden Styles 40 and 42. By default, the Style 28 became Martin's fanciest model, and there was now very little that was fancy about it, since it had exited the war minus its endearing herringbone trim. Furthermore, its diamond and square-shaped fingerboard inlays—along with Style 21's—had been replaced with simple dots in 1944.

The guitar innards also became more simplified

LEFT: Not many people remember Derry Falligant today, and that's not a name you'd be likely to forget if you had ever heard it. Derry had excellent taste in guitars, as evidenced here where he is holding a 000-28 from sometime between very late 1944 and 1946, the last years Martin used herringbone on Style 28 models. The delicate diamond and square fretboard inlays had already been phased out in favor of simple dots, which, thanks to the convenience of the drill bit, were much easier to install. Even pearl dots didn't escape Martin's scrutiny, and each one was graded with the best side marked for the "up" position. *(Photo from the Frank Driggs Collection.)*

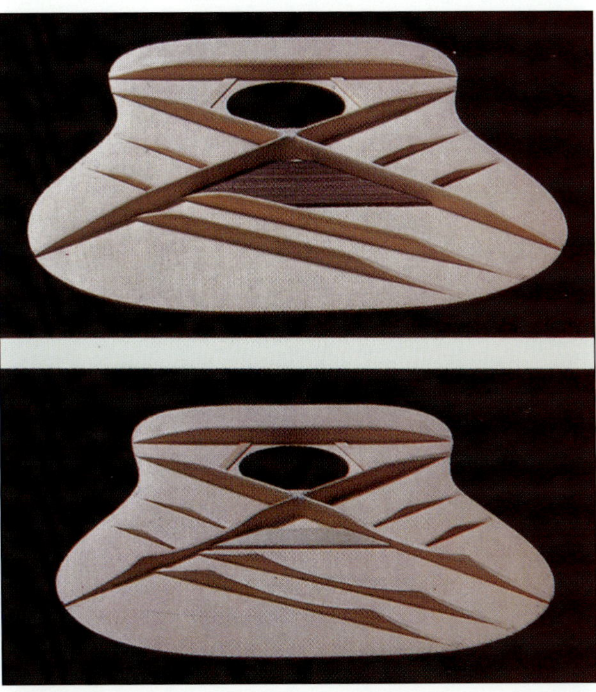

ABOVE: *Scalloped braces* is a phrase heard continually today in acoustic guitar advertising—the equivalent of "turbocharged" or "fuel-injected" in the automotive industry. The scallops, shown in the lower photo, simply take some of the stiffness out of the braces, allowing the top to vibrate more freely. Too bad guitar bracing is so anti-tech—the scooped-out sections in four of the braces underneath a pre–1945 Martin guitar top hardly seem to warrant all the fuss. Many modern manufacturers exaggerate the peaks and hollows until the top bracing looks like a series of suspension bridges. (*Photo courtesy of C. F. Martin & Company.*)

that year. Many players had begun using heavier strings, originally intended for arch-tops, to get even more volume out of their flat-tops. In the 1930s Martin had begun using a metal T-rod to strengthen the neck and, inside the body, shifted the X-brace closer to the bridge to help offset the additional strain that the string tension put on the top. (On most models this had been accomplished by 1935, with the Dreadnoughts following by 1939.) Then in late 1944, Martin halted its practice of carving scallops in its braces, as it had previously done to enhance the top's vibration characteristics. The resulting instrument held up better to the heavier strings, saved the company time and labor, and assured that future generations of collectors would have "scalloped braces" on the brain.

Along with the rosewood-backed 28s and 21s, the only other styles offered were the mahogany-backed 18 and the all-mahogany Styles 17 and 15. Those styles were each available only in select sizes. The simplification may have been Martin's way of trying to keep up with demand. Frederick later claimed that the low output during the war (no doubt coupled with the relative prosperity after it) created a demand for guitars that the company couldn't fill. Sales climbed steadily after the war until peaking at 7,000 guitars a year in 1955. (The company's biggest prewar total had been some 6,000 guitars sold in 1927, though it was selling oodles of ukes at the time.) The company's sales were often limited by the number of instruments it was able to produce, and guitars were sometimes back-ordered for two years.

ABOVE: The Martin shop crew expanded into the 1950s. The workers huddle between new and old factory additions one chilly afternoon in the early 1950s. *(Photo courtesy of C. F. Martin & Company.)*

BELOW: Frederick Martin was quite frugal, as this practical copper tube proved; it was fashioned to gain another few days from the common pencil.

Stairs and Steam

Frank Henry Martin died on April 9, 1948, at the age of 81. Born in the aftermath of a war fought with horse, saber, and cannon, he lived to see wars waged with Flying Fortresses and atom bombs. His own company had grown in his lifetime from a one-room operation worked entirely by hand to a small factory employing steam engines, gasoline-powered ones, and finally electric machinery.

But the C. F. Martin & Company his son Frederick inherited still had more in common with the way it had been in the 1800s than it did with most modern businesses, which were becoming mills of mass production in which a gray corporate structure prevailed.

Despite the factory expansions during the ukulele boom, the Martin company remained a building housing individual craftsmen, rather than an assembly machine with human parts. A completed guitar body would often be the work of a single craftsman. Employees knew the company owner because he was on the shop floor every day, and Frederick tended to make his presence known.

"You talk to some of the old-timers and you'll hear he was a stern taskmaster," C. F. "Chris" Martin IV says of his grandfather. "He struck me when I was young as someone who was very stern, the kind of guy where when he walked by, you held your breath and hoped he didn't notice you. He had this demeanor. And it wasn't until his 80s and 90s that he became this wonderful, old, grandfatherly 'Mr. Martin' that everybody remembers now."

Frederick lived a frugal life, and he expected a similar standard from his employees. One of the

ABOVE: The old North Street factory was bulging at the seams as Martin struggled to keep up with demand in the 1950s and early 1960s. Note the drying racks for wood, suspended from the ceiling, and the ample supply of natural light from the huge windows. Guitar players would sometimes wait up to two years for a D-28 like the ones on the cart. (*Photo courtesy of C. F. Martin & Company.*)

RIGHT: Except for the ill-fated electric models of 1959, the D-21 was Martin's sole addition to its catalogs in the 1950s. As with other Style 21 models, it looked just like a D-18 except for the 28-style dot pattern on the fingerboard. Viewed from the back, however, it would be hard to miss the Brazilian rosewood and checkered-pattern backstrip that Style 21 shares with the more expensive Style 28. (*Photo © Mac Yasuda Enterprises.*)

more notorious tools required at all Martin workbenches was a copper tube to hold pencils, so workers could use them down to the very nub.

Chris recalls, "He also would go around and look in your wastebasket, and if he found sandpaper that wasn't totally utilized, he'd take it out, put it on your bench, and in the morning show you that there was some sand left on it."

While demanding, he must also have been fair, because everyone at Martin there long enough to remember him speaks of him with near-universal reverence.

"He set a high standard, by example," Chris says. "He had a sense of obligation, that you don't just take—you give and take. And he gave more than he took in many respects. He very rarely took a vacation, was probably a workaholic, and also was incredibly involved in the community. He started the

Lions Club in Nazareth; helped found the YMCA; was on the bank board, the hospital board, and the library board; and helped to fund the library. His role model in life was Woodrow Wilson. He called himself a Wilsonian Democrat. He was a businessman who really did believe in creating a safety net for the disenfranchised."

We shaped the braces for the backs, then we'd glue the back on. We used hot animal [hide] glue. We had steam heat there, and we'd actually stand the wood on the radiator and heat it before putting the glue on because with hot animal glue, if you put that on while the wood is cold, it won't stick as well.

—Martin craftsman Harold Weiss

Frederick unabashedly loved the guitars that his company made, but those who knew him said that that wasn't the most important thing to him. "I don't think creating a profit was how he measured things either," says Dick Boak, Martin director of artist relations, who was friends with Frederick in his later years. "For him, the measure of success was in all the people here he was able to provide employment for. He created a sense of family."

Many on the shop floor were family, since new generations had followed their fathers or uncles into the factory. It was an insular group, and up into the 1980s it wasn't unusual to hear the Germanic strains of Pennsylvania Dutch spoken on the shop floor.

Craftsman Harold Weiss started at Martin in 1956, and in 1997 is still there. "Sure I'm proud of the work I've done," he says. "When you buy a Martin, you're buying a person's work and skill. It's not like going out and buying something that's just stamped out."

At the old North Street factory, Weiss says, a body would often be assembled by just one craftsman: "I worked on the third floor. We'd glue the two pieces of the top together, held in place on the paddle wheel [a piece of machinery used at Martin since at least the 1920s and still in use today]. We'd glue the rims together, then we had to plane them down to a right angle, all using hand tools. We shaped the braces for the backs, then we'd glue the back on. We used hot animal [hide] glue. We had steam heat there, and we'd actually stand the wood on the radiator and heat it before putting the glue on because with hot animal glue, if you put that on while the wood is cold, it won't stick as well."

After putting the back on, Weiss explained, "We cleaned and plugged on the inside, shaped the braces on the tops, and then glued the top on. It was the most complete cabinetmaking job there.

"The first floor was the heavy machinery, where they'd get the lumber in. On the second floor, back toward the Green Street side, that was the machine room. They cut the wood out into rough shape. Then it would dry in the attic for a while, then we'd bring it down to dry more in racks above us. Once we put the tops and backs on, we had to carry them down a rampway to where they frazed them—put the binding on—and then back up."

Whomp and Twang

While Frederick was busy micromanaging his company's pencil consumption, things were changing in the outside world.

The once-regional interest in country music was now nationwide. During the war, many people migrated from the southern states to defense jobs in California and the Northeast. Military men returning from the war also often resettled in

LEFT: George Jones is known as a singer, not a guitarist; but since the 1950s, he has rarely appeared without a Martin Dreadnought. Oversize pick guards were the height of fashion in country music for many years, even for singers who didn't scratch the top. *(Album cover courtesy of Sony Music Entertainment.)*

states where they'd been stationed. Along with radio, television shows in many cities were broadcasting country music, which was no longer such a corn-fed commodity. Responding to its increasingly urban audience, the music now boasted players to equal a jazz band's in technique and style.

Yet no matter how advanced the music got—and Nashville was larding string sections into its recordings by the late 1950s—people still wanted to think of their country singers as troubadours, and an acoustic guitar seemed a requisite part of the package.

The cowboy stars of the 1930s and 1940s had helped to shape the notion of the country singer and his guitar forming a self-sufficient unit, with a band merely in tow. That notion was cemented by the phenomenal success and influence of Hank Williams. Most of his records featured the chug of his strummed Martin Dreadnought. (Williams chiefly played a post-war D-28, although a D-45 now belonging to Marty Stuart and a herringbone D-28 are also believed to have been owned by him.) Beginning in 1947 Williams wrote and recorded some 100 songs before turning blue in the back of a white Cadillac

ABOVE: Country singers have come and gone, but none had as great an impact on the world's image of country music as Hank Williams. Through all the recordings of his tragically short life, including the enduring classics he wrote such as "Cold, Cold, Heart" and "I'm So Lonesome I Could Cry," Hank played a steady rhythm guitar part. It wasn't flashy guitar playing—even by Jimmie Rodgers's modest standards—but it did the job. Though he sometimes played a Gibson, Hank usually got the job done with a Martin D-28. *(Album cover from Henry Schofield, Tim Jones ©/Courtesy Polygram Records.)*

BELOW: Bill Monroe set both the pace and the style of early bluegrass, and a Martin Dreadnought was the rhythm guitar for every one of his many guitar players. The list reads like a Who's Who of early bluegrass—Clyde Moody, Lester Flatt, Jimmy Martin, and Bill's son, James Monroe. *(Album cover courtesy of MCA Records.)*

on New Year's Day, 1953. The country stars who followed him may have been more preened and less pilled, but they still wanted to do things the way ol' Hank had done 'em.

Besides, the guitar was the driving force in most country songs. The Grand Ole Opry allowed performers on its stage to wear eye-stabbingly garish suits, but it didn't allow drums. So it often fell to the singer's guitar to provide the rhythm, and the Martin guitar was already proven in that regard. While doubtless having a fine regard for a Martin's subtlety of tone, musicians also began to speak of its "whomp," of the way it was loud and percussive enough to be picked up on their vocal mike and reach a crowd.

Guitar collector Mac Yasuda—a frequent Opry performer in the 1990s—owns the world's largest collections of prewar D-45s *and* vintage Gibson J-200s (Martin's main cowboy competition). He maintains, "When you want to look good, you play a J-200. When you want to sound good and be heard, you play a Martin."

Martin's reputation among players was such that it did little to advertise in the 1950s. Hopelessly back-ordered much of the time, Martin wouldn't have known what to do with more business. Many mid-1950s country magazines had full-page Gibson and Gretsch ads but none from Martin, yet in those same magazines nearly every performer pictured with a flat-top had a Martin.

LEFT: Like Flatt and Scruggs before him, Jimmy Martin set out on his own after learning the ropes in Bill Monroe's band. Jimmy's powerful bass runs on his mid-'40s herringbone D-28 helped establish the Martin Dreadnought legend. *(Album cover courtesy of MCA Records.)*

New Tradition

While the Nashville crowd was using Martins to link its changing sound to the past, another breed of country musicians was using the guitars to exalt the past in new ways. The all-acoustic strains of bluegrass music sprang from old fiddle tunes and ballads, such as those that had comprised the Grand Ole Opry's earliest offerings.

The fiddle, banjo, and mandolin in bluegrass all sound very bright (some would say "piercing" is too kind), and the high-pitched vocals often take the tonal balance to a canine's pain threshold. The string bass—a luxury many groups couldn't afford—is the foundation, but that still leaves a bluegrass band without the ground floor. The Dreadnought was called on to do just the job it had been designed for: providing enough bass to balance the other instruments.

ABOVE RIGHT: Every young guitar picker who listened to bluegrass in the 1950s and 1960s knew that Red Smiley played a D-45. His booming bass runs and percussive chord "whomp" were easy to hear, even when competing with Don Reno's wild five-string banjo. Maybe Red could have made a D-28 sound just as impressive, but it was more enchanting to credit that acoustic power to the legendary prewar D-45. *(Album cover courtesy of Rebel Records, Roanoke, Virginia.)*

RIGHT: Doc Watson combined both hot flatpicking and dazzling "Travis picking" on his first album for Vanguard in 1961. The sound of his old D-18, translated through modern recording technology far superior to that of a few years earlier, was a revelation to an entire generation of baby boomer guitarists, who then set their sights on a Martin Dreadnought. But by the late 1960s, Martin's conservative no-endorsements policy allowed the new J. W. Gallagher & Son guitar company to gain invaluable exposure when it provided Watson with a guitar, and he has remained true to Gallagher ever since. *(Album cover courtesy of Vanguard Records, a Welk Music Group Company.)*

ABOVE: Carter Stanley's D-28 shows a custom job that was quite common in the 1960s: Leave the body alone but put binding and D-45–style pearl on the neck, resulting in a lot of flash for little money. *(Album cover courtesy of Starday-King Records.)*

ABOVE: Clarence White and brother Roland, on mandolin, were the core of the Kentucky Colonels in the late 1950s and early 1960s. Clarence used a heavy metal pick, which shredded the soundhole on his 1935 D-28. The repair enlarged the soundhole and resulted in the unique (or bizarre) Style D-28, large-soundhole guitars that became best-sellers for some of Martin's competitors. *(Album cover © Phil Melnick/Courtesy Capitol/Nashville.)*

Guitarists quickly learned that a rosewood Martin Dreadnought gave them a ground floor with room to spare. Bluegrass progenitor Bill Monroe's revolving cavalcade of guitarists played D-28s, including Lester Flatt and Jimmy Martin, who went on to broaden the field with their own bands. (Curiously, when Monroe first appeared at the Opry in 1939, it wasn't his mandolin he was playing but a D-28.)

Carter Stanley of the Stanley Brothers and Jim McReynolds of Jim and Jesse also chose the D-28. Red Smiley's bass runs, played on his legendary D-45, probably did more to create the early mythology surrounding that rare model than anyone else, and the Reno and Smiley recordings still bear testament to the unplugged wattage of an early Martin Dreadnought and a strong right hand. Though Gibson and Chicago's Larson Brothers made instruments that offered respectable competition, all of the notable bluegrass guitarists but one played Martins. The sole holdout was Bea Lilly of the Lilly Brothers, who often played a guitar he'd made himself—hardly a defection from the ranks.

Not until the 1970s did Martin's grip on bluegrass weaken, but smaller guitar companies didn't exactly storm the bluegrass fortress. Instead they sneaked in, paying Martin the ultimate compliment by building rosewood Dreadnoughts that looked exactly like a prewar D-28. Thanks to recent reissues of its early Dreadnoughts, Martin has won back many who drifted from the fold, and today the company still dominates the bluegrass stage with old Dreadnoughts and new alike.

Elvis and the D-18

Put down that damn guitar. It's going to be the ruination of you.

—Elvis Presley's boss at Memphis's Crown Electric, where Elvis drove a truck in 1954

Within a year of that dire pronouncement, Elvis Presley had become a regional sensation with his early recordings for Sun Records. His exuberant melding of Black blues and country music was most Americans' first taste of rock and roll music,

LEFT: Elvis Presley backstage with Texas Bill Strength, August 1955. As an aspiring country singer, Elvis was still embraced by Webb Pierce, Red Sovine, and others who shared the stage with him the night this photo was taken in Memphis. Within a year or two, however, Elvis and other rock and rollers elbowed country artists off the charts. His gyrations on stage and the screaming of female fans hid the fact that Elvis was a solidly effective rhythm guitarist in his early days. Since he was moving all over his body and all over the stage, he seemed to pay little attention to playing his guitar. Yet the sparse band of Elvis's pre–military-and-movies career made his rhythm playing a necessity, and pulsing hammer-ons and thumping on damped strings were an essential part of the beat that changed American music. Elvis used Martins almost exclusively in the 1950s, either a 1942 D-18 or the 1950s D-28 (shown here) encased in a tooled leather cover. *(Photo © EPE.)*

RIGHT: Merle Haggard's devotion to Jimmie Rodgers is reflected in his guitar choice shown here—a 00-21 with his name added in pearl to the fretboard. As soon as the Martin Custom Shop was a reality, Merle ordered 12-fret 000-45 models like the "Blue Yodel" original. He also recorded an excellent tribute to Jimmie Rodgers around the time this photo was taken, the album titled *Same Train, a Different Time.* *(Photo from the Frank Driggs Collection.)*

ABOVE: The Dillards brought hip humor to bluegrass, something the older groups sorely lacked. Here they show the traditional choice in instruments for a bluegrass band; Gibson wins the banjo and mandolin positions, but lead singer Rodney Dillard uses a D-28. *(Photo from the Frank Driggs Collection.)*

and it started a rhythmic revolution. It's worth noting that on the record that started it all, Elvis's reworking of Arthur "Big Boy" Crudup's "That's All Right," there weren't even any drums, just Elvis's pulsing rhythm guitar part on the D-18.

It wasn't long before Frank Sinatra was dismissing rock as "a rancid aphrodisiac." Others derided it as degrading jungle music, a communist plot, or, in Stan Freberg's immortal words, a "nasal obstruction." Whatever it was, rock and roll wouldn't go away.

Once Presley's musical career started looking as if it might work out better than driving a truck, he bought his used 1940s D-18. According to a story in the April 1955 *Country and Western Jamboree,* he purchased this guitar from a Memphis dealer, who took as partial trade the budget guitar Elvis had owned since he was 11 years old. The dealer then tossed the old guitar in the trash as Elvis was leaving.

For all of his early performing career, Elvis played either the D-18—which soon read ELVIS in gold stick-on mailbox lettering on the face—or a D-28, which he had corseted in tooled leather.

His Sun label mate Johnny Cash also got quite a rhythmic racket out of a Dreadnought. But of the post-Elvis rockers, it was TV star Ricky Nelson who got Martin the most exposure, often playing a Dreadnought on the nationally broadcast *Ozzie and Harriet* show. Nelson eventually had his Martin garbed in tone-killing leather as well.

BELOW: Ask a Hawaiian who is at the heart of the islands' music, and you'll hear about Gabby Pahinui. The late master of the slack-key guitar created some of the most inviting, peaceful, and playful music found on the globe. This distinctly Hawaiian style seemed suited to Martins, and Gabby favored several Martin models throughout his life.

More Bother from the Islands

Demand for Martins took another jump in the late 1950s when a couple of guys from Hawaii got together with a guy from California with the intent of playing music from yet another sunny clime, the island of Jamaica; hence their name, the Kingston Trio. Somehow this plan got sidetracked when they recorded an old North Carolina murder ballad: It became a hit in Salt Lake City, and the folk music boom was born.

Up to that point, America had had a love/hate

relationship with folk music. It loved the old-time revival sound of voices joining in plain harmony, as well as the image of the hard-traveled common man raising his voice in song. But listeners got a little uneasy about what those voices were telling them.

From the 1930s through the 1950s, the Dustbowl-bred Woody Guthrie was something of an American institution. His "This Land Is Your Land" became a surrogate national anthem, but people often left out the disquieting later verses that railed against private property and poverty. (Guthrie's most famous ax, a Gibson, bore a sticker reading, "This machine kills fascists." He later had a Martin, which only killed Gibsons.)

In 1949 Guthrie's friend Pete Seeger formed the Weavers, and in the early 1950s the group had national hits with such tunes as "On Top of Old Smokey," "So Long, It's Been Good to Know You," and Leadbelly's

(continued on page 172)

ABOVE: Though they often had fun in concert, the Weavers made a point of looking glum for photographers. Fred Hellerman is holding an early 1950s 00-28G Martin, intended for nylon strings, though he strung his with silk-and-steel strings. Predictably, the bridge kept pulling off under the excess tension, and it had to be bolted to the face. Though the top is seriously warped, the guitar is still functional, making it a truly exceptional 00-28G. *(Album cover courtesy of Vanguard Records, a Welk Music Group Company.)*

LEFT: Woody Guthrie, the folk singer and songwriter of the people if there ever was one, played the people's Martin, the 0-15. First offered in 1940, the 0-15 was the least expensive Martin guitar for over 20 years and brought Martin quality to folks who couldn't afford the herringbone or pearl models that made the company famous. *(Photo from the Frank Driggs Collection.)*

The Kingston Trio

Reluctant Folkies

There have been but a few musicians as consistently associated with Martin guitars as the Kingston Trio. From their first album cover in 1958 to their concert appearances today, they've been toting Martins. That loyalty was commemorated in 1997 by the company's issuance of a limited-edition Kingston Trio series D-28, 0-18T tenor guitar, and five-string banjo (made for Martin by Deering Banjo Company).

"Martin instruments have been very good to us, and in turn we've stayed true to them," says guitarist Bob Shane. "I've had maybe 50 Martins over the years. I think it's the best-sounding guitar for the stage for the kind of music we do. I play rhythm guitar, and my favorite instrument on-stage is the D-28. It's got a sound that's not too deep and not too high, but really full. And they make such good-quality guitars, consistently, that if an airline breaks one, you can get it replaced with exactly the same thing. It's that continuity that really makes a difference to a professional."

Shane and fellow founding members Nick Reynolds and Dave Guard hadn't exactly been planning on continuity or being professionals when they started. Shane and banjoist Guard were high school friends from Hawaii who met up with tenor guitarist Reynolds while all were in college in Palo Alto, California. They sang for fun and got pretty good at it. In 1958 Phyllis Diller had to cancel a San Francisco club engagement, and the Kingston Trio got the last-minute gig filling in for her. A Capitol Records exec heard them that night, signed them, and the rest is history, though a rather skewed history.

Not very long after "Tom Dooley" put folk music at the top of the charts, it became hip to hate the trio, with purist folk fans deriding their untroubled music. Shane thought the whole argument ridiculous.

"To call the Kingston Trio folk singers was kind of stupid in the first place," he says. "We never called ourselves folk singers. We started off playing calypso music, and we took our name from Kingston, Jamaica, and to this day not one of us has ever been there. We did folk-oriented material, but we did it amid all kinds of other stuff. But they didn't know what to call us with our instruments, so Capitol Records called us folk singers and gave us credit for starting this whole boom. And we got a Grammy in the country cate-

LEFT: The Kingston Trio is widely credited with bringing the folk revival into the mainstream of American popular music. With Bob Shane on D-28 and Nick Reynolds playing an 0-18T, the group also brought Martin envy to a bigger and more affluent audience than the company had ever been able to reach in the past. (*Photo courtesy of the Kingston Trio.*)

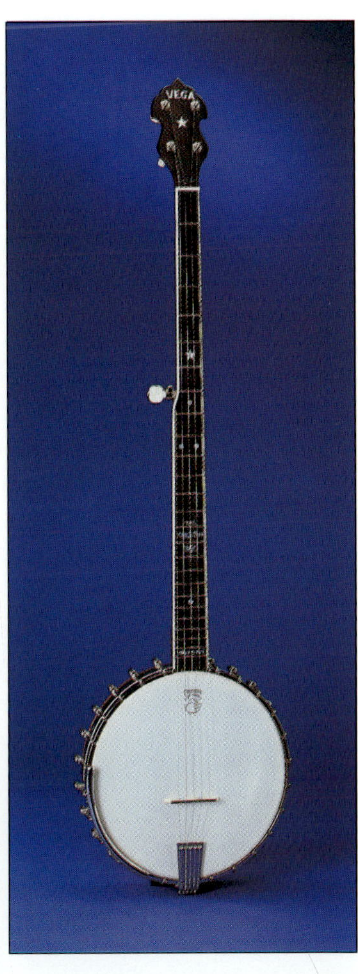

LEFT: Martin celebrated the Kingston Trio's 40th anniversary with a limited edition of 40 sets of the three instruments associated with the group—a D-28, an 0-18T tenor guitar, and a long-neck Vega (the banjo was made by the Deering Banjo Company). (*Photos courtesy of C. F. Martin & Company.*)

gory. Whatever they wanted to call us, that was fine as long as they paid us, too. We were all business majors in college."

Shane's musical career started with a koa wood ukulele (a love of that wood led him to custom-order in the 1980s the first koa D-45 in Martin history), then he moved up to a Sears tenor guitar. In 1956 he was being billed as Hawaii's Elvis Presley. It was around then he met folk-blues–playing Martin devotee Josh White, in Hawaii for a club engagement.

"Josh White essentially taught me how to play the guitar," Shane says. "And he was the one who talked me into a Martin. I'd seen most of the Hawaiian guys playing them—Gabby Pahinui usually played a 00. Josh White said that they last the best, that they had the best sound after you've played them for a while, and that they're constructed so they would take more of a beating than a Gibson would.

"And if in some of our early pictures you see that I've got double pick guards on the guitar, Josh White told me to do that, too. He said, 'When you scratch up the top side too much, just put a pick guard over it,' so that's what I did."

Shane got his first D-28 new for $180 from Honolulu's Bergstrom Music in 1956. The D-28 has been his guitar of choice since then, though he has played D-45s and toured for three years straight with a koa D-37K2.

Though known for playing five-string banjo in the group, Dave Guard also played guitar and owned at least two Martins. One was a mid-'60s 12-fret 000-28; he had chosen the shape while taking a tour of the factory.

The Kingston Trio membership has varied over the years, with Shane being the only constant (Guard passed away in the early 1990s). At this writing Shane, Reynolds, and two-decade vet George Grove (who also plays Martins) continue to entertain audiences everywhere except, evidently, in Kingston.

"Goodnight, Irene." Those also were the years, though, that Senator Joseph McCarthy was alleging that a massive communist conspiracy was at work in the entertainment business, and that did not bode well for the largely leftist folk scene. Popular though the Weavers were, their record label dropped them. Seeger's politics had already gotten him blacklisted from television in 1950, and he wasn't to appear on network TV again for 17 years.

The Kingston Trio, however, was just three clean-cut college guys who liked to sing and strum. There wasn't a speck of topicality to their huge 1958 hit "Tom Dooley," a revamped century-old murder ballad about a genuine murderer named Tom Dula. The song hit the charts first in Salt Lake City, spread through the nation, and assured the Kingston Trio a series of hit albums all the way into the 1960s British Invasion. Within three years of the trio's advent, acoustic guitar sales had more than doubled nationally.

The Kingston Trio's Bob Shane played a D-28, and Nick Reynolds played an 0-18T tenor guitar, while Dave Guard played banjo. Sales of the 0-18T jumped from 50 in 1958 to 127 in 1959 and continued upward, peaking at 251 in 1962. (Martin also introduced the budget 0-15T in 1960, selling 476 of them in four years.) Martin's standard guitars didn't make a similar sales leap, likely because they were so far back-ordered that aspiring players bought other brands rather than wait.

The national interest in folk music was a boon both for the prefab collegiate folkies who followed in the Kingston Trio's wake and for folk and blues artists—such as Josh White—who had been playing for decades without major recognition. By the early 1960s, new young fans were flocking to folk music festivals where authenticity and obscurity were measures of excellence. And what could be more authentic than a guitar with a pedigree going back to 1833, or more obscure than a guitar you couldn't even find in stores, because there was a two-year wait to buy one?

LEFT: Burl Ives's impressive vocals and unthreatening choice of material helped bring polished versions of old folk songs to a wider audience in postwar America. He's playing a 00-17, probably warming up for his biggest hit, "Wayfaring Stranger." Ives also played a Martin Dreadnought. *(Photo from the Frank Driggs Collection.)*

LEFT AND BELOW: Josh White was one of the few blues artists who didn't slip into obscurity in the postwar years, and he was one of the first genuine bluesmen to tour the "college circuit" along with clean-cut acts like the Kingston Trio. A Martin diehard, he favored the old 12-fret style, here a late 1930s 00-42. The extra pick guards were an absolute necessity, and he wore out the tops on a succession of later 00-21 models in his long career. Though many other players used the 00-21, it became unofficially known as the Josh White model. *(Photo from the Frank Driggs Collection; album cover from David Caplan © 1956/Boosey & Hawkes.)*

MEANWHILE, BACK AT THE FORT

As if the demand for Martins caused by booms in country, bluegrass, rock, and folk music were not enough, the ukulele also made a comeback in the 1950s.

"When Arthur Godfrey went on TV with a ukulele, it opened the demand up again," current Martin company head Chris Martin says. "My grandfather told me Godfrey came to visit and was extremely arrogant. Godfrey said, 'I want to play the Martin ukulele. I will endorse it, and you will pay me this much money.' My grandfather told him that that's not the way we do business, and he reportedly stormed out, not believing that we wouldn't bow down before the great Arthur Godfrey." (Godfrey instead ended up endorsing Vega ukes.)

The Martin company was so busy keeping up with demand that it didn't have much impetus or time to develop new products. The first new guitar since before the war was the D-21, built in 1955; this guitar was only an even plainer variation upon the D-28. Another sign of the stagnation was that Martin used the same cover on its catalog from 1940 until the early 1960s, and after 1946 there weren't many changes on the inside, either.

The Martin company did make some custom models for Boston's E. U. Wurlitzer store, and the instruments would later play significant roles in Martin's own roster. Boston, with its many college campuses, was one of the centers of the folk music boom, and some players were requesting a bigger version of the 12-fret, longer-bodied 00-21 shape. (Alone in Martin's line, the slot-headed 00-21 had barely changed since the late 1800s.) These younger players may not even have known about Martin's 1930s 12-fret Dreadnoughts. In 1954 Martin began making reissues for Wurlitzer from the original side-shaping forms used in the 1930s that it had found in the attic. In 1962 it began stamping the guitars D-28SW, for Special Wurlitzer. (By late 1967 Martin had 12-fret Dreadnoughts back in its own catalog, as the D-18S, D-28S, and D-35S.)

ABOVE LEFT: Even as late as the early 1970s, Martin was still offering three sizes of ukulele. It may have been a far cry from Martin's lineup during the glory years of the uke in the mid-1920s, but it was still far more than any other manufacturer, and more than sales warranted. *(Photo courtesy of C. F Martin & Company.)*

LEFT: If I had a D-28.... Peter, Paul, and Mary brought a wide range of material to audiences of the 1960s folk revival, but their most enduring hit has been "Puff, the Magic Dragon," now a children's classic. Peter Yarrow was probably the first and most visible guitarist to use a "reissue" Martin Dreadnought, and his D-28SW caused many folky guitar nuts to ask: "What's that big funny-looking Martin with the short neck and slotted peghead?" *(Photo from the Frank Driggs Collection.)*

Electric Shocks

Sometime near the close of World War II, in Fullerton, California, Leo Fender had carved up a local musician's 000-18 and mounted one of his steel guitar pickups on it, resulting in—voilà!—an electric guitar, albeit an ugly one. Other companies had been amplifying acoustic guitars—usually arch-tops—since the 1930s. With its 1950s CF-100E and 1954's J-160E, Gibson made flat-tops that had an all-but-invisible pickup mounted inside the body at the end of the fingerboard, a stylish blend of traditional form and amped-up function.

When Martin grudgingly shuffled onto the bandwagon in 1959, its design was closer to Fender's brutalized Martin. The company essentially took 00s and Dreadnoughts, sawed holes in them, and mounted big chrome-plated (or gold on the D-28E) DeArmond pickups—of the variety Gretsch had just stopped using—on the face of the guitar. On the single-pickup 00, the unit jutted clumsily over the soundhole. The two-pickup Dreadnoughts had another of the hefty units mounted near the bridge, effectively killing the acoustic tone. Martin might as well have strapped dumbbells to the spruce tops.

ABOVE: After building a single prototype in 1958, Martin made just over 300 D-18E models like this one in 1959. Even without flower decals, they must not have jumped out of the stores, for that burst of production in 1959 was the end of the D-18E. A smaller version, the 00-18E, fared only slightly better; the rosewood D-28E lasted longer, but fewer were made overall. Martin dropped all of the flat-top E series by 1964, putting its hopes for electric success in the thin hollow-body GT series. *(Photo courtesy of Steve Szilagyi/Elderly Instruments.)*

RIGHT AND INSET: In 1965 Martin introduced the GT series electrics, which replaced the F series. The modern peghead and adjustable truss rod were positive changes, but the odd body shape certainly didn't win any design awards. By the time the GT models were issued, the pickups were hopelessly out of date, and the gigantic SS-140 amp was even more of a dud. *(Guitar courtesy of C. F. Martin & Company.)*

After making one D-18E prototype in 1958, in 1959 the Martin company produced 324 00-18Es, 301 D-18Es, and 176 D-28Es—respectable numbers, but ones that certainly weren't repeated in the few subsequent years of production. Martin guitars were sold largely by musicians' word of mouth, and in this case the word was, "Egad! What have I done?" Production of the 00-18E dropped to 101 guitars in 1960, reached a low of 27 in 1962, and fell off the production roster after 1964. And it fared far better than its big brothers: only another 62 D-28Es were made before that model, too, was dropped in 1964, and no D-18Es were made. It wasn't until the 1990s that an artist of note, Nirvana's Kurt Cobain, played one of the acoustic-electrics, appearing with it on MTV's *Unplugged*.

LEFT: Even when it decided to get radical, the Martin company was still conservative. The F series electrics introduced in 1961 were true F-style Martins—the body outline and f-holes were taken straight from the F-7 and F-9 arch-tops of almost 30 years earlier. This time, however, there was a cutaway (Martin's first), the sides were only 2 inches deep, and the whole body was made of laminated woods. If introduced ten years earlier, these guitars might have had a chance. *(Guitar courtesy of C. F. Martin & Company.)*

The company soon made another stab at electrics, this time with more conventional arch-topped models, the single-cutaway, single-pickup F-50, the two-pickup F-55, and the two-pickup, double-cutaway F-65. The factory made 15 samples of each in 1961 and went into full production in 1962. These were superseded in 1965 by the awkwardly shaped GT-70 and GT-75 models, again with DeArmond pickups. Though plentiful enough to be considered a success, some would swear that the guitars must have been shipped straight from the factory to pawnshops, since they didn't seem to linger in musicians' hands very long. West Coast jump-blues guitarist Junior Watson refers to the arch-top electrics as "treble bombs." The instruments were accompanied by a short-lived line of Martin amplifiers, which would doubtless be rare if anyone were looking for them.

According to Chris Martin—who was given a GT-75 as a child—there was a lesson to be learned from this and other company missteps. "In most cases," he says, "it was a matter of our getting away from what we were good at—making flat-top guitars—because we got jealous of another company's success with an instrument."

ABOVE: It may have been short on stairs, windows, and Old World charm, but in 1964 Martin's new factory was a welcome relief from the overcrowding at the old North Street building. *(Photo courtesy of Robert A. Yoder.)*

New Blood, New Turf

In 1955 another generation of Martin came to work at the company: Frederick's son, Frank Herbert Martin, or simply Frank to his numerous drinking buddies. He was born in 1933 and joined the company even more reluctantly than his father had. Frank loved sports, played on a minor league team, and was intending a career in baseball until a knee injury limited his options, as perhaps did the birth of his son, Chris, on July 8, 1955.

Even after starting in the shop at Martin, Frank's thoughts were elsewhere. He loved race cars, so he and some cronies started a dealership selling European sportscars. One of their first shipments of cars wound up on the bottom of the Atlantic, having sunk in the famous *Andrea Doria* shipwreck of 1956. This was but the first disaster in Frank's career. Later, in the 1970s, he would inject some much-needed drama into the company history.

In the meantime, he worked his way up through the company, moving from the factory to sales, to sales manager in 1960, then vice president in 1963. From that position he instigated what would be one of the most important leaps in the company's history, the move to a new factory.

Like many others who had been through the Depression, his father, Frederick, didn't like taking financial risks, especially when they might affect his employees. As a result, Chris Martin thinks "from a business standpoint, he underutilized the opportunities the company had." By that point Martin's production was back-ordered two years on many models, and three years on D-28s, helping Frank to make a compelling argument that the company

ABOVE AND RIGHT: Judy Collins and Tom Paxton serenaded Martin workers from the loading dock at the new factory on opening day in 1964. The choice of performers shows Martin's strong ties to the Folk Revival, and with good reason: Every other popular style of music in America, except bluegrass, had turned to the electric guitar years earlier. *(Photo courtesy of C. F. Martin & Company.)*

THE NEW YORK MARTINS

ABOVE: Because of the New York stamp on nineteenth-century Martins, they were commonly called New York Martins. As a result, all small 12-fret Martins, especially those with rectangular bridges and no pick guard, were called New Yorkers. Martin simply adopted a name already in use for its folk models pictured here, the 0-16NY and 00-21NY. If they had really purchased and played the guitars they are holding, the clean-cut collegiate types in this ad from 1962 would soon have been sporting long hair and faded Levi's and worrying their parents.

Through the 1940s and 1950s, the 00-21 model remained in Martin's catalog as the company's sole link to its past. Although updated for steel strings, with "belly bridge" and celluloid pick guard, it retained the original 00 body shape and wide 12-fret neck topped with a slotted peghead.

The folk revival of the late 1950s brought the old 12-fret Martins back from the dead. In the process of looking back at older styles of music, some folkies inevitably discovered older styles of guitars as well. Unlike the McCarthy-era folk singers, who had focused their ire on heartless capitalists and warmongers, the new folk revival protested about most everything, and what better accompaniment for songs that questioned modern America than an elegant old guitar?

Not everyone could find an old Martin, however, or put up with its quirks. Martin seemed acutely aware of the folk revival in general and kindly obliged the specific need for more of its old guitars by presenting models that could be called the first "reissues" of the company's earlier styles—new guitars that looked like old Martins. The 0-16NY and 00-21NY both had satin finishes, a small rectangular bridge, and no pick guard or fretboard dots. The necks were like the stalwart 00-21, 1⅞ inches wide at the nut, and with a slotted peghead. Though advertised as suitable for either nylon or steel, these guitars sounded weak at best when strung with nylon, and most were sold with silk and steel strings, suitably dubbed "folk" strings. Like beards and sandals, C. F. Martin Sr.'s original designs were back in style, at least for a time.

LEFT: The 00-21NY was the rosewood New Yorker model, with dark binding and other typical Style 21 appointments. Though it sold quite well (275 in 1964 alone), the model was dropped in 1965. Martin historian Mike Longworth's explanation is that the total numbers of 12-fret 00 models sold, including both the 00-21NY and regular 00-21, didn't warrant keeping two versions of the same guitar on the roster. (*Photo courtesy of Fred Dusel.*)

RIGHT: Blind blues harpist Sonny Terry and singer/guitarist Brownie McGhee were staples of the college concert and folk festival circuit for many years. Conventional wisdom in the 1960s was that blues guitar players preferred Gibsons, but Brownie must not have been listening. Though Sonny went through countless harmonicas, his partner used the same battered D-18 throughout his career. (*Photo from the Frank Driggs Collection.*)

had outgrown its quaint North Street factory.

The company purchased a lot in Upper Nazareth, between where the North Street factory stood in town and where the original Martin shop had been situated on Cherry Hill. A title search revealed that the property had once been owned by C. F. Martin Sr. in the 1850s. (It's possible he had bought it to relocate the workshop there but then had moved into town instead when the Moravians opened it up to outsiders.)

Financing the construction wasn't an easy matter. Chris explains, "Nazareth National Bank is extremely conservative, and when we went to put this building in here, they just bailed out completely. We did our payroll there—still do—and a lot of us have our personal savings there, but even with my grandfather on the bank board, they freaked out, and we had to go to Philadelphia to borrow money." The new 62,000-square-foot location was a modern—by 1960s standards—single-story factory, with parts of the exterior painted a shade of blue similar to the plastic cases the company had started using around 1970.

When the factory opened in 1964, folk singers Judy Collins and Tom Paxton performed, using the loading dock for a stage. Each was given a special guitar for their efforts, a Dreadnought made with old D-45 tops found during the move that had pearl soundhole rings and herringbone trim. There also was a baby elephant on hand, who didn't get a guitar.

In the new plant Martin controlled the wood drying electronically instead of using attics and radiators as it had previously. The move also hastened the company's switch from using hide glue to white glue on the guitars. Martin worker Harold Weiss recalls, "Every time they opened a door there, they'd get a draft and the hide glue wouldn't set right."

ABOVE: The Gateway Trio displays the usual lineup of instruments—a long-neck Vega five string banjo, stand-up bass, and Martin guitar—but it is rather unusual for a woman in a folk group to be the only guitar player, and wielding a D-28, at that. Despite the suits and narrow ties on her partners, Betty Mann was ahead of her time. (*Photo from the Frank Driggs Collection.*)

CF Martin instrument catalogue

A Fat Catalog

In 1965 Martin's guitar production topped 10,000 instruments for the first time, and it continued to climb, making the new factory a very providential thing.

The 12-string guitar had become popular in folk music and became even more prominent when it was amplified and played by the likes of the Beatles and the Byrds, birthing the term folk-rock. Martin had made a total of six 12-string guitar models in its past: a 000-18 in 1913, a 000-21 in 1921, a 000-28 in 1936, arch-tops C-1 and C-2 in 1932, and an F-1 in 1941. Martin was reluctant to reenter the fray in the 1960s, however, even taking out an ad explaining that it felt the increased string tension would make a guitar structurally unsound. In 1964 the company did an about-face, issuing the 12-fret, slotted-head D12-20 (following a single prototype, the X-12). It proved a popular model, with 726 made in 1965, climbing to 1,675 in 1969.

ABOVE: The spartan look of the 1950s was rapidly disappearing by the time this 1965 catalog came out. Thanks to the folk boom, the old nineteenth-century guitar shapes and slotted pegheads were back in style. Prototypes of the D-35 were already in progress, and this would be the last catalog with the D-28 as the flagship of the Martin line.

Also in 1965 another new member joined the Dreadnought family. Recognizing that there was already a scarcity of Brazilian rosewood lumber large enough to saw into 8-inch-wide sections for the usual two-piece backs, Bob Johnson—hired in 1962 as a computer expert, later becoming a vice president of the company—came up with the idea of a three-piece back, since Martin had a surplus of 6-inch sections. After a new bracing pattern was worked out, the D-35 was born. It was marginally fancier than the D-28, with a bound fingerboard, and it listed for $50 more. In 1966, its first full year of production, 977 were made, compared to 1,827 D-28s. Martin also issued a popular 12-string model, the D12-35.

LEFT: Introduced in 1964, the D12-20 was Martin's first production 12-string. It was joined a year later by the rosewood D12-35. The 12-fret Dreadnought body and short neck were coupled with a long, slotted headstock, giving the folk world a 12-string that wasn't quite what it had been looking for. Unlike the deep, rumbling 12-string guitars of Leadbelly and earlier blues players, or the whomping bass heard on Erik Darling's 12-string hit "Walk Right In," Martin's 12-strings were better suited for light strings and a delicate touch. The D12-20 has remained the only modern Martin in Style 20 and the absolute record holder in sales for Martin's 12-string guitars—over 1,600 were sold each year in 1970 and 1971. Sales of these models then slowed dramatically, as Martin issued the D12-28 with 14-fret neck.

An invisible change took place inside Martin necks in 1967, when a square steel-reinforcement tube replaced the steel T-bar, which had been used in the necks since 1934. There was still no adjustable truss rod, making Martin one of only two major guitarmakers not to use one; the other one was the budget-brand Danelectro company. Both companies' necks, it should be noted, have held up remarkably well over the years.

Abalone addicts had been going through withdrawal pangs since Martin stopped its inlay work during World War II. Some players hired craftsmen to 45-ize their D-28s, with varying results. Perhaps the best of those craftsmen was Tennessean Mike Longworth, who was known for customizing Hank Snow's Martin—known as "the Snow Job." With a new generation of rock guitarists now seeking out old Martins, the company decided finally in 1968 to reintroduce the D-45. Though never pictured with it, one of the musicians to obtain a new D-45 was Jimi Hendrix, a far cry from the Vahdah Olcott-Bickford crowd to which Martin had once catered. Longworth was brought aboard to do the inlay work on the new D-45s. As rare a skill as that was, Longworth soon proved invaluable in other respects also.

LEFT AND ABOVE: The D-35 could be called the first modern Martin guitar. It had both design and structural elements outside the long-standing Martin tradition, and as a result it wasn't what a Martin traditionalist would have expected from a Style 35 (no dart on the back of the peghead, no pearl around the soundhole, and a three-piece back). But it was fancier and more expensive than a D-28, and the lighter bracing on both the top and back gave the D-35 a distinct sound. It was new and different, and it was an instant success. During 1974 to 1977, the D-35 even outsold the D-28. *(Photo © Mac Yasuda Enterprises.)*

ABOVE: Hank Snow may have been one of the earliest collectors of pearl-bordered Martins, like the 1930s 000-45 shown here. Other Hank Snow albums, and there were dozens, showed a wide range of fancy guitars, usually Martins. *(Album cover courtesy of the RCA Records label.)*

RIGHT: This 1966 D-28 destined for Hank Snow was sent to young Mike Longworth of Tennessee for special inlay in the D-45 style, then it went back to Martin for final finishing. A few years later Martin simplified the process by hiring Mike to help revive the D-45. Several features seen here, such as the pearl bordering on the pick guard and the Martin script logo in pearl, are now offered by Martin's custom shop and appear on many of the "over 45" limited editions. Such lavish decoration, unheard of in the 1960s, earned this guitar a nickname: "the Snow job." *(Photo from Hank Risan.)*

Perhaps those at Martin were standing too close to fully appreciate the company's singular history. Newcomer Longworth reveled in it, and his 1975 *Martin Guitars, a History* was one of the first entrants in the now-burgeoning guitar-book field. This book proved to be an invaluable tool to Martin aficionados. Longworth ultimately had the title of Consumer Relations Manager before leaving Martin to return to Tennessee in 1996.

Folk and Blokes

The Kingston Trio and their similarly radio-friendly imitators influenced thousands of kids to take up the guitar, but it became nearly as popular for those kids to disown the group. The trio had altogether too many teeth to be authentic folk musicians. They were supplanted by a hipper wave of singers who were earthier, more earnest, and concerned with controversial issues. College students didn't want to hear a trio chirruping about "Billy Goat Hill," not while they were heading out to protest for civil rights and union grapes and against the Vietnam War.

Folk festivals became big events, and insular artists who once played only for their neighbors now performed before thousands. One such musician was Elizabeth Cotten of North Carolina, virtually unknown from her birth in 1893 until she was discovered by the folk crowd in the early 1960s. Her distinctive picking style was accomplished on a right-handed Martin, flipped over and played backward. (Curiously, Cotten wasn't the only player to flip a Martin. When surf guitar pioneer Dick Dale strums country songs at home, it's on an upside-down Brazilian rosewood D-35, strung with nylon strings!)

Hammering out a warning on a 12-fret D-28, Peter, Paul, and Mary managed to straddle the commercial and controversial sides of folk, having major hits and joining in the civil rights marches, including some of the

ABOVE: Hank Snow was one of many country music stars who showed up at the dedication of the Jimmie Rodgers Memorial in Meridian, Mississippi. *(Photo from the Frank Driggs Collection.)*

RIGHT: The D-41 was another of Martin's careful readings of what consumers wanted. Martin historian Mike Longworth suggested that the company offer a pearl-bordered Dreadnought at a lower price than the D-45, something similar to the position of the old Style 42. Eliminating the pearl around the end of the fretboard (Style 40) saves a lot of time, and pearl on the back and sides is rarely seen by the audience. By putting an almost-Style 45 neck on a Style 40 top, Martin created the D-41. Introduced in 1969 at $800, when the D-45 was $1,200, the D-41 proved to be a winning combination—the look of a D-45 at only two-thirds the price. Over 400 were sold in 1970, the D-41's first full year of production, and it has been the most popular pearl-bordered Martin since. *(Photo © Mac Yasuda Enterprises.)*

RIGHT: Besides getting the Style 45 guitars back in production, Martin historian Mike Longworth helped the company rediscover its rich past. His book, *Martin Guitars, a History*, helped to make Martin guitars of the past a known quantity, spurring collectors' interest in rare Martins, at a time when the vintage guitar market was just beginning to awaken. *(Photo courtesy of C. F. Martin & Company.)*

FAR RIGHT: The reintroduction of the D-45 in 1968 made sloppy D-28 conversions like this one for Webb Pierce unnecessary. At the time, however, the need to "fancy-up" his D-28 was obvious, as Pierce's elaborate suits and custom cars were befitting an Opry star, making a plain D-28 stick out like a sore thumb. Webb's devotion to the guitar included having a guitar-shaped swimming pool at his home in Nashville. *(Photo © Mac Yasuda Enterprises.)*

BELOW: "Get Rhythm" sang Johnny Cash, and he got his from a Martin Dreadnought. Like his early Sun Records label mate Elvis Presley, Cash had such a locomotive drive to his rhythm guitar playing that few noticed when there wasn't a drum on his records. *(Photo from Michael Rougier/Life Magazine © Time Inc.)*

ABOVE: The Clancy Brothers and Tommy Makem brought Irish folksongs to the folk revival, keeping rhythm on a 000-18. If they seemed to sing a lot about returning to the Emerald Isle, it was perhaps because those heavy fisherman's sweaters are murder when you're under hot stage lights. *(Photo from the Frank Driggs Collection.)*

more dangerous ones, such as Selma, Alabama, in 1962. Some of the songs they made palatable to mainstream America were by a young rocker from Hibbing, Minnesota, Bob Dylan, who reinvented himself as the prototypical folkie.

Dylan and Joan Baez became the undisputed king and queen of the new "protest" singers—most of whom despised that label and all other labels. Dylan played Gibsons or Martins indiscriminately, but Baez was married to a striking 1920s 0-45. Baez explains, "In spite of all my radical leanings, I'm an old traditionalist, I think."

Indeed, much of the folk movement was stiff with tradition. When Dylan, inspired by the Beatles and the Byrds (who had been inspired by the Beatles and Dylan), started performing with electric guitars, he had to contend with booing and cries of "Judas!" from folkies in the audience.

Dylan's producer at Columbia Records, Tom Wilson, hoped to strike folk gold again with another act. Simon and Garfunkel, originally a rock duo called Tom and Jerry, were now aspirants in the Greenwich Village folk scene and recorded an album with Wilson featuring a tune called "Sounds of Silence," on which the pair's voices were accompanied by Simon's Dreadnought. The record went nowhere, the pair split up, and Simon went to England, where he performed solo in folk clubs.

Back in the states, folk-rock had become big. In Los Angeles, a gang of folk and bluegrass players saw the Beatles' *A Hard Day's Night,* bought electric guitars, including a jangly 12-string, recorded Dylan's "Mr. Tambourine Man," and put folk-rock on the charts.

More on that gang later. The pertinent thing here is that Columbia producer Wilson heard that sound and called in some studio musicians—including New York session ace Vinnie Bell with a 12-string Danelectro—to overdub a rock accompaniment on Simon and Garfunkel's flop. Columbia reissued it as a single, it went to Number 1 in early 1966, and

(continued on page 188)

Joan Baez

Strumming Society's Changes

In 1959 America's growing folk music movement found a home at Newport, Rhode Island. The Newport Folk Festival became an overnight institution, but its debut that summer was all but overshadowed by another debut that took place on its stage, that of singer Joan Baez.

She sang like a dusty gold angel, had such a striking appearance that everyone to the left of Barry Goldwater fell in love with her, and was clearly not someone who was willing to wait a couple of decades for men to become comfortable with the idea of an outspoken, opinionated woman. Baez's fearless stands on civil rights, Vietnam—she refused to pay taxes for a time during the war—and other issues were headline stuff, and she was even attacked on the funny pages in the *Lil' Abner* comic strip.

All of which did rather tend to distract from the fact that she was a fine self-accompanist on guitar. Her rhythm patterns flowed and there was the sort of single-note detail that put leaves on a song and birds in its branches, without ever drawing undue attention to itself. Listen sometime to her early version of "Babe, I'm Gonna Leave You," and see if Jimmy Page didn't nick a few licks for Led Zeppelin's subsequent version of the song.

Baez has never given herself much credit as a guitarist. "I never pushed the guitar playing," she said recently. "I learned exactly what I needed to know to accompany myself on the early ballads, and moved on a little bit from there, but I never really expanded much. I don't mean to downplay it. I think maybe now having worked with the best musicians in the world, I see that my job is singing, and accompanying the singing. So that's why when people talk about my

TOP RIGHT: Joan Baez presented the Folk Revival with one of its most enduring images, that of a small, lithe woman playing an elegant little guitar delicately embroidered with pearl. She would often kick off her shoes while on stage and ask that the house lights be turned up so she could see the audience, preferring not to sing into a black abyss that only hinted at life through applause. For many members of the audience weaned on folk songs by the Weavers, the soft gleam of abalone at the edges of her guitar was the first hint that Martin guitars hadn't always been plain utilitarian instruments framed in black or white celluloid. (*Photo from the Frank Driggs Collection.*)

RIGHT: Despite the appearance of delicacy, Joan Baez had a huge voice, and her messages—at protest marches and rallies—were often demanding and urgent in support of the disenfranchised or powerless. (*AP/Wide World Photos.*)

guitar playing, the tiny little portion of me that's self-effacing comes out."

She's self-taught, having picked up Travis picking and other basics from watching other guitarists in Harvard Square while she was living in Boston. She picked up her style from those unknown players and from such influences on the folk scene as Eric Von Schmidt, Leadbelly, and Odetta.

"When I first started playing, I would simply fall asleep with the guitar on my stomach while I was lying on my back. I'd wake up that way. I had fallen in love with the whole folk scene and the ballads and the guitar," she recalls.

If people had to wake up with a guitar on their stomachs, they could do a lot worse than to find Baez's trademark 0-45 there. While most other players were working behind a Dreadnought, Baez was playing this tiny jewel from the 1920s.

While going to high school in Redlands and Palo Alto, California, her folk career started with singing "Scarlet Ribbons" on a Sears Silvertone guitar. Then she graduated to a Gibson. When she saw her Martin, though, "I think it spoke to me," she says. "I remembered a lady-sized Martin a neighbor had that was just laden with pearl. It was like a bracelet, in a wooden box, a tiny, beautiful thing. And I think that's when I fell in love with Martins, this hand-made thing. After that I don't think I would have considered anything else."

She bought that first guitar for $250. It's some indication of the impact Baez made with the guitar that when she bought a second one a few years later—actually a simpler 0-42—she had to pay $700 for it. Those were the only two guitars she owned for two decades, she notes.

She was down to one guitar for a time. "It was stolen once, you know," she says of the cherished 0-45. "It was stolen at Woodstock out of the car, which was locked, and I played the duplicate. And I would just say in concert after that, 'Whoever has it, either play it and enjoy it or, if not, send it back.' And it came back, all very mysteriously on a Greyhound bus."

Baez eventually retired the guitar from the road after it became too fragile, and she had a Canadian luthier build her an exact copy. She gave the 0-42 to friend David Bromberg.

In 1996 the Martin company contacted her about putting out a limited edition Joan Baez 0-45, and it offered to repair her old one. She'd had it repaired before by various non-Martin craftsmen, and one of them apparently wasn't a huge Baez fan. When the luthiers at Martin put a mirror in the soundhole to check out the top bracing, they were surprised to find that a previous visitor had written "Too bad you are a Communist" on the underside of the top. Baez was merely amused. She says, "I'm just very excited to see it again. I don't know whether to put it in a glass case or play it. It feels sort of like the crown jewels to me. Maybe I'll play the limited-edition one."

She doesn't expect she'll fall asleep playing it anymore, saying, "I'm really involved in a whole bunch of other things. I put playing with my dogs, my chicken and goats, first. I will, however, sit and look at my Martin guitar and have my ongoing love affair with it that way."

LEFT: Joan Baez's 1929 0-45 led a hard second life, and the modern pick guard and bridge were added as the rigors of life on the road took their toll. *(Guitar courtesy of Joan Baez.)*

someone eventually remembered to call Simon in England and tell him he had a folk-rock hit.

Paul Simon is nearly as accomplished a guitarist as he is a songwriter. His finely wrought, introspective songs prefigured the singer-songwriter trend of the early 1970s. Except in Simon's case, it was an introspective singer-songwriter with a guy standing next to him. Simon's deft playing style was no doubt responsible for several guitar sales.

By 1967 Beatles John Lennon and Paul McCartney had achieved a higher consciousness that directed them to leave their Gibson acoustic-electric J-160Es behind and buy a pair of D-28s. Lennon was first seen strumming his at the November 10, 1967, taping of the *Hello Goodbye* video. When the Beatles went to the Maharishi Mahesh Yogi's retreat in northern India in February of the following year, their D-28s went along, and several of the songs composed there on the guitars wound up on the *White Album*.

According to Beatles expert Bob Mytkowitz, who has researched the guitars that the Beatles recorded with, their D-28s can be heard on the finished versions of several *White Album* songs, including "Julia," "Mother

ABOVE LEFT: Elizabeth Cotten was discovered while working as a housekeeper for the Seeger family, who thrust her into the limelight of the folk revival for some overdue recognition. She played on right-handed guitars but played them left-handed. Her song "Freight Train" has become a classic, and many young folkies have been introduced to the fingerpicking style by learning her song. *(Photo © B. Spremo/Toronto Star, courtesy of Mike Seeger.)*

LEFT: Robert "Pete" Williams, shown performing at the Newport Folk Festival, was first discovered at Angola State Penitentiary in 1959. Williams was an idiosyncratic, of-the-moment blues singer highly regarded by fans looking beyond the typical blues formula. Here he is playing a Style 45 Martin, probably loaned for the performance by guitarist Stefan Grossman. Grossman's fancy Martins saw action in the hands of many great country blues artists of the 1960s. *(Photo from Frank Driggs Collection.)*

ABOVE: The muttonchop gang, better known as Crosby, Stills, Nash, and Young, was the mainstay of folk-rock. David Crosby clearly wasn't going to wait for Martin to issue a 14-fret 12-string model, as here he is playing a converted D-18 with a lengthened peghead. Some D-28 models were similarly hot-rodded, until Martin took the hint and offered the D12-28 in late 1970, followed by the D12-18 in 1973. Regardless of what guitar model from Nazareth they played, this group probably did more to boost Martin's sales among folk-rockers than all other bands combined. *(Photo from Henry Diltz/Corbis.)*

Nature's Son," and "Blackbird." McCartney's D-28 was a right-handed model he'd flipped over and restrung left-handed, and one can only presume he had the bridge modified left-handed as well. Otherwise "Blackbird" would have become a discordant flock of crows as he moved up the neck.

By 1968 California's Byrds were revisiting their acoustic roots by leading the pack into another hyphenated movement, country-rock. Singer Gram Parsons was inducted into the band, as was Clarence White, who had been terrifying every other bluegrass picker in Southern California since he was in his teens. White was tragically killed when he was struck by an automobile in 1973, but his stunning flatpicking and seemingly endless flow of ideas made him a legend.

Though the late '60s were dominated by ever-louder rock bands with refrigerator-sized amps and a DNA chain of effects pedals, there was also a strong retrograde movement. Perhaps as a revolt against the polluted progress of industrialized life, hippies and others began to exalt the antique, sporting Elizabethan clothing and moving into funky old houses.

In L.A. another group of old folkies had formed the Buffalo Springfield. Guitarist Neil Young fancied fringed buckskin coats, and both he and guitarist Stephen Stills were nuts for old Martins.

With ex-Byrd David Crosby, Stills subsequently formed Crosby, Stills, and Nash (former Hollie, Graham Nash), who were sometimes Crosby, Stills, Nash, and Young when Neil was in the mood. Their performance alone assured that Martins were well represented at the 1969 Woodstock festival. Other Martin players appearing before the half-million or so in attendance included Joan Baez, Arlo Guthrie, and Country Joe McDonald.

With Martin exiting the 1960s with such credentials and the acoustic singer-songwriter movement aborning, there was every reason to expect the company was heading into its biggest decade yet, which it was. There was no guessing, though, that Martin would barely make it out of the 1970s.

Expansion, Decline, and Just HANGING ON

1970–1986

The 1970s started auspiciously enough for Martin. The company sold 15,630 guitars in 1970, a new peak, and that was just the latest summit in a steady climb that began with the 6,299 guitars made in 1964 when the new factory opened.

ABOVE: Though C. F. Martin III and Frank Martin had dramatically different approaches to running the family business, at least they agreed on their pants. Father and son are pictured here in a 1970s ad for Haggar slacks. (*Photo © Haggar Clothing Company.*)

The employees didn't exactly have time to stop and celebrate in 1971 because production leaped then to a staggering 22,637 guitars. The company was now making more guitars in a single year than it had in the entire first quarter of the century. That level of production would have been impossible had not Frank Martin urged the company to move out of its old factory in the 1960s.

As Chris Martin sees it, "Without my father making the new building happen, we couldn't have been able to capitalize on the guitar boom as we did. But he didn't create the demand—that came from previous generations' maintaining this extraordinary level of quality that performers respected. They bought Martins more for the way my grandfather built them than for anything my father did."

In 1970, while still a vice president, Frank Martin had set about building Martin into a musical empire, pushing the company into ambitious expansions. That year the company first imported the budget Sigma guitar line from Japan (and later Korea). It purchased the Boston-based Vega company—primarily making banjos then—moving its operations into Martin's Sycamore Street factory the following year. Before 1970 was over, Frank had also orchestrated the acquisition of the Darco String Company from the D'Addario family and that of Fibes Drums, a Long Island–based firm whose clear Plexiglas drums were a brief sensation with the Mahavishnu Orchestra's Billy Cobham and other influential players.

In 1971 Frank was named president of C. F. Martin & Company when Frederick (C.F. III) stepped down. Though Frederick stayed on as chairman of the board and CEO, he clearly deferred to his son's very different manner of steering the venerable ship.

By the mid-70s, Frank had also purchased a drumstick

ABOVE: In this 1971 photo, it was all smiles at Martin during the guitar boom. Despite the company's growth, a family mood still prevailed. That was not to remain so as the decade progressed. Shown, left to right, are: Herbie Knauss; "Schmidty" Lester Smith; Dave Bostich; John Werner; Jim Schott; and Elwood Gradwohl. *(Photo courtesy of John Rowe Photography, Fort Lauderdale, Florida.)*

LEFT: When guitar fanatics began comparing current Martins with old ones, one of the most obvious differences was the heavily rounded corners on pegheads from the 1960s and 1970s. Was this blasphemous alteration the work of a saboteur? A Communist plot? Would you believe a heavily worn template? It seems that the pattern for the peghead shape got more and more rounded with time, but since it happened so gradually, no one at Martin noticed. The original sharp corners are once again the standard on vintage series Martins. All Martins made today have a peghead much like what the company used in the 1930s. *(Photo courtesy of Fred Dusel.)*

RIGHT: Martin's flagship, the D-28, had suffered only minor cosmetic changes as the 1960s wound down. In 1966 the ivory-grained celluloid bindings were replaced by plain white, and the tortoiseshell celluloid pick guard was changed to plain black acetate, bringing Martins to an even more monochromatic color scheme than before. But these changes were nothing compared to the switch in 1969 from Brazilian rosewood to Indian rosewood for the backs and sides. This change would have a dramatic effect on the value of rosewood Martins made before that date and on the value of Brazilian rosewood itself. *(Photo courtesy of Fred Dusel.)*

manufacturer and the Swedish guitar company AB Herman Carlson Levin. On the production side, in 1974 Martin built a state-of-the-art sawmill right behind the factory that was capable of taking in raw logs and milling guitar-thickness tone woods.

Under Frank, Martin was chugging full speed ahead, but by the end of the decade, it would be clear that Martin had become a locomotive without a track.

Frank's heavily financed expansions were predicated upon the Martin guitar remaining a cash cow. He had no reason to believe it wouldn't. The era of the singer-songwriter was coming into full flower, with Neil Young, James Taylor, Joni Mitchell, the now-solo Paul Simon, Van Morrison, Cat Stevens, Jackson Browne, and even John Denver going all sincere and sensitive with an acoustic guitar—and with more of them than not playing a Martin guitar.

There were odes to "goin' back to the country" and finding a simpler life. Though "back to the country" for some of them meant a Laurel Canyon home 15 minutes from the Sunset Strip, it was a sentiment that resonated through the nation. Few people actually moved onto a farm, but they did buy a lot of herbal shampoo, macramé, and granola. In music, a natural-looking instrument became as much a part of the uniform as faded Levi's—many a '60s metalflake Stratocaster was sanded down to the naked wood.

LEFT: The N series, introduced in 1968, was Martin's attempt to introduce a true Spanish-style classical guitar. The shape looked Spanish enough, as did the soundhole rosette, but for the first two years they still had the squarish Martin peghead and 25.4-inch-string scale of the C series. In 1970 the N guitars got a whopping 26⅜-inch scale length and a fancier peghead shape. The whole project would probably have been forgotten, but one of the early N-20s wound up in the hands of Willie Nelson, and though highly modified, it has become one of the best-known Martins of all. The N series sold moderately well at first, but sales virtually disappeared by the mid-1970s. *(Photo courtesy of C. F. Martin & Company.)*

LEFT: Martin historian Mike Longworth prepared two N-40 prototypes, including the one pictured here, about the time Martin unveiled its new N series classical guitars. The idea of a fancy N-40 was rejected because the classical guitarists whom Martin polled didn't want any inlay on their nylon-stringed guitars. In the long run, classical guitarists largely rejected Martin's new N series anyway. *(Photo from Hank Risan.)*

Competition Hot and Heavy

Martin guitars had never been anything but natural-looking, and they were there ready for the picking. Unfortunately, so were a lot of other guitars that looked almost exactly like Martins.

Well into the 1960s, manufacturers prided themselves on making their instruments with a discernible personality,

ABOVE AND RIGHT: The Vega company of Boston was not able to maintain its earlier standards of quality in the postwar years. Were it not for the popularity of the Pete Seeger long-neck five-string, the PS-5, it probably would have died in the late 1950s. That model became a virtual flagpole for every folk-revival group that followed. But when Martin bought the Vega company in 1970, the folk-rock that powered acoustic guitar sales had no use for folky long-necks, and Vega bluegrass-style banjos lacked the pedigree to crack that market. The four-string (tenor and plectrum) banjo had largely disappeared; so despite the improved quality of Martin's Vega banjos, there was no existing market to notice the improvement. *(Banjo courtesy of C. F. Martin & Company.)*

RIGHT: Though the singer/songwriters of the 1970s each went their individual ways, they at first seemed like a Martin-wielding movement. The stage of 1969's Big Sur Folk Festival—featuring Joni Mitchell; Joan Baez; Crosby, Stills, Nash, and Young; and others—presented a unified wall of spruce and rosewood to rival the Grand Ole Opry. Soon Mitchell—pictured here with David Crosby and a D-28—emerged as one of the most distinctive and fearlessly creative artists of the times. *(Photo from Henry Diltz/Corbis.)*

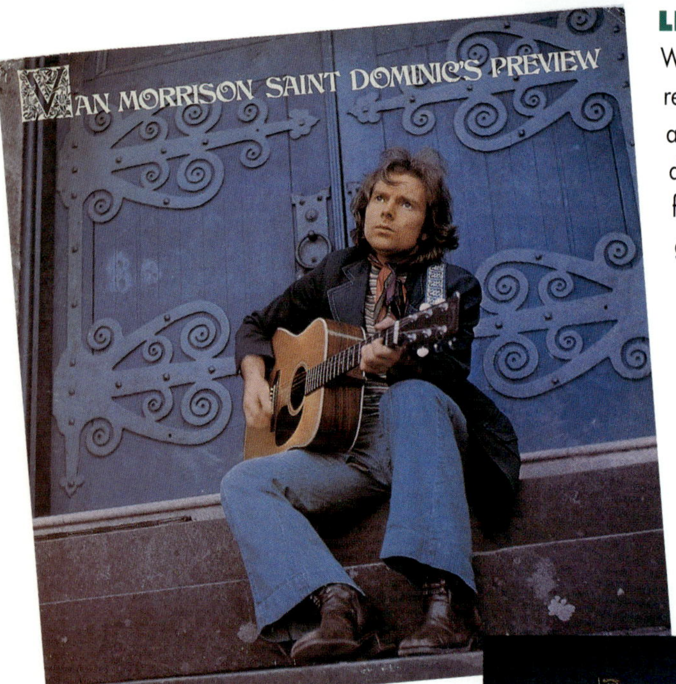

LEFT: Though not as influential a guitarist as Stephen Stills or Doc Watson, Van Morrison was a highly respected musician who sold a lot of records. Martin guitars (here a D-28) kept showing up everywhere, and album covers like this one from 1972 seemed to prove that the company didn't really need any kind of artists' promotion program. Everybody famous played Martins just about every time they played an acoustic guitar anyway. *(Album cover courtesy of Van Morrison.)*

recognizable from across the hall at trade shows. That's not to say that companies didn't nick each other's ideas—that had been happening to Martin since before the turn of the century—but up to that time, competitors at least had made their absconded designs look a little different.

During the '70s, though, importers began marketing slavish knockoffs of other makers' once immutable designs. Armadas of Dreadnoughts floated over, not just with similar dimensions to Martin's, but often with identical headstocks, even with squiggly gold-lettered decals easily mistaken for Martin's.

Frank had the foresight to stave off some of the foreign competition by bringing in the Sigma line, which—no surprise, since they were designed and inspected by Martin—offered some remarkably good-sounding, solid-playing guitars, particularly the model DM-18.

There was also new competition

RIGHT: American manufacturers such as Harmony and Kay produced less-expensive guitars than Martin or Gibson, but their models had a separate identity. In the early 1970s, a flood of Japanese imports was marketed in the United States. They looked exactly like Martins, except for the widespread use of laminated woods. No wonder myths began circulating that Martin had been bought by the Japanese. *(Catalog courtesy of Kaman Corporation.)*

at the other end of the scale, from a generation of luthiers weaned on Martin's classic designs. Along with Gallagher and Mossman, which both started making high-quality Dreadnoughts in the '60s, the '70s saw the birth of such enduring makers as Santa Cruz, Goodall and Taylor, as well as the short-lived Lo Prinzi, Gurian, and other craft-minded makers.

LEFT: If you can't beat 'em...import your own Martin copies! Beset by low-priced competition from foreign imports that looked like Martins, the company began importing Sigmas from Japan (the Greek letter sigma looks like an M lying on its side). This catalog cover from the 1980s shows a D-41 copy with imitation abalone bordering.

Martin had never given much attention to artist relations. Indeed, they not only didn't seek artist endorsements but even rebuffed offers from artists interested in endorsing Martins. Other makers found it not so difficult to woo players away. Doc Watson, for example, began to play and endorse the Gallagher Dreadnoughts.

Martin's fiercest competitor was its own past. Its new success and growth ran counter to the quaint image that musicians cherished of Martin's North Street days and only fueled the well-deserved reputation of its golden-era instruments. There were enough things markedly different on old Martins—the scalloped braces, the herringbone trim, the Brazilian rosewood (replaced by the Indian variety in 1969)—that it was easy for musicians to create a mythology around them.

The vintage guitar phenomenon took off in the 1970s, when everyone wanted a '50s maple-necked Strat like Clapton's or a sunburst Les Paul like Jimmy Page's. But the vintage craze had started a decade earlier for Martins, with bluegrass players who craved a Dreadnought like Lester Flatt's or Jimmy Martin's. Now, with the prominent likes of Stephen Stills and Neil Young strumming the praises of old Martins, weather-checked D-28s took on a godlike luster to rock-era players as well.

Another thing fueling the interest in both vintage and import guitars was the sad fact that nearly all American guitar manufacturers had let their quality slip in the '70s. After the maelstrom of the '60s, there seemed to be a consensus that the nation was going to nurse its hangover and not aspire to much in the following decade.

ABOVE: In the early 1970s, with Frank Martin at the helm, Martin guitars finally got the glossy, full-color catalog they deserved. But only Frank would use an exotic Italian sports car in livid yellow as a backdrop for three Style 18 Martin guitars that hadn't changed since the invention of the jeep. Perhaps the D-45 and D-41 made a better match with a Rolls, but Frank Martin's jet-set mentality would continue to be a mixed blessing for the company.

Dick Boak

THE HIPPIE IN THE WOODPILE

Dick Boak, Martin's director of artist relations, is a prime example of how a person with will and ability can rise through the company ranks, given that Boak was first known there as the longhair rooting through the trash Dumpster for scrap wood.

Boak had done the hippie thing, living in the California commune of former Limeliter Lou Gottlieb and hitchhiking four times across the nation before returning to his hometown near Nazareth. Though interested in guitars, he first heard of Martin while passing its billboard on his way to work.

"I stopped in for the tour and was blown away by the place," Boak recalls. He asked if he could go through Martin's scrap wood and was soon a frequent sight Dumpster-diving out back.

He started making guitars and dulcimers from the scrap wood and teaching his art students how to as well. He recalls, "One day out back at Martin they asked what I did with the wood, and I showed them several instruments. They were real impressed and thought I should apply for a job. I went around the front and asked if they had any openings. I had very long hair and maybe wasn't what they wanted to hire. They said they only had one job opening, for a design draftsman, and didn't think I would be qualified. And I said, 'I've been teaching design drafting for years now, and I happen to have examples in my car.'"

"'Well, that's interesting but we're really looking for somebody who has woodworking experience.'"

"Well, I've been doing that for ten years. Here's some lathe turnings and things I've made of your scraps."

"'Well, we really need someone who knows about music and guitarmaking.'"

"'Well, here's two instruments I just completed, and I'll play you a song on them.' I did, and they ended up hiring me on the spot."

The number of skills Boak pulled out of his hat to get hired pale beside the number of tasks he was put to once he was on the job. His first task was drafting the specifications for all Martin's models, haphazardly kept in the foremen's pocket notebooks until then.

Next, Boak got himself fired for insubordination, having complained about policies he felt were detrimental to the company.

Fortunately, Frederick Martin (C.F. III) had already become fond of him, and he was hired back.

That was during the strike in 1977, and Boak joined management in the factory—gluing bridges, scraping bindings, and setting actions. Halfway through the strike, he was given the job of designing a new line of solid-body electrics for the company.

Next he started Martin's retail store, the 1833 Shop, and the Woodworker's Dream, which sold guitar kits and woods from the sawmill.

He next ran The Sawmill. Then in the late 1980s he went to Mexico to set up the division where Darco strings are made. Upon returning he was offered the chance to work on the company's advertising. Boak convinced Martin to do its advertising in-house and says the company saved $125,000 the first year and revamped its image.

That established, Boak then became the first director of artist relations in the company's history, and he scored Martin's most prestigious and successful artist association, with Eric Clapton. Boak says some at the company doubted the expensive limited edition model would do well. When it sold out, he says, "It gave me more credibility at a time when people here were thinking I was little Vincent Van Gone. And I was, and I am. But I really love these guitars we make."

"I don't think anything was worth crap in the early '70s—guitars, amplifiers, cars, you name it," claims country picker Marty Stuart. "I think for the most part the Martin is the most consistent instrument in the history of the guitar. However—though I do know of a few pretty good early '70s Martins out there—they slipped for a while, too. Hell, they'd been making them since 1833...they should be allowed a few lazy years."

With Gibson, Fender, and others, the quality dip could be attributed to their acquisition by large corporations, whose lawyers and accountants had no feel for the guitar business. While there was no heedless corporation running the show in Nazareth, the company did have Frank Martin.

Decline

Perhaps Frank thought the Martin company's sales were going to continue as a near-vertical line on the sales chart, but 1971's 22,637 total was a peak that was as steep going down as it had been going up. Except for two brief sales spikes in 1972 and 1979, the numbers took a steady plunge, until bottoming out at just barely over 3,000 guitars in 1982. Sales hadn't been so low since 1939.

What caused the decline? There was Martin's competition, though virtually all guitar companies—acoustic and electric—hit the skids in the early '80s; there was a recession; there was the rise of disco music and of synthesizers that allowed players to get hundreds of sounds instead of the acoustic guitar's one. While all these factors played a part in Martin's slump, an institution doesn't crash that hard without somebody stepping on the gas.

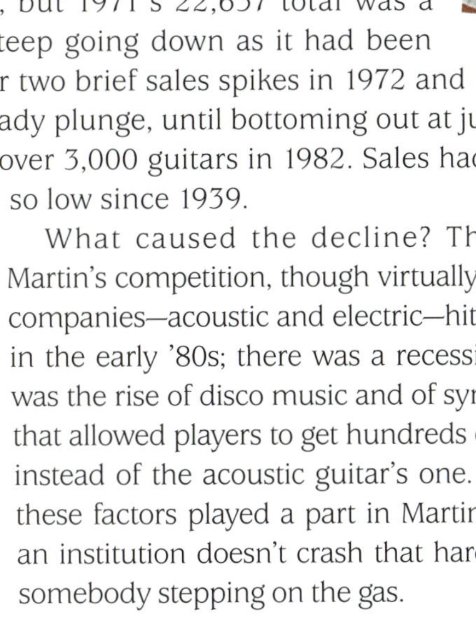

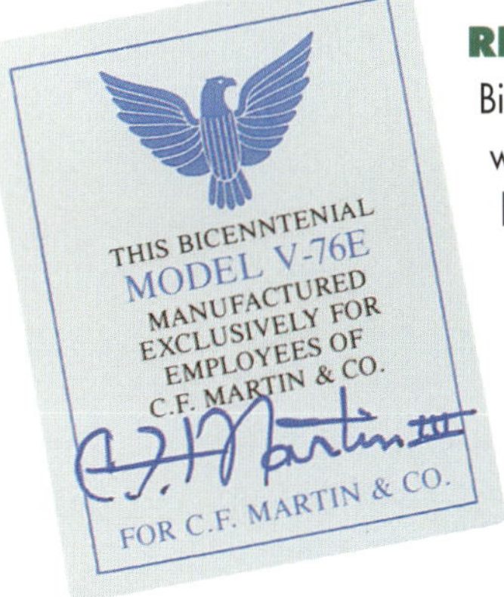

RIGHT: Martin's first limited edition was the D-76 guitar celebrating the Bicentennial of the United States with 1,976 guitars. Based on the D-35, it was an odd model to choose for commemorating longevity—the D-35 was barely ten years old at the time and it was more of a favorite with rock and rollers than flag-draped patriots in the heartland of America. It was also an ambitious number of guitars for a first-ever limited edition, and combined with the steep price—higher than the pearl-bordered D-41—the result was a new D-76 model that was still on dealer shelves long after the rest of the Bicentennial was forgotten. Seventy-six Bicentennial Vega banjos were also made.

David Lindley

A Man for All Sessions

Few guitarists have touched as many musical bases as David Lindley. He started off as a Southern California bluegrass prodigy in the 1960s, winning so many competitions on several instruments that he was often made a judge just to give the other players a chance. In the late 1960s he belonged to the rock group Kaleidoscope, for whom the psychedelic mood of the times was an excuse to work bluegrass, Bulgarian rhythms, and harp guitars into their act.

Through the singer/songwriter era, Lindley was Jackson Browne's right-hand man, lending empathetic support to the singer with his fiddle and acoustic, electric, and slide guitars. He formed the band El Rayo X in 1981. He also became part of Los Angeles's active studio scene, playing on everything from Grammy-winning hits, such as the Emmylou Harris–Dolly Parton–Linda Ronstadt *Trio* album to friend Ry Cooder's moody soundtracks.

In recent years he's embarked on adventurous musical meldings with experimental guitarist Henry Kaiser, recording with native musicians in such far-flung locales as Norway and Madagascar.

When Lindley performs, there is usually a thicket of stringed instruments on stage, from 12-string fretless Turkish banjos to Hawaiian koa wood Weissenborn slide guitars to '60s drugstore electrics. And Martins have been a constant in his arsenal.

He says, "There's a Martin X-braced tone, especially for bluegrass and stuff, and it's kind of a growl and projection I look for. It's real characteristic."

Among the '60s Los Angeles folk crowd that gathered at the Ash Grove and McCabe's music venues, Martins were already collector's items. Lindley recalls, "Out on this coast, Martin was the one, because the player was Clarence White. If Clarence played one, and he was the best, why dispute him? Our standards for Martins were real high, and there were a lot of them available—used ones that were just monsters, prewar herringbones, and all that. You might pay $375 for an old D-28 or $600 for a really special Martin.

"The first one I had was a 00-18 in 1962. At the Claremont folk music center out here, the owner really knew his stuff. He had old ivory bridge ones, even had Stauffer-style ones. I got to have a hands-on thing with some of the best Martins ever made, and I own one of the best ones, which is a 000-21 herringbone.

"To me the most consistently good-sounding guitar is the 000 series. You can get a great-sounding 000-18. Even people who say they don't like Martins—who don't like the amount of air that a D-size moves—say the 000s are an exception. I use my 000-21 whenever there's a call to do solos or fancy work. I used it on the *Trio* album. It has a wonderful recording sound."

Lindley has owned several Martins—he's also partial to some all-mahogany models and still mourns a stolen '70s 12-fret 12-string, maintaining "it was the best 12-string in the world"—but he has recently been paring down his collection, feeling some instruments might be played more by others. At present he's only kept his essential 000-21.

"They'll have to pry that one from my cold, dead hands."

(Photo from Kim Upton.)

"My father was more aggressive than his father, and initially he hit the nail on the head," Chris Martin says. "You build a new factory, you build more D-28s. Then he got heady about it and expanded where he should have stuck to his knitting. Where he really failed was, they stopped reinvesting in this business. We were profitable, but not that profitable—you could either put more money into this or make more acquisitions. And when they were making acquisitions, this business suffered.

"I think they took their eye off the ball and stopped talking about the goal of making a better guitar. They all bought into Martin as just the foundation to make us a bigger player in the music business, and doing it through acquisition."

Frederick didn't like to cross his son's (Frank's) decisions, and sometimes didn't have the opportunity to:

"My grandfather [Frederick] was in the hospital, supposed to die from leukemia until they gave him this experimental drug. He was in there all hooked

ABOVE: This photo from Martin's 1970 catalog shows braces being glued to the soundboards in a sea of clamps and cauls. Production was way up, but many of the old procedures and old tools remained unchanged. Today this operation is done with vacuum clamping. *(Photo courtesy of C. F. Martin & Company.)*

RIGHT: After the success of the D-45 and D-41, a reissue of the earlier Style D-28 seemed like an obvious choice, but it wasn't until 1976 that Martin brought back both the sorely missed herringbone top trim and the equally mourned scalloped braces under the soundboard. Bass response and overall volume were further aided by the use of a small maple bridgeplate, rather than the large rosewood plate introduced in the late 1960s. Five hundred HD-28s were made in 1976, then production tripled the following year. Ten years later the HD-28 was Martin's best-selling model of all, a position it has maintained ever since. It was a significant turning point for Martin because the company recognized not only the visual appeal of its older models but also the guitar player's desire for the sound of the older guitars as well. *(Photo courtesy of C. F. Martin & Company.)*

RIGHT: Another of Martin's great ideas of the 1970s was the *1833* magazine, first introduced in 1973. The confusing array of Martin body shapes, style designations, and other details unique to Martin history were carefully explained along with the usual information helpful to new owners of Martin guitars. Unfortunately, declining sales cut deeply into the budget for such extravagance and only two issues were produced.

up and dying, and my father comes in and says, 'We have this marvelous opportunity to buy this amazing drum—patented, unbelievable—everybody thinks it's the best drum in the world.' And my grandfather lectures that we really need to look into it better and see if it makes sense. My father's champing at the bit, and finally goes, 'I hate to tell you, but-the-guy-told-me-if-I-didn't-buy-it-today-I-couldn't-have-it, so we bought it!' That was kind of the dynamic at work there. He'd ask permission after he already had done it," Chris says.

Frank also made some early attempts to automate the factory, where the methods of guitarmaking had changed little over the decades. He brought in an automated neck-carving machine and other devices that didn't especially work and only alienated workers, who weren't involved at all in the selection process. Though they

LEFT: Introduced in 1977, the M-38 was the first new flat-top body shape from Martin since 1934, though its origins as the outline for the ill-fated F-7 and F-9 arch-tops dated back to the mid-1930s as well. With an abalone rosette and bound fretboard and peghead, the M-38 was the showiest model below the D-41. The D-35–inspired M-36 was a less-expensive version introduced in 1978. However, Martin traditionalists frowned at the use of a rosewood bridge and the bright orange tint on the top. The long scale and scalloped bracing, plus the wider body, gave the M series much more clout than the 000-28s being made at the time, so Martin buyers finally had a more viable alternative to the Dreadnought. *(Photo courtesy of C. F. Martin & Company.)*

ABOVE: Like his onetime bandmates and co-Martin strummers Stephen Stills and David Crosby, Neil Young strode from the folk-rock scene of the 1960s into the singer/songwriter era of the 1970s. In the 1990s, Young was embraced anew by the grunge generation for his uncompromising, emotionally scarifying music. *(Photo © Jay Blakesburg.)*

cost $50,000 to $70,000 a pop, the machines were deemed a bad idea; so, as Chris puts it, "We became more insular and bought more drawknives."

There were only a few new Martin models introduced in the mid-'70s, the first being the company's 1975 nod to the pending U.S. Bicentennial, the D-76. The guitar featured a three-piece back with herringbone backstrips, a herringbone rosette on the top, star-shaped fret markers, and an eagle emblazoned on the headstock. Martin made 1,976 (as well as 98 for employees, stamped D-76E). Seventy-six Vega banjos with similarly appointed necks were also made. Despite the patriotic theme, the instruments were not popular.

In 1976 Martin celebrated its own heritage by reissuing the venerated herringbone D-28, now dubbed the HD-28. The new model was a somewhat modernized version of the prewar legend, and it reintroduced scalloped braces. In 1978 the D-35 was also offered in a herringbone model.

After years of prompting by players and dealers, Martin introduced a new flat-top size that also had its origins in the 1930s. In the mid-1960s New York guitar dealer Mark Silber had taken an old Martin 16-inch arch-top—an F-7 or F-9 model—with a damaged top, got a new Dreadnought top from Martin, and created the biggest Martin flat-top yet. Then dealer Matt Umanov made a similar conversion for guitarist David Bromberg, this one with a longer-scale neck. The instrument's uniqueness—and no doubt Bromberg's prowess on it—resulted in a demand for more of these conversions.

Martin finally capitalized on that demand in 1977 with the M-38, and the following year it introduced the three-piece–backed M-35 (which soon got a name change to the M-36).

Even with Martin's sales declining after the 1971 peak, the company was still cranking out a huge number of instruments. Meeting those numbers contributed to the quality slip, but there were also some conscious decisions hastening that slide. Martin guitars came with a lifetime warranty, and to

cut down on the number coming back needing repair, workers began building them to be sturdier, to the detriment of the tone. A large rosewood bridgeplate, for example, was implemented to keep the bridge and top stable. For a time, the company even shortened its famous lifetime guarantee to five years. The Martin name sold so well that one of its salesmen at the time bragged that they could stamp the name on toilet paper and get $1 per roll.

The Martin string division that Frank had created by purchasing Darco Strings was very successful for the company. But the Fibes Drums fad went the way of the Plexiglas guitar, and the plant was finally sold in 1979.

The Sawmill was a victim of bad timing. It had been built primarily to process logs of Indian rosewood, but the year after it was completed, India suspended the exportation of logs, wanting them instead to be processed in Indian mills. Rather than let its sawmill sit idle, Martin began importing other exotic woods to market to the domestic upper-end furniture market, and the sawmill workers took on odd jobs. They cut wood into rough shapes for marimba bars, cutlery handles, buck knife handles, and veneer for Steinway pianos.

Frank's acquisition of the Levin guitar factory proved a misstep, too. "Sweden was just an abominable failure," Chris says. "We had no comprehension of the socialist system there. Once the boss, Mr. Levin, got his money, he went on permanent vacation, and the factory was just a mess. We'd send people over to try to resurrect it, and the attitude of the workers was so lackadaisical. They wouldn't come to work—they'd get paid just as much if they stayed home. It almost put us over the edge financially, having to keep pumping additional hundreds of thousands into it.

"We finally told them we were shutting it down, and they didn't cry a lot. Someone asked them, 'Aren't you upset?' and they

ABOVE: The image of picking and grinning together at the Martin factory, as seen in this early 1970s ad, was more fantasy than reality. Management and the workforce got along about as well as ukuleles and a Fibes drum kit, and it all came to a head in the eight-month strike in 1977.

said 'Yeah, this is really sad, and, you know, you're going to have to continue to *pay* us for another two years.' Huh? So it took another two years until we were out from under it, paying their unemployment compensation."

The C. F. Martin Organisation, as it was now called (with organization intentionally spelled the old-fashioned way, but with a modern corporate-looking logo to contrast it), wasn't content with only a series of music business failures, branching further into computer software ventures. Unlikely as it seems, Martin poured several hundred thousand dollars into a glitchy software system intended for veterinarians' offices.

Blackout

Frank Martin was decidedly more colorful than the previous generations of ramrod-straight Martins who had led the company. If those Martins had deferred their share of worldly pleasure while establishing the Martin name, Frank more than made up for lost time.

"Frank liked alcohol and he liked women," Dick Boak recalls. "He could be very smart and shrewd in one breath, and whimsical and quick to make decisions not necessarily based on fact in the next."

Frank's son, Chris, also saw two sides to him:

"He could be very compassionate. He was a very likable person, unless you were family. As long as you were a friend, you could love Frank. When you were family, it became a love/hate kind of thing. The closer you got, the more he would abuse the relationship. But from a friendship standpoint he was a great guy. He had a great sense of humor. He loved to golf, loved to drink, loved to laugh. And if that's what you did, he was a great friend. 'Want to play golf?' Sure. 'Want a beer?' Sure, let's have three."

Frank married four times. He sported a goatee and dressed hip, looking much like Peter Sellers in a swinging '60s comedy. He loved sports and race cars. He didn't, however, seem to have any special love for the guitar bearing his last name.

He had even less cause to love Martin guitars by 1977, when he announced that the guitar division hadn't turned a profit in three years. He blamed worker inefficiency, telling a reporter, "Five years

(Courtesy of John Rowe Photography, Fort Lauderdale, Florida.)

Stephen Stills

Radical Traditionalist

In the rock-inspired guitar boom of the 1960s and early 1970s, Martin guitars had no emissary more effective than Stephen Stills. On recordings like "Bluebird" with the Buffalo Springfield; "Suite: Judy Blue Eyes" with Crosby, Stills, and Nash (CS&N); and "Change Partners" in his solo career, Stills introduced the crisp report of a herringbone Dreadnought to a generation.

In interviews, Stills praised scalloped braces, prewar D-45s and such, driving the price of D-45s up before he even bought one for himself. He's still enthusing about the company's works.

"They're works of art. They're the Stradivarius of American musical instruments. The best Martins that I've heard—with dense Brazilian rosewood and cross-grain ripple to the top, lightly braced—sound better than anything else ever made. There's an artisanship in them that just can't be replaced," Stills said in 1997, the same year he was recognized as something of a treasure himself: Stills became the only artist to be inducted into the Rock and Roll Hall of Fame twice in the same year, with the Springfield and CS&N.

Stills grew up with a varied musical background, as his father's business often had the family moving. They lived for years in Latin America, "but all the gut-string guitars didn't get it for me," he recalls. "It was back in a New York shop, Fretted Instruments, that I first grabbed a Martin, and it just sounded better than anything with wood around it."

He couldn't yet afford one, though. "When I was playing the coffeehouses, I'd try to position myself so I was playing after guys who had Martins, and I'd try to use them," he says with a laugh. "Then virtually the first money I made in music was used to buy a really good old herringbone D-28."

That's the guitar—a mid-1940s model—that was used on most of the Buffalo Springfield and early CS&N recordings. As soon as CS&N signed its record deal, Stills bought his first D-45, a 1939. He bought his second vintage one in a bidding war with a Japanese collector who, Stills claims, wanted to saw the guitar in half to study it.

Stills keeps 12 Martins around now, including the 1939 D-45 and a 1942, a 1938 D-28 (serial #71358), a 1-26 and 1-45, a 00-42, a 00-45, and a 000-45. "That 000 sings like nothing you've ever heard," he remarks. He rarely takes his old Martins on the road, but he records with them. He doesn't hobnob with other collectors, he says, "because envy is one of the seven deadlies."

He convinced his friend Jimi Hendrix to order a left-handed reissue D-45, while one of the 000s Eric Clapton used on his *Unplugged* performance was a gift from Stills. "I don't know what possessed me to do that!" Stills exclaims. "I think it was in return for coming and playing on my record [*Stephen Stills*]. God bless him, I really loved seeing him play those things."

Stills sees no dichotomy in the fact that in the 1960s he and others were in bands branded as radical while revering vintage instruments:

"That's because of our granddads: One of the reasons we revolted is our granddads would never have put up with the bull we had over the Vietnam War and all that. They really instilled in all of us this reverence for honor and dignity and tradition and craftsmanship. And in our time, there was a healthy debate going on within the country about a very serious issue, and we were treated like we were ignorant scumbags. But we were the ones paying attention to our past.

"And you could feel the past in those guitars. The craftsmanship, and the handmade-ness of things, you can tell the love and care the guys put into those things, particularly Martins from the '30s and '20s. You can really feel someone's spirit in them."

(Photo from Henry Diltz/Corbis.)

Martin Union a Sour Note?

6-7-78

guarantee those privileges.

Frank Woodrow, personnel director at ... said the men who have been ... the old wage

By the end of May, 110 workers were back at their jobs and others placed their names on recall lists. The recall list now includes 50 names, Woodrow said.

Martin Won't Meet with Union

5-26-78

EAST LAWN — Now that C.F. Martin Inc. is back in the business of making Martin guitars, the company is refusing to meet for a scheduled negotiating session with representatives of the 69 craftsmen still out on strike, according to union officials.

may be cause for filing charges of unfair labor practices. Marvin Wright, union district council representative, said he will investigate whether any legal action will be taken against the company.

Company officals this morning declined comment on their apparent unwil- ... that 111 former

Woodrow added that from five to ... former strikers who wished to co... back to work have been temporarily l... off.

"But hopefully, our sales effort w... soon support anyone who wants to com... back," Woodrow said.

The company official noted that he wil... back nearly all of the 69

Guitar Co. Strike Takes Toll Of Livings, Town, Marriage

ABOVE: Newspaper headlines from the time of the Martin strike tell of tensions and strains.

ago, the guitar division was in great shape. It took 18 hours to make a guitar then. Now it takes 20." He particularly blamed the younger workers, claiming, "They just do not want to work."

Dealing with productivity on the factory floor was not nearly as engaging as following the race car team he sponsored or the semi-pro Allentown Jets basketball team he had bought. Others noted that Frank's own productivity wasn't enhanced by his long lunches in local taverns.

In 1976 he brought in a new "get tough" personnel manager, Frank Woodrow, to ride herd over the factory. Up to that point, management and workers had held informal monthly meetings. The workers were the best paid in the industry and, along with standard benefits, also could expect free shoes and shop aprons, a $25 Christmas bonus, full tuition for work-related study, company bus outings to a Broadway show and baseball game, and, for newlyweds, a week's paid vacation to honeymoon.

Woodrow canceled the monthly meetings. Workers accustomed to speaking to Frank or Frederick were directed to address all matters to Woodrow. As one worker put it, "Now there's only one way you can go that leads to just one individual. And his door is closed."

A wall of distrust grew. An exasperated Frank claimed the workers in tiny Nazareth "can't comprehend" progress or the company's growth. Workers claimed it was Frank who was out of touch, unconcerned with Martin's quality and squandering its resources. Dick Boak notes, "If you looked at Frank's racing team, the basketball team, and some of the hiring he did [basketball players went on the company payroll in the off-season], that would have been enough to raise anyone's eyebrows."

When the informal meetings were replaced by formal documents drawn up by the company lawyers asking workers to make concessions, workers got some outside help of their own, joining the locally prominent, AFL-CIO–affiliated United Cement, Lime and Gypsum Workers union. And on September 13, 1977, the factory stood empty as 180 workers went out on strike.

Strike

Men who had spent their adult lives at Martin's workbenches—many whose fathers had done the same—walked the picket line outside, while they and their families tried to subsist on the $50 a

ABOVE: The profits from all those Martin guitars sold in the late 1960s and 1970s went toward building the music industry empire that Frank Martin and his cronies were sure would lead the C. F. Martin Organisation [sic] toward Fortune 500 status. Bad management and even worse timing, however, led to a flood of red ink from all but the Darco acquisition. All that was salvaged from Vega was the trademark for strings, while Fibes and Levin resulted in disastrous losses.

week doled out by the union's strike fund. Inside the eerily abandoned factory, management did its best to remain open, piecing together a trickle of guitars. Without the string division and the imported Sigma line, Martin would have folded.

The rift between workers and management wasn't over money or the major differences that typically lead to a strike. Indeed, two decades later, those on both sides are hard-pressed to even recall what the particular issues were. Records of the time reveal what amounted to minor quibbles compared to most labor strife issues.

The company had sought concessions from the workers, one being that it wanted all employees to take their two-week vacations at the same time in the summer so the factory could shut down for that time and save money. It also wanted a management-rights clause, giving the company final say over layoff procedures, when holidays would be taken, and other matters.

More than any one issue, though, the striking workers complained about a shifting mood at the company, one in which they were made to feel as if they didn't matter. Though Frank may have faulted the younger workers, those who were unhappiest with the firm were the older ones, who pined for the old days when Frederick was actively running things.

In local papers, one veteran employee after another spoke out: "This place was one big happy family. No matter how busy he was, the Old Man found time to talk to you," said one, while another offered, "With the Old Man, the business was his life. But Frank Martin doesn't want the headaches. He just wants to have a good time."

Frederick, 83, was heartbroken by the strike. While he needed to go to work, he couldn't bring himself to drive across the picket lines at the parking lot. Instead he had someone drop him off at the front entrance.

While largely peaceful, the strike wasn't without its unpleasant moments. Chris Martin, home from college for a business meeting, found the paint on his car scratched and his tires slashed. One night, he says, thugs showed up at Frank's home and beat Frank. On May 9, pickets blocked the parking lot exit for three hours.

TOP: Unlike the previous generations of Martins that preceded him, C. F. Martin IV (*right*) did not grow up in Nazareth with the Martin factory as home. When he moved in with his grandfather (*left*) and began working full-time at the factory in 1978, however, Chris quickly made up for lost time. In the early 1980s he began traveling around the country giving clinics on the history and philosophy behind the Martin guitar. *(Photo courtesy of C. F. Martin & Company.)*

ABOVE: Chris Martin (*left*) and Dick Boak (*right*) man their table at the 1979 Boston Luthier's Convention. *(Photo courtesy of Roger Sadowsky.)*

Martin still shipped a few guitars during the long strike, but they weren't produced by the rank and file. Members of Martin management, many of whom hadn't actively built guitars for years, went from desks to workbenches to keep a few models coming off the line.

Finally on May 18, 1978, 22 strikers broke ranks and returned to work. One told a reporter, "I knew if I ever wanted to work at Martin again, to work with wood, I had to go back. I had put my name in for a job at many places, but I never wanted to work anywhere else."

In the following weeks others also returned, and on June 1, after assurances that the company would hire the strikers back, the strike was called off. It had lasted eight and a half months. "It's like a bad dream. I'd like to forget it," said one returning worker. It was years before the scars entirely healed, though, and by then Frank Martin was the one on the outside.

From C.F. III to C.F. IV

When he was growing up, Chris Martin didn't dream of being the head of the Martin company. He didn't even want to be a fireman. "No, I had this desire to be a hermit. I'm still a very shy, insular person, and my dream was to live by myself—not in a Unabomber shack, but in a nice cabin somewhere," he says.

Instead he would wind up a leader and figurehead, the latest C. F. Martin to have to live up to an American legend bearing his name.

Chris was born on July 8, 1955, in New Jersey. While his parents were in college, his mother became pregnant; both quit school, and Frank then went into the family business. The young family moved into a Martin-owned house across the street from the old factory in Nazareth.

Chris recalls, "I lived there until I was three, and it must have been a traumatic three years because I blocked it out completely. My first memories are of being back in New Jersey after my mother left my father. My mother has a temper, my father had one, too, and I can imagine they were two screaming banshees," Chris says.

Growing up, Chris would come to Nazareth for two weeks in the summer and an occasional weekend. He recalls, "I actually was much closer to my grandfather than to my father. My father and I always had a strange relationship. I don't think he ever knew what to do with me."

Chris said his grandparents were "spoiling me rotten." Frederick (C.F. III) spent a lot of time grooming Chris for the family business. "I think he found in me what he never found in my father in terms of a love for the Martin guitar and a desire to learn what it stood for."

Chris's grandfather and father gave him a little 5-18 acoustic and a GT electric, and he took lessons to learn some basic chords for summer camp. The teacher knew he was

ABOVE AND LEFT: This 1982 OM-45 with koa back and sides and "tree of life" inlay came from Martin's Custom Shop, opened in 1979 so customers could order guitars with a unique combination of features. Most orders were for new versions of old Martins, and the company realized the popularity of features found on its 1930s instruments. The Custom 8 and Custom 15 (so named because they were the 8th and 15th orders the Custom Shop processed) proved so popular that they eventually became stock models. Today such 1930s D-28 reissues have been superseded by the HD-28VR. *(Photo above courtesy of C. F. Martin & Company; photo at left from Hank Risan.)*

ABOVE AND LEFT: Unlike earlier Martin attempts at building electric guitars, the E series solid-bodies introduced in 1979 actually worked, and quite well at that. But the electric guitar market moves from one fashion to another at a rapid pace, and the natural-wood look of these guitars was already on the way out by the time the E series made it to market. The EB-18 at left is an early prototype. The 28 series electric Martins (*far left*) were the second generation of solid-body instruments, introduced in 1980. The sculpted mahogany body and active electronics may have improved the guitars, but did little to improve sales. *(Guitar at far left courtesy of C. F. Martin & Company; guitar at left courtesy of Cliff Cole.)*

C. F. Martin IV, though, and felt obligated to make an Andrés Segovia of him, which soured Chris on the guitar for a time.

When he was a senior in high school, he came to live with his dad and endeavored to make his own guitar in the factory:

"So the word went around that Chris was going to make this guitar, a D-28S because my grandfather liked those, but with a narrow neck. I went out in the shop, and they'd take my part and shape it perfectly. Then they'd pull out a couple of D-18 necks and say, 'Here you try it,' with those. So my guitar was perfect, but I didn't build it—it was what the craftspersons had made demonstrating the techniques for me."

As college neared, Chris toyed with studying marine biology at the University of Miami. Instead, Fred Walecki, owner of Westwood Music in Los Angeles, suggested that Chris go to UCLA and work in his store, as well.

"What I learned there was that I didn't know anything," says Chris. "I didn't know who being C.F. Martin was. I'd be in the back trying to help John Carruthers doing repair

BELOW: The electric guitars that could have been? In the 1970s Dick Boak produced several electric prototypes that never hit the factory floor. Perhaps his designs were a bit too progressive for the conservative company. (*Guitars courtesy of Dick Boak.*)

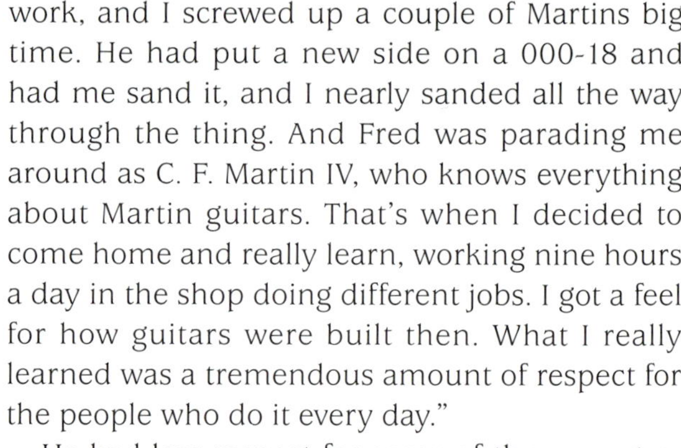

work, and I screwed up a couple of Martins big time. He had put a new side on a 000-18 and had me sand it, and I nearly sanded all the way through the thing. And Fred was parading me around as C. F. Martin IV, who knows everything about Martin guitars. That's when I decided to come home and really learn, working nine hours a day in the shop doing different jobs. I got a feel for how guitars were built then. What I really learned was a tremendous amount of respect for the people who do it every day."

He had less respect for some of the managers running the company with his father: "They had arranged to buy guitars from a factory in Holland that we were going to market as the Vega brand, right between the Martin and Sigma lines. We displayed these samples at a trade show, and they were terrible. They had just grabbed a bunch of stuff and thrown it together. And these management people were standing there telling people how wonderful these Vega guitars were.

"That was the beginning of my father's generation coming to understand that something wasn't clicking between them and [me]. I was getting really angry at these people abusing this business under the pretense of their marketing brilliance. And I was saying, 'I know a guitar, and that ain't a guitar.' Certainly it wasn't a guitar *we* should be selling," Chris says.

Chris finished college, earning a degree in business administration from Boston University. He returned to the company in 1978 and moved in with Frederick.

"Living with my grandfather, I was getting indoctrinated into the philosophy of the company. He said you should always treat your smallest customer the way you would your largest. He treated the employees differently than I do, in that I don't think he ever encouraged participative management. It wasn't the thing back then. But he did treat people very fairly. He was very concerned about fairness in the organization and against favoritism. My grandfather wasn't a very aggressive businessman. He was pretty conservative, tended to react a little late to things, and never really exploited or understood how powerful the brand was. All he tried to do was make really great guitars, and he was really good at it."

TOP: The 1983 "A Century and a Half of Fine Guitar Making" catalog was the first time Martin used its vintage guitars as a marketing tool. Along with Martin historian Mike Longworth's 1938 D-28 shown at the far right, an original D-45, 0-28K, F-9, and 12-fret 000-45 were pictured with contemporary Martin models. Since the company was not yet making a concentrated effort to reproduce the look of a vintage Martin, however, some of the pages served only to emphasize the greater appeal of the old styles.

MIDDLE: Martin always seems to celebrate important milestones in the midst of calamity. In 1933, the company marked its 100th year in the depths of the Depression, with many of its workers laid off and production cut to half of what it had been a few years earlier. Yet those were the good ol' days compared to the precarious position Martin was in as it celebrated the 150-year mark. That year, production was less than 25 percent of what it had been a decade earlier, and this time the depression Martin suffered was partly of its own making.

BOTTOM: As in the past, when sales were slow, Martin tried to entice guitar players with something new. In 1980 it introduced koa guitars in six different models. The koa models were offered in two styles, 25K and 37K (shown here), and those with a "2" after the K also had a koa top. Style 25K had appointments similar to Style 21, while Style 37K had more deluxe features than Style 28, including a pearl rosette and the fretboard inlay pattern of the old Foden Special Style D guitars. Although Martin still makes limited runs of koa guitars, not many of the 25 and 37 Styles were made after 1987. *(Photo courtesy of C. F. Martin & Company.)*

LEFT: In 1981, Martin finally began building guitars with a cutaway. The oval soundhole was the result of moving the brace beneath the end of the fretboard down to avoid the cutaway. The MC-28 was the plainest of the M series, and it proved to be more popular than the cutaway Dreadnought. Both models have since been redesigned and now have a round soundhole.

CHANGING OF THE GUARD

Chris worked a number of positions in the factory and offices. He feels that going on the road as a sales representative would have been good for his career development, but "I was scared to death to leave. I was afraid I'd come back and there'd be nothing here. It was that bad."

What had been a slide in sales in the late '70s became a rout in the early '80s. In 1982 production sank to a mere 3,153 guitars, worse than the company had even done in most years of the Depression. The entire musical instrument business was soft, but acoustic guitars were faring particularly poorly in this era of synthesizers and arena rock. The company cast about for alternatives, such as the barely remembered Shenandoah violin and a series of solid-body electrics that, unfortunately, couldn't find a place in the already crowded market. Martin had bankrupted or sold off most of its bad investments, but it was still paying for them.

Chris eventually wound up as assistant to his father. Sometimes they'd get along, sometimes not, Chris explains. "Too much business was done over a four-hour lunch at a local tavern. Everybody else managed to stay more or less sober enough that they could come back and apparently do their job for the rest of the day, except my father, because there were no constraints on him. Who was going to fire him?" he says.

Actually, Martin's board of directors was going to, for Martin was now a privately held corporation.

The company had been family-held until Frederick gave stock to Princeton University, to a secretary, and to Frank and his sister Pam. In the early '70s, some of the firm's officers were given shares. To finance his divorces, Frank would sell off stock, while more shares came back to the company as restitution for money

RIGHT: Though sales were bleak overall, in 1982 Martin was able to purchase a supply of Brazilian rosewood and began making the most accurate reissues of its famous Dreadnoughts from the 1930s that it had made, well, since the 1930s. The D-28V, released in 1983, helped pave the way for more reissues in the future. Thanks to Martin historian Mike Longworth, the D-28V had other special features besides just Brazilian rosewood. These included the diamond and square fretboard inlays, X-bracing moved closer to the soundhole, ivoroid binding, and the more squared-off peghead typical of prewar Martins. (*Photo courtesy of C. F. Martin & Company.*)

borrowed to pay his basketball team.

On May 5, 1982, the company board voted to ask for Frank's resignation. He wasn't present for the meeting—he was off having a drink at the time. Later, he accepted their vote without a fight. After leaving Martin, Frank opened a health and exercise center in Nazareth, which never really got off the ground. In 1983, when that business failed, he retired to Cape Canaveral, Florida, where he died on November 25, 1993.

"I definitely was part of the decision to let him go," Chris says. "Something had to change; he was so far gone at that point. The person has to be willing to change, and he had no desire whatsoever to change."

Over Chris's sole nay vote, Hugh "Tigger" Bloom (who had been hired as a computer consultant in 1964, had been made a vice president in 1970, and had sired the veterinarian software) was named president. At the next board meeting, Frederick made a rare appearance.

Chris remembers, "He was nearing 90, and didn't want to have to be involved in this. But he was still the chairman, and he started off the board meeting by saying, 'I've been thinking a lot about how the organization is structured, and it's appropriate now that we make Chris a vice president. All in favor say aye.' He realized he had to do something to get me on some sort of footing as an officer."

Along with business being abysmal, employees being laid off, and the debt of bad investments weighing on the company, there was another problem. The bank that Martin had done all its borrowing from was sold to another bank, which called in the sizable loan.

"The only reason we didn't declare bankruptcy was my grandfather decided he

ABOVE: C. F. Martin III (Frederick) was one of the few Martins who actually took the time to play the instruments his company made. He treasured the precious legacy that had been passed on by his great-grandfather, and he carefully passed it on to his grandson, Chris. He lived through the ukulele craze and the roundup of flashy cowboy singers. It's an irony that he died just as the acoustic guitar was coming back in popularity. *(Photo courtesy of C. F. Martin & Company.)*

LEFT: In 1985, just when things looked bleakest, Martin introduced another new model, the brainchild of Chris Martin IV. By combining the body outline of the M series with the deep sides of the D, Martin came up with a new, powerful model that didn't look like a Dreadnought but still had plenty of power and bass response. Thanks to a rave review by Rick Turner in the May 1985 issue of *Guitar Player* magazine, the new J-40M brought new attention to the company, and the wide array of maple and 12-string versions brought new respect from players who had written the company off as hopelessly stuck in the past. *(Guitar courtesy of C. F. Martin & Company.)*

would allow the value of his stock to go to zero before we declared bankruptcy, and it got very close. A prudent businessman would have either declared bankruptcy or sold the company. But he wouldn't let the company die," Chris says.

So C. F. Martin & Company lived on, while C. F. Martin III passed away on June 15, 1986. The previous June he had made a rare speech, appearing with Chris Martin at the Symposium of American Lutherie held in Easton, Pennsylvania. He made it up to the stage, assisted by a cane of rosewood that Dick Boak had made for him, with Martin fingerboard markers inlaid on it.

For the last time, Frederick spoke of the family passion: "I confess, I am in love with wood. Wood to me has personality. It talks to me in its grain, in its consistency, in its hardness or softness, in its music. The vibrating wood...just a plain reed vibrating in the wind is musical. And if you put it into a properly designed soundbox, as Chris said, you can wrap wood around the sound, you get the guitar tone."

He continued at length and sometimes so emotionally that his eyes teared up, recounting the company history—telling of going to the New York City lumberyards with his father at the turn of the century; of how he would daily traverse the stairs in the old North Street factory; of how they'd choose spruce for the tops ("we like medium-narrow grain; maybe 12 to 13 grain lines to the inch, with the tighter grain at the edge of the body and the wider grain in the center of the top"). He spoke of the Depression and the recession; of the then-current lay-offs, concluding, "We're very optimistic for the future. The Martin business is not over. Chris is right—the future is his."

LEFT AND BELOW: Martin introduced new maple models in 1985, with both a 6-string and a 12-string jumbo and a shallow-bodied M-64. These were joined two years later by a maple Dreadnought, the D-62. Guitar critics loved them, but the public couldn't seem to warm up to the idea of a maple Martin guitar. The J-65 was the most popular, with sales peaking at 91 in 1988, but by the mid-1990s sales had essentially disappeared, and the entire 60 series was discontinued. *(Photos courtesy of C. F. Martin & Company.)*

RIGHT: The D-45LE was the first "over 45" Dreadnought issued as a limited edition. Offered in 1987 in Brazilian rosewood at a list price of $7,500, it had more pearl than a normal Style 45, especially on the neck, and a list price almost double that of a stock D-45 at the time. Fifty D-45LEs were sold, and special versions of the D-45 continue to be among the most popular limited editions year after year. *(Photo courtesy of C. F. Martin & Company.)*

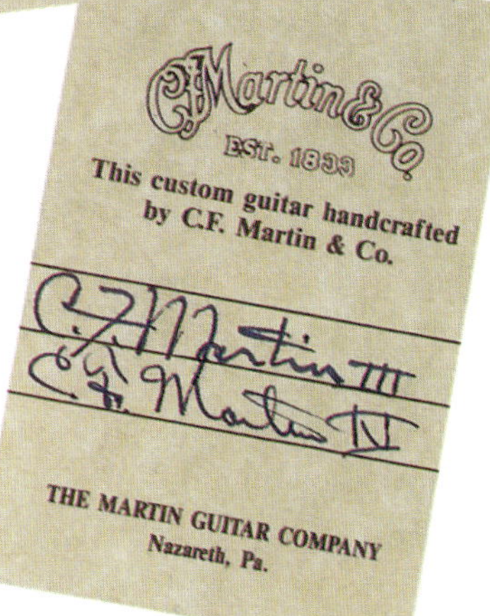

ABOVE: Martin's new Guitars of the Month series saw the return of paper labels visible through the soundhole. In 1984 and 1985, the labels were signed by both C. F. Martin III and C.F. IV. Since the death of his grandfather in 1986, Chris signs all of the labels.

By the time Frederick died, Chris had given up on the hermit idea. Wanting to follow in his grandfather's footsteps, Chris put himself forward for the CEO position.

"The board realized something had to change, took a deep breath, and put me in charge," is how he succinctly puts it.

In the four years after Frank's ouster, business had improved somewhat, to producing over 7,000 instruments a year; but things were still precarious. A settlement of Frederick's estate required a stock evaluation. The accountants took one look at the books and advised that the company be liquidated.

According to Chris, "That's when we decided, 'Let's focus this thing like a laser beam on flat-top guitars and their accessories.' And business picked up. It was like serendipity. The phones started ringing." Within a decade the company was to surpass the 22,000 mark it had hit in 1971; and today it just keeps climbing.

MARTIN *in the* MODERN WORLD

1987 – Present

A visitor to the Martin factory today will find it a very changed place from days past. Craftsmen still use drawknives to hand-sculpt the final shape on a great many necks, but the drudge work of revealing its rough form from a block of mahogany is mostly done on computer numeric control (CNC) machines.

Five of these large, pricey machines are now on the Martin shop floor. Wood braces, instead of being hand-glued to the tops, are joined via a vacuum clamp. The edges of the bent rosewood sides, once leveled with hand planes, now meet a huge rotary sander. Other stages of manufacture are similarly automated.

It is not the place it was, but neither is the Martin company the soulless machine it could have become. Rather, it is an example of what a business might be—modern, competitive, and still very human.

People matter at C. F. Martin & Company. Chairman and CEO Chris Martin's office door is literally open most of the time. A worker of no particular standing can offer an idea for a plant improvement or guitar design and stand a fair chance of seeing it implemented. There is a profit-sharing plan in place as well.

RIGHT: As the company Chairman and CEO who led Martin back to prosperity in the late twentieth century, Chris Martin (C. F. Martin IV) has reason to smile. (*Photo courtesy of C. F. Martin & Company.*)

ABOVE: Old-time country music has dedicated advocates in Norman and Nancy Blake, who often choose to recreate songs from the 1920s and 1930s with 12-fret Martins of the same era. Here they pose with a 00 and a 000, both Style 45s. Norman often puts several other old Martins to good use, including 12-fret Dreadnoughts and a C-3 arch-top with round soundhole. (*Photo courtesy Tom Rowland/Copper Creek.*)

"I think feelings have changed," says Elaine Dilliard, who has been both a worker and a manager at Martin. "On the floor years ago you didn't know what the office was thinking or doing. Being on the floor and then moving into management, you realize a lot more than if you come in here as management. I know how those people who work the floor think. I know what it feels like when something is put to you in a manner that is *telling* you rather than asking for your input and your involvement. Chris absolutely has worked very hard at avoiding that. His door's always open, and I don't think anybody is afraid to go in there and ask him a question."

There are people at Martin who have done the same job nearly all their lives and are content with that. Others have worked nearly every station in the place or have risen through the ranks to assume managerial roles in the company.

For many firms, pride is mentioned only in their advertising campaigns. At Martin you hear it from the CEO *and* from the guy with the lip ring who files nuts. Each feels the responsibility to live up to a legend, to make a product that's a standard by which others are measured and from which artists draw inspiration.

Many Martin players and dealers speak of the company's entering its second Golden Age in the 1990s, making the most consistently excellent guitars in its history. Some few others decry that the master stroke of the craftsman's hand is now missing from some stages of production. But there are instances when that hand is best used for designing and refining a machine to do the work. The vacuum clamp, for example, applies a uniform pressure that acoustically marries the braces to the top in a manner that hand clamping cannot achieve. And the vacuum clamp wasn't designed by cost efficiency experts but was championed in guitarmaking by the late renegade luthier Richard Schneider in his small workshop, because it worked best for his $10,000 guitars.

There are not many names in American business as long-lived as C. F. Martin & Company, and fewer still that exist as more than a brand name owned by a faceless corporation. Martin has a long history, having been nearly bankrupted by its attempt in the '70s to be like other businesses and having been jeopardized by a bitter strike. These experiences seem to have given the workers at Martin today an understanding of just what a rare thing they are a part of.

Martin People

The C. F. Martin name on a guitar headstock tells a player what he or she might expect to get out of the instrument, but there's only one guitar that tells the full story of what went into it. That instrument is an HD-28P, serial number 500,000, made in 1990. This instrument bears the signatures of the entire Martin workforce, commemorating their half-millionth guitar.

There are now some 500 people working for the Martin company. An employee could get lost in such a number, but instead Martin workers seem to have a sense of belonging, knowing they're contributing to something rare and unique in the world.

"I really believe there is a spirit in this factory that keeps great guitars coming out of it, something magical about that shop out there," says employee Richard Starkey. "There is a spirit

RIGHT: In 1990 Martin produced this HD-28 with serial number 500,000. Like the company itself, the guitar is a mixture of old, new, and somewhere in between. The herringbone top trim and the soundhole rosette pattern date to well before the Civil War. The shape is a 1934 adaptation of a 1916 original, and many other details such as the bridge and pick guard were also refined in the 1930s as Martin switched from gut to steel strings. The signatures on the soundboard represent Martin's entire workforce in 1990, yet the neat rows of names remind one of the careful ledger entries from a century and a half earlier by the individual who founded it all—C. F. Martin Sr. (*Guitar courtesy of C. F. Martin & Company.*)

that seems to look over everybody's shoulder to make sure that it is done correctly all the way down to the final inspection. They're amazing guitars."

Harold Weiss started with Martin in 1956. (His account of working in the old factory is on page 162.) The new factory took some getting used to for him, and the new machinery took even longer. He used to assemble bodies, likening the craft involved to the individual strokes of a master painter. In 1997 he instead is overseeing the functioning of a neck-carving CNC machine.

Is the individual's input still there?

"Oh yeah," he says. "There's a lot that has been changed, but it still has to come down to handwork. To do the roughing out, sure, use a machine. But it's the hand work that makes a difference."

After 41 years with Martin, Weiss says, "I don't want to retire. This work matters to me. And you get out here, you meet the kids working here, you talk with them. You're doing something. Who'd want to sit home?"

Mechanization isn't the only thing that has changed in Weiss's time. The factory, once exclusively the province of men, now has women working in virtually every aspect of guitarmaking.

This isn't entirely new: During World War II women filled several positions, but as Chris Martin notes, "The soldiers came home, the women went

ABOVE: Beginning in the late 1980s, singer/songwriter Diane Ponzio provided the musical portion of the Martin Guitar clinics conducted by Chris Martin. This led to her joining other women at the company in the Women & Music Committee in 1996. One result of this unique focus group was the 00-16DB, a limited edition of deep-bodied small guitars more comfortable for most women to hold. Response from dealers at the January 1997 trade show was so favorable that a second version with rosewood back and sides was added as a stock model several months later. *(Photo from Pete Shaheen/The Allentown Morning Call.)*

ABOVE: Women were Martin's prime customers in the 1800s, and they may well be again in the 2000s. The Indigo Girls, seen here with Joan Baez at an Earth Day concert, perform with their Jumbo models. (*Photo © John Bellissimo.*)

RIGHT: Though her guitar playing is often overshadowed by other instrumentation on recordings, on tour singer/songwriter Shawn Colvin exhibits considerable prowess on her '70s D-28. (*Photo © Gary L. Hacking, Photography G.*)

OPPOSITE PAGE: Martin's 00-16DB, introduced in 1997, was the brainchild of the company's Women & Music Committee. Combining the narrow 00 body with the deep sides of a J or D size results in the warm bass response contemporary players want, but in a small guitar more comfortable for women to hold. Since a similar combination was used at Gibson over 60 years ago for their Nick Lucas model, the 00-16DB will probably find favor with lots of males as well. (*Photo courtesy of C. F. Martin & Company.*)

ABOVE: Elaine Dilliard started working at Martin in 1976, and worked in almost every department before becoming a manager. One of the first women to tackle guitarmaking tasks usually performed by men, she has paved the way for many others. Today Martin's workforce is 48 percent women.

back to being housewives, and—as happened in so many other businesses—people conveniently forgot that women could do the work."

Enter Elaine Dilliard. She started at Martin the day her granddaughter was born, thinking she'd work a couple of years to help her husband buy his own business and then she'd leave Martin.

"But it didn't happen that way," she says. "You start to work here and then you get this feeling of belonging, and you get the pride in what you do, and you don't leave."

Dilliard started in pearling—as they call the inlay work in the shop—and could well have stopped there, too, since it and string-winding were considered the two jobs women were capable of.

Chris recalls, "Elaine was one of the first women to take on some of the jobs that people were doubtful about. They'd say, 'Sure, women can do inlay, but they probably can't assemble bodies.' And Elaine was like, 'Oh yeah? *Watch me.*' She set the tone, showing that women can do that work."

"I got into assembly, putting tops and backs on rims, shaping the braces," Elaine says. "No women were doing that at the time. I'd go home from here and I couldn't make a fist, my hands were so sore from holding a plane all day, and a chisel. There were some of those older guys there and they were old-fashioned. It was tough to break in. But I really got to enjoy the job and I earned some respect from them."

She went on to work in almost every department before becoming a manager. She says, "I'm really a people person. That's our main thing here, our people, and our end product, of course."

LEFT: Master repairman Dave Musselwhite drives over 70 miles to get to the factory each morning, spends the day fixing guitars, and then drives back home to strum around on his collection of 30 Martins. He got his first when he was 12 years old. (*Photo courtesy of Dave Musselwhite.*)

A lot of those people are women now. As the area's blouse mills closed when jobs went overseas, more women came to work at Martin, and there is almost parity in the workforce now. A similar shift has been seen with guitar-toting women in the popular music charts. Martin responded to this shift, first by forming the Women & Music Committee of employees in June 1996 (composed of 20 female employees, including Dilliard, and 5 males) to promote women's involvement in guitar playing. And in 1997 the company issued a model—a deep-bodied 00—designed primarily for women.

"Let me tell you how happy I am to be here," says Dave Musselwhite, "I drive 144 miles a day round-trip to work here. And I used to drive that about twice a month, just coming up here in the hopes they'd hire me. The consensus here is that Martin treats its employees with a lot of respect. It's like a family in my department."

ABOVE: Since Martin historian Mike Longworth's retirement in 1996, Rich Starkey has had the task of answering five to eight highly technical calls and letters each week from Martin owners about their beloved guitars. In total, Martin receives an average of 50 inquiries each working day.

Inspired by an uncle who collected guitars, Musselwhite got his first Martin when he was 12. "By the time I was 16, I had my first dozen Martins. I love the quality of the workmanship, the *whoom!* when you strum them. I had toured the factory several times, and it became my lifelong desire to get a job here," he says.

Now with Martin for over a decade, Musselwhite is one of its master repairmen and, as such, sees a lot of its classic models on his workbench.

"It impresses me how structurally sound they are after decades and decades," he says. "The thing that *depresses* me is the way some people abuse their Martins. We get guitars in here that are loaded with dirt. We don't know where to start on them sometimes. I've seen guitars come in with bullet holes in them, guitars that went down with a ship and swelled up, guitars that have been in barroom fights, and one guitar that a wife accidentally ran over, completely, with her car, and asked if we could get it fixed before her husband came home from a business trip. Our turnover isn't *that* fast."

One of Hank Snow's name-inlaid D-45s also ran afoul of some car tires and had to be put to rights. A ripple of excitement went through the factory when Marty Stuart's 1940 D-45—previously owned by both Johnny Cash and, reportedly, Hank Williams—came in for repair. Other guitars have come in bearing Frankenstein-like bolts and Bondo from botched home repair jobs. Martin workers have found everything from rattlesnake rattles to marijuana in the cases, and one busted guitar arrived packed in a box with a slice of pizza and a half-finished Coke.

Musselwhite now has some 30 Martins, dating back to 1860, in his collection but says, "The new guitars are still exciting to me. I can tell you the old ones were very, very good for the technology they had at the time, but the new ones are far superior."

Richard Starkey was also a precocious guitar nut, starting at age 5 while growing up in Connecticut. In 1971, when he was 15, his parents took him on a tour of the Martin factory. "I had a

(continued on page 226)

Willie Nelson

Nylon-String Martin Maverick

If Willie Nelson had never penned a word or sung a note, it would be a grievous loss to the music world. But then perhaps more people would have noticed that he's also one of the most distinctive guitarists in American music.

Nelson's sound is unique, even to the casual ear: a country musician playing a strangely amplified nylon-string guitar with a pick. The guitar tends to stand out visually as well: an unpopular fan-braced nylon-string model made by the most famed steel-string guitarmaker on earth, with a primeval bridge pickup added to it and scores of signatures scrawled on its top (except for the spot where Nelson's pick has worn a hole so big it looks as if the spruce was rammed by a U-boat).

The playing that Nelson accomplishes on Trigger—named after Roy Rogers's horse—is easily as expressive as his voice. Accompanying said voice, his picking becomes like a second voice, so closely joined to his singing one that it recalls the six-string symbiosis of Robert Johnson, in passion if not in style. And when Nelson solos on Trigger, the playing is pure personality, phrased like no one else, but with the passionate vibrato of his idol Django Reinhardt.

With the guts from a 1960s Baldwin electric jury-rigged into it and pumped through an equally archaic Baldwin amp, his 1969 Martin N-20 has a singularly sweet rasp to its tone, one that's ragged but right.

RIGHT: Willie Nelson's trusted sidekick Trigger, featuring the most famous hole this side of the Grand Canyon. (*Photo © Kwaku Alston.*)

"Grady Martin says it sounds like a road grader, and that's good enough for me," Nelson says with a laugh. "It's got real sweet tone to it, and you can rock and roll on it, too.

"The tone is what makes it what it is. It's a miracle to find a tone like this. The Baldwin pickup didn't have it, not until the pickup was put on the Martin. The guitar by itself has everything you need without any amplification. I did my whole *Spirit* album without any amplifier at all. That's when it sounds the best," Nelson says.

His first guitars were a budget Stella; a Sears, Roebuck; and a Harmony. "I didn't know anything like a Martin or Gibson existed until I was half-grown. Then someone came along with a Martin, and right away you know the difference. They're great guitars," he says.

Nelson wound up with his Martin only by accident, though, and bought it sight unseen. In the late 1960s he had eschewed steel strings for nylon, and he says "the Baldwin company gave me a Baldwin amp and classical electric guitar with a special three-cord stereo pickup. I busted the guitar so I sent it up to Nashville to get it fixed, to Shot Jackson. And he called to say, 'I can't fix it. It's broke too bad.' I said, 'Well what have you got around?' He said he had a Martin up on the shelf for $750. I asked if he could put the pickups in the Martin. And that's how I got it, right off the shelf, unseen from a thousand miles away.

"When I got it I knew that I had picked up something special. I like to just sit around in a room and play it. I like to write on it. I just like the sound of it. It goes all the way back to the old Django sound. I'm definitely a kicked-in-the-head Django Reinhardt fan. Him, Grady Martin, and Hank Garland—to me, those were the guitar players."

Nelson estimates he has 100 signatures on his Martin, beginning ages ago with Leon Russell's autograph. Nelson recalls, "He got me to sign his one day. I asked why, and he said, 'It'll make it valuable.' So I said, 'Well, do mine then.' All the signatures on it are of friends, both musician friends and friend-friends. It's got Roger Miller, Kris Kristofferson, Gene Autry, Waylon Jennings, lawyers, football coaches, all sorts."

Nelson chuckles at the thought that Martin might conceivably issue a Willie Nelson model, as it has with Eric Clapton and other guitarists. "People would have to get their own signatures," he says.

He also doesn't know what they'd do about duplicating the hole he's worn in his N-20. It's still a living, changing thing.

"I think with all the varnish and paint jobs it's had, the hole may have stopped some, but it still grows a little bit. The fingers and pick both have at it. And I don't care if it gets bigger," he says, laughing again. "I'd just put another piece of wood in there or something. I really don't care."

BELOW: On the road again: Nelson has scarcely done a recording or performance in three decades without Trigger. (*Photo © Paul Natkin.*)

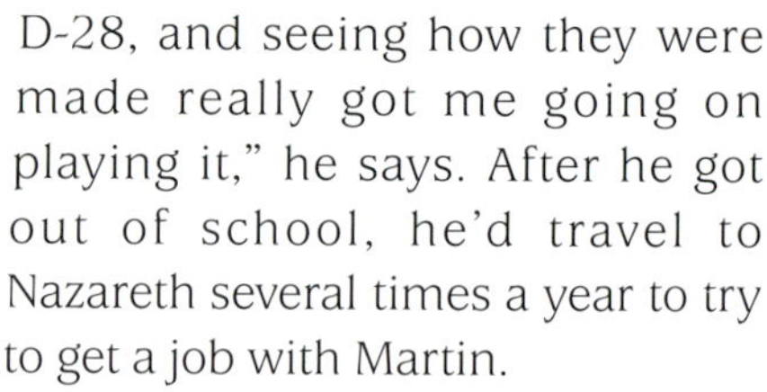

RIGHT: If these guitars could talk.... Even Martin guitars have fallen prey to overly ambitious, do-it-yourself repairmen. The tacked-on braces and splints must have done wonders for the tone of this Dreadnought. In this case, it looks like the warranty has been voided. (*Photo courtesy of Dick Boak.*)

D-28, and seeing how they were made really got me going on playing it," he says. After he got out of school, he'd travel to Nazareth several times a year to try to get a job with Martin.

Starkey did guitar repair at home and one day visited Ovation Guitars because he'd heard that an executive there had a prewar D-45 and Starkey had never seen one. He wound up being offered a job there, "so I got my job at Ovation because of a Martin guitar," he chuckles.

Starkey kept checking with Martin, though, and was eventually hired in 1992. In a four-year span there, he went from shaping necks to setting up actions, to working in repairs, then to research and development, and finally he became a clinician, doing workshops and performing on the guitars in music stores. When Martin historian Mike Longworth retired in 1996, Starkey also took on the daunting job of answering players' technical questions. Most who write in want information about their old Martins, but Starkey's favorite letter is from a player who claimed the vibrations of his D-16 gave him an upset stomach.

Starkey finds the company to be very receptive to input. A method he devised of simulating string tension is now used when the truss rods are set, and the factory has also adopted nut-slot gauges that he designed. He also submitted the idea for the three-piece rosewood headstock face used on the D-35 anniversary model.

At 21, Chris Eckhart is one of the younger people working at Martin. He took some getting used to for the older employees, because of his multiple earrings, lip ring, rockabilly haircut, and tattoos.

Though he listens to bands that

BELOW: Harold Weiss and Chris Eckhart (*left to right*) represent a wide generation gap of Martin employees, bridged by a love of the Martin guitar.

most employees have never heard of, he's also an Elvis Presley fan and is awed by Martin's past.

"Seeing that D-45 come in that had belonged to Hank Williams and Johnny Cash, that was amazing. I'm really proud to tell people where I work. I don't want to work in a really crappy factory job. I've done that already. There's a special feeling to working here. I'd like to make it my career," he says.

ABOVE: Elvis Costello emerged amid the British punk scene of the 1970s, going on to become one of the most versatile, questing, and accomplished songsmiths and performers of his time. Though he has forayed from country to classical, his affection for Martins has been consistent throughout. (*Photo © Jay Blakesberg.*)

People do tend to linger at Martin. Martin's Director of Artist Relations Dick Boak recalls a recent trade show where six people from Martin went out to dinner with six people from another American guitar institution. "We got to adding up how long each person had been with their respective companies. Our six people's years in the company added up to 120 years; theirs added up to 5 years."

The Environment

As guitars have grown in popularity, the materials they are made from have been in dwindling supply. In the past 20 years, the cost of Indian rosewood has tripled, the cost of ebony has increased to five times what it was, and a back-and-sides set of Brazilian rosewood has gone from $50 to over $1,000 for the same-quality wood.

Except for the beloved Brazilian, this increase is not as significant to the cost of an instrument as labor costs are. Nonetheless, Martin is aggressive about using resources responsibly. If, as C. F. Martin III described it, the wood in the guitar is the voice of the tree, the Martin company couldn't very well ignore the cry of alarm over clear-cutting and other forest-decimating practices.

"We've tried to be responsible and ahead of our time, and at the same time we're dealing with an audience that demands the traditional materials for guitarmaking," says Dick Boak. Balancing those concerns has become a fine art.

Boak continues, "We buy our mahogany from Peru and Bolivia, trying always to purchase from a sustainable-yield vendor. We don't buy it from Brazil because we don't want to contribute to the deforestation there. Spruce comes largely from fall-down trees. Our spruce vendors will take core samples from trees usually in state forests or in Canadian provincial parks. Then, working with the park rangers, they'll get permission to remove a fallen tree. After they've determined that the grain orientation is correct, they'll cut it on site and remove it in billet form. I can't say spruce has been managed well, and probably the American government is the biggest culprit, especially in the 100-year treaty with Japan that provides for unlimited logging at ridiculously low prices from Alaska. That's very distressing to us, but nothing we've been able to do has amended that treaty."

The Indian government has been progressive in effectively managing its rosewood. Again, most of the wood Martin uses comes from fall-down trees sold at government auction. Maple, used for bridgeplates or for bodies on limited-edition or

ABOVE AND TOP RIGHT: Oak is one North American hardwood that can be used for the back and sides of steel-string guitars, yielding excellent tone. The different appearance of the guitar is the only obstacle for buyers to overcome. North American walnut also works well for the backs and sides of guitars, and Martin has used it for limited editions as well as for a run of 100 D-16W models in 1987. (*Photos courtesy of C. F. Martin & Company.*)

ABOVE AND LEFT: When a rare wood does go into a Martin guitar, it certainly sounds better than it would have looked as a coffee table. The limited edition D-40FMG from 1995 is made of rare quilted mahogany. (*Guitar courtesy of C. F. Martin & Company.*)

custom-shop models, is in no danger, since it's a plentiful and fast-growing domestic tree. Spanish cedar, used in small amounts for linings, is not endangered either.

"The most difficult wood in respect to environmental impact is ebony," Boak says. "We get it from India, Africa, Madagascar, and Sri Lanka. It's disheartening to hear that a lot of ebony is downed when they're cutting for highways, and it's just left to rot. We would hope they'd realize they have a valuable resource and take care if it, but it wouldn't appear they're doing that. And we don't know how to have an impact. We don't feel boycotting ebony is the way to convince them that their resource is valuable."

Between the harvesting of Brazilian rosewood and Brazil's long slash-and-burn forest-clearing policies, the wood is in danger of extinction; and international treaty prohibits its importation. Martin can only use wood that was imported from Brazil before the treaty was signed in 1992.

As such traditional tone woods become unavailable, Martin has experimented with using other woods, including larch, redwood, cedar, and poplar for soundboards. Bodies have been made of ash, cherry, several types of maple and walnut, Australian blackwood, red and white oak, mesquite, the koa-family monkey pod, and California acacia. An all-spruce guitar was even built as a prototype.

Another guitar still in the prototype stage at this writing is a "sustainable-yield" model, made of readily replenished woods. Some new woods have made it into production, such as the limited-edition figured claro walnut model and the Style 16 ash model. "The ash one looked kind of like what you'd expect of a kitchen table," Boak says, "but it sounded great. All the woods are potential tonewood; it's just a matter of working with them in the appropriate way, modifying bracing etceteras."

ABOVE: The soundboard of this LHD-28 looks like spruce, but it isn't. In 1991 to 1992 Martin used larch for guitar tops on a limited number of HD-28 models (and now, the larch model). Though the larch-top Dreadnoughts sounded fine and the wood looked like good old spruce, people still wanted spruce tops on their HD-28s. In 1990 Martin made 200 to 300 HD-28s with backs and sides of morado, a close substitute for rosewood from Bolivia. *(Photo courtesy of C. F. Martin & Company.)*

New Growth

A funny thing happened to the acoustic guitar on its way to "extinction." Predicted to follow the woolly mammoth to the tar pits in the early to mid-1980s, when high-tech electronic keyboards dominated the music industry, it instead soared to unprecedented popularity in the 1990s. Perhaps the people who bought synthesizers realized that 540 processed sounds don't equal one rich, expressive one. Perhaps the resurgence of country music helped, or the progressive "newgrass" sounds of a new generation of super pickers. The persistent emotionality of artists like Neil Young reaching across generations may have helped, too. Or maybe it was the 1989 advent of MTV's *Unplugged,* from which a new audience realized the best songs were the ones that could survive being stripped down to just voice and guitar.

Whatever the reasons, C. F. Martin's sales began a steep climb in the 1990s, and the company had the biggest year of its then–164-year history in 1997, producing 31,869 guitars.

RIGHT: Martin's MTV model, unveiled at the January 1996 trade show, is the most radical departure from traditional acoustic guitar construction and styling the company has ever offered. Though the bracing and body outline are that of a standard Dreadnought, one side (and adjacent half of the back) is rosewood, while the opposite side (under the treble strings) is mahogany. The MTV logo on the headstock and the letters spelling "UNPLUGGED" down the neck are equally unusual. All that's missing is Beavis and Butthead, heh-heh, uh, heh-heh. (*Photo courtesy of C. F. Martin & Company.*)

It probably didn't hurt that the company met the new acoustic boom with its reputation redeemed and with a dizzyingly broad line of instruments; there were nearly 50 models in the standard catalog. These included limited-edition guitars that are the most ornate in the company's history, and there are others made to the specifications of famed Martin players. There are low-priced utilitarian models with bold new bracing and neck joint designs. There are exacting copies of models from the first Golden Era. In 1997 there was even a limited-edition reissue of an 1830s Stauffer-style Martin, with a coffin case, no less. There is the Backpacker travel guitar, a glorified toothpick with a surprisingly big tone. Then there is the Guitar of the Month series, which was begun in 1984 to bring out several specialty guitars each year. Even without Martin's Custom Shop, which will indulge hundreds of option variations, there have been more Martin models made since 1985 than were made in all the years previous in the twentieth century.

Martin had begun its journey back from near-dead in 1985, with the introduction of the Jumbo M series, a deeper brother to the M "Grand Auditorium"–sized guitars. It kept the large M body size that had been derived from Martin's 1930s arch-tops but now added the depth of a Dreadnought to the equation, making for *one* big-sounding guitar. It was the brainchild of Chris Martin, who has taken an active hand in designing instruments ever since then, including a "CEO's Choice" limited-edition series of instruments for 1997.

The company exists in a competitive market, and Martin has had to make changes to stay abreast of younger companies that don't have the weight of tradition on their shoulders. Taylor Guitars and other competitors were quicker to make the slimmer necks that modern players want. Chris says, "The one place that the competition hasn't poked us is tone. They leave us alone on that one, but they were able to poke us on playability. We were still making big fat honking necks for people who play on the first three frets. The more we understood that people who were accustomed to electric guitars needed better action, the more we changed."

LEFT: As awareness of the company's past became more pronounced, it wasn't just the famous Martins from the 1930s that customers began to ask about. In 1996, Martin built a prensentation-grade 00 with black Stauffer-style neck and commissioned Larry Robinson to execute a special inlay for the fretboard. The inlay commemorates the old factory and C. F. Martin Sr.'s 200th birthday.

The J-40M was the first Martin model with the new, "low-profile" neck shape, a feature now standard throughout the Martin line, with the exception of the Vintage series. The slimmer neck was made possible by another long-overdue feature, an adjustable truss rod that replaced the square steel tubing neck reinforcement. As the acoustic guitar recovered from its mid-1980s slump, the more modern neck shape allowed Martin to attract electric guitarists switching to acoustic guitar.

More recently, in 1995, the quest for electric-like action also caused Chris to institute a policy of delaying the shipment of finished guitars for two weeks and then giving them yet another inspection before sending them out into the world. Though Martin was setting up its guitars with their lowest action ever, retailers complained that they were arriving too high. Tests showed that the wood shifted after being set up, so now guitars are stored in-factory for two weeks and adjusted yet again before being shipped.

Chris Martin is the first to admit that the inspiration Martin has provided to other makers is sometimes a two-way street. "I have to thank Bob Taylor [of Taylor Guitars] for giving us a reason to respond to competitive pressures," Chris says. "Without that, businesses are not as responsive. We only put our first CNC machine in place after Bob had his up and running, and he was very accommodating in sharing information on it."

ABOVE: In 1997 Martin offered two limited-edition size 00 guitars with Stauffer-style necks: a 00-40 in Indian rosewood and a 00-45 in Brazilian rosewood. For guitarists who wish to travel down Martin's historical memory lane with period luggage, a black wooden "coffin" case is included. (*Photo courtesy of C. F. Martin and Company.*)

Marty Stuart

Country Picker Extraordinaire

Marty Stuart is an altogether rare breed of country performer, one who is more than able to hold his own in the contemporary country scene but who is also thoroughly based in the traditions of the music.

Stuart was given three albums when he turned five—the Beatles, Johnny Cash, and Flatt and Scruggs. "I liked the Beatles record, but it didn't hit my heart the way those other two records did. There was something about the excitement and the sound of Flatt and Scruggs band, and there was something about the darkness and mystique of the Johnny Cash world, his storytelling abilities. And oddly enough those are two bands I've played with down through the years," Stuart says.

A fretboard prodigy, he landed a gig as Lester Flatt's mandolinist long before he was old enough to drive, at age 13. Even then he was a total guitar hound, judging bands by their instruments along with what they played on them. He got his first Martin at age 14, and it was an auspicious beginning to his guitar collection.

"I got in pretty good," he says, with a laugh. "The first Martin I ever owned was that famous Lester Flatt guitar. He gave it to me. When I put Lester's guitar on, I knew even when I was 14 that I'd never fill the shoes, but there was a responsibility to damn well try to fill them."

"When I started playing with Lester, I moved to Nashville—my mom and dad still lived in Mississippi—and he let me move in with him and his wife, gratis. I was always curious and found this guitar with no strings on it in the spare room of the house. It was leaning up in a corner, not even in a case. I immediately recognized it as the guitar I grew up watching on TV. I took it into the kitchen and said, 'What's the deal on this guitar?' I asked permission to string it up and play it, he let me, and I adopted it." The Flatt guitar was a D-28 that had been heavily modified over the years, by a teenage Mike Longworth, among others.

Just to spoil him for good, Stuart's next Martin was a 1939 D-45 that Johnny Cash gave him, a guitar believed to have once been Hank Williams's. Though Stuart has a considerable guitar collection now, Martins are the only flat-tops he plays, and he has 15 of them.

"It's kind of an all-purpose guitar. If

LEFT: Marty Stuart knows how to strike a pose with his namesake guitar, but he's even better at playing the devil out of it. (*Photo © Ron Keith, Nashville.*)

you're a singer-songwriter, your guitar is you and your song's best friend. And Martin is a very singer-songwriter–friendly guitar. And it's a bluegrass player's guitar. And it's not just a rhythm instrument, but a lead guitar as well. It's like a Fender Telecaster without a pickup. It's a real cannon.

ABOVE: Stuart and fellow performer Travis Tritt (*far left*) check out production of the Marty Stuart Limited Edition. Chris Martin (*holding the guitar*) and Dick Boak (*back*) lead the tour. *(Photo courtesy of Ronnie Ricci Simpson/C. F. Martin & Company.)*

"Clarence White and Doc Watson really established it as a lead instrument, but you can trace it back to people like the Delmore Brothers and find lead players. An overlooked fact is that Hank Williams was a great southern blues guitar player. If you'll check the solo he did on the record *My Bucket's Got a Hole in It,* he did a brilliant solo on that record, a real testimony to the Martin guitar," Stuart says.

What's the best Martin he's ever played?

"I would be hard-pressed to find any guitar better than a prewar D-45," he says. "I mean it's just like playing a grand piano, like the difference when you play an upright piano and a grand. Then without a doubt the greatest herringbone I ever played is under glass at Hank Williams Jr.'s museum. It's his dad's herringbone. I picked it up after it hadn't been played in 25 years. I tuned it up and the first chord I hit was an E major. And it sounded like a shotgun going off. It was just brilliant. So you walk away thinking you couldn't possibly top this. But then I play that '39 prewar D-45, and it just goes to another level, like straight to your heart."

The main Martin he's been touring and recording with of late, though, is a model bearing the same name as his driver's license. The limited-edition Marty Stuart model—with production limited to 250—is one of the most ornate guitars the company has ever made, with a distinctive ring of pearl herringbone around the soundhole and 103 pieces of several varieties of pearl on the fingerboard—in the shapes of horseshoes, steer horns, dice, and such—not counting Stuart's signature. Sales of the $5,400 list guitar raised over $20,000 for Stuart's chosen charity, the children's education fund of the Oglala Lakota College District Learning Center.

Stuart said, "I told Dick Boak I wanted a guitar that looked like a country guitar or a country-rock guitar—with a lot of character—that played like a bluegrass player's dream," Stuart says. "Without a doubt the best neck I've ever played on a Martin guitar is that prewar D-45, so we took the neck specs from that guitar. I drew out the neck inlay pattern on a napkin. I was really interested in getting them to do the pearl herringbone because I knew Martin had never done that before. It's gorgeous, but the sound of the guitar is what I'm most impressed with.

"I love guitars that are workhorses, that have a personality and a sound, that play like a dream and write songs by themselves. And Martin's one of those things that's like a gunfighter with his pistol. I love guitars that you strap on and you don't think about. You know they're going to do their part. They're there to work. And we take off—I do my part, and it does its. And at the end of the night everybody's happy. A Martin gives me that feeling.

"It is a tradition to play a Martin guitar. And the thing that makes me feel good as the new millennium approaches is that they're still doing good work. I get a feel from Chris Martin and Dick Boak down to the custodian, a feeling of dedication and integrity that runs through that plant. It shows in the net result. It's something that America can be proud of anywhere in the world. Martin guitars are a great representative of America."

LEFT: The J-40BK was introduced in 1988. With gleaming black lacquer finish, white bindings, gold tuners, and colorful abalone fretboard inlays, the black jumbo is a visually stunning example of a modern Martin guitar. *(Guitar courtesy of C. F. Martin and Company.)*

RIGHT: There was a lot of resistance to the acoustic bass guitar from some factions at Martin, with predictions of high costs and months devoted to development. This prototype—produced in a couple of days by Dick Boak, Martin's director of artist relations—was intended to prove the workability of the 34-inch scale length as well as the 17th-fret neck-to-body joint. The tone was considerably better than what had been expected. Like the production models, this prototype has a nonscalloped X-brace, but its other braces are scalloped as usual. *(Guitar courtesy of Dick Boak.)*

LEFT: As the unplugged craze spread to bass guitars, Martin responded with acoustic bass versions of the J-40 and J-65 (maple) jumbos called the B-40 and B-65. Though highly regarded, the stiff price kept production numbers low. The B-1 has the same Martin jumbo body but uses D-1 materials and construction, with a price less than half that of the B-40. *(Guitar courtesy of C. F. Martin & Company.)*

New Models, New Strategies

Chris jokingly credits another competitor with causing Martin to introduce its incredibly successful, low-cost D-1 model. Desiring a midline instrument between the Sigma and Martin brands, the company began importing guitars in kit form from Japan and assembling them in Nazareth in 1983. The new line was dubbed Shenandoah. There were production problems—the guitars weren't made to the tolerances required of Martin's light lacquer finishes—and then the yen started climbing, until an $899 Shenandoah ultimately jumped to $1,199.

Then, Chris says, a competitor followed suit but went too far, having the guitars arrive in the United States nearly completed. "It got to Customs and they said, 'This isn't parts. This is a Japanese guitar.' The competitors complained, 'Well Martin does it,' so then Customs decided *ours,* too, was a Japanese guitar. We had to label them 'parts from Japan,' and it was no longer perceived as an American guitar. Sales just dived. Someday I'm going to write the competitor a letter thanking him because that caused us to invent the D-1. People in the shop were so fed up with the Shenandoahs that they were saying, 'Let us do it from scratch.' Then [engineer] Mike Dresdner joined us, and he was able to cut through the tradition to say we had to look at it differently, that we couldn't make it with a dovetail neck. He helped us to design the D-1 so we were able to make it more efficiently and price it accordingly. And that's where our bigger market is now. We were able to sell a few more D-28s, but we're selling thousands and thousands of the less expensive Martins. The DM is over six months backordered and is part of why we're running at about 150 guitars a day now. We've never done that in our history."

Something else Martin had never done before was artist endorsements. Dick Boak, whose position as director of artist relations didn't exist prior to his creating it, can persuasively argue the need for the change, as can Chris Martin, who says, "For what my family wanted out of the business years ago, [the old] policy made sense. But today, if we

ABOVE: In the 1980s Michael Hedges rewrote the rules about how acoustic guitars could be played. A dynamic performer and prolific songwriter, Hedges changed musical directions several times in his long career, which sadly ended with his death in 1997. One constant in his music was his workhorse 1970 D-28. Though he owned several guitars, his Dreadnought was in constant use and may rival Willie Nelson's "Trigger" as one of the most-traveled and most-heard Martins of modern times. *(Photo © Jay Blakesberg.)*

BELOW: The Shenandoah Series Martins, introduced in 1983, were the company's attempt to fill the enormous price gap between its imported Sigma line and the Martin guitars. Martin lacked the high-tech tooling necessary to build mid-price guitars efficiently, so it began importing unfinished guitar bodies and necks from Japan. After lacquering and final assembly in Nazareth, the company added tuners, a hard-shell case, and under-the-saddle pickup as well, thus contributing more than 50 percent of a Shenandoah's value and qualifying the guitar for a "Made in USA" label. But the laminated backs and sides, laminated neck heels, and dyed rosewood fretboards and bridges made a D-2832 quite unlike a regular Martin D-28, both in sound and in the quality of materials. Less than a decade later, Shenandoah models were replaced by the D-1 and similar models made from scratch in the Martin factory.

BELOW AND RIGHT: The new low-cost DM brings a made-from-scratch-in-Nazareth Martin to buyers who previously couldn't afford such a prestigious brand. The mahogany back and sides are laminated, the finish is low-gloss, and the decoration is almost nonexistent. But thanks to a solid-spruce soundboard and careful bracing design, the DM sounds far more impressive than it looks. Since CNC machines don't care about models and prices, the neck feels just like that of the DM's solid-wood brother, the D-16T. *(Guitar courtesy of C. F. Martin & Company.)*

don't pay more attention to artist endorsements and do it more formally, I have this tremendous fear that we'll be on the outside looking in. That's so much a part of doing business now. Look at Nike—without endorsements they wouldn't be Nike. What we're trying to do now is do it with taste."

Martin's first signature-model artist guitar likely wasn't done with the intent of cashing in with the rock video crowd. The 1993 Guitar of the Month issue was an OM-28 Perry Bechtel model, signed by the widow of the 1920s guitarist/banjoist.

Rather than indiscriminately showering free guitars on anyone who can give it some exposure, the company has embarked on a series of limited-edition guitars that are either designed in conjunction with artists long associated with their Martin guitars or are artist-associated models reflective of milestones in the company's history.

The second such instrument was the 1994 limited-edition replica of Gene Autry's first-ever D-45, which, of course, Autry had had to pay for when he bought it back in 1933. It wasn't a bad investment—he's reportedly turned down an offer of one million dollars for it. It resides still in Autry's Western Heritage Museum in Southern California.

BELOW: A long ride: In 1933 cowboy star Gene Autry ordered the first D-45. Sixty-one years later, in 1994, the company presented Autry with one of its exacting reissues of that guitar. *(Photo courtesy of Roy Kidney/C. F. Martin & Company.)*

ABOVE AND RIGHT: There are few makes of guitar that Bob Dylan hasn't played during his four decades of influencing American music, but he keeps coming back to Martin. In 1995 he ordered his custom HD-28 with Englemann spruce top, joining thousands of other musicians of all levels in making the HD-28 Martin's most popular model. (*Photo from AP/Wide World Photos.*)

Chris Martin says, "I'd always wanted to see his D-45, so before the Anaheim NAMM show [the National Association of Music Merchants trade show] one year we went to the museum, and there it was. The thing that struck me was the gift shop, packed with Gene Autry watches and penknives, really commercializing him." Martin called the museum's chairman and suggested the decidedly classier idea of a reissue D-45, with a couple of hundred dollars from each sale going to the museum. The idea clicked, and it set the pattern for future artist guitars, where an artist's chosen charity benefits.

Whereas the Autry guitar sold largely to collectors and the Bechtel model to longtime fans of the OM model, the next signature model brought in new converts. Eric Clapton's 1992 MTV *Unplugged* performance and subsequent multi-platinum-selling album had given acoustic music a big boost, and it didn't hurt that he was playing old Martins.

"As advertising manager then, I'd gotten calls from all over asking what the guitars were that Clapton was using on MTV," Boak recalls. "I didn't really know. Mike Longworth didn't know exactly.

RIGHT AND BELOW: Eric Clapton's prowess on old Les Pauls and Stratocasters increased awareness and demand for those instruments. But where could fans turn when he showed up on his wildly successful 1992 MTV *Unplugged* performance playing a Martin that hadn't been made in over half a century? The company responded in 1995 with the limited edition 000-42 model. A herringbone 000-28 EC is a popular stock model today. (*Photo of Eric Clapton © John Bellissimo.*)

RIGHT: The most unusual looking Guitar of the Month came in 1988, when Dick Boak designed this double cutaway M2C-28. Essentially an MC-28 with cutaways on both sides, it was too radical for Martin buyers, and only 20 were sold. *(Photo courtesy of C. F. Martin & Company.)*

Gradually we found out what they were, and it turns out one was even a guitar Longworth had modified years ago. [One had been a gift to Clapton from Stephen Stills in the early 1970s.] I asked permission from Chris to contact Clapton about doing a guitar. I did, and I proposed a contribution to a children's charity. There was some emotion behind it, and he immediately responded positively. We came up with some neat blended specifications that Clapton liked of the two guitars he had. I loved the project so much that I put my order in first and got number 2, which Clapton borrowed to record the 'Change the World' video in the Hoboken, New Jersey, train station."

The initial deluxe 000-42 model (the 000-28EC—a stock model with herringbone in place of pearl—was introduced in 1996) was limited to a run of 461, to tally with Clapton's *461 Ocean Boulevard* album. It was an expensive guitar ($8,100), and some quarters both in and out of the company doubted it would fare well. No other limited-edition project had sold more than 200, and the Clapton model—some on Martin's sales staff argued—was essentially a 000 with Style 42 appointments that listed for more than a Style 45.

When unveiled at the Winter NAMM show, Japanese dealers alone would have taken the entire run of the Clapton model. It became the company's most successful limited edition, and some $92,000 was raised for The Eric Clapton Charitable Trust for Children.

Since then the company has issued limited edition Jimmie Rodgers and Kingston Trio commemorative models and has collaborated with Paul Simon, Marty Stuart, and others to make their dream guitars available to the public.

Martins were also in the dreams of players in countries where they could only see the guitars in photographs. But with the fall of communism in Europe, new markets opened.

Chris Martin says, "Our dealer in Berlin, a great dealer, has almost made his fortune since the wall came down, servicing all the pent-up demand. People came in from the East with a very specific knowledge of the particular Martins they wanted. They'd done their homework in the years they couldn't get one. And he'd say, 'Geez, I'm all out of those,' and they'd say, 'Okay, I'll take one of *those*!' They'd take anything. This one fellow in East Berlin had wanted an M-38 so badly he'd gotten all the specifications for it and gone to Mark Neukirchen and had a guitarmaker

RIGHT: Maple binding and a maple peghead facing make this D-18MB, a Guitar of the Month from 1990, easy to distinguish from any typical D-18. Almost 100 were sold, proving the public's increasing acceptance of deluxe mahogany guitars. *(Photo courtesy of C. F. Martin & Company.)*

LEFT: Martin recently completed two custom-shop models, a 6-string and a 12-string, for guitarist Steve Miller. His Pegasus logo adorns both guitars. *(Photos courtesy of C. F. Martin & Company.)*

ABOVE: Both with Simon and Garfunkel in the 1960s and as a solo artist since, Paul Simon's intricate, finely executed six-string arrangements inspired many to take up the guitar. In 1997 Martin commemorated his contribution with a limited edition model. *(Photo courtesy of John Sterling Ruth/C. F. Martin & Company.)*

there build him a copy of one."

Chris took them the real thing, traveling to Mark Neukirchen and presenting an HD-28 to the town museum. It's still an instrument-making town, and while there, he passed on an opportunity to buy for $1 a failing factory making guitars for the Eastern Bloc countries if he would guarantee employment for 1,000 people. One wonders what the Violin Makers Guild would have thought.

In Space, No One Can Hear You Strum

In 1994 Martin began offering the Backpacker, a distinctive dwarf travel guitar designed by New Jersey luthier Bob McNally. It was the first instrument manufactured in Martin's plant in Mexico, where its Darco-brand strings had been made since 1991. Introduced with few expectations at the 1994 Winter NAMM show, Martin came home with initial orders for 5,000. Backpackers have since been to both the North and South Poles and to the top of Mount Everest. But no other has yet gone quite so far as one went on March 14, 1994, when astronaut Pierre Thuot took a Backpacker into space on Flight STS-62 (and you thought Martin's model numbers were confusing) of the space shuttle *Columbia*.

It wasn't the first guitar in space—the Russians

won that race, too. But it was the first American guitar in space and probably the first to have Beatles's songs played on it.

Thuot had played bass in an all-astronaut rock band, doing Rolling Stones and Beatles covers as well as the original "What to Do in Orbit on a Saturday Night." He got the notion to take a guitar into space with him. Thuot knew Rickenbacker head John Hall socially, and he asked him if he knew of any guitars small enough to fit NASA's size restrictions. Hall pointed him at Martin, and Martin had McNally build a slightly smaller model for Thuot. A bag of flame-retardant Nomex was made for it because NASA has rules about flammable materials in its spacecraft (and had perhaps seen the film of Hendrix at Monterey).

What happens if you drop your pick in space? "Nothing," according to Thuot. "It just stays right there, floating. You don't have to worry about hunting for it. The other nice thing is you can play guitar on the ceiling."

Picking on his space porch, Thuot didn't lack inspiration. He says, "Seeing the Earth like that is just an awesome sight. It really makes you realize there's no lines between countries, and the planet is the only thing we've got. You can see very graphically in space how if a fire is burning somewhere, the smoke can carry for thousands of miles. It makes you step back and think."

In its 13 days, 23 hours, and 16 minutes aloft, the Backpacker traveled even farther than Willie Nelson's battered Martin, Trigger, has on his tour bus, logging 224 orbits and 5.8 million miles.

RIGHT: The Martin Backpacker was meant to travel, but none has traveled as far as this one, which accompanied astronaut/ guitarist Pierre Thuot on the space shuttle Columbia in 1994. *(Guitar courtesy of C. F. Martin & Company.)*

Legacy and Lift-off

It took C. F. Martin Sr. months to cross the Atlantic on a wind-powered ship. Pioneer though he was, his imagination probably wasn't big enough to conceive of a time 161 years in the future when a guitar bearing his name would orbit the entire planet in a mere 90 minutes.

Dealing with that amount of change is challenge enough for Chris Martin, the sixth generation of his family to head the company. C. F. Martin & Company may have a greater legacy than any other guitarmaker, but there's also some strain involved in dragging a century and a half of tradition behind you.

"It's something we wrestle with all the time," Chris says. "We're rarely on the leading edge of technology. We wait for someone else to bang us on the head with it and say, 'You guys might want to look at a CNC machine!' Well, yeah, I guess we should. Now we have five of them.

"And something I wonder regarding the tradition is how much of an obligation do we have to improve the product when we find a way that would be noticeable? Fortunately just about everybody I've asked, dealers and others, say you have to improve the product. Don't get so stuck in your tradition that you continue to make them in a way that may fail eventually. My feeling is that a lot of our design is still based on gut strings; and because we put steel strings on them and didn't beef them up that much, we continue to have problems that other companies with no history don't have."

Observing the generations of Chris Martin's family is almost like viewing a history of the

ABOVE AND RIGHT: The old Martin factory now houses the Guitarmakers Connection, formerly "A Woodworker's Dream," and small goods shipping warehouse. Shown are Ruth Piasecki, Mike Dickinson, and Frank Finocchio of the Guitarmaker's Connection. (*Photo by Robert A. Yoder; artwork courtesy of Dick Boak.*)

United States in microcosm. The first several generations were busy carving a place in the New World, establishing the family business and weathering hardships that made dedication and integrity a necessity, not an option. They put the company on a solid footing, giving one generation the latitude to make mistakes (which it did). That mirrors much of American business in the 1970s, when companies began acting as if their whole story could be told with a line on a graph.

And Chris Martin is a new breed, subtly different from past generations. He's more studied and self-aware. Like many of his generation, he seems less a product of instinct than the result of years spent finding himself: When his grandfather made the rounds of employees at their workstations, it was simply because that's what he did. When Chris does it, it's part of a well-considered management philosophy. It also happens to be the right thing.

"I love participatory management and empowerment," Chris says. "Some people have joined us recently and said one thing they like here is that nobody is trying to sabotage their success. I have coffee with the employees to find out what's on their minds. We're an open company. We share the books. We have profit sharing. Of all the things I instituted when I took over, that may be the one thing that let people know they mattered."

The long days he spent with his grandfather as he was growing up have stayed with him. He says, "That instilled in me the philosophy of what the Martin guitar is and how the company should be run in terms of the employees and the dealers. If you aren't doing right by both of them, there is no Martin guitar. My grandfather stressed that we're as beholden to the little dealers as to the big ones. That's why we don't offer quantity discounts to Martin dealers—the big would get bigger and the small would go away. And I really think he convinced me that our goal is to try to make a better guitar tomorrow than we do today.

"I'm just so thankful that people want to play

LEFT: For 1997 one of the limited-edition Guitars of the Month is this CEO-1R, designed by Chris Martin. Though it employs the neck joint, "A-frame" hybrid top bracing, and other details of Martin's new Style 16 T guitars, the hexagon outline inlays are a modern echo of the classic Martin designs of the 1930s. And of course it is still a Dreadnought, the most copied guitar shape in the world since 1934. *(Photo courtesy of C. F. Martin & Company.)*

the guitar. I'm afraid they'll stop thinking it's cool. If the guitar went the way of the whalebone corset, I don't know what we'd do," Chris says.

The Martin guitar began as a contemporary of the whalebone corset, and it exists in a world today that could never have been imagined by C. F. Martin Sr. as he crossed the Atlantic in months of nights lit only by stars.

Between 1833 and now, the world has become unglued. Life—which had changed little for thousands of years, moving no faster than the horses or sails that conveyed us—has been cast into dizzying, seemingly endless change; from steam to atomic power; from telegraph to Internet; from leeches to microsurgery. National borders have changed. Political systems have risen and fallen. A single bomb can now kill millions, while probes are sent millions of miles into space. Resources once considered inexhaustable—varieties of trees that have survived for literally millions of years, the mighty elephant with its valuable (and now protected) ivory tusks—are now threatened with extinction.

Yet the fragile wooden boxes bearing the C. F. Martin name have endured and thrived. Styles of music have shifted. The audience has grown—guitar performances once audible only in a parlorlike setting can now be broadcast around the world.

Despite all the change in modern life—perhaps even directly because of it—the desire for a simple, honest, direct form of expression abides. And as it has been for gold rush pioneers, freed slaves, Hawaiians, hillbillies, bluegrass brethren, country troubadours, rock rebels, folk music iconoclasts, Woodstock rockers, Birkenstock rockers, newgrass virtuosos, New Age soothers, unplugged punks, and others, the Martin guitar will be here for players in the twenty-first century.

MAKING A MARTIN

ABOVE: The neck templates are traced onto the planks of 3-inch thick genuine mahogany before Randy Wagner cuts them out with the band saw. Careful layout and cutting make full use of the expensive lumber.

If you ever get to Nazareth, don't forget to stop by the Martin factory. Every day at 1:15 P.M. the staff gives a tour through the factory so that you can see, firsthand, how they make a Martin. Some days they get tour buses coming through, and other days you might just get your own personalized tour. Either way, you won't soon forget the smell of rosewood in the air or the look of pride on the faces of the employees—each one a craftsperson making one of the best acoustic guitars in the world.

Until you get there, you'll have to settle for this photo tour. Not all of the stages in a Martin's construction are represented, just the ones that are easy to show in a photo. The computer numeric control (CNC) machines that rough-cut the necks have to be seen and heard to be appreciated.

ABOVE: Ed Golden joins book-matched spruce tops and rosewood backs on a huge "paddle-wheel" of clamps. Though modified over the years, this same fixture was used in the old North Street plant. No one remembers when it was acquired, since it has been at Martin longer than any of the workers.

ABOVE: Larry Fehnel bends a rosewood side over a heated pipe. Many custom orders still begin the old-fashioned way, using the templates you see on the right. Most of the sizes produced over the years are still available; as a result, Martin offers more guitar shapes than all other major American manufacturers combined.

ABOVE: Joanne Messinger is clamping the neck and tail blocks that connect the bent sides of a D-1. Both mahogany and rosewood 1 series side assemblies can be seen in the background.

ABOVE: Sometimes it isn't the tools you use but how you use them. David Anthony is gluing kerfed cedar linings to the rosewood sides of a series of Dreadnoughts, using high-tech clamping devices—wooden clothespins.

ABOVE LEFT: Susan Cummings scallops the spruce braces on the underside of a guitar's top. In the background you can see the mortise in the bodies of 1 series guitars (which do not have scalloped braces). Susan is the granddaughter of Earle Hartzel, pictured on page 98 working at the North Street plant in the 1920s.

ABOVE RIGHT: After the top and back are glued to the sides, a ledge is routed into the edges of the body for the binding. Here Sophie Eckhart is gluing the binding into the notch, holding it in place with small strips of tape. The binding is then clamped with cloth strapping, as seen on the cutaway Dreadnought bodies in the background.

RIGHT: Despite the high-tech machinery, many steps in building a Martin remain unchanged. Here Frank Werkheiser uses good, old-fashioned sandpaper on the back of a Dreadnought. The guitar bodies in the background show the traditional dovetail neck joint.

ABOVE: Though most Martin necks are now rough shaped on a CNC machine, necks for many custom orders or limited editions are still hand-carved with a drawknife, as wielded here by Willard "Buddy" Silvius. Years of practice (and a very sharp blade) make this process go much faster, and more accurately, than an amateur woodworker can imagine.

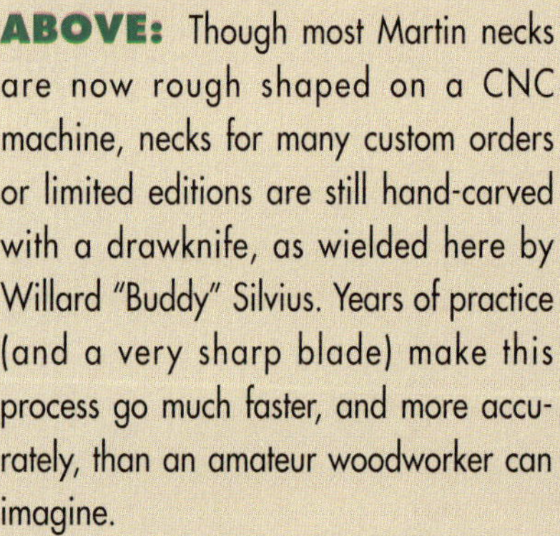

ABOVE AND LEFT: One of the most critical aspects of guitar making is fitting the neck to the body. The centering and the pitch of the neck affect the height of the bridge saddle, and hence the playability and tone. Nathan Hoffman removes thin slivers from the dovetail of the neck until a perfect fit is achieved.

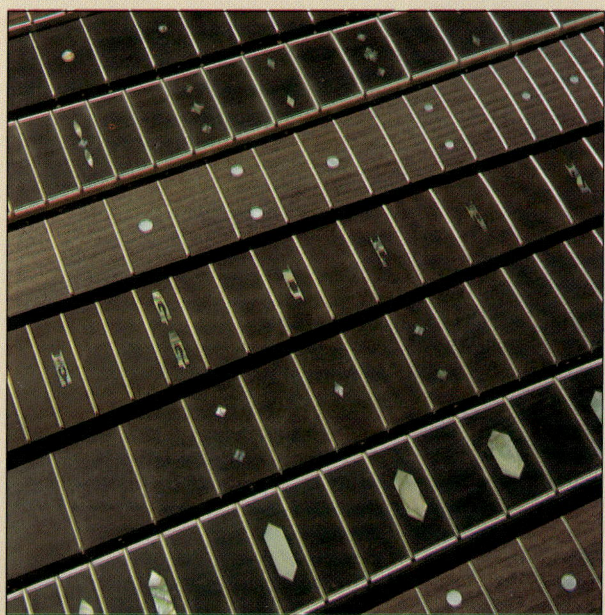

ABOVE: Martin fingerboards are fretted before being glued to the necks. The ebony one with the letters as fret position markers is for the MTV model.

ABOVE: Melanie Hoffert fits the nut to the neck before finishing. On the table are 1 series necks, with the truss rod assembly showing. Martin necks and bodies are finished separately after matching and fitting, then assembled.

LEFT AND ABOVE LEFT: After the binding on a D-45 is installed, Phyllis Klein removes a Teflon strip and replaces it with strips of abalone (you can see the Teflon still in place around the soundhole). A thin "compression strip" is placed at the bottom of the slot so the pearl can be glued in with the upper surface flush with the binding.

ABOVE RIGHT: After final sanding, the bodies go through the finishing process separately. Gluing the neck onto the body is one of the last steps in completing a Martin guitar. All that remains after Jim Miller has finished his job is gluing the bridge to the soundboard.

ABOVE AND LEFT: A Martin 000-28 herringbone in final setup. Gluing on the bridge and installing the tuning machines are the final operations before tuning up a guitar for the first time. Virgil Remaly will check the string action; then the guitar will be stored for two weeks and the action will be checked again before the instrument is shipped.

MARTIN FACTS AND FIGURES

MARTIN GUITAR SERIAL NUMBERS

YEAR	LAST SERIAL NUMBER	YEAR	LAST SERIAL NUMBER
1898	8348	**1950**	117961
1899	8716	**1951**	122799
1900	9128	**1952**	128436
1901	9310	**1953**	134501
1902	9528	**1954**	141345
1903	9810	**1955**	147328
1904	9988	**1956**	153225
1905	10120	**1957**	159061
1906	10329	**1958**	165576
1907	10727	**1959**	171047
1908	10883	**1960**	175689
1909	11018	**1961**	181297
1910	11203	**1962**	187384
1911	11413	**1963**	193327
1912	11565	**1964**	199626
1913	11821	**1965**	207030
1914	12047	**1966**	217215
1915	12209	**1967**	230095
1916	12390	**1968**	241925
1917	12988	**1969**	256003
1918	13450	**1970**	271633
1919	14512	**1971**	294270
1920	15848	**1972**	313302
1921	16758	**1973**	333873
1922	17839	**1974**	353387
1923	19891	**1975**	371828
1924	22008	**1976**	388800
1925	24116	**1977**	399625
1926	28689	**1978**	407800
1927	34435	**1979**	419900
1928	37568	**1980**	430300
1929	40843	**1981**	436474
1930	45317	**1982**	439627
1931	49589	**1983**	446101
1932	52590	**1984**	453300
1933	55084	**1985**	460575
1934	58679	**1986**	468175
1935	61947	**1987**	476216
1936	65176	**1988**	483952
1937	68865	**1989**	493279
1938	71866	**1990**	503309
1939	74061	**1991**	512487
1940	76734	**1992**	522655
1941	80013	**1993**	535223
1942	83107	**1994**	551696
1943	86724	**1995**	570434
1944	90149	**1996**	592930
1945	93623	**1997**	624799
1946	98158		
1947	103468		
1948	108269		
1949	112961		

MARTIN MANDOLIN SERIAL NUMBERS

YEAR	LAST SERIAL NUMBER	YEAR	LAST SERIAL NUMBER
1895	23	**1947**	18303
1896	112	**1948**	19078
1897	155	**1949**	19559
1898	359	**1950**	20065
1899	577	**1951**	20496
1900	800	**1952**	20902
1901	881	**1953**	21452
1902	1171	**1954**	21952
1903	1348	**1955**	22254
1904	1507	**1956**	22629
1905	1669	**1957**	22985
1906	2026	**1958**	23111
1907	2357	**1959**	23262
1908	2510	**1960**	23512
1909	2786	**1961**	23663
1910	3098	**1962**	23938
1911	3431	**1963**	24139
1912	3847	**1964**	24339
1913	4162	**1965**	24439
1914	4462	**1966**	24564
1915	4767	**1967**	24639
1916	5007	**1968**	24839
1917	5752	**1969**	24989
1918	6370	**1970**	25039
1919	7237	**1971**	25139
1920	8761	**1972**	25289
1921	9627	**1973**	25339
1922	10196	**1974**	25679
1923	11020	**1975**	25895
1924	11809	**1976***	26045
1925	12520	**1977**	26101
1926	13359	**1978**	26101
1927	13833	**1979**	26112
1928	14170	**1980**	26156
1929	14630	**1981**	26215
1930	14892	**1982**	26225
1931	15290	**1983**	26247
1932	15476	**1984**	26254
1933	15528	**1985**	26263
1934	15729	**1986**	26273
1935	15887	**1987**	27279
1936	16156	**1988**	26281
1937	16437	**1989**	26283
1938	16580	**1990**	26291 Total
1939	16747	**1991**	26297 (6)
1940	16957	**1991†**	509122 (11)
1941	17263	**1992**	509122 (0)
1942	17405	**1993**	533213 (6)
1943	—		
1944	—		
1945	—		
1946	17641		

** 1976 also includes serial numbers 259996–260020.*

† Note: Beginning in 1991 Martin put mandolins in the same serial number sequence as guitars.

GUITAR DIMENSIONS: 12-FRET MODELS (in inches)

	SIZE 7 (Modern 7/8 D, 14-fret)	SIZE 5	SIZE 4	SIZE 3 1/2	SIZE 3	SIZE 2 1/2
Total Length	36 1/16	33	33	33 1/2	36	36 1/2
Body Length	17 1/2	16	16	16 7/8	17 3/8	17 7/8
Width of Upper Bout	10	8 1/4	8 15/16	8	8 1/8	8 1/4
Width of Lower Bout	13 11/16	11 1/4	11 1/2	10 11/16	11 1/4	11 5/8
Depth of Upper Bout	3 31/64	3 1/4	3 1/4	3 1/8	3 1/8	3 1/8
Depth of Lower Bout	4 3/8	3 7/8	3 3/4	3 7/8	3 13/16	3 7/8
Fretboard Width at Nut	1 5/8	1 5/8	1 3/4	1 3/4	1 3/4	1 13/16
Soundhole Diameter	3 3/4	3 1/4	3 1/4	3 7/16	3 11/32	3 1/2
Scale Length	23	21.4 OR 22	22	22	23 7/8	24.5

GUITAR DIMENSIONS: 12-FRET MODELS—CONTINUED

	SIZE 2	SIZE 1	SIZE 0	SIZE 00	SIZE 000	SIZE D
Total Length	37	37 3/4	37 3/4	37 3/4	39 9/16	39 9/16
Body Length	18 1/4	18 7/8	19 1/8	19 5/8	20 7/16	20 15/16
Width of Upper Bout	8 1/2	9 1/4	9 1/2	9 3/4	10 3/4	11 1/2
Width of Lower Bout	12	12 3/4	13 1/2	14 1/8	15	15 5/8
Depth of Upper Bout	3 3/4	3 3/8	3 3/8	3 1/4	3 1/4	3 15/16
Depth of Lower Bout	4	4 3/16	4 3/16	4 1/16	4 1/16	4 3/4
Fretboard Width at Nut	1 13/16	1 7/8	1 7/8	1 7/8	1 7/8	1 7/8
Soundhole Diameter	3 1/2	3 9/16	3 5/8	3 3/4	3 7/8	4
Scale Length	24.5	24.9	24.9	24.9	25.4	25.4

Note: Variation of up to 1/4 inch is not uncommon on pre-1930 instruments. Smaller variations occur even today. Martin also made a size 1/4 (6 5/8 inches wide at lower bout, with 17-inch scale length) and a size 1/2 (7 3/8 inches wide at lower bout, 20 7/8-inch scale length). Many early 12-fret 00 models are long scale, and some 12-fret 000 models are short scale. Many new (post-1970) 00 models are long scale. Classic models (stamped G or C) have wider necks.

GUITAR DIMENSIONS: 14-FRET MODELS (in inches)

	SIZE 0	SIZE 00	SIZE 000 (OM)	SIZE D	SIZE M (0000)	SIZE J
Total Length	38 3/8	38 5/8	39 3/8	40 1/4	40 3/8	40 3/8
Body Length	18 3/8	18 7/8	19 3/8	20	20 1/8	20 1/8
Width of Upper Bout	10	10 7/8	11 1/4	11 1/2	11 11/16	11 11/16
Width of Lower Bout	13 1/2	14 5/16	15	15 5/8	16	16
Depth of Upper Bout	3 13/32	3 11/32	3 11/32	3 15/16	3 5/16	3 15/16
Depth of Lower Bout	4 1/4	4 1/8	4 1/8	4 7/8	4 1/8	4 7/8
Fretboard Width at Nut	1 11/16	1 11/16	1 11/16	1 11/16	1 11/16	1 11/16
Soundhole Diameter	3 5/8	3 3/4	3 7/8	4	4	4
Scale Length	24.9	24.9	24.9	25.4	25.4	25.4

Note: OM and earliest 14-fret 000 models are long scale. All 14-fret models have 1 3/4-inch fretboard width prior to mid-1939. Post-1970 reissue OM and other Vintage models often have pre-1939 specs.

UKULELES (in inches)

	STANDARD UKULELE	TENOR UKULELE	BARITONE UKULELE	TARO-PATCH AND CONCERT UKE	TIPLE
Total Length	21	26 1/4	30 11/16	25	27 1/4
Body Length	9 7/16	12 1/16	14	11	12 1/16
Width of Upper Bout	5	6 5/8	7 1/2	5 5/8	6 5/8
Width of Lower Bout	6 3/8	8 15/16	10	7 5/8	8 15/16
Fretboard Width at Nut	1 13/32	1 11/32	1 3/8	1 9/16	1 1/2
Scale Length	13 5/8	17	20 1/8	14 7/8	17

Note: Except for the longer peghead and wider neck on the taro-patch, dimensions for the taro-patch and concert uke are the same.

GOLDEN ERA PRODUCTION TOTALS FOR SELECTED GUITAR MODELS

YEAR	000-28*	000-42	000-45	OM-28	OM-45	D-28* 12-FRET	D-28* 14-FRET	D-45
1920	3							
1921	5	5						
1922	4	1	3					
1923	3		2					
1924	20		19					
1925	8	4	3					
1926	25		12					
1927	44		20					
1928	48		25					
1929	82		20	11				
1930	2	1	21	235	19†			
1931	57		1	166	10	1		
1932	1	1		50	5	4		
1933				25	6	12		1
1934	129	1	14			21‡	52‡	1
1935	52		24			2	81	
1936	72		24			1	61	2
1937	113		18				148	2
1938	97	27	19				121	3
1939	48	31					123	14
1940	86	12	6				134	19
1941	36	24	12				183	24
1942	48	12	6				96	19
1943	96	6					192	
1944	133						231§	
1945	147						183	
1946	134						425	
1947							24‡	

Please note: There are no structural differences between 1946 and 1947 rosewood models with herringbone and guitars without herringbone that immediately followed. In total, there were twenty-seven 000-28s, two 000-42s and sixteen 000-45s made before 1920. In 1934, 000 guitars switched from standard 12-fret necks to 14-fret necks. One 14-fret 000-42 was made in 1932.

**000-28 and D-28 totals are for herringbone models only. Martin began producing nonherringbone 000-28 and D-28 models sometime in early 1947.*

† In 1930 there were also fourteen OM-45 Deluxe and two OM-42 models made.

‡ These numbers are estimates only.

§ Number reflects 219 with old bracing and 12 with new bracing. Some late 1944 000-28s also have new bracing.

MARTIN PREFIXES AND SUFFIXES IN MODEL CODES

Beginning with the introduction of koa guitars in 1917, Martin began adding letter suffixes to the model code. By 1930, when model codes began to be stamped inside the guitars, the suffixes K, H, T, and P were already in use.

In modern times (post 1960), the use of letters, or letters and numbers combined, has often been used instead of adding a new number to the original model code. For instance, an SP000C-16TR is hardly a Style 16 at all, as it has a pearl soundhole ring, snowflake inlay pattern, rosewood body, and gold tuners. However, since the SP000C-16TR doesn't have the standard features of the higher Martin models either, it is probably just as well that Martin chose to label these new guitars in its Technology (T) series as it has. (An exception to the company's increasing use of prefixes and suffixes for new models was the series of maple guitars added in 1985, which were given model numbers in 60s—60, 62, 64, and so on—rather than being designated with an M.)

Below is a brief list of the letter and number prefixes and suffixes commonly found on Martin guitars. Extremely rare examples, such as one-of-a-kind prototypes, are not listed.

Models listed in parentheses are examples and not necessarily the sole use of the letter in question.

Now that Martin has begun issuing models designed by contemporary performers (Paul Simon, Eric Clapton, and Marty Stuart, to name a few) and to commemorate famous players who used Martins (such as Jimmie Rodgers), many more initials will probably be added to this list.

A	*Ash* back and sides.
B	*Brazilian* rosewood back and sides.
BK	*Black* finish (usually on entire guitar, including top).
BLE	Same as B, but a *limited edition.*
BSE	Same as B, but a *signature edition.*
C	Means *classical, cutaway,* or *cedar,* depending on where the C is placed in the model code. C after the style number (00-28C) means classical (intended for nylon strings), while C after the body size code (000C-16) means cutaway. (The exceptions are the first Jumbo cutaways, such as the J-40MC, changed in 1990 to JC-40.) When the C is before the body size designation (CHD-28), it means the guitar has a cedar, rather than spruce, soundboard. C followed by a hyphen and a number indicates an arch-top model.
C.T.B.	*Custom Tortoise Bound,* see "Martin Guitars of the Month" on page 255.
D	In 1975, Martin made some D-18 and D-28 models with pickups that were given a D suffix (D-18D).

DB	*Deep body,* a new suffix used with the 1997 00-16DB women's model.
E	*Electric* flat-top model with magnetic pickups mounted in the top in the late '50s through early '60s. Beginning in 1970 piezo pickups were mounted under the saddle, or under the top; when ordered with a pickup before production was begun, or when made as a special run, these are also often stamped E. Since the mid-1980s, however, many Martins have pickups installed just before being shipped, and these have no E in the model code. The E suffix can also mean a special model made for Martin employees.
EC	*Eric Clapton* 000 models.
FMG	*Figured mahogany.*
G	For *gut* (later nylon) strings.
GE	*Golden Era,* referring to modern Martins made in the style of the 1930s. Features are similar to Vintage series.
GM	*Grand Marquise.*
GOM	*Guitar of the Month,* usually a limited edition or special style made for a limited time.
H	*Hawaiian,* meaning set up at the factory with a high nut and often with a high saddle without compensation (angle).
K	*Koa* wood for top, back, and sides (1917 to early 1940s) or for back and sides only (after 1980).
KLE	*Koa* back and sides, *limited edition.*
K2	*Koa* top, as well as back and sides. Since 1980, the 2 has been added to the K designation when the top is also of koa.
L	*Left-handed* version. Any Martin guitar stamped with an L not only has a left-handed nut and bridge (modern versions with pick guard and fretboard side-dots) but also has the transverse braces under the top reversed. L as a prefix means *Larch* soundboard (LHD-28), a wood very similar to spruce.
LE	*Limited Edition.*
LSH	*Large soundhole.*
M	*Mahogany* back and sides. On the early J models, an M suffix was to indicate that it was a deep (jumbo) version of the *M body* (J-40M). As this was redundant (the J was offered only in the M shape), that suffix was deleted in 1990.
MB	*Maple binding.*
MBK	Black J-40 models made before 1990.
MC	Pre-1990 Jumbo cutaway model (see M and C above).
MP	*Morado* rosewood back and sides. This wood was used around 1990 when Martin was using the P suffix to denote low-profile necks.
NY	*New Yorker* model, with wide, 12-fret neck with slotted peghead, no fretboard markers, usually with no pick guard.
P	*Plectrum* or *low-profile.* Plectrum refers to models with a long-scale 4-string neck, mostly made in the 1920s and 1930s. From 1985 through 1989, the P suffix indicated a low-profile neck with adjustable truss rod, usually found only on D models since they were the only ones still offered with other neck shapes.
PSE	*Signature Edition* with low-profile neck. See "Martin Guitars of the Month" on page 255.
Q	This appears only on models made after 1985 with the old-style nonadjustable neck.
R	*Rosewood* back and sides, usually appears only on a lower style number (such as 16 or 18) that normally is associated with another wood.
S	*Special,* or special order. Most frequently appears on dreadnoughts with the long body shape and 12-fret neck (D-28S). Also occasionally appears as a prefix (SOM-45). In the days before Martin processed special orders through its Custom Shop (beginning in 1979), the S designation could mean almost anything, such as a wider fretboard or special run of instruments for a certain retailer.
SE	*Signature Edition.*
SP	*Special.* Beginning in 1995, Martin introduced a fancier version of its popular 16T series, with SP as a prefix before the body code (SPD-16T).
SW	*Special Wurlitzer.* Made for the Wurlitzer company of Boston.
T	*Tenor,* a 4-string model with short string scale (0-18T). Beginning in the 1990s, T on a 6-string model stands for "technology" and was added to 16 series Martins made with the 1 series neck joint. (A few tenor guitars also have other suffixes after the T.)
TR	*Rosewood* back and sides on a 16T model (see above).
V	*Vintage,* which often includes a V-shaped neck. Martin first began using the V-for-Vintage suffix in 1983. See page 258.
W	*Walnut* back and sides.
2R	*2 rings* of herringbone around the soundhole (HD-282R).

PRE-1898 MARTIN STYLES

Prior to the late 1880s, most styles were offered only in one size. As demand for larger guitars increased, styles previously listed only in size 2 or size 1 begin to appear in larger sizes. This is particularly true of styles 30 and higher, which were offered only in size 2 on the 1870s Zoebisch price list.

The earliest date given below for each style merely indicates the earliest surviving written record; since Martin sales records from before 1873 are incomplete, earlier examples were probably made. Sales records from the 1850s show the wholesale cost evolving into the style code, but the specific features of each style were not always consistent, especially before 1867 (black necks were still appearing on higher models in the late 1850s, for example). Martin records from 1885 to 1898 are also missing; but because many guitars from this period have dates penciled on the underside of the top, we have some idea of what models were popular.

Please note that Martin often had requests to build guitars in an earlier style or with a particular feature that had been discontinued years earlier. Dating a Martin by its earliest features may thus result in attributing a date decades before the guitar was actually constructed. For example, the "screw neck" and purfling that bisects the sides are features commonly associated with the 1840s and early 1850s, but one Martin with these features has a serial number placing it in 1898! Another example of a Martin "reissue" made in the early 1890s is pictured on page 61.

There are no markings on pre-1898 guitars, inside or out, as to the style. The size and style were written on a paper label on the inside of the case; but these labels often fell off, and cases can be switched. To identify a Martin with no serial number, first determine the size, using the chart on page 249. Then compare the soundhole rosette and edge binding to the photos on pages 52–54 and 79–81, and check the descriptions given below. All of these guitars originally had the following: Brazilian rosewood back and sides, spruce top, ebony fretboard with barstock frets, and ebony or ivory pyramid bridge.

Martin did make a very few guitars on special order for steel strings beginning in 1900, but there are no surviving records of Martins built for the higher tension of steel before that date. It is safe to assume that all pre-1898 Martins are for gut (and later nylon) strings.

STYLE	CHARACTERISTICS
STYLE 17 *From 1850s through 1897 (reappears in 1908 as first mahogany model)*	Offered in sizes 2½ and 3. Black neck with cone-shaped heel. Fan-pattern top bracing at least through early 1890s. Rosewood binding, no binding on back. Single-line white backstripe. Brass tuners with ivory buttons. Soundhole rosette varies, usually with colored purfling in center ring.
STYLE 18 *From 1850s*	Similar to Style 17, but offered in larger size 2. Back bound with rosewood until late 1890s.
STYLE 20 *1850s through 1897*	Offered in size 2. Fan-pattern top bracing common. Cedar neck (all higher styles also have cedar neck). Rosewood bindings, 5-ply on top, 3-ply on back. Multicolored herringbone rosette and backstripe.
STYLE 21 *From 1850s*	Very similar to Style 20 listed above, but offered in larger size 1. Always X-braced. Multicolored herringbone changes to black & white at least by 1890s. Larger sizes in Style 21 common beginning in mid-1880s. This style continued virtually unchanged until after World War II.
STYLE 24 *1850s through 1880s*	Offered in size 2, early versions usually fan-braced. Rosewood binding with white line on sides. Colored wood purfling around soundhole and edge of top. Multicolored purfling in backstrip.
STYLE 26 *1850s through 1897*	Offered in size 1. Ivory binding on body (lowest style to get ivory edges). "Half-herringbone" top purfling. Rosette like Style 28. Backstrip usually "zigzag" pattern like later Style 28.
STYLE 27 *1850s through 1898*	Offered in size 2. Ivory bound body and fretboard. Pearl soundhole ring. Narrow band of colored wood purfling around top edge. Multicolored backstrip, often with long arrow-pattern in center. Styles 27 and higher usually had ivory bridge pins with pearl dot.
STYLE 28 *From 1870s*	Originally offered in size 0 only, seen in 00 by mid-1880s (first 00-28 in 1873). Listed in 1850s as 0-27 (because of $27 wholesale cost), but 0-27 did not have bound fretboard and pearl soundhole like 2-27). Soundhole rosette with "5-9-5" pattern. All Martins without pearl soundhole after 1988 have this rosette. Though the Zoebisch price list suggests that the 0-28 was "inlaid with pearl" like the 2-27, this is probably an error (no early 0 size with Style 28 features and pearl soundhole have been reported). Herringbone around top edge. Often has multicolored backstrip (as found on Styles 40 and higher from teens on to present). Later with "zigzag" pattern. This style continued virtually unchanged until mid-1940s.
STYLE 30 *1850s through 1917*	Originally offered in size 2, larger sizes seen by mid-1880s. Very similar to Style 27 but with "German silver" (nickel silver) tuners. Not shown on 1897 price list but appears again in 1898 catalog in larger sizes. Colored wood purfling around top usually wider than Style 27.
STYLE 34 *1850s through 1898*	Originally offered in size 2, larger sizes seen by 1890s. Same features as Style 30 but with ivory bridge.
STYLE 40 *1850s through 1880s*	Originally offered in size 2, reappears as Hawaiian model 1928–1939. Features identical to Style 42 described below except pearl border does not extend around end of fretboard.
STYLE 42 *From 1850s*	Originally offered in size 2, larger sizes common by 1890s. Listed as with "screw neck," but this feature rarely seen after 1880s. Pearl border around top edge, end of fretboard, and soundhole. Multicolored backstrip with long "arrowhead" patterns in center. Ivory binding on body and fretboard. Nickel-silver tuners with pearl knobs. The most common pearl-bordered Martin, style continued virtually unchanged until discontinued in 1942.

POST-1898 MARTIN STYLES

Thanks to the serial numbers that Martin began stamping on the neck blocks sometime in 1898, twentieth-century Martins are easy to date (see "Martin Guitar Serial Numbers" on page 248). Until October 1930, however, there were still no model designations on the instruments. Before the late 1920s, Martin models remained much the same as they had been in the nineteenth century. Features common to virtually all 6-string guitar models before 1930 are:

- Neck with 12 frets clear of the body.
- Slotted headstock with three tuners on each side, *or* solid peghead with friction pegs (rare after 1916).
- Rectangular bridge, higher models with pyramid tips (tips were flattened, Washburn style, on a few Style 18 and 21 models around 1916).
- Necks change from cedar to mahogany beginning in 1916.
- Except for Style 17, bridges change to belly style in 1930 (many exceptions).

Beginning in 1934, the 14-fret design that began with the "Orchestra Models" a few years earlier replaced the old "Standard" style (12-fret) Martin guitar. From this date on, most Martins, except for Hawaiian models and a few 12-fret holdovers, are as follows:

- Neck with 14 frets clear of body.
- Solid peghead with right-angle geared tuners.
- Belly bridge with pick guard on top.
- Shaded tops listed as optional.

This reference section does not cover every change in every Martin style, and structural and stylistic changes that occurred to most Martins in general are listed separately on page 259. Most features that differentiate one style from another are listed, as are important changes that mark the evolution of each style over the years. Exact dating for many of these changes can be difficult, for the following reasons:

- We don't have *dated* catalogs for each year. Martin often didn't issue a new catalog, instead inserting an updated price list into the previous year's edition.
- Martin frequently made changes in production but didn't change the wording in the catalog, and catalog descriptions are often very general and brief.
- Catalog illustrations from previous years were sometimes used (this is common for all instrument manufacturers of the period).
- Receiving lots of orders for a particular model, or special feature, was often what prompted Martin to add that style to a later catalog. Unlike Gibson, Martin was reluctant to dictate change, instead preferring to respond to what dealers and musicians were requesting.
- Even after a change was made, certain dealers or customers would order the earlier style.

We have not included 4-string guitars, tiples, Hawaiian models, arch-top models, or the N series (nylon string) in this summary due to space restrictions. Classical models (G suffix, changes to C in 1962) are not noted separately; all have the wider, flat fretboard and pinless "loop" bridge with rounded ends. Because of the difficulty in describing tuning machines and the wide variety used by Martin, they are not included. A more thorough description is planned as a part of the Martin Guitar Company web site that will be devoted to historical models.

STYLE	CHARACTERISTICS
STYLE 15	First offered as all-mahogany size 0 in 1940. No binding, low-gloss finish, rectangular bridge. Small single celluloid dots on neck from 5th to 12th fret. Deleted from catalog in 1961. D-15 model added in 1997.
STYLE 16	First offered as 12-fret 0-16NY in 1961. Classical (nylon-string) model, 00-16C, added in 1962. Style 18 binding on top, no binding on back. Slotted peghead, no neck dots. Low-gloss finish, no pick guard. D model added in 1986, 14-fret neck, scalloped bracing. Up through 1991, different woods, finishes, and binding offered each year on D-16 (trade-show specials). 000-16 and 000C-16 (cutaway) added in 1990. Style 16 becomes 16T in 1995, with 1 series neck joint. Style 16 becomes 16T in 1995, with 1 series neck joint. Rosewood version (16TR) added in 1995. SP series added in 1996, with pearl rosette and snowflake inlays.
STYLE 17	Not offered from 1898 to 1905. Reintroduced in 1906 as first mahogany model. During this period offered in sizes 1, 0, and 00. Described in catalogs as identical to Style 18 except mahogany back and sides. Discontinued again in 1917 (when Style 18 became mahogany).
STYLE 17, MAHOGANY TOP	Introduced in 1922 in size 2 only, as Martin's first stock steel-string model. Peghead now has slots rounded at the ends. Single-ring rosette. Rosewood binding on top (3-ply) and back. Rosewood fretboard (small dots all the same size) and pyramid bridge. Bridge remains rectangular, but with flat tips, and rosewood bindings deleted in 1929 (bridge probably changed earlier). This simpler size 2 in Style 17 was called #25 (price was $25) in 1929 and 1930 only. Offered in sizes 1, 0, and 00 in 1930. By 1935 has small celluloid dots from 5th to 15th fret, with two at 7th and 12th. Darker stain on mahogany, glossier finish than 0-15.
STYLE 18	Spruce top with 3-ring rosette (1-9-1 grouping). Ebony fingerboard (single pearl dot at 5th, 7th, and 9th frets by 1900). Rosewood back and sides until 1917, when switched to mahogany. Rosewood binding on top edge only, binding on back added by 1919. Cedar neck (with dart) until 1917, mahogany neck (no dart) after. Slots in peghead change from square to rounded ends by 1917. First listed in catalog with steel strings in 1923. Rectangular bridge changes from pyramid to flat tips by 1928. Dot inlays on neck extended to 15th fret (2 at 12th) in 1932. Binding changes from wood to celluloid in 1932, with black outer layer. New 14-fret "orchestra model" 0 replaces old models starting in 1934. Outer layer of binding changes to tortoiseshell color by 1936. Style 18 models were switched from ebony fretboards and bridges to rosewood starting around 1935, first 0, then 00, 000, and finally D. D-18 switched to rosewood in late 1946. In each size, examples with ebony may turn up with higher serial numbers than examples with rosewood. Binding and pick guard change to black by 1967. 12-string D12-18 (14-fret neck) added in 1973. J-18 added in 1987.
STYLE 19	Introduced in 1977, size D only. Style 28 rosette, spruce top stained brown. Extra white-black lines around back, all other features like D-18. Discontinued in 1988, most were made from 1977 to 1981.
STYLE 20	Introduced in 1964 as D12-20, 12-string, slotted peghead, 12-fret neck. Like Style 18, but with extra white-black lines around back, with checkered backstrip.
STYLE 21	Rosewood back and sides, spruce top. Rosewood binding (both edges), herringbone rosette and backstrip. Ebony fretboard and pyramid bridge, small
STYLE	CHARACTERISTICS
STYLE 21 CONTINUED	slotted diamond inlays at 5th, 7th, and 9th frets. This was the one style exempt from the switch to 14 frets in the early 1930s (except for special orders). 14 fret 000-21 added in 1938. Diamond inlays change to dots in 1944. Fretboards go to rosewood and herringbone disappears from soundhole in late 1946. Herringbone backstrip changes to checkered (Style 28) in 1947. Color of outer binding changes in same sequence as Style 18. D-21 added in 1955, "NY" version of 00 in 1962. OM-21 added in 1992 (does not conform to standard Style 21 specs).
STYLE 25K	Introduced in 1980 in sizes D and 00. Koa back and sides with toned spruce top, K2 version has koa top. Style 28 rosette, all other features like Style 21. Very few made after 1988.
STYLE 27	Dropped from catalog in 1898, but a few made through 1907. See "Pre-1898 Martin Styles" on page 251 for details.
STYLE 28	Like Style 21, but ivory binding, herringbone around top, zigzag backstrip. Rosette of 5-9-5 pattern of white and black lines, 2 ivory strips in center. Ivory switched to celluloid in 1918. Neck inlays: 2 small slotted diamonds at 5th and 9th frets, larger single diamond at 7th. Inlay pattern is extended to 15th fret by 1933, changes to dots by 1945. Herringbone changes to black and white lines by early 1947. Zigzag backstrip changes to checkered style shortly after. Retains dart on back of peghead to present. D12-28 added in 1970. Herringbone returns to some models, starting with HD-28, in 1976.
STYLE 30	This nineteenth-century style remained in the catalog until 1917, and a few were made up to 1921. See "Pre-1898 Martin Styles" on page 251 for details. Except for the addition of inlays on the neck, the style remained largely unchanged after 1900.
STYLE 35	Introduced in size D in 1965, appointments like Style 28 except: three-piece rosewood back, two back strips of white-black-white wood lines. No dart on back of peghead. Fretboard bound, extra white-black-white-black lines on sides of body. Top braces not scalloped, but same size as 00, with 000 size back braces. HD-35 added in 1978 (herringbone, scalloped braces).
STYLE 36	Introduced in 1978 in size M only, appointments like Style 35 except: rosewood bridge with ebony fretboard, scalloped top braces. Fretboard dots all same size starting at 3rd fret. Top tinted yellow-gold, tortoise-style pick guard. First few were stamped M-35. Discontinued in 1997.
STYLE 37K	Introduced in 1980 as size D and size 7 (mini-D). Figured koa back and sides with tinted spruce top, K2 version with koa top. Pearl rosette, Style 28 binding with white-black-white-black lines on sides. Ebony fretboard with diamonds and wedges (Foden Style D) inlay. No dart behind peghead, black pick guard. Discontinued from catalog in 1989.
STYLE 38	Introduced as size M in 1977 (old F arch-top shape). Rosewood bridge, pearl rosette, top tinted yellow-gold. White binding, extra black-white lines on sides, white binding next to neck heel. Neck and peghead bound in white-black-white. Fretboard dots all same size starting at third fret, dart on peghead. 7-ply white-black binding on top, Style 45 backstrip. Scalloped top braces, back more highly arched. Renamed 0000-38 in 1997.
STYLE 40 PRE-1942	Same as Style 42 but pearl border on top doesn't extend around end of fretboard. Rarely made until 1928, when offered as Hawaiian 00-40H, without fretboard binding. 00-40H last listed in 1941 catalog.

STYLE	CHARACTERISTICS
STYLE 40, 1985 TO PRESENT	Introduced in size J in 1985, J-40M 6-string and J12-40M 12-string. Pearl rosette, no pearl around top. White binding with more black-white lines on top and back than Style 28. Bound fretboard with 4/5 size D-45 hexagons. Style 45 backstrip. "M" suffix dropped in 1990. Style 45 headstock binding and inlay added in 1995.
STYLE 41	Introduced in 1969 (D only), same woods as Style 28. Pearl bordering around top and soundhole, but not around end of fretboard. Binding on neck, bound Style 45 headstock with MOP C. F. Martin letters. Hexagons on fretboard from 3rd to 15th fret. Style 45 backstrip. Hexagon inlays change to J-40 style in 1987, headstock same as D-45.
STYLE 42	Same woods as Style 28. Ivory bound body and fretboard, ivory bridge. Pearl bordering around soundhole and top edge, including end of fretboard. Snowflake pattern starting at 5th fret, cat's-eye at 12th. Multicolored backstrip. Ebony bridge by 1919 (binding changes to celluloid). Discontinued in 1942, last made in 1943. Returns as special order in 1980s.
STYLE 44	See "Vahdah Olcott-Bickford" on page 97.
STYLE 45	First appears in 1904 catalog, listed earlier as special Style 42. Pearl bordering added around sides, back, endpiece, and neck heel. Headstock bound (white-black-white) with scroll inlay, fretboard like Style 42. Inlay on head changes to "torch" (sometimes called flowerpot) by 1906. Fretboard inlay is extended from 1st to 17th fret by 1910. Ebony bridge by 1919 (binding changes to celluloid). Headstock inlay changes to C. F. Martin letters on 14-fret models in 1934. D-45 gets hexagon fretboard inlays by 1939. Last made in 1942. D-45 revived in 1968, but now with plastic black-white-black lines next to pearl border. Style 45s have gradually "evolved" closer to prewar details.
STYLES 60 THROUGH 65	Maple models added in 1985, discontinued by 1997. All have tortoise color bindings, spruce tops with scalloped bracing, no dart on peghead, and ebony fretboards and bridges. The maple is often lightly stained. Model summary: D-60, bird's-eye maple, Style 42 snowflakes, maple headplate. D-62, flamed maple, plainer and lower-priced than D-60. M-64, Style 45 backstrip, neck dots like M-38. J-65, J-size version of M-64 with gold tuners. J12-65, 12-string version, nonscalloped braces.
STYLE 68	Introduced in 1985, oval soundhole, rounded cutaway. White bindings on body and neck like D-35, checkered backstrip. Style 45 peghead, dart on back. M series dots on fretboard. Often finished in sunburst on top, back, and sides.
STYLE 76	Bicentennial D-76, see page 197.

INSTRUMENTS MADE BY MARTIN FOR OTHER FIRMS

Martin made many instruments for other companies, especially in the period from 1916 to 1925. Some of these instruments were marked as made by Martin while others had no hint as to their origin. The most important of these accounts are described in Chapter 4. Most of Martin's "custom brand" business ended in the mid-1920s because the demand for Martin ukuleles had the company heavily backordered.

Some of the early instruments for Ditson and Southern California Music Co. had a separate serial number series, but later guitars for both companies used regular Martin numbers. Some custom brand guitars had no serial numbers. Most of this information was gathered from Martin records by Mike Longworth.

FIRM	SUMMARY
BACON	A few guitars without Martin stamps were made for the Bacon Banjo Co. around 1924. Most guitars sold under the Bacon trademark, however, were made by larger manufacturers such as Regal of Chicago.
BELLTONE	This was a trademark of Perlburg and Halpin, New York City. Only a few Martins were made under this name, including 15 guitars, 10 mandolins, and 12 Style 3K ukuleles.
VAHDAH OLCOTT-BICKFORD	See page 97.
BITTING SPECIAL	Mandolins and guitars were made under this name for a well-known teacher in Bethlehem, Pennsylvania, from 1916 to 1919.
BRIGGS SPECIAL	A flat-back mandolin made for Briggs Music, Utica, New York.
BRUNO	C. Bruno was an early partner of C. F. Martin Sr.
OLIVER DITSON CO.	This was Martin's most extensive custom order account, lasting from before 1915 to 1930. Included were guitars, bowl and flat mandolins, ukes, tiples, and taro-patches. See page 112.
CARL FISHER	New York City retailer and music publisher Carl Fisher ordered some special 0-18T guitars in 1929.
WILLIAM FODEN	See page 96.
JENKINS	Kansas City, Missouri, dealer. They purchased Martin Style 1 and Style 2 ukes and used their numbers #35 and #40, respectively.
KEALAKAI	Measurements for a model with this name are on Martin spec cards from 1917 and 1923, giving it the same dimensions as the Ditson Dreadnought. An "extra large 17" guitar was made for "Major Kealakai" in early 1916 (#12210). At least two other guitars with the same description were made without serial numbers, the last in June of 1917. No other details are known.
MONTGOMERY WARD	In about 1932 this well-known firm sold guitars, flat mandolins, and ukes, all of mahogany. No sales figures are available, and letters found in the North Street attic indicate several disagreements over price increases and returns.
PARAMOUNT	See photo on page 116.
ROLANDO	These were a series of koa Hawaiian guitars, and possibly ukes as well, made for Southern California Music Co. after the "M. Nunes" models.
RUDICK	A firm in Akron, Ohio, that ordered some 00-17 guitars with the number 0-55 stamped in them around 1934 to 1935.
SCHOENBERG	In 1986 C. F. Martin agreed to produce a line of Schoenberg "Soloist" models, based on early OM-28s. Materials were supplied by the partnership of Eric Schoenberg and Dana Bourgeouis (later replaced by T. J. Thompson); top bracing, final setup, and some detailing was done outside Martin. Most were OM shape, usually with wood binding and a rounded cutaway. The project ended in 1994 with about 250 guitars, all with Martin serial numbers.
H & A SELMER, INC.	The Selmer stamp showed up in the Martin archives, but there is no record of what instrument was made for them.
WILLIAM J. SMITH	This New York City firm had Martin-made ukes, taro-patches, and tiples in their line around 1917.
SOUTHERN CALIFORNIA MUSIC COMPANY	See page 115 and *Rolando* above.

FIRM	SUMMARY
STETSON	A trademark of W. J. Dyer in St. Paul, Minnesota. Martin made at least 3 guitars for them in 1922, but most Stetson guitars were made by the Larson Bros. of Chicago.
S. S. STEWART	Buegelelsen and Jacobson of New York City had Martin make ukuleles and related instruments with the S. S. Stewart label from about 1923 to 1925. Other manufacturers also made similar instruments for the firm.
JOHN WANAMAKER	Around 1909, special models were made for this large Philadelphia department store.
H. A. WEYMANN & SON	Martin made some ukuleles and taro-patches for this Philadelphia banjo company around 1925. Weymann also marketed guitars, but they were not made by Martin.
WOLVERINE	This brand of guitars and mandolins was made for Grinnell Brothers of Detroit. They had regular Martin serial numbers.
RUDOLPH WURLITZER	The well-known music store chain, based in Boston, had a wide range of special guitars made by Martin during the period of 1922 to 1924. See page 116.

MARTIN GUITARS OF THE MONTH

Though Martin initiated its Custom Shop in 1979, five years later there was still no catalog of options and prices. Part of the problem in marketing custom orders was the paperwork, customer deposits, and long delays in completing unique guitars. In a society accustomed to instant gratification, the Custom Shop was able to satisfy only the patient, plan-ahead guitarist.

In 1984 the Guitars of the Month program began, essentially offering custom Martins in small batches. The idea of a different guitar for every month of the year was abandoned in favor of fewer unveiled all at once, but Martin kept the plan's original name. These instruments are announced at the January trade show, with others unveiled at the July show (since 1995), but no guitar is assigned to a particular month. In 1984 and 1985, C. F. Martin III and his grandson, C.F. IV, signed the special labels. Since C.F. III's death in 1986, only C.F. IV signs the labels, unless otherwise noted.

Guitars offered in this program have ranged from simple Style 18 models to pearl-encrusted limited editions that make the original Martin Style 45s look humble. Vintage reissues from the 1930s have been the most popular, and many are now stock models.

Following is a list of the Guitars of the Month from 1984 through 1997, followed by the list price when issued and the number of guitars sold. The following statement from C. F. Martin & Company may shed some light on the production totals of limited editions.

As a general rule, Martin has produced two prototypes of each limited edition in order to develop the model specifications. These prototypes are initially not for sale, but many prototypes have already or eventually may be sold. Prior to 1997 the Limited Edition Program produced separate labeling for the domestic and foreign editions (e.g., the 1990 HD28BLE domestic edition probably had a label that read 1 of 100, 2 of 100, etc., while a separate foreign-edition label read 1 of 8, 2 of 8, etc.) Separate foreign-label editions are included in the totals given below. [This explains why the numbers are often somewhat higher than the figures originally published. —Ed.] *In 1997 Martin stopped issuing separate foreign labeling in favor of one label worldwide.*

Some editions are "fixed" and some are "open-ended." Fixed editions have a predetermined total, whereas open-ended editions are open to orders taken within the particular calendar year (cutoff date for dealer orders is usually October 31). All numbers below are as accurate as possible but must be viewed as approximate. [Prototypes are NOT included in the "number sold" totals given below because we do not know for certain if they were sold and how they were marked. —Ed.]

Due to space restrictions, descriptions of the Guitars of the Month (GOM) are limited to features that differ from stock Martins of the same year with a similar model designation. **Unless otherwise stated**, all the guitars listed have the same body dimensions, woods, and trim as stock models of the same model code (during the same year) and share the following features:

- 14 frets clear of the body, 20 frets total
- Mahogany neck with solid peghead, neck width 1$^{11}/_{16}$ inches at the nut (all other neck measurements given here are taken at the nut as well)
- After 1986 all necks have adjustable truss rod.
- "Belly" bridge, short inlaid saddle, standard 2$^{1}/_{8}$ -inch string spacing, with "teardrop" pick guard; after 1984, all pick guards on top of finish.
- Satin finish on neck, gloss finish on body; most models with pearl-inlaid headstocks have a gloss finish on that surface.
- Spruce top with scalloped X-bracing 1$^{5}/_{8}$ inches from soundhole. Scalloped bracing is always accompanied by the small maple bridgeplate.
- Fingerboard and bridge of same wood.
- Since 1993 most vintage-style GOM guitars or limited editions have been available with a dark sunburst top, at an additional charge. From 1994 on, that option is not listed here, but the total sold with sunburst top is also given.

The following abbreviations are used in this list:

- **Brazilian** means Brazilian rosewood back, sides, and headstock veneer.
- **high X** means the X-braces on the top intersect 1 inch below the soundhole, instead of 1$^{5}/_{8}$ inches. This pattern is always scalloped.
- **long saddle** means the saddle slot is a saw kerf in the bridge, open at both ends, as found on Martins in the 1930s to 1950s.
- **toned top** or **aging toner** refers to gold-toned lacquer, on the soundboard only.
- **V-neck** refers to the neck shape when viewed in cross section; this feature is always accompanied by a **squared-tapered peghead,** as used in the 1930s.
- **tortoise** means the pick guard or binding is of tortoiseshell plastic.
- **ivoroid binding** (usually includes neck heel cap) is off-white celluloid with ivory-like graining.
- **pearl bordering** is actually abalone shell. Unless other inlays are described as "white pearl" or "MOP" (mother-of-pearl), they are also of abalone shell.
- **Style 45 peghead inlay** refers to the C. F. Martin letters in pearl; the "torch" style is noted as such.
- **vintage-style tuners** refers to the open-gear tuning machines with "butterbean" knobs, or buttons, similar to the old Grover G-98 tuners used in the 1930s.

1984

STYLE	CHARACTERISTICS
00-18V	Prewar style, with ebony fingerboard and bridge, tortoise binding and pick guard, scalloped bracing, and V-neck. **List Price:** $1,520. **Number sold:** 9.
D-28 CUSTOM	Scalloped braces, Style 45 "torch" peghead inlay without binding, snowflake Style 45 fretboard inlay without binding, stamp on back of peghead. **List Price:** $2,000. **Number sold:** 43.
M-21 CUSTOM	Tortoise bindings and pick guard, M-38 top stain with Style 28 rosette. **List Price:** $1,600. **Number sold:** 16.

1985

D-18V Prewar Style D-18, with ebony fingerboard and bridge, tortoise binding and pick guard, scalloped bracing, and V-neck. **List Price:** $1,640. **Number sold:** 56

D-21LE Tortoise binding and pick guard (under finish), rosewood fingerboard and bridge, nonscalloped bracing, long saddle. **List Price:** $1,550. **Number sold:** 75.

HD-28LE High X, ivoroid binding, tortoise pick guard (under finish), V-neck, diamonds & squares fretboard inlay. **List Price:** $2,100. **Number sold:** 87.

OM-28LE Ivoroid binding, scalloped bracing, tortoise pick guard (under finish), 1¾-inch V-neck, diamonds & squares inlay. **List Price:** $2,180. **Number sold:** 41

1986

J-45M DELUXE First "over 45-style" Martin, with the exception of custom-shop orders. Englemann or European spruce, tortoise binding, Style 45 pearl bordering on body with pearl back strip. Pearl-bordered tortoise pick guard, pearl hexagon outlines on fretboard and bridge tips. Neck has pearl bordering on top and sides of both peghead and fretboard and on sides of heel. Style 45 Martin letters on head. **List Price:** $6,900. **Number sold:** 17.

D-62LE First maple Dreadnought. Flamed maple, lightly stained, for sides and back, tortoise bindings and pick guard, Style 42 snowflakes on neck. 1⅞-inch neck, $1\frac{11}{16}$-inch optional. **List Price:** $2,100. **Number sold:** 48

J-21MC First J model with cutaway. Black binding, tortoise pick guard, ebony tuner buttons. **List Price:** $1,750. **Number sold:** 56.

HD-28SE Autographed on the underside of top by C. F. Martin III, C.F. IV, and all the foremen in the plant. High X, ivoroid binding, toned top with tortoise pick guard (under finish), 1¾-inch V-neck, diamonds & squares inlay, ebony tuner buttons. **List Price:** $2,300. **Number sold:** 138.

1987

D-45LE High X, Brazilian, typical pearl bordering on body, including pearl backstrip. Neck has pearl bordering on top and sides of peghead and fretboard and sides of heel. Pearl hexagon outlines on fretboard and bridge tips, Style 45 head, ebony tuner buttons. **List Price:** $7,500. **Number sold:** 50.

HD-18LE D-18V (see page 253) with herringbone top trim, diamonds & squares neck inlays, low-profile neck. Aging toner, tortoise pick guard, 1⅞-inch neck standard, $1\frac{11}{16}$-inch optional. Ebony tuner buttons. **List Price:** $2,250. **Number sold:** 51.

HD-28BSE Signed on the underside of the top by supervisors and C. F. Martin IV. High X, Brazilian, 1¾-inch V-neck with Style 42 inlay, ivoroid binding, aging toner, tortoise pick guard, gold gears with ebony buttons. **List Price:** $3,300. **Number sold:** 93.

00-21LE Scalloped braces, aging toner, 14-fret neck with slotted peghead. Rectangular ebony bridge, tortoise binding, herringbone rosette and backstrip, optional without tortoise pick guard, 1¾-inch neck, short (24.9-inch) scale, chrome 3-on-plate gears with pearloid buttons. **List Price:** $2,350. **Number sold:** 19.

J-40MBLE Brazilian J-40 with Style 45 snowflakes on neck, aging toner, tortoise pick guard, pearloid tuner buttons. **List Price:** $3,000. **Number sold:** 17.

1988

D-42LE High X, Style 42 top bordering, J-40 neck inlay, M-38 binding on sides and back. Tortoise pick guard, ebony tuner buttons, signed on underside of top by shop foremen and C. F. Martin IV. **List Price:** $3,300. **Number sold:** 75.

HD-28M High X, HD-28 binding and backstrip, Style 28 neck with diamonds & squares inlay, aging toner, light stain on mahogany, tortoise pick guard, gold tuners with pearloid buttons. **List Price:** $2,170. **Number sold:** 81.

M2C-28 MC-28 with double cutaway, pearl single-ring rosette, gold self-locking tuners with small ebony buttons. Pick guard optional. **List Price:** $2,700. **Number sold:** 22.

HD-28PSE High X, ivoroid binding, low-profile (P) neck with Style 45 snowflakes, aging toner, tortoise pick guard, underside of top signed by shop supervisors, chrome gears with ebony buttons. **List Price:** $2,750. **Number sold:** 96.

1989

D-41BLE Englemann spruce top with high X ¼-inch bracing, Brazilian, Style 45 headstock, $\frac{4}{5}$-sized hexagons (J-40) on fretboard, both bordered on top edge with pearl. Aging toner, tortoise pick guard, underside of top signed by shop foremen and C. F. Martin IV, ebony tuner buttons. **List Price:** $4,800. **Number sold:** 39.

HD-28GM "Grand Marquis" decal on back of peghead. High X, herringbone top trim, rosette, and backstrip, tortoise binding and pick guard. Style 45 peghead inlay and snowflakes on neck and bridge. Gold gears with engraved "M" buttons. **List Price:** $3,198. **Number sold:** 120.

HOM-35 Herringbone OM with Brazilian (3-piece back), scalloped ¼-inch braces, ivoroid binding, zigzag backstrips, aging toner, 1¾-inch neck, diamonds & squares inlay, Martin stamp on back of peghead, small tortoise OM pick guard, "Kluson-style" gold tuners. **List Price:** $4,000. **Number sold:** 60.

D-18GOM (D-18 SPECIAL) High X, rosewood bindings, diamonds & squares inlay, tortoise pick guard, Grover tuners. **List Price:** $1,950. **Number sold:** 28.

1990

D-40BLE Style 41 pearl bordering, Englemann spruce top with high X, Brazilian, Style 45 inlay on pearl-bordered headstock, Style 45 snowflake inlays on neck and bridge, tortoise pick guard, tuners with "M" buttons. Label signed by C.F. IV and Mike Longworth; Mark Leaf case. **List Price:** $5,598. **Number sold:** 58.

HD-28BLE Herringbone top trim, rosette, and backstrip, ¼-inch high X, Brazilian, ivoroid binding on body and headstock (not on neck), 1¾-inch neck, diamonds & squares inlay, aging toner, tortoise pick guard. **List Price:** $3,900. **Number sold:** 108.

OMC-28 Scalloped ¼-inch bracing, rounded cutaway, single-ring rosette around oval soundhole, C. F. Martin decal design inlaid in MOP on headstock, 1¾-inch neck with M-38 style inlay, no herringbone on top, zigzag backstrip, tortoise pick guard, gold gears with pearloid buttons. **List Price:** $3,148. **Number sold:** 81.

D-18MB Flamed maple binding, backstrip, and peghead veneer, shop foremen signatures on underside of Englemann top with high X, aging toner, Style 16 small neck dots, ebony tuner buttons. **List Price:** $2,300. **Number sold:** 99.

1991

D-45KLE	Englemann top with "bear claw" figure, high X, signed on underside by employees. Flamed koa back and sides, ivoroid binding, Brazilian rosewood head-stock veneer with Style 45 inlay, Style 45 snowflakes on neck and bridge, aging toner, tortoise pick guard, "M" tuner buttons; Mark Leaf case. **List Price:** $7,800. **Number sold:** 54.
D-28LSH	High X ¼-inch bracing, 4¼-inch-diameter soundhole with 2 abalone rings, signed on underside of top by C.F. IV and employees. Ivoroid binding, herringbone top trim, Style 45 back strip, Style 42 snowflakes on 22-fret neck and bridge, aging toner, tortoise pick guard, snowflake inlays on ebony buttons. Label signed by Les Wagner (retiring after 47 years with Martin). **List Price:** $4,398. **Number sold:** 211.
OM-21 SPECIAL	Herringbone rosette and backstrip, ¼-inch top bracing, mitered white-black side inlays, tortoise binding, OM pick guard, 1¾-inch neck, striped ebony (Macassar) fretboard, MOP diamonds & squares inlay, MOP Martin decal logo on headstock, gold tuners with pearloid buttons. **List Price:** $3,998. **Number sold:** 36.
D3-18	Vintage Style D-18 with 3-piece back. High X, herringbone backstrips, tortoise-bound ebony fretboard with MOP diamonds & squares, diamond inlays on bridge, Style 28 lines inside top binding, tortoise pick guard, "M" tuner buttons. **List Price:** $2,398. **Number sold:** 80.

1992

D-45S DELUXE	Modified reproduction of 1937 D-45S (12-fret version with solid peghead). Style 45 pearl bordering on sides and front of peghead, fingerboard, and neck heel with usual 45 bordering on body. Style 45 headstock inlay, 45 snowflakes on 1¾-inch neck and bridge, ivoroid binding, aging toner, ¼-inch top bracing, 19 frets total, pearl "M" on ebony tuner buttons, leather cover for case. **List Price:** $9,760. **Number sold:** 60.
HD-28 C.T.B. (CUSTOM TORTOISE BOUND	High X ¼-inch braces, tortoise binding with black-white side inlay, herringbone backstrip, MOP diamonds & squares neck inlay, Martin logo inlaid at 12th fret, headstock with enlarged 5K uke inlay in MOP, gold tuners with "M" buttons, Martin stamp on back of peghead. **List Price:** $3,800. **Number sold:** 97.
HJ-28	Vintage herringbone Style 28 appointments on J size. High X, ivoroid binding, diamonds & squares neck inlay, aging toner, "M" tuner buttons. **List Price:** $3,050. **Number sold:** 69.
D-18 VINTAGE	High X, long saddle, aging toner, stamp on back of headstock, Grover tuners, lower profile V-neck, other prewar features similar to current D-18VM. **List Price:** $1,998. **Number sold:** 218.

1993

D-45 DELUXE	Spruce top with "bear claw" figure, high X ¼-inch bracing, Brazilian, ivoroid binding. "Tree of Life" inlay on neck and black pick guard, Style 45 headstock inlay, pearl backstrip, pearl borders on all edges of neck and peghead. "Island scroll" inlay on bridge, fossilized-ivory nut and saddle, "M" tuner buttons. **List Price:** $18,200. **Number sold:** 60.
OM-28 PERRY BECHTEL	Label signed by Mrs. Perry Bechtel. Scalloped top bracing in original pattern, wood purfling in rosette, 1¾-inch V-neck, diamonds & squares inlay, pyramid bridge with long saddle and 2¼-inch string spacing, "M" tuner buttons, Brazilian headstock veneer. Ivoroid binding and other features of current OM-28VR. **List Price:** $4,000. **Number sold:** 94.
D-28 1935 SPECIAL	1¾-inch V-neck, long saddle in bridge with 2⁵⁄₁₆-inch string spacing, Brazilian headstock veneer, optional dark sunburst, other features like current HD-28 VR. **List Price:** $3,800. **Number sold:** 237.
D-93	High X ¼-inch top bracing, herringbone rosette and backstrip, white binding on body, neck, and peghead, ebony fretboard with diamonds & squares inlay, "CFM" in MOP at 3rd fret, diamond inlays in bridge tips, Brazilian headstock veneer, tortoise pick guard, gold tuners with ebony buttons. **List Price:** $3,000. **Number sold:** 165.

1994

GENE AUTRY D-45	Replica of first D-45. Brazilian, Style 45 bordering with wood purfling, 12-fret 1⅞-inch neck, Martin decal on back of head. Torch inlay in slotted peghead, Waverly gears. Fossilized-ivory nut and long saddle, snowflakes in bridge. Label signed by Gene Autry; leather-trimmed case optional with original "Gene Autry" pearl script on neck, or Style 45 snowflakes and small "Gene Autry" signature in MOP at 19th fret. **List Price:** $22,000. **Number sold:** 66.
OM-40LE	Double row of pearl bordering around top and sound-hole, ¼-inch top bracing, "CFM" pearl script on headstock, Style 42 snowflake neck inlay, bone nut and short saddle, tuner buttons with snowflake inlay, other features of current "Vintage Series" OM. **List Price:** $7,100. **Number sold:** 57 natural, 29 sunburst.
HD-28 LSH "GRAND MARQUIS"	Double herringbone rosette, 4¼-inch soundhole, high X, herringbone backstrip, tortoise binding with black-white side inlay. Style 45 peghead and snowflake neck inlays (not bound), "Grand Marquis" in MOP at 12th fret, bone nut and saddle, snowflakes in bridge, tortoise pick guard, gold tuners with "M" buttons. **List Price:** $4,500. **Number sold:** 115 natural, 36 sunburst.
HJ-28M	Vintage series HD-28 features on a mahogany jumbo. High X, striped (Macassar) ebony fretboard and bridge, ivoroid binding, ebony tuner buttons with "M" inlay. **List Price:** $3,900. **Number sold:** 72.

1995

D-35 30TH ANNIVERSARY	Standard D-35 appointments except: Brazilian center wedge of 3-piece back and matching headstock veneer. Scalloped ¼-inch top bracing, ivoroid binding, mitered binding on fretboard with "1965–1995" inlaid at 20th fret, bone nut and saddle, tortoise pick guard with beveled edge, gold tuners with "M" buttons. **List Price:** $4,000. **Number sold:** 207.
D-18 GOLDEN ERA	Many features copied directly from a 1937 D-18, including: original mahogany stain color, small abalone dot pattern on neck, Brazilian headstock veneer and old-style decal, hot stamp burned in reinforcing center strip, cloth strips on sides, 1¾-inch V-neck, 2⁵⁄₁₆-inch string spacing at bridge, long bone saddle, bone nut; other features of current D-18VM. **List Price:** $3,100. **Number sold:** 272 natural, 48 sunburst.
000-42EC LIMITED EDITION SIGNATURE SERIES	Style 45 neck with snowflake inlays, snowflakes on tips of bridge with 2¼-inch string spacing, short scale (24.9-inch) V-neck 1¾ inches at nut, tuners with "butterbean" buttons; other details like current Style 42 vintage series reissue. Eric Clapton signature in MOP at 20th fret. **List Price:** $8,100. **Number sold:** 433 natural, 28 sunburst.

HD-28 SO 45TH ANNIVERSARY OF *SING OUT!* MAGAZINE	12-fret HD-28 with slotted peghead, *Sing Out!* logo MOP on fretboard, ivoroid binding, long saddle, and other features common on vintage series. Label signed by Pete Seeger. **List Price:** $4,500. **Number sold:** 45.

1996

D-45 C. F. MARTIN SR. COMMEMORATIVE EDITION (200TH BIRTHDAY OF MARTIN FOUNDER)	High X, pearl backstrip, snowflake neck inlays, ivoroid binding with wood inlay beside pearl bordering, toned top, 1¾-inch neck with bone nut, snowflakes on bridge tips (bone saddle), "butterbean" tuners. C.F. Sr. signature in MOP at 20th fret. **List Price:** $11,000. **Number sold:**114.
D-45 DELUXE C. F. MARTIN SR. COMMEMORATIVE EDITION	Same as above guitar but with Style 45 Deluxe pearl bordering on neck and peghead, fossilized-ivory nut, saddle, end pin, and bridge pins, signature at 19th fret. **List Price:** $19,500. **Number sold:** 91.
000-28 12-FRET GOLDEN ERA	5⁄16-inch X-bracing with ¼-inch tone bars, fine-pattern herringbone, wood rosette, linen strips on sides, short pattern diamonds & squares inlay in 1 13⁄16-inch neck, long scale, pyramid bridge with 2 5⁄16-inch string spacing, fossilized-ivory nut, saddle, and bridge pins, pick guard optional; other features like current S models in vintage series. **List Price:** $4,000. **Number sold:** 367.
HD-40MS MARTY STUART LIMITED EDITION	Soundhole rosette of pearl in herringbone pattern, high X, regular herringbone top trim and backstrip, ivoroid binding, 5 custom position markers on neck of Dice, Horseshoe, Steer Horns, Hearts, and Flowers. Gold vintage-style tuners. **List Price:** $5,400. Edition limited to 250, still in progress.
MTV-1 "MTV UNPLUGGED"	Style D-16T top bracing and neck joint, Style 18 tortoise binding with herringbone backstrip, ebony fretboard with letters spelling "UNPLUGGED" as position markers. MTV logo in MOP and abalone on peghead. Body is half rosewood and half mahogany (rosewood on bass side) but with standard spruce top with pearl rosette. **List Price:** $2,200 in satin finish, $2,450 in gloss. **Number sold:** 697.

1997

000-45JR JIMMIE RODGERS "BLUE YODEL" LIMITED EDITION	Replica of Rodgers's custom 1928 000-45: Brazilian 12-fret 000 with Adirondack spruce top. Style 45 pearl bordering with wood purfling, "Blue Yodel" in headstock, MOP "Jimmie Rodgers" in fretboard, ebony straight-line bridge with snowflakes in tips, other "vintage" features similar to 000-28 GE described above. Includes facsimile of original label by C.F. III, available with optional "THANKS" printing on back. **List Price:** $25,000. Limited to 100 instruments.
OM-42 PS PAUL SIMON LIMITED EDITION	Tortoise binding on all edges, Style 42 pearl on top and soundhole, Style 42 snowflakes on neck and bridge, high X, bone nut and saddle, OM-style pick guard, Waverly tuners with ivoroid buttons, Paul Simon signature at 20th fret. **List Price:** $8,000. Edition still in progress.
00-40 CFM/ STAUFFER	Adaptation of early Martin 12-fret with Stauffer headstock and "ice-cream cone" neck heel shape. Current Style 40 ivoroid binding (pearl only around soundhole), unbound 1¾-inch neck and headstock finished in black, Style 45 snowflake neck inlays, hybrid pyramid/belly bridge, short scale, wood "coffin" case included. **List Price:** $7,900. Edition limited to 75.
00-45 CFM/ STAUFFER	A Brazilian Style 45 version of the above. Style 45 snowflakes in bound neck, unbound headstock with C. F. Martin script logo inlaid in pearl, fossilized-ivory nut, saddle, and bridge pins. **List Price:** $20,000. Edition limited to 25.
00-16DB "WOMEN AND MUSIC" MODEL	14-fret 00 body, extra-deep sides, with slotted peghead and classical-style wood mosaic rosette. N-20 (classical model) black binding, ebony fretboard, diamonds & squares inlay, Style 16 top bracing with lighter transverse braces, black OM-shape pick guard. **List Price:** $2,100. **Number sold:** 97.
CEO-1	An SPD-16T model with the following differences: hexagon outline inlays on ebony fretboard and bridge, C.F. IV's signature in MOP at 20th fret, N-20 black binding, ebony buttons, tweed case included. **List Price:** $2,600. Edition still in progress.
CEO-1R	Rosewood version of the guitar described above. **List Price:** $2,800. Edition still in progress.
D-28KT KINGSTON TRIO	High X, standard D-28 binding in ivoroid, checkered backstrip, Brazilian headstock veneer with old-style decal, long bone saddle, bone nut, dot on neck with "The Kingston Trio" inlaid between 11th and 13th frets, "1957–1997" inlaid at 20th fret, gold vintage-style gears. Set of 3: $12,500. Edition of 40 (sold with 0-18T and Vega PS-5 banjo) with label signed by surviving members of the Trio. Extended-edition label (for D-28KT models sold separately) signed by Bob Shane.
0-18T KINGSTON TRIO	Standard 0-18T (4-string tenor guitar) but with ebony fingerboard and bridge, neck inlays as on D-28KT described above, Brazilian headstock veneer with old-style decal. Edition of 40 sets.
VEGA 5-STRING BANJO KINGSTON TRIO	A Vega long-neck 5-string banjo, as played by Dave Guard (later by John Stewart) in the Kingston Trio, was marketed by the Martin company as part of the Kingston Trio set of 3 instruments.

Late 1997

(GUITARS NOT AVAILABLE UNTIL 1998)

D-42JC JOHNNY CASH	Gloss black lacquer on body and neck, Style 42 pearl bordering on top and rosette, 3-piece rosewood back with Style 45 backstrips. Body bound in ivoroid, Style 45 headstock, bound fretboard with pearl star inlays, Johnny Cash signature in pearl at 20th fret. High X ¼-inch top bracing, bone nut and saddle, vintage-style tuners.
0000-28H AG ARLO GUTHRIE	Similar to M-38, but with herringbone top trim, ivoroid binding, unbound neck and peghead. Engraved pearl representation of church (Alice's Restaurant in Stockbridge, MA) on headstock, "circles & arrows" inlays on fretboard with "Alice's Restaurant 30th" [anniversary] between 11th and 14th frets, with "Arlo Guthrie" at 20th fret. Comes with blue-jean–covered case. Edition limited to 30.
00012-28H AG ARLO GUTHRIE	12-string with same theme as above. Edition limited to 30.
HD-28LSV	Vintage-series D with large soundhole, similar appointments to 1934 D-28 once owned by Clarence White. Adirondack spruce top (fine-pattern herringbone), high X, 4½-inch-diameter soundhole with rosette missing innermost ring, ivoroid bound 21-fret fingerboard extends over soundhole, modified 1¾-inch V-neck, 2¼-inch string spacing on bridge with long saddle, tortoise pick guard, Waverly tuners with ivoroid buttons.

LIMITED EDITIONS AND VINTAGE MODELS NOT ISSUED AS GUITARS OF THE MONTH

From 1983 to 1987 Martin built many rosewood models with Brazilian rosewood. In the first few years, they were stamped with a V, for "Vintage," after the model code. Beginning in 1985, some models with Brazilian rosewood were stamped B, for

"Brazilian." Some of the B models did not have the vintage features, such as V-shaped neck with diamonds & squares inlays, but some were nearly identical to models stamped V. So a 1983 D-28V and a 1986 Custom 15B (HD-28 with vintage features) would be nearly identical guitars.

In summary, not all "V" models from 1983 to 1986 are Brazilian, but all have "Vintage" features. All "B" models are Brazilian, but not all of them have the vintage appointments.

SPECIAL PRODUCTION RUNS

D-18LE	Quilted mahogany back and sides, herringbone backstrip, other details like D-18V. About 30 were made in 1986-87.

Other models with special woods have been made, especially since 1985, including: 2 D-28 and 2 HD-28 models with cocobolo back and sides (1987); 3 D-45 models with African tulipwood backs and sides (1990); short runs of models with figured walnut backs and sides; and vintage series guitars with Adirondack spruce tops. Many of these production runs with special woods are simply stamped "Custom" on the neck block.

CHANGES TO MARTIN GUITARS

YEAR	CHANGES
1916	Mahogany 1-piece necks begin to replace cedar (2-piece).*
1918	Ivory binding "discontinued in favor of celluloid." Some ivory bridges and ivory soundhole rings seen into 1919.
1919	Style 21 guitars get same pattern neck as Style 18 (no dart, rounded slots in peghead).
1930	Style stamp added to neck block between October 1 and October 15.
1934	Neck with T-frets and T-shaped steel bar first used #57305.
1935	Stamp in back of neck discontinued between #59044 and #61181.
1939	Narrower neck (1 11/16") begins with #72740.
1942	Ebony neck reinforcement gradually implemented #80585.
1944	Scalloped braces discontinued #89926.
1944	Dots replace slotted diamonds on fingerboard of D-28.
1947	Herringbone trim discontinued in set containing #98223.
1947	Old zigzag backstrip on Style 28 discontinued between #99992 and #100240.
1958	Chrome Grover Rotomatic tuners appear on D-28.*
1964	Bridge pin holes moved back from saddle 1/16" #197207.
1965	Loose, short bridge saddle replaces long, or through-cut, saddle #200601.
1965	Grover Rotomatic tuners on all D guitars #205251.
1966	First use of Boltaron bindings (black or white), replacing ivoroid and tortoiseshell-color celluloid. Tortoiseshell-color pick guards changed to black shortly after.
1966	Bridge pin holes moved to center #216736.
1967	Square neck bar replaces T-shape.
1967	Last hand-stamped serial and model numbers #220467.
1968	Rosewood bridgeplates on all guitars starting with #235586.
1969	Rosewood bridgeplates become larger on D guitars starting with #242454.
1969	East Indian rosewood replaces Brazilian starting with #254498.
1975	Micarta nuts and saddles replace plastic.
1979	Schaller machines on some models #416625.
1984	Self-adhesive pick guards replace the under-the-finish style in regular production.
1985	Adjustable rods gradually implemented #453181.
1986	D-45 returns to scalloped braces and maple bridgeplates #467626.
1986	New bracing and maple bridgeplates on 12-string guitars #446127.
1986	Extra-low profile necks on M, J, and all P series guitars (P is code for low profile), specs start 1/28/86. This quickly became standard for D size as well. P designation dropped beginning in 1988.
1988	Return to maple bridgeplates on all guitars #478093.
1988	All models in Style 21 and lower changed to the same "5-9-5" soundhole rosette as Style 28.
1988	Style D guitars get taller 3rd and 4th back braces like those used on M- and J-size guitars.
1992	Cross-link finish (a catalyzed finish) begins to be used on the necks of standard series Martins.
1994	Gold foil logo replaces old-style decal on regular production guitars (except vintage series).
1995	Style 16 guitars get Series 1 neck joint and "hybrid" A-frame bracing above soundhole (model code changed to 16T).

*Note: The information in this table was taken from notes made by earlier shop foremen at the Martin factory and gathered by Mike Longworth. Recollections of recent changes are from current managers and foremen. A few dates were taken from notes written in catalogs kept at the factory. There are often exceptions to these changes, and any guitar stamped S or later "custom" may have been ordered with earlier features. Items noted with an * are when changes have been noticed on Martin guitars, meaning the change could have appeared earlier or could not have happened until later on other styles. Consider this list as a general guide as to when changes occurred to most Martin guitars.*

LABELS AND STAMPED MARKINGS ON 19TH-CENTURY MARTINS

1833-1839	Paper labels affixed to the inside of the back, C. F. Martin, Martin & Bruno, Martin & Schatz, etc. There is much variety in the wording. Some guitars are stamped "C. F. Martin / New York" on the outside of the back, just below the neck heel.
1840-1867	Those with a cedar neck may have "C. F. Martin / New York" stamped on back of peghead as well as on center backstrip inside the guitar and on the neck block. Those with black stained necks have a stamp on the back of the body, just below neck heel and inside the guitar but not on back of peghead. Models from the 1840s may have only a paper "Martin & Coupa" label. From the 1850s to 1867 no paper labels were used. It is widely assumed that all Martins from at least 1850 on are stamped as mentioned above.
1867-1898	The stamp inside the body is changed to "C. F. Martin & Co./ New York." The stamp on the back of the peghead (cedar neck) or on the back of the guitar below neck heel (black neck) remains "C. F. Martin / New York."
1898	Stamp changed to "C. F. Martin & Co. / Nazareth, PA." on center backstrip, neck block, and back of peghead. (Some early 1898 stamped "C. F. Martin / 1833 / New York" on back of peghead.) Serial numbers now appear on the neck block (sometimes also on top edge of peghead).

INDEX

Photo Credits

C. F. Martin & Company thanks **John Sterling Ruth** for supplying many of the photographs.

Jim Bollman, Music Emporium, Lexington, MA; **Fred Dusel, Frank Ford, Richard Johnston,** and **Michael Simmons,** Gryphon Stringed Instruments, Palo Alto, CA; **Gary L. Hacking,** Photography G, Minneapolis; **Hank Risan,** Washington Street Music, Santa Cruz, CA, photo styling by **Bianca Soros;** International Guitar Research Archives, **Dr. Ron Purcell,** Director, Music Department, California State University, NORTHRIDGE; **Roger Kasle Collection,** Dearborn, MI; **Fred Oster,** Vintage Instruments, Philadelphia; **Starday-King Records,** Nashville (615) 889-8000; **Steve Szilagyi/Elderly Instruments,** Lansing, MI; **Mac Yasuda Enterprises,** Laguna Beach, CA.

Many of the album covers pictured were supplied by **Jim Washburn** and **Frank Ford.**